Sacrifice Regained

Sacrifice Regained

Morality and Self-interest in British Moral Philosophy from Hobbes to Bentham

Roger Crisp

CLARENDON PRESS · OXFORD

OXFORD
UNIVERSITY PRESS

Great Clarendon Street, Oxford, OX2 6DP,
United Kingdom

Oxford University Press is a department of the University of Oxford.
It furthers the University's objective of excellence in research, scholarship,
and education by publishing worldwide. Oxford is a registered trade mark of
Oxford University Press in the UK and in certain other countries

© Roger Crisp 2019

The moral rights of the author have been asserted

First edition published 2019

Impression: 1

Published in the United States of America by Oxford University Press
198 Madison Avenue, New York, NY 10016, United States of America

British Library Cataloguing in Publication Data
Data available

Library of Congress Control Number: 2019931645

ISBN 978-0-19-884047-3

Printed and bound in Great Britain by
Clays Ltd, Elcograf S.p.A.

In memory of Daphne May Crisp
(25 February 1932–24 October 2017)

Acknowledgements

I am deeply grateful to the British Academy for awarding me a Thank-Offering to Britain Fellowship for 2015–16, and to the Association of Jewish Refugees for so generously endowing the fund supporting this fellowship. Without it, this book would not have been written. I must also thank the University of Oxford and St Anne's College, Oxford, for granting me sabbatical leave for 2016–17. For continuing support and encouragement, I am indebted to the Uehiro Foundation on Ethics and Education and the Dianoia Institute of Philosophy at the Australian Catholic University. As always, I have benefited greatly from the advice and professionalism of librarians in Oxford. For providing a peaceful and scholarly environment at certain important points in my research, I thank the librarians at the International House of Japan and my colleagues at the Institute.

For comments on drafts and/or discussion, I thank the following: Robert Audi, Ralf Bader, Nigel Biggar, Paul Bloomfield, Nigel Bowles, David Brink, Sarah Buss, Krister Bykvist, Tony Coady, Dale Dorsey, Julia Driver, Aaron Garrett, Lorenzo Greco, Brad Hooker, Thomas Hurka, Terence Irwin, David Killoren, Richard Kraut, Paul Lodge, David McNaughton, George Monbiot, Martha Nussbaum, Takuya Okada, Catherine Paxton, Tyler Paytas, Nalin Ranasinghe, Andrew Reisner, Richard Rowland, Philip Schofield, Bart Schultz, Luděk Sekyra, Rob Shaver, John Skorupski, Daniel Star, Marcel van Ackeren, Ralph Wedgwood, and David Wiggins. I am grateful also to Derek Parfit and Daniel Robinson, and it is a great regret to me that they did not live to see the book in print. Thanks also to Peter Momtchiloff at Oxford University Press for his enthusiasm and wise guidance, to the Press's three readers for insightful and constructive comments, and to Elissa Connor and Jonathan Rowley for their sharp eyes and excellent advice.

Chapter 12 includes material from 'Hume on Virtue, Utility and Morality', in S. Gardiner (ed.), *Virtue Ethics Old and New* (Cornell University Press, 2005): 159–78. I am grateful to the editor and to Cornell University Press for permission. Chapter 14 is based on 'Richard Price on Virtue', in D. Brink, S.S. Meyer, and C. Shields (eds), *Virtue, Happiness, Knowledge: Themes from the Work of Gail Fine and Terence Irwin* (Oxford University Press, 2018): 254–69. I thank the editors for their permission.

Contents

1. **Introduction: The Morality Question**   1
    1. Self-interest and Morality   1
    2. Psychological Egoism   4
    3. Rational Egoism   6

2. **Hobbes: The Return of Gyges**   10
    1. Psychological Egoism in Hobbes   10
    2. Rational Egoism in Hobbes   14
    3. Hobbes on Morality   17
    4. The Response to the Foole   22

3. **More: An Enthusiasm for Virtue**   27
    1. Virtue and Hedonism   27
    2. The Pleasures of the Boniform Faculty   29
    3. Who is the Competent Judge?   31

4. **Cumberland: Divine Utilitarianism**   33
    1. Egoism as a Natural Necessity   33
    2. The Law of Nature   36
    3. The Will of God   38
    4. Agreement and the Rationality of Maximization   41
    5. The Birth of Utilitarianism   42
    6. Deontology and Self-interest   46

5. **Locke: The Sanctions of God**   49
    1. The Response to Hobbes   50
    2. The Law of Nature   51
    3. Morality and Self-interest   54
    4. Well-being, Morality, and Pleasure   57

6. **Mandeville: Morality After the Fall**   60
    1. The *Fable* and Mandeville's Rigorism   61
    2. Worldly Virtue and the Invention of Honour   64
    3. Private Vices, Public Benefits   69

7. **Shaftesbury: Stoicism and the Art of Virtue**   74
    1. Repression, Acceptance, and Badness   75
    2. Human Nature and Motivation   78
    3. Ethical Aestheticism   82
    4. Pleasure and Virtue   84

8. **Butler: The Supremacy of Conscience**   92
    1. Human Nature and the Supremacy of Conscience   93
    2. Self-love and Benevolence   97

    3. Butler's Ethics   103
    4. Self-love and Virtue   105

9. Hutcheson: Impartial Pleasures   110
    1. God, Morality, and the Will   111
    2. Impartial Beneficence and Subordinate Virtues   115
    3. Two (or Three?) Grand Determinations   119
    4. The Highest Pleasures   123

10. Clarke: Virtue and the Life Hereafter   128

11. Reid: The Goodness of Virtue, and its Limits   132

12. Hume: Morality as Utility   137
    1. Hume, the Moral Anthropologist?   139
    2. Ethics of Action, Ethics of Motive   142
    3. *Maximandum* and Maximization: Two Objections   146
    4. Utilitarian Impartiality and the General Point of View   150
    5. Hume's Dualism of the Practical Reason   154

13. Smith: The Delusions of Self-love   158
    1. Sympathy   158
    2. Normative Standards and the Impartial Spectator   160
    3. Smith's Ethics   164
    4. Smith's Dualism   166

14. Price: Morality as God   170
    1. Price's Deontological Pluralism   170
    2. Moral Motivation and Moral Worth   173
    3. Virtue as Law, and Supererogation   179
    4. Virtue and Egoism   181
    5. Virtue and Happiness   183

15. Gay, Tucker, Paley, and Bentham: Variations on the Theme of Happiness   187
    1. Gay: Virtue and its Associations   187
    2. Tucker: Regulus and Virtue Re-enlarged   191
    3. Paley: Rules for Happiness   195
    4. Bentham: Legislating for the Good   198
    5. Conclusion: The Shaping of Modern Moral Philosophy   205

Bibliography   207
Index   231

1

Introduction:
The Morality Question

1. Self-interest and Morality

By the time the sixth edition of Henry Sidgwick's masterpiece, *The Methods of Ethics*, was published, its author was dead. But its editor, E.E. Constance Jones, included within the preface (1907: xvi–xxiii) some notes she had found for a lecture by Sidgwick on his philosophical development. Sidgwick describes how he was initially attracted to Millian utilitarianism, later coming to see the force of the rational or normative egoist view that each of us has reason never to act against our own self-interest or well-being.[1] This resulted in his notorious 'dualism of the practical reason', a dualism that, since he could not resolve it, led him to philosophical despair. Sidgwick claims that he found that dualism in the work of Butler, and it was re-reading Butler in the light of Sidgwick's suggestion that led me into writing this book.

Two questions arise immediately. First, is Sidgwick's interpretation of Butler correct? Second, does the dualism occur in writers before Butler? If we take dualism to be the view that reasons to act are grounded both in our own good or self-interest, and in morality, duty, or the good of others, Butler is certainly a dualist. But then so are many philosophers in the western tradition since Plato and Aristotle, including all the writers I shall discuss before Butler, except the egoist Hobbes and perhaps Cumberland, if he is read as an extreme impartialist. I shall argue against Sidgwick for the traditional interpretation of Butler, according to which, if we are to imagine a conflict between self-love and duty, the latter must win.[2]

The subject of this book, then, is the relation of self-interest on the one hand, and morality or the interest of others on the other. I have focused on that group of philosophers often known as 'the British moralists' not only because they form an

---

[1] I take these notions as essentially equivalent, noting that 'self-interest' implies more straightforwardly a contrast with 'other-interest' (or 'morality', which I am taking as equivalent *not* to other-interest but to 'duty'), while 'well-being' is more at home in discussions of what makes life good for the person living it, happiness, and so on.

[2] For a very helpful discussion of various conceptions of self-love employed in the eighteenth century, see Maurer 2009.

unusually self-contained group,[3] but because the brilliance and imagination of their respective works are often insufficiently recognized or utilized in current debates. My selection of authors was guided initially by the canon as partly created or at least conceived by L.A. Selby-Bigge in his *British Moralists*, first published in 1897, and reshaped by D.D. Raphael in his *British Moralists 1650–1800* in 1969. I have omitted some of the canon, usually because their work focused on issues other than the potential conflict between self-interest and morality, and for the same reason said less about some authors—primarily Clarke and Reid—than others. I have also added More and Tucker, because of their intrinsic interest, and, in the case of Tucker, his influence on Paley. Doubtless there are important authors I could, and perhaps should, have included, and I regret greatly that all those I discuss are male. I would certainly welcome advice from readers on potential omissions.

It would not be an exaggeration to describe this period in philosophical ethics as a response to Hobbes, though his influence naturally declined as time went on and his egoism was (it was standardly thought) reshaped by Mandeville.[4] Hobbes's view of human nature was not as pessimistic as some of his early interpreters suggested, and he allowed for action caused by immediate benevolent concern for others. But the ultimate source of our motivation is self-interest, and subjective self-sacrifice—that is, action which we believe will be overall detrimental to our well-being—is impossible. The British moralists after Hobbes, and in particular after Shaftesbury, tended to be more optimistic, and to allow at least for ultimate moral normative reasons and what we might call 'mundane' subjective self-sacrifice (that is, action that we believe will make our life on earth worse than it would otherwise have been). But the majority of these writers—those who believed in divine reward and punishment in the afterlife—then faced the problem that the virtuous would, if they were religious, be unable to sacrifice themselves overall (not just on earth), not only objectively, but subjectively, unless some complicated account of virtuous motivation, involving inattention to the ultimate rewards of virtue, could be made plausible. The great change came with the atheism of Hume, who was ready to accept moral reasons and to deny the egoistic veto according to which one never has reason to act against one's own self-interest. Hume, less driven than Sidgwick by the need to find a single ethical principle which will guide agents in every case, allowed that moral reasons could sometimes trump those of self-interest (as well as vice versa), thus recovering for philosophy the possibility of overall sacrifice, both subjective and objective, which had been ruled out by the ancient view that virtue and self-interest coincide and by the doctrine of divine reward and punishment.

To discuss the relation of self-interest and morality of course requires some discussion of the conceptions of each of these notions held by each writer. So what follows

---

[3] See Sidgwick (1902: xxiii): 'For the century and a half that intervenes between Hobbes and Bentham the development of English ethics proceeds without receiving any material influence from foreign sources'.

[4] See also Maurer's discussion of Archibald Campbell's attempt to rehabilitate self-love in British moral philosophy (2009: ch. 6).

might serve as something of an introduction to the prudential and moral theories of the British moralists, though I shall largely avoid issues of metaethics and religious confession except where they impinge on these first-order matters. The period is, perhaps surprisingly, dominated by evaluative hedonism, especially about self-interest or well-being, the rare exceptions being Cumberland, Mandeville, and Reid. Few of these authors, though most tend to stress the pleasures of virtue and the pains of vice, sought to deal with the apparent conflict between self-interest and morality by incorporating virtue into their account of self-interest, and here we see a stark contrast with ancient ethics. In more recent philosophy, hedonism has fallen into decline, to be replaced largely by conceptions of well-being which incorporate not virtue, but self-regarding elements such as accomplishment or personal autonomy. Those who wish to allow for genuine overall subjective and objective sacrifice, then, must follow Hume not in his hedonism but in his allowing for ultimate moral reasons of sufficient strength to outweigh self-interest, at least on some occasions. Since one of the important sources of contemporary moral philosophy is British moral philosophy, and since most contemporary moral philosophers appear to allow for both subjective and objective self-sacrifice, here we see yet another debt owed by moral philosophy to Hume's insight and integrity.

Though this particular road leads to Hume, the chapter on him is not the last in the book. That is primarily because the authors I discuss after Hume had interesting things to say about the relation between self-interest and morality, and the possibility of self-sacrifice. But it is also because one hope I have is to encourage further work on the British moralists as sources of inspiration for work on self-interest or well-being and normative or first-order ethics in general. The ordering of chapters is by the date of birth of the philosopher in question, except in the case of Clarke, whom I discuss in the light of Hutcheson, and Smith, because of his relation to Hume. I chose Bentham's date of birth to determine the place of chapter 15 because he is the latest of the four utilitarians discussed and he was born after Price.

Let me now flesh out the philosophical background a little. Early in Plato's *Republic* (2003: 359c–360b), Glaucon tells Socrates the story of a Lydian shepherd, Gyges. Gyges, having found a ring which made him invisible, used its powers to enter the royal palace, where he seduced the queen, killed the king, and himself assumed power. Glaucon suggests that many in Gyges's circumstances would do the same, believing that immorality is more profitable than being moral and to be avoided only through fear of being caught.

A key question arising from Glaucon's story is whether there are self-standing or ultimate normative reasons for action grounded in morality itself or in the well-being of others—which we might call *M-reasons*—that might count against what Gyges does with the ring. Is there a principle forbidding killing, for example, or should Gyges take into account the fact that he is depriving the king of the rest of his life? Or are all our reasons *S-reasons*, that is, ultimately non-moral and entirely self-interested? The relation of M-reasons to S-reasons (which we might call the *morality question*) is what

Sidgwick called 'the profoundest problem of ethics' (1907: 386n4), and it is the starting point for this book.[5]

Many different answers to the morality question have been canvassed. One is rational or normative egoism, the view that all our ultimate reasons are S-reasons, there being no M-reasons. As Glaucon implies, egoism has immediate intuitive plausibility, and, according to William Frankena (1983: 169), 'it has been the prevailing [view] throughout the history of thinking about why we should be just or good or do what is right'. Egoism so stated allows for the possibility that we may have ultimate reason to violate moral principles or to harm others, and this is indeed the kind of position lying behind Glaucon's presentation of the story of Gyges. But even if egoism is correct, it does not follow that Gyges had strongest reason to use the ring as he did. Socrates's own response to Glaucon can plausibly be read as an egoistic defence of morality, according to which the agent's own self-interest or well-being consists in virtue.[6] This position—*moralistic egoism*—is characteristic of ancient philosophy in general (Sidgwick 1907: 91–2). As I shall suggest in the first chapter, our period begins with a robust defence of egoism which provided a focus for, and shaped, discussion of the morality question in British moral philosophy for many decades.[7]

The morality question received little direct discussion during the twentieth century, though there were exceptions (e.g. Williams 1972: 17–28; Scheffler 1982; Parfit 1984: pt. 1; Nagel 1986: chs 9–10). The standard view during that time was that the correct moral theory provides a comprehensive account of an agent's strongest, or indeed only, reasons for action, and that morality, in any conflict with an agent's self-interest, is overriding. This was particularly clear in the work of utilitarians, according to whom an agent's well-being provides reasons only as a constituent of the overall good, impartially construed. But the view that morality is overriding is also implicit in the work of non-utilitarians, such as W.D. Ross or John Rawls. The overridingness of morality, however, was largely assumed without argument, or incorporated into the definition of morality itself (see e.g. Hare 1981: 53–7), and the time has come to return to the morality question, to consider exactly what it is and how serious a challenge to morality it constitutes.

2. Psychological Egoism

Before discussing Hobbes in particular, some clarification of egoism in general is called for. One basic distinction between forms of egoism is that between *psychological egoism* and what I shall call *rational egoism*. Both theories focus on human action, rather than, say, human character or human lives, and both are universal, in that their

---

[5]   Sidgwick is speaking in particular of the relation of 'rational egoism' to 'rational benevolence'.

[6]   One possible exception here is Socrates's view stated later in the *Republic* (Plato 2003: 520c) that the philosophers should return to the cave; see Crisp 2003: 67–71. If this is understood as a sacrifice, Socrates may be understood as a non-ego-restricted pluralist (see below p. 6).

[7]   See Sidgwick 1902: 163.

claims are intended as exceptionless. Psychological egoism is a *descriptive* theory, and its central concern is the *motivation* of human action. In its strict form, it can be broadly stated as:

PE: The sole ultimate motivation of all voluntary human action is self-interest.

The restriction to voluntary action is to avoid counter-examples based on non-voluntary action, such as that resulting from hypnosis or insanity.[8]

A motivation's being 'self-interested', as I have implied above, I shall take as its being one that advances the agent's own good or well-being. Note that psychological egoism is consistent with the claim that some human motivation is non-self-interested, as long as that motivation is non-ultimate. Consider, for example, someone who makes high-profile donations to charity solely because they enjoy being thought well of by others.

'Self-interest' can be understood as 'real' or 'apparent'. An *objective* form of psychological egoism will be based on the former, a *subjective* form on the latter. Objective psychological egoism, if it is to be at all plausible, should be understood as the combination of a descriptive view, equivalent to subjective psychological egoism, with an evaluative theory concerning the human good, according to which what appears to humans to be in their self-interest is indeed so. Psychological egoism, when considered independently of such an evaluative theory, should be construed subjectively. Subjective forms may differ in the account they give of actual human decisions, such as the role played by probability judgements or attitudes to time. But they must agree that ultimately, given an array of options, humans will choose that which appears to them to advance their own interest.

Do such choices have to be 'maximizing' (Kavka 1986: 38–9)? That is, must psychological egoism involve the view that the ultimate motivation is to promote the *greatest* apparent good for the agent? That is certainly a theoretical option, but it runs immediately into the problem of weakness of will. Even if we consider cases in which only their own interests are concerned, it seems that human beings are often motivated to act in ways that they themselves believe are not best for them. Of course, one might follow Socrates and claim that cases of weakness of will are in fact cases of maximization based on ignorance, but this is very hard to believe. What matters primarily for proponents of psychological egoism is that the only ultimate goal for any agent is the good of that agent, and not the good of others or adherence to moral principle (Gert 1991: 6).

A further issue, again independent of evaluative theory, is what account of self-interest is offered within any version of psychological egoism. By far the most common view here has been *psychological hedonism*, according to which the ultimate motivation for human action is to promote the balance of the agent's pleasure over pain. As implied above, broader views will allow for non-hedonic ultimate aims, such as accomplishment

---

[8] Other ways to avoid such examples would be to insist that action properly understood must be voluntary, or to develop an account of motivation according to which only voluntary actions are motivated.

or posthumous fame, or virtue itself. Psychological hedonists may claim that agents who believe themselves to be pursuing such ultimate aims are self-deceived: in reality, what motivates them is the pleasure of accomplishment or of thinking about one's reputation after death, or fear of painful sanctions. Again, this view is hard to accept.

Also significant is the position taken by the psychological egoist on the self-awareness or self-consciousness of human agents. In its most extreme form, psychological egoism may be interpreted as the claim that every agent is continuously, and with full awareness, seeking to promote their own good. Few if any philosophers have held such an extreme view. Most psychological egoists will permit, for example, good-promoting strategies (I decide that playing tennis will promote my good, and then put that thought from my mind to concentrate on the game), in which the agent's good serves as a background check or veto on decisions made independently of it (I am attracted by the idea of playing tennis and decide to do so, but then as I am playing reflect on how badly I have been affected by losing in the past and feign an injury to end the game). Motivation by concern for morality or the good of others, then, without any explicit attention to the good of the agent, need not be a counter-example to psychological egoism if the agent has, perhaps even without recognizing that they are doing so, adopted a strategy of acting on moral principle or altruistically in the belief that this will promote their good, and if that belief remains as a dispositional check on any action, such that if it becomes clear that they are putting their own good at risk through moral or altruistic action they will, if possible, change course. We might call this *split-level* psychological egoism. At the most fundamental or global level, an agent's motivation is egoistic; but this motivation may itself lead to non-egoistic motivation on occasion.

This brings me to a final and important distinction. According to the strict form of psychological egoism, the only ultimate aim of any agent is their own self-interest. But one might construct a weaker position which will allow for direct motivation by moral or other-regarding considerations, without any splitting of levels, but will insist that such motivation is always subject to egoistic oversight. I may, for example, be directly motivated to help some other person out of unmediated concern for their well-being; but I will do so (or will do so reflectively, or whatever) only if acting in that way appears to promote my expected good, or at least to promote it as much as any other action available to me. This view contains the egoistic restriction that an agent will never knowingly act in a way that they believe to be against their own self-interest; so we may prefer to call it *ego-restricted pluralism*. Another pluralistic view—*non-ego-restricted pluralism*—will claim that egoistic motivations are weighed against, and sometimes overcome by, non-egoistic.

3. Rational Egoism

Psychological egoism is a descriptive view. Let me now consider *rational egoism*. This view is normative or prescriptive, and concerns grounding, or justifying, reasons *for* agents, not reasons *why* agents act in a certain way. It is the reference to reasons here that explains the name given to the view; it need not involve commitment to, say, some rationalist epistemology, or cognitivist conception of practical reason.

It might be thought that psychological egoism is inconsistent with any normative theory, since any such theory requires the possibility of decision between options. But we have already seen that Hobbes himself allows that an agent may choose between options which vary in how effectively they promote that agent's own good. But what about M-reasons? Can there be ultimate M-reasons if agents can never be motivated to act on them? Some philosophers will deny that there can. But this is itself a controversial metaethical position. Take the common view that reasons are properties of actions that count in favour of acting (see e.g. Scanlon 1998: 17). Now consider the claim that the fact that some action conforms with a moral requirement to benefit others counts in favour of it. If psychological egoism is true, no agent can act *for* that reason. But it may be that in certain cases the action in question will also be the action they view as in their interest. So they can perform the action, and if they do so it may be said that one of the properties that counted in favour of their doing so was the action's conformity with morality. Nevertheless, it is true that on a common view of reasons, according to which an agent cannot have a reason they are unable to act on, psychological egoism limits the options available for any normative theory. In other words, though it is a merely descriptive theory, it *may* have significant normative implications.

It is important to distinguish between a weaker, merely substantive form of rational egoism, concerning derivative reasons, and a stronger, explanatory form, concerning ultimate reasons. Consider the view that any agent has strongest reason to obey the commands of God, *because* these are the commands of God. That is, the justification for doing what God commands—the ultimate reason for doing so—is that it is God who is issuing the command. Now combine this view with another: that God's sole practical command to each of us is maximally to promote our own self-interest. This combination of views gives us a substantive form of rational egoism, according to which each of us always has strongest reason to pursue our own good. But that reason is itself only derivative; our ultimate reason is to obey God's commands. One might, however, combine a substantive version of rational egoism with an explanatory account according to which the very fact that some course of action promotes my interest is itself what grounds or justifies it. If we again employ the notion of ultimacy, this gives us a strict form of rational egoism:

> *RE*: The sole ultimate reason for all voluntary human action is the promotion of the agent's self-interest.

RE will apply to any agent at any point where there is a plurality of options open to that agent. Note that the theory does *not* involve any claim about decision-procedures, except in so far as following such procedures involves acting in a certain way. Because of the possibility of split-level views, a rational egoist is not committed to the view that agents should always *try* to promote their own self-interest. Many have recognized the so-called *paradox of egoism*, according to which one's own good is best promoted by aiming at something else (such as victory in a game of tennis), and so recommended indirect decision-procedures as themselves the best strategy to promote one's own good. Indeed RE is consistent with the view that agents should never deliberately try to maximize their own good.

Several of the distinctions noted above in connection with psychological egoism are relevant also to understanding the different forms rational egoism may take. Note first that the view allows for non-egoistic normative reasons as long as as they are derivative. Recall the earlier example of the person who enjoys being thought well of. They have a reason to make charitable donations, but this reason is derivative from the ultimate egoistic reason grounded in their own self-interest.

Rational egoism is usually restricted to voluntary actions. This again raises the question of the nature of reasons. Consider a case in which you interfere with my brain in such a way that you have complete control over my behaviour. I am unaware that I am about to be bitten by a dangerous spider, and you manipulate my arm so that I kill the spider. Many would be unhappy with the claim that there was a reason for me to act in this way, preferring to say, for example, that it is good or good for me that I so acted.

Again, self-interest here should be understood narrowly, to refer to the agent's well-being only, and not, for example, states of affairs which involve the agent but not the advancement of their well-being.

Rational egoists may have in mind actual or apparent self-interest. Indeed, they may incorporate conceptions of both into their account, for example by distinguishing between objective and subjective reasons. Agents have objective reason to promote their actual self-interest (I have objective reason to take this pill, e.g., because it will in fact entirely cure me, though there is a very high risk of dangerous side-effects), and subjective reason to promote their apparent self-interest (I have subjective reason to take this other pill, which will not cure me entirely, because there is no risk of dangerous side-effects). RE may allow a role for probability in elucidating self-interest. My self-interest, that is to say, may be understood as my 'expected self-interest', where the value of different outcomes varies according to the likelihood of the relevant goods or bads coming about.

Probability considerations aside, the most common versions of rational egoism will be temporally neutral. I have strongest reason to promote my self-interest, understood as the total amount of well-being in my life, regardless of when it occurs. And most versions of rational egoism will understand promotion in terms of maximization. But temporally non-neutral and non-maximizing positions are also available.

Rational egoists have held a variety of views of well-being, including hedonism, desire-satisfaction theories, and so-called 'objective list' views, according to which certain things, such as accomplishment, are good in themselves, independently of any pleasure they may involve or any desires they may satisfy or fulfil. And strict rational egoism is monistic: an agent's *only* reason is to promote their own good. Proponents of rational egoism less strictly construed may allow that moral or other-regarding considerations also provide reasons, and again this pluralism will be ego-restricted, never allowing for the rationality of genuine self-sacrifice.

These clarifications made, we may now turn to the egoism of the 'Beast of Malmesbury', as Hobbes came to be known after the publication of his great work, *Leviathan*.

2
Hobbes:
The Return of Gyges

Thomas Hobbes (1588–1679) is best remembered as a hugely influential political philosopher, and in particular for his *Leviathan*, published in 1651, the last year of the Civil Wars which had dominated English social and political life for the previous decade. Hobbes was a royalist, and had left for Paris in 1640, where he was tutor to the future King Charles II and played an important role in the intellectual circle of Marin Mersenne. Hobbes was a brilliant polymath, and developed a materialist world view which led him in the direction of metaphysical reductionism. But his scepticism about morality was tempered by a clear recognition of its value. As Michael Oakeshott aptly put it (1975: 11), '[b]oth the energy to destroy and the energy to construct are powerful in Hobbes'. The morality question was, then, one of Hobbes's concerns, but he approached it primarily with a view to justifying near absolute sovereignty. His aim was to explain how, given human nature and human capacities, each person is rationally required to give obedience to a sovereign with vast coercive power.

1. Psychological Egoism in Hobbes

Although the traditional view of Hobbes as a psychological egoist has recently been widely doubted,[1] I believe it to be correct.[2] Hobbes holds a version of what I called in

---

[1] See e.g. Gert 1967; 1972: 5; 2001: 243–4; 2010a: 88; 2010b: ix, 9, 30–46, 62–4, 112; McNeilly 1968: chs 5–6; Raphael 1977: 54, 64–6, 68–9, 77–80; Sorell 1986: 96–100; Hampton 1986: 19–24; Baumgold 1988: 7–8; Lloyd 1992: chs. 1, 7; 2014: Abstract.

[2] For accounts closer to the traditional view, see e.g. Peters 1956: 143–9; Warrender 1957: 91, 274; Nagel 1959: 69, 79; Mintz 1962: 81; Plamenatz 1965: 75–6; Gauthier 1969: 17–18; Watkins 1973: 77, 83; Frankena 1983: 172; Farrell 1985: 276–7; Johnston 1986: 34–5, 55, 93, 106–8, 121, 214–16; Herbert 1989: 86 (though cf. 152); Tuck 1989: 64–5, 70; De Stier 1993; Shaver 1999: 3; Parkin 2007: 6–7; Irwin 2008: 113; Olsthoorn 2014: 158. For an excellent discussion of the issues, see Kavka 1986: 44–51. Kavka himself concludes: 'If we put greatest weight on explicit statements, we shall be more inclined to regard *Leviathan* as an egoistic work' (51). I shall focus primarily on *Leviathan* (L), in the English version, because this was seen, by readers and Hobbes himself, as the central statement of his position, and it has had by far the greatest influence of all his works. I shall refer also to other works—in particular, the *Elements of Law* (EL), *De Cive* (DC), and *De Homine* (DH), and the Latin version of L—for elucidation and support. This strategy

the previous chapter 'split-level' psychological egoism, according to which: agents pursue their apparent good, taking probabilities into account and often exhibiting temporal non-neutrality; all other aims are subservient to that of promoting the agent's own good; agents often seek to maximize their good, but not always; all agents are hedonistic; and agents do not always consciously aim to promote their own good, sometimes immediately pursuing moral or altruistic aims.

The basic role Hobbes gives to desire and goodness in his account of voluntary action does not appear to imply psychological egoism (L 6.78-82; see EL 1.7).[3] The origin of any such action is a conception in the imagination of a goal, a conception which can be described as 'endeavour' or 'desire', and the word 'good' is used by agents of the objects of their desires. There are three kinds of goodness: promised goodness (*pulchrum*); goodness in the achievement of the desired end (*iucundum*, or the delightful); and goodness as means (*utile*, or the profitable). Delight, or pleasure, is itself the sense of the motion of desiring. So all desire is accompanied by pleasure, and aversion by displeasure. Hobbes is not here claiming that the *object* of every desire is pleasure, let alone the pleasure of the agent themselves (see e.g. Hampton 1986: 19–24).

Elsewhere, however, Hobbes's commitment to psychological egoism is clear: the object of all voluntary action is some good to the agent (L 14.202; 15.230; 25.398; see DC 5.1; 6.11). Now it might be thought that we should understand the goodness here merely to follow from the goodness of the desired object, and that such objects might extend beyond merely the good of the agent (Lloyd 2009: 84). But Hobbes is again explicit about this: 'every man is presumed to do all things in order to his own benefit' (L 15.238; see EL 1.12.6; 1.14.10; 1.19.1; DC 1.2; 1.7; 2.8; Olsthoorn 2014: 161–3). Further, agents choose what appears good or best for themselves 'by necessity of Nature' (27.456; see 14.214; EL 1.14.6; 1.16.6; DC 1.13; 6.4; 9.3; 13.16; DH 11.6; 12.6).

What, more precisely, is it that agents aim at? One thing is clear: we aim at the apparent rather than the actual good, in the sense that we can misjudge what is really best for us (L 6.94). But how do we understand that good? Hobbes sees the happiness of non-humans as consisting entirely in their 'enjoying of their quotidian Food, Ease, and Lusts' (L 12.164), but perhaps humans may pursue non-hedonic ultimate goals, such as achievement or knowledge?[4] In fact, Hobbes's view appears consistently hedonistic. The ultimate end of our voluntary actions is 'a contented life', understood in terms of 'delight', and it is for this that we desire 'Power after power' (L 11.150; see EL 1.7.2; DC 1.2; DH 11.1). But what about apparent counter-examples, such as the case of someone who seems to be sacrificing opportunities for pleasure for the sake of posthumous

---

also has a dialectical advantage, since several interpreters have claimed that works other than *Leviathan* provide stronger evidence of egoism (e.g. McNeilly 1966; 1968: 116–17, 127–9; Gert 2010: 30).

[3] For a helpful critical discussion of Hobbes's physiology and psychology of action, see McNeilly 1968: 100–36.

[4] Non-human action is also presumably to be understood in terms of psychological egoism. Voluntary action, for Hobbes, is willed action, and since will is merely the desire immediately preceding action it can be found in non-humans (L 6.92).

fame (see DC 9.15)? Hobbes suggests that this is not a 'vain' object of desire, since we enjoy imagining our being well-regarded and the benefits this may bring to our descendants (11.152). Hobbes does not here claim explicitly that this enjoyment is the actual ultimate object of our desire, rather than its cause (McNeilly 1968: 119). This, however, is how he must be understood if his claim is to be consistent with that concerning delight on the previous page. But, because he accepts a split-level version of psychological egoism, Hobbes need not be committed to the highly implausible claim that this delight is the conscious aim of the agent when they are reflecting on their posthumous fame. In other words, Hobbes can respond to Butler's point (2006: *Sermon* 11.6) against psychological hedonism, that we must have desires for objects other than pleasure to gain pleasure, by accepting it, but noting that these desires are not ultimate.[5]

Because survival is necessary to experience pleasure, and because of his wish to highlight the hugely increased risk of death in a state of nature lacking a sovereign, Hobbes tends to emphasize the value of self-preservation rather than the (further) goods it makes possible.[6] But he does not believe that what is taken to be good by each person is merely to survive: we desire preservation for the sake of a contented life, that is, for 'delight' (L 17.254).[7]

Agents necessarily prefer what seems best for themselves. But Hobbes allows both that decisions based on that preference can be distorted through irrational assessment of options, and that agents can be hindered from putting their choices into action by irrational passions. Each of these can be seen in what Derek Parfit (1984: 159) has called our 'bias towards the near'. At L 18.282 (see also DC 3.32), Hobbes says of our attitude to taxation for defence purposes:

[A]ll men are by nature provided of notable multiplying glasses, (that is their Passions and Selfe-love), through which, every little payment appeareth a great grievance; but are destitute of those prospective glasses, (namely Moral and Civill Science), to see a farre off the miseries that hang over them, and cannot without such payments be avoyded.

That is to say, the 'present goods' which are irrationally chosen are still goods for the agent.[8] Hobbes cannot allow the possibility of voluntary action unmotivated by any self-interested good:

---

[5] Butler's claim is anyway an exaggeration: in some situations, e.g. when buying a ticket for the roller-coaster, we clearly are motivated by the anticipation of pleasure.

[6] See e.g. EL 1.17.14; Olsthoorn 2014. For defence of the 'standard' view that Hobbes held that death was the greatest evil, see Murphy 2000b. Sidgwick notes (1902: 166n) that at L 14.202 the transferring of rights in the state of nature is said to be 'the security of a man's person, in his life, and in the means of so preserving life, as not to be weary of it'.

[7] See e.g. Warrender 1957: 219. This enlarged end should also be that of the sovereign for his people: DC 13.4; 13.14.

[8] *Pace* Irwin (2008: 110), Hobbes appears not to allow for genuine weakness or incontinence, in which the agent acts in a way that they believe, at that time, will be worse for them (see L 6.92; Olsthoorn 2014: 160). I am assuming that the 'weakness' Hobbes speaks of at DC 14.18 is merely a desire to keep the law of insufficient strength to win out against competing desires.

I conceive not how any man can bear *animum felleum*, or so much malice towards himself, as to hurt himself voluntarily, much less to kill himself. For naturally and necessarily the intention of every man aimeth at somewhat which is good to himself, and tendeth to his preservation. And therefore, methinks, if he kill himself, it is to be presumed that he is not *compos mentis*, but by some inward torment or apprehension of somewhat worse than death, distracted.[9] (EW 6.88, *A Dialogue of the Common Laws*)

Hobbes would probably account for the bias towards the near by suggesting that the internal motion caused by present sensory impressions or images of the near future is stronger than that caused by images of the distant; but since he allows that the passions can to some degree be corrected or resisted by reason (DC 3.32; DH 12.1–2), it will be not be irrational to seek to overcome such bias.[10]

Given the foregoing evidence, why have some recent scholars been led to deny the traditional view of Hobbes as a psychological egoist (e.g. Gert 1991: 8–9; Lloyd: 2009: 79)? The main reason is his allowing for non-self-interested motivation. The desire of good to another he describes as 'BENEVOLENCE, GOOD WILL, CHARITY', and of good to humanity in general, 'GOOD NATURE' (L 6.84; see e.g. DH 14.2). Hobbes does, however, show a tendency to introduce self-regarding elements into his explanation of other-regarding emotions. Grief at the 'calamity of another' he calls 'PITTY', and suggests that it arises from the agent's imagining that they may meet with a similar calamity (L 6.90). Now it is true that he may be read as claiming not that pity *is* self-regarding fear, merely that it originates in that (Gert 1967: 509).[11] Nowhere, however, does Hobbes explicitly allow for *ultimate* non-self-interested motivation of the kind we might find in conscious sacrifice of one's overall good or well-being. In other words, if we are not to ignore or dismiss his clear assertions of psychological egoism, we must assume that he believes that non-self-regarding motivations are non-ultimate. Benevolence can also be explained on the split-level model, with reference to the agent's enjoying helping others or wishing to decrease their own compassionate suffering. I can immediately act out of concern for another, but only because this is a strategy I have adopted to advance my own overall good. If my benevolent inclination at any point disposes me to action I believe to be against my self-interest, I will, by

---

[9] Here we see again Hobbes's exaggeration of the importance of self-preservation. If I am driven by some 'inward torment' to kill myself, and this torment is itself not understood as a desire or aversion, we can see the action as involuntary. But if I believe that remaining alive will be worse than dying now (perhaps because I know that I shall be tortured to death), my desire to die is quite consistent with my intention to do what is best for myself. Indeed at DH 11.6, Hobbes allows that the pains of life can make people count death as a good.

[10] Schmitter (2016: sect. 6) plausibly argues that the contrast here is best understood as not so much between two entirely distinct faculties, as between unbridled passions and an architectonic or 'organizing' passion.

[11] At EL 1.9.10, pity is identified with the imagination of the future calamity to oneself; and at 1.9.17, charity is said to be the conception of one's own power, and affection for strangers to be an attempt to win friendship or peace. But the apparently purely cognitivist reconstruction of the emotions in such passages may be read in the light of Hobbes's view of an imaginative conception as itself a desire.

natural necessity, resist that inclination. At no point does Hobbes allow non-self-interested motivations to interfere with the promotion of self-interest.[12]

There is more to be said about Hobbes's view of morality, and we shall return to the issue below. But already we can see the strength of the evidence for the traditional reading of Hobbes as a psychological egoist. Robert Shaver (1999: 38) has complained at the lack of arguments in Hobbes for egoism. But, as suggested above, egoism has a great initial plausibility.[13] Despite the fact that Hobbes often criticizes Aristotle, he was working in the Aristotelian tradition, and Aristotle—like most ancient philosophers—was a psychological egoist. In the *Rhetoric*, for example, he says: 'It may be said that every individual man and all men in common aim at a certain end which determines what they choose and what they avoid. This end, to sum it up briefly, is happiness' (1959: 1360b4–5; tr. Roberts (Aristotle 1984)). And the first sentence of the *Nicomachean Ethics* is: 'every action and rational choice is thought to aim at some good' (2014: 1094a1–2). That good, we soon learn, is happiness, and it is clear that Aristotle means the happiness of the agent. As with Hobbes, nowhere in the large Aristotelian corpus is there a reference to an agent's sacrificing their own happiness for the sake of morality or the good of others.

But it has to be said that psychological egoism now has few if any philosophically sophisticated supporters. Because we are less in the grip of the Aristotelian ethical tradition, because we are now aware of the evolutionary advantages of self-sacrificial behaviour by individuals (see e.g. Sober and Wilson 1998: esp. ch. 10), and because of empirical evidence from psychology (see e.g. Batson 2011: esp. pt. 2), we are less willing than many of our predecessors to deny that agents are knowingly able to sacrifice their own well-being (Tiberius 2015: 38–43). What seems much more plausible is the view Kavka (1986: 64–80) calls 'predominant egoism', according to which self-interested motivations tend to predominate in human action.

2. Rational Egoism in Hobbes

The traditional view that Hobbes is a rational egoist has also been denied in recent years (e.g. Gert 2010: 35–8, 62–4), but again I shall argue that it is correct.[14] Hobbes accepts rational egoism in the following form: agents have sole ultimate reason to

---

[12] Hobbes responds to Bishop Bramhall's objection—that Moses, St Paul, and the Decii are counter-examples to psychological egoism—that the first two acted out of long-term self-interest (i.e. eternal life) and the Decii for posthumous reputation (AB: 378). *Pace* Lloyd (2009: 188), we should expect Hobbes to take the same position on the 'final' law of nature, which requires each to protect the sovereign even in time of war (L Review.1133; see 26.423). He notes that the sovereign preserves the individual's strength, as well claiming that it is contradictory to assume a right of nature to preserve oneself and to will the destruction of the person who is doing just that (see below pp. 24–5 on the 'inconsistency' arguments against the Foole).

[13] At L Intro.20, Hobbes asks his reader to introspect, suggesting that this is the only 'demonstration' of his doctrine available.

[14] For modern statements of positions closer to the traditional view, see e.g. Peters 1956: 162; Gauthier 1969: 61; Nunan 1989; Shaver 1999: 3; 6; Irwin 2008: 114, 119.

pursue their actual self-interest; probabilities are relevant to understanding apparent self-interest;[15] self-interest is to be understood in a temporally neutral way across an individual's life; and self-interest consists in the balance of pleasure over pain.

Hobbes's anti-Aristotelianism emerges in his claim that there is no '*Summum Bonum* (greatest Good), as is spoken of in the Books of the old Morall Philosophers' (L 11.150). Hobbes has in mind, however, not the concept of happiness, but a conception of it as consisting in 'the repose of a mind satisfied'. Such tranquillity is unavailable in our lives, because that life itself consists in motion, and in particular the motion constituting desire (L 6.96; see EL 1.7.6–7; 9.21; DH 11.15). Happiness, or 'felicity', for Hobbes, then, consists in the continual satisfaction of desire over time, such satisfaction issuing in 'continual delight' (EL 1.7.7).[16]

As shown in the previous section, Hobbes believed that this *is* the goal of all voluntary action. Does he believe also that this is a goal we *ought* or have *reason* to pursue? Since Hobbes denies any notion of 'rational will', and because his conception of deliberation appears to involve merely balancing desires for and against the outcomes of acting or not acting in certain ways (L 6.90; EL 1.12.1–2; DH 11.2; see Gauthier 1969: 21–2; Irwin 2008: 104–5), it may be thought that Hobbesian egoism is merely psychological.

But, as we have already seen in connection with temporal neutrality, Hobbes's view allows for rational requirements on action.[17] Appetites can impede reason, and the emotions militate against the 'real' good in favour of the immediate. But perhaps these claims concern merely instrumental rationality, and reason is silent on which ends we should pursue (Darwall 1995: 58–9; Hampton 1996: 19–20, 34–42; Malcolm 2002: 15, 30–1, 52)? At L 14.198, Hobbes defines a law of nature as 'a Precept, or generall Rule, found out by Reason, by which a man is forbidden to do, that, which is destructive of his life'.[18] The reference of 'which' here is ambiguous: it could be 'Precept' or 'Reason'. The 'qua' in the Latin version, however, makes it most plausible that Hobbes

---

[15] Hobbes distinguishes between necessary and probable beneficial or harmful consequences of actions at L 25.404.

[16] Happiness is the satisfaction of desire, but its goodness need not be understood merely as its being desired. Nor, *pace* Hampton (1986: 35), is this view inconsistent with Hobbes's account of goodness at L 6.80–2. Goodness is always non-absolute in the sense that its sincere attribution is always related to the desire of the speaker. But this does not imply that goodness itself is identical with the property of being desired. Hampton also refers to DH 11.4. Here Hobbes claims that nothing is 'simply good'; goodness is always goodness for some individual. Again, this is consistent with the view that the goodness of happiness does not consist merely in its being desired. Hobbes draws a clear distinction between the desirable and the desired at 1889: App. 1, 208.

[17] At DC 7.18, the relation between reason and desire is compared to that between man and beast (see Plato 2003: 588c–e).

[18] And '[a]ll these *natural precepts* are derived from just dictate of reason, that presses on us our own preservation and security' (DC 3.26). Note that the rest of the sentence in L might suggest that Hobbes has in mind subjective as well as objective reasons here. Kavka (1986: 340–1) plausibly claims that we should not so read the text, since it is not up to each agent whether or not to act on any law of nature. What is up to each person is how best to conform with each law of nature.

intended the latter.[19] So reason requires self-preservation, and 'this is that good…, which not every man in passion calleth so, but all men by reason' (EL 1.17.14).[20] So when Hobbes says that the laws of nature are 'simply the dictates of right reason' (DC 3.25; see L 13.196; DC 1.7; 2.1; 14.16;), he is saying not merely that they are instrumental to some non-rational goal; rather, the goal they help us achieve is itself one we are required by reason to pursue.[21] We have already seen Hobbes's readiness to include more than mere survival in his account of our ultimate goal, and can therefore conclude that he will accept rational egoism.

It is of course true that Hobbes gives reason an important instrumental role: 'the Thoughts, are to the Desires, as Scouts, and Spies, to range abroad, and to find the way to the things Desired' (L 8.110). But he nowhere explicitly limits reason to this role, whereas he does claim that reason requires us to pursue our own good. Hobbes describes deliberation as a series of desires and aversions guided by reflection on the good and bad consequences of the options under consideration (L 6.90; see 3.40). But he does not rule out deliberation's itself being required by reason to postulate as its goal the happiness of the agent. Each agent has, by natural necessity, a desire that their self-interest be promoted; but this desire is itself rational.

At this point, it may be objected that Hobbes cannot be read as offering such a substantive and significant role to reason, since for him reason is purely 'formal', rather than 'material':[22]

REASON … is nothing but *Reckoning* (that is, Adding and Subtracting) of the Consequences of generall names agreed upon, for the *marking* and *signifying* of our thoughts. (L 5.64)

Here it is important to note what Hobbes himself is willing to include in 'reckoning'. He allows that it can involve the 'adding together *two Names*, to make an *Affirmation*' (L 5.64; see EL 1.5.9). The 'first Items in every Reckoning … are the significations of names settled by definitions' (L 5.66). The claim that our rational end is our own self-interest is nothing more than an affirmation, or a definition. Further, reason can, through reflection on 'consequences' or implications, 'reduce the consequences … to generall Rules, called *Theoremes*' (L 5.68). At L 15.242, Hobbes notes that, strictly

---

[19] 'At Lex Naturalis Praeceptum est, sive Regula generalis Ratione excogitata, qua unusquisque id quod ad damnum suum sibi tendere videbitur facere prohibetur.' See Newey 2008: 90. It is possible that the 'qua' refers to 'Regula', but this would be odd, given that this is the second of a pair of disjuncts, the other of which is the neuter 'Praeceptum', and that 'Ratione' is closer to 'qua' than 'Regula'. See also L 15.224: 'Justice … is a Rule of Reason, by which we are forbidden to do any thing destructive to our life'; and note 'the postulate of natural reason, by which each man strives to avoid violent death as the supreme evil in nature' (DC: Ep. ded. 10).

[20] See also DC: Ep. Ded. 6. At EL 1.14.6, Hobbes makes the weaker claim that it is not against reason for someone to seek self-preservation. At DC 3.29 and 31, we are told that the end of reason is peace (see L 14.198–200). I take it that Hobbes means by this a state of peaceful and tranquil self-preservation.

[21] See Gert 2010: 48–53. Note that at L 15.222, the 'Foole' speaks of 'that Reason, which dictateth to every man his own good', and Hobbes does not quibble with this usage.

[22] See Deigh 1996: esp. 39–40, 50; also Boonin-Vail 1994: 54; Darwall 1995: 58; Murphy 2000a: esp. 260–1; Deigh 2003: esp. 98, 109. For a discussion of Hobbes's use of the term 'reason', see Kavka 1983: 120–1. For another rationalist interpretation, see Gert 2001: esp. 248, 253, 255.

speaking, his natural 'laws', considered merely as the 'dictates of Reason', are not laws, but 'Theoremes concerning what conduceth to... [men's] conservation and defence of themselves' (see Harrison 2003: 89–90; 100). In other words, Hobbes's conception of reason is material as well as formal, and extends to the issuing of fundamental requirements on any human action.

3. Hobbes on Morality

Hobbes, then, accepts S-reasons. But what about M-reasons? It is true that nowhere in Hobbes is genuine self-sacrifice recommended as rational or reasonable.[23] But it could be that this is because he saw self-interested reasons as entirely consistent with non-self-interested, ruling out conflict and hence the very possibility of self-sacrifice. As noted above, on one plausible reading this is Aristotle's position on the relation between happiness and the exercise of moral virtue.

Morality is an obvious potential source of normativity, and it is easy to see why many have thought Hobbes accepts ultimate moral reasons. He often speaks of right and wrong, moral obligations, moral law, and so on, and most who use such concepts believe in self-standing moral reasons. But Hobbes's position on morality, I shall suggest, is a descendant of that outlined by Glaucon. Morality's value is, in effect, instrumental, as a social system to create conditions for co-operation which would be unavailable through unco-ordinated actions by self-interested individuals; it is, that is to say, 'nothing more than a system of common, or universal, prudence' (Gauthier 1969: 98; see also Watkins 1973: 55–6; Hampton 1986: 50, 56–7; Nunan 1989: 59; Irwin 2008: 132–3). As John Locke later put it: '[A]n Hobbist... will not easily admit a great many plain duties of morality'.[24]

The key text here is L 14. Hobbes begins the chapter by linking himself to the natural rights tradition. But it turns out that his conception of a natural right is quite different from that of other natural rights theorists. A right of nature, he claims, is each person's liberty to do whatever is necessary to preserve their own life. Liberty is then defined as the absence of external impediments. So the right of nature turns out to be equivalent to a version of so-called 'negative' liberty. If my liberty to preserve myself is limited in some way, my right is also limited, since my liberty and my right are identical. But it would be quite misleading to say that my right has been 'violated', even if it is the action of others that has limited it. There is nothing evaluative or normative to this right: it is merely the absence of impediments to the exercise, to some degree or other, of my power to preserve myself. If the impediments are such that there is *nothing* I can do to

---

[23] See Hampton (1986: 94), who rightly notes that it is not essential to a morality that it allow for self-sacrifice. Gert (1996: 169) suggests that Hobbes does not rule out rational sacrifice, referring to his claim at DH 13.9 that all virtues can be placed under the headings of charity, along with that of justice. If Gert means overall sacrifice of well-being rather than of certain goods, then the passage appears not to support his interpretation.

[24] Quoted from an article of 1677 in King 1830: 1.191.

preserve myself, it is again not the case that my right has been violated. Rather, I no longer have any right of nature, since I have no power to do anything towards preserving myself.

So far, then, Hobbes has not committed himself to any normative claim.[25] He then goes on to offer the definition of a law of nature we have already encountered, as a rational requirement to take the means to preserve oneself. He contrasts law, which 'determines' or 'binds' us, with right, which consists in liberty—that is, with not being bound. We are bound, then, not by any moral or other-regarding reason, but a self-interested one.

He then returns to the idea of the 'state of nature' described in the previous chapter, the 'condition of Warre of every one against every one'. Here, each person is governed only by their own reason, and no object is such that they might not use it to preserve themselves. So each has a right to everything, even to the bodies of others. Hobbes does *not* mean that in a state of nature each person has reason to do whatever they wish. Though one may have the right of nature or liberty to act in whatever way one likes, reason requires one to act only to further one's own good.

Now, given that human beings are rational, the result of their each exercising their reason in the state of nature will be war and insecurity for all. Hence arises the first law of nature: to seek peace where possible, and where not possible to engage in war. The second law of nature concerns the means to peace and self-defence, and requires each man to 'lay down' his right to everything and '*be contented with so much liberty against other men, as he would allow other men against himselfe*' (14.200).

We cannot understand the idea of laying down here as equivalent to 'waiving' a moral or legal right, since Hobbes has postulated no such rights. Any limitation on my right must arise through the presence of some external impediment, and so laying down must consist in the placing by the individual of some external impediment on their exercise of their power to promote their own good. Imagine some situation arises in the state of nature in which A can promote their good only by harmfully using the body of B. They have the liberty to do so, in the sense that there is no external impediment; and reason also requires them so to act. If A lays down their right to use B's body, they are in effect allowing B the liberty to use B's body for B's own purposes—that is, they are removing an impediment from B which previously existed. But they should do so, Hobbes insists, only if B is also prepared to allow A to use A's body for A's purposes.

---

[25] Hobbes sometimes speaks of rights more narrowly, as limited by what the agent has reason to do (EL 1.14.6; DC 1.7). He is led to this through his willingness to equate what is right with what is in accordance with right reason (see Gauthier 1979: 550; Hampton 1986: 54). This narrower notion of a right can also be understood in terms of liberty from external impediments, in this case to do what one has reason to do. There are then two senses of 'right' and 'wrong' at work in Hobbes: the rational sense, and the moral sense (see the distinction between a *peccatum* (error) and *malum culpae* (culpable evil) at DC 14.16–17; see also Gert 1991: 26). By distinguishing them, we can see that Hobbes is not contradicting himself when he claims, e.g., that on the one hand there is no right or wrong in the state of nature, and on the other that what is done for self-preservation in the state of nature is done rightly (DC 2.27n).

At this point, it might appear that Hobbes is allowing for M-reasons, for he goes on:

[W]hen a man hath...abandoned, or granted away his Right; then he is said to be OBLIGED, or BOUND, not to hinder those, to whom such Right is granted, or abandoned, from the benefit of it; and that he *Ought*, and it is his DUTY, not to make voyd that voluntary act of his own: and that such hindrance is INIUSTICE. (L 14.200–2)

It is tempting to think that Hobbes is using the notion of obligation or being bound, here, in the same way as we saw him using it to describe our relation to reason and the law of nature. If I lay down my right, in other words, I am morally bound not to act as if I had not.[26] But if this were Hobbes's view, then we might expect him to claim that a 'covenant' in the state of nature is morally binding, in the sense that each party has moral reason—binding moral reason—to keep it. In fact, in the state of nature, '[t]he notions of Right and Wrong, Justice and Injustice have there no place' (L 13.196). Indeed any covenant made in the state of nature in which contractors promise future performance is 'voyd', because of the absence of 'a common Power set over them both' (L 14.210; see EL 1.15.10).[27]

---

[26] One important passage, used by deontological interpreters of Hobbes (e.g. Taylor 1938: 408–9; 424; Gert 1967: 517; 2010: 32 (for a clear statement of the deontological view itself, see e.g. Ross 1930: 18–19)), might seem to commit Hobbes to ultimate moral normativity: 'Some have thought that being obligated and being kept to one's obligation are the same thing and that consequently this is a verbal not a substantial distinction. So I will put it more clearly. A man is obligated by an agreement, i.e. he ought to perform because of his promise. But he is kept to his obligation by a law, i.e. he is compelled to performance by fear of the penalty laid down in the law' (DC 14.2n; italics removed; see DC 2.22). In DC 14.2, Hobbes is seeking to distinguish between agreements on the one hand, and laws on the other. An agreement might be, e.g., a 'crowd of men declaring rules for living by common consent'. Such agreements, however, 'do not obligate anyone and are therefore not laws' until a coercive sovereign power is established. Since Hobbes explicitly says that mere agreements do not obligate, we cannot read 14.2n as an assertion of deontology. Hobbes must be speaking of agreements made when there is a coercive power to compel performance, and his main point is that '[i]n *agreements* one says, *I will do*; *laws* say, *Do*'. If, when a sovereign power exists, I say 'I will φ', then that is an agreement, and I am obligated to φ; and the *explanation* of the existence of my obligation is that I have, by saying those words in that context, made a promise. Before I said those words, I was not so obligated (see EL 1.15.9; DC 2.13). My being obligated, however, itself consists in no more than my now being bound to φ through fear of the consequences. The law requires contractors to fulfil their contracts, and by commanding that, and threatening sanctions for disobedience, the law thereby 'keeps me' to my obligation.

[27] Kavka (1986: 139–40, 351) suggests that Hobbes's response to the Foole (15.224) implies that the second party to a covenant in the state of nature, once the first party has performed, is bound to perform. But Hobbes begins his response by stating that he and the Foole are not discussing 'promises mutuall' in the state of nature, since such promises are not covenants. So when he goes on to mention the case of first-party performance, we must understand this to be the fulfilling of a genuine covenant, made in the presence of a coercive power. Indeed in the Latin version Hobbes made this clear with this addition of 'existente Potentia, quae cogat' (L 15.225). Darwall (1995: 72) claims that it is 'reasonable suspicion' that voids a contract, and, since the second party can no longer harbour any such suspicion once the first party has performed, they are obligated. But the text of 15.210 makes it clear that the reasonable suspicion of both parties during the initial contract would already have made it void, and that it is the presence of a power to compel performance which makes a contract non-void.

In an especially problematic passage at L 14.212, Hobbes claims that '[c]ovenants entred into by fear, in the condition of meer Nature, are obligatory', giving the example of my promising a ransom to an enemy in return for my life (see EL 1.15.3; DC 2.16). The main point Hobbes wishes to make is that the fact that some covenant is made through fear does not invalidate it. If we are to avoid attributing a serious and straightforward contradiction to him within a few pages, we must understand him to be speaking only of

The bonds Hobbes has in mind here, then, are not rational or moral. They 'have their strength, not from their own Nature, (for nothing is more easily broken than a mans word,) but from Feare of some evill consequence upon the rupture' (L 14.202; see L 18.268).[28] That the primary motivation for keeping one's promises is fear of the consequences of breaking them explains why Hobbes insists that certain rights are 'inalienable' (L 14.202; see DC 6.13). If I promise to φ, then I am willing the placing of an obstacle to my not φ-ing in the form of some threat to my own happiness if I fail to φ. Consider a case in which I promise not to resist you if you try to kill me. I can be making that promise only because I believe it will advance my own good. But, Hobbes suggests, it is obvious that such a promise can bring me only harm, so it has to be assumed that I do not understand what I am doing. For the system of contracts to operate successfully, it must insist on understanding by the contracting parties of what it is they are binding themselves to.

By establishing a common power to punish us if we fail to keep our covenants, we are in effect creating a morality.[29] But this morality has no normative force in itself; if it did, it would surely have such force in the state of nature. The laws of nature are based on a single dictate of reason: that of self-preservation (broadly construed) (DC 3.26; see 2.1).[30] Here, then, we find another form of split-level egoism in Hobbes, this time a normative version. On any occasion, I have reason only to advance my own good.[31]

cases in which there is some sanction for non-performance—that is, of covenants that are not 'voyd'. (Nunan 1989: 48 suggests that it is in the prisoner's interest to keep the promise because it helps establish the general principle, and the prisoner might be captured again at some future point. This argument, though weak, does resonate with Hobbes's somewhat hopeful response to the Foole: see sect. 4 below.) Of the case in which I agree to pay a highway robber if he spares me, Hobbes says: 'There are times when an *agreement* like that should be held to be invalid; but it will not be held to be invalid simply because it was motivated by fear' (DC 2.16). The invalidity he has in mind is likely to be that arising from lack of security of performance. At DC 8.1, Hobbes claims that a vanquished person who promises obedience to the victor 'owes the victor service and obedience, as absolute as may be, except for what is contrary to the divine laws'. Divine law is identical with the law of nature, which requires us to promote our own good. It is tempting, then, to understand Hobbes to be speaking of cases in which it is in the vanquished's interest to obey the victor.

[28] Hobbes also uses the notion of 'binding' to make the point that, if the laws of nature are being generally disobeyed in the state of nature, an individual should not just forget about them. They oblige '*in foro interno*; that is to say, they bind to a desire they should take place' (15.240; see DC3.27). In the Latin version, Hobbes says that in such cases one may call action in opposition to the laws of nature 'vitium' rather than 'crimen'. I take it that he is here using 'vitium' in a non-moral sense, to mean something like 'defect, blemish, fault' (Lewis and Short 1879: s.v.). Note also that Hobbes later allows that there may be another motive to keeping one's word: 'Glory, or Pride in appearing not to need to break it' (L 14.216).

[29] Justice has its origin in human agreement rather than nature: DC: Ep. ded. 9; DH 10.5. See Gauthier 1977a: 435–7, and for a modern account influenced by Hobbes, Gauthier 1986: esp. 115, 160. It is part of the role of the sovereign 'to be Judge, or constitute all Judges of Opinions and Doctrines', and to prescribe the 'Rules of Propriety...of *Good, Evil*...in actions of Subjects' (L 18.272, 274).

[30] Lloyd (2009: 112) cites the claim at DC 15.5 that reason requires the surrender of the right to all things 'for the preservation of the human race' as evidence that the laws of nature are grounded on the common good, not self-interest. The passage after that she quotes continues: 'However, if anyone had been so much more powerful than all the rest that they could not have resisted him with their united strength, there would have been no reason whatsoever for him to give up the right'. The preservation of the human race, in other words, is assumed by Hobbes to be in the self-interest of the individuals surrendering their rights.

[31] On this interpretation, Hobbes's position is not, as Kavka (1986: 358–9) claims, a version of 'rule egoism'. According to Kavka, the laws of nature are themselves grounded on the following principle (REP):

But I will succeed over time in advancing my own good most effectively if I can make certain covenants with others. Those covenants will indeed impose certain restrictions on me; but since others will also be subject to those restrictions, we shall all do better than we would in the absence of morality.

Is Hobbes restricting morality merely to acting in certain ways? The laws of nature, reasonably enough, are all stated in terms of actions alone, without requiring any particular motivation. Nevertheless, it is tempting to read Hobbes as claiming that it is rational for individuals to take steps to direct their own character and motivational dispositions towards virtue (see Boonin-Vail 1994: esp. 106–23; cf. Ewin 1991: 189). For example, at L 15.226–7, Hobbes distinguishes between the righteous man, who does just actions because they are just, and the unrighteous, who, if he does just actions, does them out of fear of the consequences of not doing them (see EL 1.16.4; DC 3.5; 14.18). And he then goes on (L 15.242; see EL 1.17.14) to claim that the virtues, including justice, are the means to peace. The laws of nature, that is to say, require one to become a virtuous person.[32]

Structurally, Hobbes's two-level egoism mirrors that of two-level consequentialism. There are difficulties for two-level consequentialism in cases in which an agent has strong evidence that some course of action will promote the good overall, but that course of action is forbidden by the principles constituting their non-consequentialist decision-procedure (see e.g. Smart 1956; Williams 1985: 106–8). One consequentialist response is to claim that such cases will never occur in the real world, so agents should never give up their decision-procedure for the sake of promoting the overall good.[33]

'Each agent should attempt always to follow that set of general rules of conduct whose acceptance (and sincere attempt to follow) by him on all occasions would produce the best (expected) outcome for him'. Kavka says that he is explaining Hobbes's 'moral theory', contrasting rule egoism with act egoism, act consequentialism, and rule consequentialism. There is no suggestion that REP concerns only pro tanto rather than overall reasons for action; so the principle is best understood as the claim that the right or rational action for any agent on any occasion depends on whether that action is in accordance with this set of general rules. There are two significant problems with this interpretation (the same problems arise for the suggestion by Worsnip (2015) that covenants are entered into for self-interested reasons but can then provide reasons to act against one's self-interest). First, if Hobbes were a rule egoist, we might expect him to have used the view to respond to the Foole that we should follow rules even if on certain occasions we do worse by so doing. Second, Hobbes's psychological egoism predicts that any agent, absent distorting factors, will seek to act in accordance with act egoism; it is not possible for an agent to do anything other than what they believe to be best for them on that occasion, whether or not doing so is in accordance with some set of rules (see Hampton 1986: 93). (Kavka refers to Moore 1971; 1972 for support. Moore appeals to passages in which Hobbes argues that those who have gained their freedom through promising a ransom should pay; that one should follow the principle of trying to requite benefits; that one should be just—that is, fulfil contracts for their own sake rather than to advance one's own self-interest. To avoid the two problems just mentioned, and for the sake of consistency with Hobbes's statements of rational egoism elsewhere, it is best to read these passages as expressions of split-level act egoism, and to assume that Hobbes would use the same arguments against objections based on apparent exceptions as those he uses against the Foole.)

[32] This does not make Hobbes a 'virtue ethicist' in anything other than a weak sense. One's reasons for becoming virtuous are entirely self-interested, and Hobbes's conception of self-interest is hedonistic rather than an 'objective list' account (Parfit 1984: app. I) which includes virtue on the list.

[33] Hobbes himself insists that the laws of nature are immutable and eternal, not because they state universal ultimate reasons, but because 'it can *never* be that Warre shall preserve life' (L 15.240 (my italics); DC 3.29).

This response is implausible. Such cases may be rare, but they will occur. The same issue will of course arise for the Hobbesian two-level egoist, and in a potentially more serious form. In the consequentialist case, the issue is which moral principle an agent should follow—that of common sense, or that of moral theory. In the egoist case, the question is whether the theory justifies going against morality entirely, if morality is understood as a possible source of reasons independent of the agent's own well-being. What, then, should a Hobbesian agent do in a case in which the morality they have rationally agreed to abide by goes clearly against their own interest? Hobbes faces just this problem in his famous discussion of 'the Foole' (L 15.222–6).

4. The Response to the Foole

Hobbes begins chapter 15 (L 15.220) with the third law of nature: 'That men performe their Covenants made'. He then explains how it is only through a valid covenant (one made by parties whose performance will be enforced by an independent coercive power) that justice and injustice come into being. Injustice, in other words, can be defined as the failure to perform what one has covenanted to do. And because, before any such covenant, there is no moral restriction on what any agent can use to pursue their own good, it is only through the establishment of such a coercive power (that is, a commonwealth) that the institution of property can emerge.

The Foole is happy to speak of covenants, and to use the word 'unjust' to describe the breaking of them. But he denies the existence of justice and injustice, and claims that sometimes, when breaking a covenant will benefit an agent, that agent is required by reason to commit injustice (that is, break the covenant). This is especially so when the profit of injustice puts one beyond the powers of other men completely—that is, through making one king. The Foole goes on:

The Kingdome of God is gotten by violence; but what if it could be gotten by unjust violence? were it against Reason so to get it, when it is impossible to receive hurt by it? and if it be not against Reason, it is not against Justice: or else Justice is not to be approved for good.[34]

One immediate oddity here is the Foole's speaking of God and of justice, when he believes in neither. But his argument is presumably directed at those who do believe in both. The question appears to be why I should not, if I can, usurp God himself, since once I have succeeded I cannot be punished. Hobbes himself notes here that such reasoning has led some to describe successful vice as virtue. And, he concludes (probably

---

[34] In implying that any moral principle, if it is to have normative weight, must be in line with self-interest, the Foole commits himself to something close to what Baier (1991: 201–3) calls *ethical egoism*. This view is not a version of rational egoism, since it allows for non-egoistic sources of normativity. It is important to remember that both the Foole and Hobbes deny the existence of justice and injustice as sources of normativity (see Darwall 1995: 73). Shaver (2017: sects. 1–2) defines ethical egoism as the view that it is necessary and sufficient for an action to be morally right that it maximize one's self-interest, and notes that one could argue for ethical egoism from RE and the not implausible claim that the best moral theory must tell me what I have most reason to do. See also the reference to Hare 1981: 53–7 at p. 4 above.

speaking of the Foole's position as well as the claim that gaining a kingdom through the kind of force usually described as unjust is in fact virtuous): 'This specious [that is, attractive] reasoning is nevertheless false'.

At this point, if Hobbes believed in independent moral normativity, we might expect him to mention it,[35] and also to claim that the kind of action recommended by the Foole—except when God himself has been supplanted—will be punished by God in the afterlife. He assumes that the Foole is also an atheist, but this of course would not undermine a theistic response. As we have seen, however, such a response is not available to Hobbes, and he does not attempt it. If the Foole is right about what reason dictates, then it will be in accordance with natural law, and *failing* to break a covenant will be punished by God, since the laws of nature are themselves commands of God (L 15: 242).[36]

Hobbes has several responses to the arguments of the Foole and those based on the Foole's position. Each is problematic. The first is that a man's breaking a covenant 'tendeth to his own destruction', whatever the evidence suggests, so that it would be unreasonable to do it even if in fact some unexpected event will result in the action's benefiting the agent overall.

But why should the Foole accept that covenant-breaking is *always* more likely than not to lead to destruction? Support is required for the claim that it does indeed have that tendency, and it could be that the following two arguments are meant to provide that support.

The second argument is that it is dangerous, by the very breaking of a covenant, to advertise the fact that one is willing to break covenants, since one will be unable to benefit from the advantages of making covenants, unless one's fellow covenanters are ignorant enough of their own good to co-operate. And this is something one cannot reasonably rely on.

This argument is a good one against a defaulter's letting others know his position, whether through openly breaking a covenant or in any other way. But that position, as Hobbes himself suggests, is stated by the Foole 'in his heart'. There is no argument here against secret injustice (Farrell 1984: 309).[37]

[35] *Pace* Shelton (1992: 60), van Mill (2001: 132), and Lloyd (2009: 296), there seems no good reason to expect Hobbes to offer only arguments that the Foole himself is likely to accept. Hobbes's aim is to persuade his reader, not the imaginary Foole.

[36] At L 15.226, Hobbes considers such a position, and objects that we are ignorant of the afterlife and of what may be rewarded or punished there (see main text below). This claim appears to be in tension with that on the previous page that keeping covenants is the only way imaginable of gaining heavenly happiness. His view is perhaps that it is more plausible to believe that keeping covenants will be rewarded than not, but that even this belief is not well justified.

[37] Hoekstra (1997) argues that Hobbes is responding only to the 'explicit' Foole, who advertises his position. But Hobbes is clear that the question he is addressing is whether, in a case where one party to a covenant has performed or will be coerced into performance, 'it be against reason, that is against the benefit of the other to performe, or not' (L 15.224). He is defending the third law of nature as a law of reason without exception. For an extended defence of the rationality of a disposition of 'constrained maximization' rather than one of straightforward case-by-case maximization, see Gauthier 1986: esp. ch. 6. At 183, Gauthier claims: 'A straightforward maximizer...must expect to be excluded from co-operative arrangements

Hobbes then turns to the argument that it is both reasonable and just to acquire the kingdom of God by any means, and in particular to what we can now see to be its underlying assumption: that if one acquires the kingdom of God one will gain 'secure and perpetuall felicity'. This argument, he says, is 'frivolous', since the only conceivable way to such happiness is through keeping covenants.

This, however, is mere assertion on Hobbes's part. As we have seen, were he to allow independent moral normativity, and to claim that God—unless usurped—punishes the breaking of a moral law even when it benefits the agent, his argument would have purchase. But he does neither.

Hobbes has two final arguments in L 15, directed at the general argument in favour of winning sovereignty through rebellion. The first is a version of the initial 'tendency' argument: it will not have been reasonable to seek to acquire sovereignty in this way even if one is in fact successful, since one can reasonably expect only to fail. Again, no support for that claim is offered by Hobbes.

The second argument, though it again has some weight, and generalizes to other cases of injustice, is also ultimately insufficient. The argument is that success in injustice may encourage others to act unjustly, and so (presumably because the unjust agent's interests overall will be harmed) injustice is 'against reason'.

Just as a potential defaulter would be well advised to consider the consequences of publicizing his position verbally, so they should take into account the effects of its becoming known through their acting on it successfully (in the short term). Hobbes is right that there will be occasions on which the danger of imitation by others will make it subjectively or objectively irrational to break a covenant. Equally, however, there will be cases in which, despite that danger, it is egoistically rational to act as the Foole recommends.

Hobbes does have a further line of argument against the Foole, which he outlines independently. If someone breaks a covenant, Hobbes suggests, he 'willeth the doing and the not doing of the same thing, at the same time; which is a plain contradiction' (EL 1.16.2; see DC 3.3; L Rev: 1133; LeBuffe 2003). There are several problems with this argument.[38] First, the defaulter may claim not to be willing to keep their agreement. They may be fully intending throughout not to keep it if it is in their interest to do so. Second, Hobbes appears to be exploiting an ambiguity. In the quotation above, the phrase 'at the same time' may be taken to apply to 'willeth' or 'the not doing'. Let us grant that willing the doing and the not doing of the same thing at the same time is a contradiction. The defaulter may claim, however, that they never do this. At time t, they initially will, let us allow, that they will keep their agreement at $t1$. They do not will that they will break that agreement. At time $t1$, they will that they will break the agreement

which he would find advantageous. A constrained maximizer may be expect to be included in such arrangements'. This claim is plausible only of those whose dispositions are known to others. For further criticism of constrained maximization, see Superson 2009: 23–37.

[38] For an excellent discussion of these problems, see Harrison 2003: 114–19.

made at t. They do not will that they will keep that agreement. So their will is in fact never in conflict. Finally, even if we allow that there is a contradiction in the defaulter's will, it is not clear, in the absence of further argument, what kind of practical reason they have to avoid such contradiction, unless it is in their interest to do so.

There is a slightly different argument at DC 3.2:

[I]n making an agreement, one denies by the very act of agreeing that the act is meaningless. And it is against reason knowingly to take away the meaning of anything. If he does not believe the agreement should be fulfilled, by the very fact that he so believes he affirms that the agreement is meaningless.

This argument runs into the same difficulty as the second argument against the Foole. It would indeed be problematic were the defaulter to assert, while promising to φ, their intention not to do so. It may be, that is, that any genuine agreement between two individuals requires that each not believe that the other will break the agreement. But the Foole will of course recommend against any such assertion. If Hobbes is then to claim that a false promise is no promise, he will require a good deal of further argument; and even if that argument were to succeed, the Foole can insist that he is advocating not promising, but false promising.

We have been considering whether those in the state of nature, or citizens in a civil society, might have morally normative obligations. But what about the sovereign themselves? Can a sovereign, given that their position makes acting unjustly possible, themselves act in this way? Hobbes is clear that this is not possible (L 18.270), since the sovereign has been given authority by each of their subjects to act as they wish. Nevertheless, they *do* have certain duties; sovereigns are bound by natural law like anyone else, and in their case the law requires that they 'procure, to the uttermost of their endeavour, the good of the people' (EL 2.9.1; DC 6.13n; 7.14; 13.2). So it might appear that here we have an obligation with independent moral weight (Taylor 1938: 415–16).

But we are required by parsimony and charity to understand natural laws as applying to the sovereign in the same way as to their subjects. If they fail to promote the good of the people, then they are acting against reason, against natural law, and against God (DC 6.13). This is because they are not advancing their own interests by so acting. The divine punishment for breaking the law of nature is 'eternal death', and the good of the sovereign herself correlates with that of their subjects: 'governing to the profit of the subjects, is governing to the profit of the sovereign' (EL 2.9.1).[39]

Hobbes's denial of a conflict of interest between the sovereign and their subjects is clearly too optimistic. It is easy to imagine cases in which the overall balance of pleasure over pain in the life of an extremely powerful sovereign will best be promoted by their inflicting severe suffering on their subjects, or at least the majority of them.

So far, we have been discussing non-self-interested moral normativity. What about the normativity that might be found in the commands of God? Could Hobbes believe

---

[39] The law of nature is also the moral law: DC 3.31; see EL 1.18.1; 2.10.7.

that the mere fact that God has commanded me to φ *in itself* gives me a reason to φ independent of my own self-interest? Hobbes claims frequently that it is by virtue of God's commands that dictates of reason concerning self-preservation *become* laws (L 15.242;[40] EL 1.17.12; 2.2.3; 2.10.7; DC 3.33). He also makes it clear that God's commands are to do what reason independently requires (EL 1.18.1–2; DC 13.2), but this of course is consistent with its being the case that God's command does provide an additional reason to further one's own good. And indeed this turns out to be the case, but not in the sense that the reason generated is independent of the agent's good. The absolute right of God is grounded not in, say, gratitude but God's 'irresistible power' (L 31.558; see DC 14.1; Hampton 1986: 95–6). We should conclude, then, that our obligation to obey again rests on nothing other than the consequences of disobedience and our fear of those consequences.[41]

Hobbes restates Glaucon's challenge to morality in an especially stark and sustained way. Many will agree that self-interest is at least one important human motive, and that it constitutes one source of normative reasons. Hobbes seeks to persuade us that action based on immediate concern for morality, or for the well-being of others, is issuing in fact from a long-term, self-interested disposition, and that any moral or altruistic desire is vulnerable to overthrow by self-interest at any point. Further, he suggests, reason requires us maximally to promote our own good. And though he argues vigorously against the view that reason so understood can justify immorality, the relative weakness of those arguments is part of the explanation of why Hobbes came to be seen as such a danger to the common good. Extremes, it has been said, beget extremes. In chapter 3, we shall see that one of the earliest responses to the extreme partiality of Hobbes's views was an extreme form of impartiality. But before that we must consider Henry More's attempt at closing the gap between morality and self-interest.

---

[40] In the later Latin translation, Hobbes drops the reference to God here.
[41] See Warrender 1957: 315, cited in this connection by Gauthier 1969: 191; Nunan 1989: 63–4.

3

More:

An Enthusiasm for Virtue

The most well-known and distinguished of the so-called 'Cambridge Platonists' was Ralph Cudworth (1617–88), whose main ethical work was *A Treatise Concerning Immutable and Eternal Morality*, posthumously published in 1731. This is primarily metaethical, defending the views that goodness is prior to the will (including the will of God) (e.g. 1.2.1), and that moral principles are, in a sense, innate, though our understanding of them depends on experience and the exercise of an active intellect (e.g. 4.2.15, 4.6.4). The *Treatise* was to be part of a larger work on ethics, which was never completed, but it is likely that Cudworth's views on normative ethics were close to those of his colleague and friend Henry More (1614–87), whose *Enchiridion Ethicum* was published in Latin in 1667 and in an English translation of 1690 as *An Account of Virtue*.[1] Some have thought that More used Latin, which he found difficult, so as to leave room for Cudworth to publish in English (Henry 2016: sect. 5). Unlike Cumberland's *Treatise of the Law of Nature*, which appeared shortly after the *Enchiridion*, More's book does not advertise itself as a direct response to Hobbes, though he is mentioned. But More and his readers would undoubtedly have seen his ethics as offering a securer foundation for virtue than that of Hobbes.

1. Virtue and Hedonism

More begins his book (1.1.1–3) by distinguishing between living well and happiness, claiming that the Pythagoreans were right to see a difference between 'perfection according to nature' (that is, virtue) and 'perfection according to life' (happiness) and to allow that virtue does not always lead to happiness. This is primarily because virtuous dispositions alone are not enough: the virtuous person also requires both the opportunity for virtuous action (which may well involve a certain provision of goods 'external' to virtue) and success in those actions (1.3.11).[2]

---

[1] Unattributed references are to this translation.

[2] Certain external goods can also increase happiness in their own right, but—with the possible exception of health—only in an insignificant way (2.10). Further, virtue itself can increase one's holdings of external goods, including subtlety of wit, memory, knowledge of the divine, strength, health, liberty, sufficient wealth, nobility, and true friendship (3.9).

More sees three virtues as 'primitive' or basic (2.1–3). *Prudence* involves rational dominion over the passions, and is clearly close to Aristotelian *phronēsis* in its enabling the virtuous agent to find the 'Golden Mean' (Aristotle 1894: 2.6). Once that decision has been made, the virtue of *sincerity* is exercised in the agent's actively willing the action in question, assisted if necessary by *patience* in overcoming the desires of our 'animal nature' to avoid suffering. There are then three main 'derivative' virtues: justice (which to God constitutes piety and to humans 'probity'), fortitude, and temperance (2.4–7). Finally, there are various virtues which can be 'reduced' to the three deriva-tive virtues, including liberality, gratitude, modesty, and love of humanity (2.8). Early in his work, More seeks to capture the essence of his ethical views in twenty-three 'immediately and irresistibly true' principles, or *noemata*, analogous to mathematical axioms (1.4.2–4). It is clear from noemata 14 and 15 that More saw his ethics as based on the 'golden rule' of Matthew vii.12, and there is no reason to think that he was recommending anything other than the standard common-sense Christian morality of his day. Further, More held that these common-sense moral principles captured ultimate M-reasons: right reason is consonant with divine reason, which 'does nothing partially for the sake of this or that particular: but as she generously dictates...such Laws as tend...to the Happiness of all Mankind' (1.3.6). We have independent duties to others, which are not grounded in the promotion of our own self-interest (1.4.3).

The opening of More's book is strongly reminiscent of Aristotle's discussion of hap-piness in the first two books of the *Nicomachean Ethics*, and indeed More refers to Aristotle at this point as he does frequently throughout his book (there are few refer-ences to Plato). So one might expect his view of well-being to incorporate virtue—or the successful exercise of virtue—as a significant and independent component. But, perhaps surprisingly, More, like Hobbes, is a hedonist, citing Aristotle in his support (1.2.4). More's very first noema (1.4.2) states: 'Good is that which is grateful, pleasant, and congruous to any Being, which hath Life and Perception, or that contributes in any degree to the preservation of it'.[3] Goodness is straightforwardly aggregative (the value of two people's being happy is twice that of one person's (1.4.3 (noema 18)), goods and evils are commensurable (1.4.2 (noema 7)), and the balance of good over evil is to be maximized neutrally across time (1.4.2–3 (noemata 5, 8–11, 13).

There is, however, an important difference between the claim that it is pleasure alone that makes someone happy, and the weaker Aristotelian claim that the virtuous life is pleasant. According to More, 'Happiness is that pleasure which the mind takes in from a Sense of Virtue, and a Conscience of Well-doing' (1.2.2; also 2.7.6; 2.3.9; 3.3.6). He is, then, what we might call a *substantive hedonist*, in that he believes that well-being con-sists only in pleasure.[4] But there is little reason to attribute to him a full or *explanatory*

---

[3] See also noema 2. The distinction between non-instrumental or final good and instrumental good may be implicit in both noemata; see More's comments on the evaluative neutrality of self-preservation at 1.5.8.
[4] It is hard to read Aristotle as a substantive hedonist of this kind. For him, happiness is a matter of activity, albeit pleasurable activity (1894: 1098b18–22). More's conception of happiness is better

version of hedonism, according to which the only good-making property of the pleasure of virtue is its pleasantness. More is also a perfectionist, and uses Aristotelian perfectionist arguments, within a religious context, to support his view of happiness (1.2.5; 3.3.14). Virtue consists in the exercise of our rational capacity, and it is that capacity that makes us human. Hence the exercise of virtue perfects our nature. Aristotle tells us that pleasure can be understood as the return to a natural from an unnatural state.[5] We know that the state of humanity before the Fall was intended to be eternal, and hence (given God's beneficence) the most perfect and natural state. So, through virtue, we can in effect return ourselves to a prelapsarian state of 'the most intrinsick and peculiar Pleasure'.

What about non-moral pleasures and pains? At 1.2.3, More allows that pleasure completes the activities of all animals, and that the pleasure peculiar to any species is the 'supreme happiness' of members of that species. When he claims that human happiness consists in the pleasure of virtue, then, he is probably best understood to be speaking of this as 'supreme happiness', as the most important pleasure among others.[6] So 'external Comforts...do much conduce to the making happiness complete' (1.2.2) not just through facilitating the pursuit of happiness, but partly through constituting that happiness. This raises the question of the relative hedonic weights of moral and non-moral pleasures.

2. The Pleasures of the Boniform Faculty

Given More's belief that virtue brings us into a prelapsarian state, his enthusiasm for it as a pleasure is not as surprising as it would otherwise be. Also important to note here is his view of the 'boniform faculty'. More distances himself from the Aristotelian account of virtue as a disposition acquired by habit (1.3.1). Rather, it is an intellectual power that enables us to see what is best and to take pleasure in it (1.2.5(2)[7]). The good in question here is 'absolute', rather than 'particular' to any individual or inclination (1.3.3; also 1.5.8; 1.12.2–3; 2.1.6). We are bound by reason and divine law 'never to make our own Pleasure or Utility to be the Measure of human Actions' (3.2.14). The boniform faculty is not purely or passively intellectual, 'but much resembles that part of the Will which moves towards that which we judge to be absolutely the best, when, as it were with an unquenchable thirst and affection it is hurried on towards so pleasing an Object; and being in possession of it, is swallowed up in satisfaction that cannot be exprest'. It can indeed be described as '*Intellectual love*' (2.9.18). The boniform faculty involves a 'Divine Sense', and inspires and enables us not only to 'pant after God' but, as

captured by the claim that it consists in pleasure rather than the claim that it consists in pleasures (see Owen 1971–2).

[5] More here refers to *Magna Moralia* 2.7. The authorship of this work is disputed, and the claim anyway appears to be that of an imagined objector to hedonism.

[6] At 3.8.10, he refers to it as 'the most perfect Happiness'.

[7] The translator misnumbers the sections in 1.2, including a second section 5.

far as our nature will allow it, to make ourselves like him (1.5.1; 2.1.9; 2.3.4; 2.9.15–16). As a sense, it does not involve the application of 'certain and distinct Principles' (1.3.8) or a 'List of Precepts' (2.10.4). Further, just as for Aristotle, the divine aspect of contemplation vastly increases its value, so for More this is true of the exercise of the boniform faculty. Indeed one of More's rare criticisms of Aristotle is that his conception of the divine life is excessively intellectualist, restricting happiness to an élite and failing to make room for God's beneficence (1.2.6; 1.3.10–11).[8]

The pleasures of virtue can be placed in two broad categories. The first are those of the calm contentment and satisfaction which arise through awareness of one's own virtue: 'a wonderful Peace and Tranquillity to the Mind; a permanent sweetness and complacency which is never to be repented of' (1.6.12). We might also include here the pleasure taken in the 'charm' of beautiful proportions of the internal components of virtue (1.9.2). But the sense of virtue and virtuous action itself, along with the awareness they bring of one's consequent relation to God, can involve active pleasures of great intensity: 'Raptures of joy' (2.10.12; 3.3.14); 'Joys that [are] unspeakable' (3.3.17). And these pleasures are of immense value, both absolutely and relatively: 'it is plain, that when we open our Eyes, such are the Charms of this Joy, that a man would rather venture a thousand deaths, than by any base prevarication to hazard his portion in a state of life, which is so desirable and so divine' (1.5.6). Nor is death the only price worth paying for the pleasures of virtue: the same is true of infamy, exile, poverty, oppression, loss of liberty, as well as pain and torment (2.1.10; 2.3.12; 2.5.1; 3.5.6; 3.9.17–18). Indeed these evils can themselves be instrumentally beneficial overall, in creating opportunities for bearing them virtuously (2.10.19; 3.5.10).

Non-moral, bodily pleasures may be valuable to some extent, but we must remember their essential bestiality (1.5.3–4), and the need to approach them temperately and continently so as to achieve the significantly more valuable pleasures of virtue (2.3.6; 2.7.6). Continence is one species of the virtue of patience, another being 'suffering', through which we can 'easily and constantly endure whatever is harsh and vexatious unto our natural Life'.

In effect, then, More is claiming that the 'Relish and intrinsick Feeling of the *Boniform faculty* within' (2.9.16) is incommensurably or discontinuously more valuable than any other good: it is worth any price (see Griffin 1986: 5.6.d). And his conception of divine moral inspiration leads him to claim that a truly virtuous person is capable of enduring anything for the sake of the pleasure of virtue:

[A]s soon as we advance to the Knowing what appertains to Virtue, and become *Masters of the Divine Sense*, there is a certain Power above all that is Human, that associates with us and gets into us.... [T]hose who, with Sincere Affections, do even pant and thirst after Virtue, They on the sudden are caught up by *that Intellectual Spirit, which replenishes every Thing*; They are animated and supported by it, and finally therewith join'd in the strictest association of Love.

---

[8] Restriction to an élite, More is probably assuming, is itself inconsistent with God's benevolence.

So that, to conclude in the Words of *Plato, They are as Men rapt up, and inspir'd by some Divinity*; and they are easily and spontaneously led on to every Good Work. (3.3.10)

More gives examples of such inspiration (3.10.10): Spartan boys allowing themselves to be beaten to death for religious reasons without crying out, the practice of suttee in India, Egyptians choosing death rather than killing certain animals, and so on. And we might reasonably expect those with true Christian virtue to be capable of even greater 'patience' (3.10.11–12). But More is sufficiently realistic to recognize that virtue is not always heroic:

[S]ince *Happiness* consists in that *Pleasure*, which good men take in the Sense of Virtue, and a Conscience of Well-doing; no man can possess this *Happiness*, if any pain be so intense upon him, as to distract the Mind, and extinguish all present Sense of Pleasure. Whence it plainly follows, that we must not lie under acute Diseases, or want the Food that is needful. For the want of a Sufficiency for Nature; or a State of Captivity; or any Degree of Vassalage; are able to depress, as well as distract, the Mind by Cares and Anxiety. (1.2.10)

In other words, More cannot provide a self-interested reason to act virtuously in all cases, except to moral heroes.

3. Who is the Competent Judge?

Who is to judge the relative pleasantness of different courses of action? Here More again follows Aristotle. The competent judge is the virtuous person, who will judge according to 'right reason' exercising prudence and their boniform faculty (1.3.4; 1.12.2; 2.2.6; also 1.4.2 (noema 12); Aristotle 1894: 1176a15–19).[9] As we have seen, the pleasures of virtue are 'unspeakable', and so it is important that 'learners' of virtue believe the ordinal judgements of the virtuous even if, as learners, they cannot conceive of the experience of virtue itself. If they make such judgements on their own, there is a risk they may seriously undervalue virtue and face punishment in the afterlife (1.2.9). More also provides an epistemic justification in noema 6 (1.4.2): 'In things of which we have no experience, we must believe those who profess themselves to have experience'. As did J.S. Mill when describing his 'competent judges' of higher pleasures (1998: 2.5–8), More almost certainly has in mind Socrates's claim in Plato's *Republic* (2003: 582) that the pleasantness of different lives is to be assessed by those who have experience of the pleasures of each.[10] Mill's judges rate the intellectual pleasures as higher than the bodily, to which Alan Ryan (1974: 111) objects: 'The philosopher who is a half-hearted sensualist cannot estimate the attractions of a debauched existence, any more than the sensualist flicking through the pages of Hume can estimate the

---

[9] ''Tis better to obey God than Men' (1.4.3 (noema 21)), but the boniform faculty is of course itself divine and cannot conflict with the judgement of God. On the relation of the boniform faculty to right reason, see Dolson 1897: 600–1; Vienne 1995: 400–1.

[10] More's fourth noema (1.4.2) is: 'One Good may excel another in Quality, or Duration, or in both'.

pleasures of philosophy'. The problem for More is perhaps even more serious. In Mill's comparison, it is not clearly implausible to claim that the majority of philosophers would agree that proper appreciation of Hume is more enjoyable, and hence more valuable, than certain basic bodily pleasures. But it seems unlikely that the majority of virtuous people would agree with More on the pleasantness of acting virtuously, especially in standard or mundane cases (perhaps in certain cases of extremity people can experience some kind of inspired euphoria). Imagine you have promised a friend to post a letter for her by 5 p.m. and you now have to walk out into freezing rain to the post-box: these are not conditions conducive to ineffable rapture.

The weight More attaches to the pleasure of virtue has some dialectical advantages. He may be able to fend off the so-called 'experience machine' objection (Nozick 1974: 42–4) by arguing that someone apparently performing virtuous actions on such a machine would still be in communion with God, so that the machine poses no genuine threat. If offered a choice between the machine, and a life of apparently virtuous action, and a life of genuine virtuous action but at a lower hedonic level, it may seem that, from the self-interested point of view, choosing the machine is rational. But if choosing the machine is sinful, because of the loss of benefits to others, then God is likely to punish one once one's soul moves from the machine into the afterlife. More is also in a stronger position than most hedonists to fend off the objection that certain pleasures, far from constituting the good, are in fact evil; indeed he may well have seen such pleasures as not only valueless to the individual, but bad in themselves.

But his hedonistic superstructure does creak at various points. Just as Mill (1998: 2.6) speaks of the value of 'dignity', an apparently non-hedonic value, so More claims that one of the rewards of dying for God or for virtue is 'glory' (3.4.5). And as we have seen there is a further question about the plausibility of More's claim that the pleasure of virtue is more valuable than any amount of physical suffering, a question which seems especially pressing in cases of mundane virtue which are enjoyed. Here More's argument rests solidly on his appeal to the immortality of the soul and the 'ineffable pleasures' (3.10.19) and punishments of the afterlife (3.3.4; 3.3.12–13; 3.3.20; 3.4.5; 3.10).

The need for that appeal highlights the essentially religious underpinning of More's ethics. The pleasure he attributes to virtue is best understood not as that of the appropriate performance of duty itself, but as that of communion with God. He is preaching to all, but when it comes to the unconverted his arguments will persuade only those willing to put their faith in the testimony of the converted.

4

Cumberland:

Divine Utilitarianism

We have seen that Hobbes's contractualist attempt to ground derivative M-reasons on rational egoistic hedonism fails to explain why an agent should be moral when they have more to gain from violating than from respecting moral principles. Partly because of that very failure, many found his radically individualist political morality deeply worrying, and the philosophical clergyman Richard Cumberland (1631–1718), who like More had close links with the Cambridge Platonists, devotes a great deal of his first publication, *De Legibus Naturae* (1672), to criticism of Hobbes, much of it *ad hominem*.[1] In opposition to Hobbes's extreme partialism, Cumberland develops a theologically based, non-hedonistic welfarist impartialism, of so extreme a form that he can plausibly be seen as the first systematic utilitarian.

1. Egoism as a Natural Necessity

Cumberland directly addresses Hobbes's psychological egoism at 470–4. His objection is deeper than that of many modern critics, who merely point to non-self-interested motivation, in reality or within Hobbes's own text.[2] Cumberland's account of rational action is value-based, in the sense that our rational capacity leads us, by natural necessity, to desire and pursue what we see as good, and usually best overall, unless we are overcome by 'the Appetite, and the *corporeal* or animal *Affections*' (257):

There is nothing which can super induce a *Necessity* of doing or forbearing any thing, upon a Human Mind deliberating upon a thing future, except Thoughts or *Propositions* promising Good or Evil, to ourselves or others, consequent upon what we are about to do. But, because we are *determin'd, by some sort of natural Necessity, to pursue Good foreseen*, especially the Greatest; and to *avoid Evils;* hence those Dictates of Reason, which discover to us, that these things will

---

[1] The best complete translation is that of Maxwell, originally published in 1727. All unattributed textual references in this chapter are to Cumberland 2005. An excellent discussion of the political context of Cumberland's arguments can be found in Parkin 2002.

[2] Both strategies are also found in Cumberland, the former at e.g. 421–30 and the latter at e.g. 466–7.

follow from certain of our Actions, are said to lay upon us *some kind of Necessity* of performing or omitting those Actions. (554; also 466–7)

Cumberland accepts that an agent entirely concerned with their own good is conceivable, but also insists that some may judge as good things other than the advancement of their own self-interest. Then, by a matter of natural necessity, they will desire and will those goods, and may indeed pursue them.

The passage quoted above goes on to claim that the dictates of reason in question not only necessitate action, but *oblige* us to act. The obligation here, however, does not emerge from the goodness of the outcome or its being required by reason. Rather it is grounded on a law which requires us to pursue the goods in question, a law with sanctions such that the goods in question 'are necessarily connected with our Happiness, which we naturally desire, and our Actions are evidently necessary to the attainment of them'.[3] Cumberland's conception of obligation, then, is similar to that of Hobbes: it involves being bound to act by sanctions affecting one's own self-interest.[4]

---

[3] For discussion of Maxwell's objection that virtue must be obligatory independently of sanctions, see Irwin 2008: 230–2. Cumberland might respond that what is fundamental is whether there is an overall normative reason to be virtuous, not whether one is obligated (see e.g. the contrast between law and 'necessary practical Truths' at 303; see also below sect. 2; Irwin 2008: 235n57, 237). As Irwin notes, Cumberland's view may be closer to that of the Scholastics on 'intrinsic morality' than he realized. Irwin claims that it is difficult to justify making morality posterior to normative rationality, and dependent on God's will. Cumberland might justify his doing that with the claim that morality is a matter of law, and law requires sanctions. And there may be, for imposing a law, reasons which can be stated without reference to any further law (see Crisp 2006: ch. 1).

[4] At 571, Cumberland says: 'the *intrinsick Force of all those Arguments, with which the Legislator* (God) *uses to enforce Universal Benevolence,* is, in my opinion, all that is meant by the *Obligation of Laws*', and it is probably this passage that leads Schneewind (1998: 11) to claim that Cumberland 'does not derive the obligation of law from the sanction'. Maxwell's note on 'intrinsick Force' reads: 'The *intrinsick* Force of these Arguments consists in the *necessary* Connexion, according to the establish'd Course of Nature, between Virtue and Happiness, Vice and Misery'. This is borne out by what follows the passage above, after a colon: 'The *Rewards* annext to Universal Benevolence by the *right Reason of Men*, chiefly *oblige*, because they promise, beside the Favour of Man, the Friendship of the *Chief of Rational Beings*, God'. In an earlier paper (1995: 94), Schneewind cites Haakonssen 2000 in support of the same claim. According to Haakonssen, Cumberland is 'adamant that the obligation of the law of nature does not arise from the sanctions', citing the following passage (2000: 38–9; Parkin (2002: 83) refers to Haakonssen and also 5.22 in support of the same view, and presumably also has this passage primarily in mind): 'Mens *care of their own Happiness,* which causes them to *consider,* and be *moved* by, Rewards and Punishments, is no *Cause of Obligation;* That proceeds, wholly, from the *Law* and the *Lawgiver*: It is only a *necessary Disposition* in the Subject, without which the Rewards and Penalties of the Law would be of no Force to *induce* Men to the performance of their Duty. As Contact is necessary in the Communication of Motion from Body to Body; tho' Force impress'd be the only Cause of that Motion' (543–4). This passage claims not that obligation does not arise from sanctions, but that it does not arise from men's concern for their own good, which leads to their being moved by the sanctions. It does say that obligation arises from the law and the lawgiver, but a law's existence itself involves the imposition of sanctions by a lawgiver. Just before the passage cited by Haakonssen, Cumberland says: 'I, therefore, resolve *Moral Obligation,* (which is the immediate *Effect* of Nature's Laws,) into their First and Principal *Cause,* which is the *Will* and Counsel of *God* promoting the Common Good; and, therefore, by Rewards and Punishments, *enacting* into Laws the *Practical Propositions* which tend thereto' (543). In a second passage cited by Haakonssen ('Altho'. therefore, this be *last* discover'd... *inverted* Method of Reasoning' (607)), Cumberland draws the same distinction between our self-love and God's will. As Haakonssen notes, on his interpretation of the text, '[t]he clarity of Cumberland's theory is not helped by the many places where he talks as if obligation is founded upon the sanctions of law'. Why would

This raises a question about cases in which an agent is in a position to advance some non-self-interested good, but it is not obvious that their doing so will promote their own self-interest or well-being. As we shall see, Cumberland believes that promoting the overall good is a central component of well-being. So it is tempting to think that, even if the non-self-interested good to be promoted in the case in question were not the greatest possible, the agent would be obliged to some degree (by natural law) to pursue it, since its promotion would advance their own well-being to some extent. But the obligation to promote the greatest good would override it.

Cumberland accepts ultimate M-motivation, even in non-human animals (409–10). Does he, then, allow for the possibility of subjective self-sacrifice, that is, of actions that agents themselves believe will be against their overall self-interest? He does accept that there may be occasions when it appears that the sacrifice of an individual by God or by others may promote the greatest good (277–8). The relation of an individual to society is like that of a hand to the body, and there are times when a hand must be sacrificed for the sake of some more important part or the body as a whole (278; also 554–5)—when the 'Detriment' of one person is the means to achieving the common good (277).[5] There will be times when an individual will be required voluntarily to sacrifice their own life for the greater good (341), and this is something that has often been done (360).[6] Are these possible cases of subjective self-sacrifice? Apparently not, since Cumberland also believes that '*every one* necessarily seeks *his own* greatest Happiness' (556; also 312). That is, those giving up their lives must be assuming that

Cumberland do that—in 'many places'—if he did not believe it? Haakonssen (2000: 39) claims that often, after talking in this way, Cumberland will offer a hasty clarification: 'Thus in talking of punishment, he typically mentions "the Obligation thence arising, or rather discover'd"' (336). In the passage from which this quotation comes, Cumberland is suggesting that Hobbes's right to war will ground a right to punish, and that this will have as an 'effect' the obligation to avoid the crime in question. So his disjunctive 'discover'd' clause cannot be read exclusively, as implying that the obligation does not arise from the sanction. He must mean that, in some sense, claiming that the obligation is 'discover'd' is preferable to claiming merely that it arises. Cumberland's original Latin reads: 'inde natam (aut potius indicatam)'. *Indicare* is also used by Cumberland to claim that the obligation to promote the common good is 'discover'd naturally by the Punishments and Rewards annex'd to Actions' (560). In the original passage quoted by Haakonssen, then, Cumberland wishes to stress that punishment not only gives rise to obligation, but provides evidence for its existence—evidence Hobbes should have seen. Cumberland goes on to claim that Hobbes '*does not see*, that *Men* are *obliged*, for *fear* of that War as of a *Punishment*, to the *outward Acts* of those same Virtues, whose *inward Acts* only will not preserve Peace and mutual Defence, which Nature dictates are to be pursued' (336).

[5] The fact that Cumberland does not just ignore, or rule out, the possibility of one person's being genuinely sacrificed for the common good, along with his view of that good as aggregative, are difficulties for Irwin's suggestion (2008: 228) that Cumberland is speaking of the common good as what is good for everyone in common. Maxwell (362) suggests that Cumberland should have claimed that, since the good of any individual usually lines up with the good of the whole, the uniformity of nature in general suggests that this will be true even in the case of these apparent exceptions (he may perhaps be thinking of posthumous rewards).

[6] Cumberland sees humanity as 'one System of Bodies', and the action of any one person may affect others 'as the Motion of every Body in the System of the World, communicates its Motion to many others, especially neighbouring ones' (395).

they will be compensated, perhaps in the afterlife.[7] We can will at the same time to act to promote the good of others or the common good *and* our own good (412, 612).

2. The Law of Nature

Let me now turn from issues of motivation to Cumberland's normative theory. Cumberland's work sits alongside that of other leading natural lawyers of the seventeenth century, in particular Grotius and Pufendorf, and like the latter he was especially concerned to provide an alternative conception of natural law to that of Hobbes. Cumberland begins the book with an account of his method (247–54). One can support claims about the laws of nature, he suggests, by examining either the effects of those laws, or their causes. The effects he has in mind are human sentiments, practices, or beliefs, and he cites Grotius as an example of an author who took this approach. The general idea is that, on the assumption that human beings have some rational capacity to grasp and to act on normative truth, we can make inferences about normative truth on the basis of empirical evidence about human beings. Cumberland sees merit in such arguments, and is ready to defend them against objections (indeed Cumberland's arguments in general are clearly deeply influenced by Grotius), but believes that the cause-focused approach will be more fruitful. He is also doubtful about the possibility of basing a natural law theory on any assumption of innate ideas, whether in the human or the divine mind.

When he is outlining his own approach, Cumberland moves from talking about the laws of nature themselves to their being 'imprinted' on our minds (252). At least one important proximate cause of that is the rewards and punishments attached to the laws in question, and these will provide the basis for one of Cumberland's most important arguments: that we can ascertain the content of natural law by examining the sanctions attached to it by its legislator, that is, God. And of course a fuller account of our knowledge of natural law, and indeed natural law itself, will give the most important role to the ultimate or first cause of everything—that is, again, God, whose perfection itself gives authority to the laws he issues. As Cumberland puts it, his aim—on the basis of 'sense and daily experience'—is to demonstrate:

That the Nature of things, which subsists, and is continually govern'd, by its first Cause, does necessarily imprint on our Minds some practical Propositions, (which must be always true, and cannot without a Contradiction be suppos'd otherwise,) concerning the Study of promoting the joint Felicity of all Rationals. (253; also 384–5)[8]

---

[7] Cumberland claims also that the demand by some society for such sacrifice is only reasonable, given the gains that any individual has already received from it (601–2). This argument can serve only to allay any regret by an agent required to sacrifice themselves that things have not turned out even better for them than they already have. By natural necessity, they cannot sacrifice themselves if they believe it will be worse for them.

[8] Cumberland continues: 'And that the Terms of these Propositions do immediately and directly signify, that the first Cause, in his original Constitution of Things, has annex'd the greatest Rewards and

Cumberland, in Cartesian fashion, sees philosophical ethics as analogous to mathematics, and his aim is to provide 'the Rules of its Practice, and the whole substance of its Art, in a few universal theorems' (489; also 296–7, 544–6). In particular, through careful attention to the nature of things (which include the supernatural (499)), he is seeking necessary normative, value-based truths in the form of laws, the sanctions of which are independent of civil law (281–2, 289). These laws are not self-evident 'without proof' (384)—that is, justified in themselves, without reference to argument or evidence—but as dictates they can be grasped through the exercise of an entirely natural capacity—reason (368–9). Cumberland allows these laws to be stated in various forms (483–6): 'It is best to φ'; 'φ!'; 'φ ought to be done'.[9] In the case of the first, because according to Cumberland the true laws of nature require a person to advance their own good (as well as that of others), failure to do what is best will impose a cost on the agent themselves and this can be seen as a sanction. The imperative statement of the law can be understood in terms of an analogy between a person's understanding and a magistrate authorized to make laws. Cumberland sees this analogy as somewhat 'metaphorical' rather than philosophical, but claims that it has a 'very just Foundation in Nature'. As the text below explains, the authority Cumberland has in mind behind our understanding is God, who will punish us if we disobey. The third, gerundive form can be elucidated in a similar way, though the analogy here is with an 'inferior Judge', who is requiring conformity to a law already made. 'Ought'-statements of natural law, then, are acceptable to Cumberland only in so far as they are made against a background in which natural law is based on God's will and the understanding imposes that law on itself:

The *Nature* of Things *represents* to the Mind, what is *best* to be done. The *Mind*, considering the Government of Things, does, from the Idea of God, conclude, that he wills, or *commands*, them to be done, and, in his *Name*, imposes the Command on it self, in the second Form. In the third, it reflects upon the two former, and pronounces, that an *Action agreeable to that Command*, will be *just;* the contrary, *unjust.*

Cumberland explicitly avoids any appeal to the authority of scripture (258, 280–1). The theistic premise in his argument relies on that version of the so-called 'cosmological' argument according to which the existence of the universe must be explained by reference to a 'first cause', and that cause must be God (e.g. 253, 283). The 'chief authority' of the laws of nature is that—like everything else—'they are known to proceed from God' (502). One might be tempted to attribute to Cumberland a divine command

Punishments to the observance and neglect of these Truths.' He might be taken here to be arguing in a circle: from the sanctions of natural law to natural law, and from natural law to its sanctions. But the passage immediately following suggests that his point is to emphasize that it is the imposition of these sanctions that make the requirements in question into laws.

[9] Cumberland rejects a fourth form—'φ-ing is most agreeable to human nature'—on the grounds that it may suggest that what is required is attention to the agent's *own* nature and hence happiness, that it may be understood to exclude God, and that the notion of agreement is itself best understood with reference to the first form.

theory, according to which God's authority rests on his being creator or on his power. Cumberland admits that he himself found this position attractive, but rejected it on the ground that it would itself require the postulation of a natural law prior to that he himself sees as fundamental, which makes no reference to any such grounding for authority (672–3). Rather, God's dominion is itself justified by natural law, which demands that God assume the power of governance. Of course it does not bind him through sanctions to be imposed by some superior. Rather, it has the 'essential Force of a Law' since that law 'is a true Proposition formed by the supreme and most perfect Being, concerning the best End and the Means necessary thereto' (670). So in a sense God imposes the law on himself; but Cumberland is not an extreme voluntarist—the law, or perhaps the dictate of reason underlying it, may 'exist' only because like everything else it is caused by God, but its truth, like that of certain mathematical propositions, is independent of God's will. This analysis enables us to see that the theistic element in Cumberland's account of natural law could be removed without its collapsing: it could be, that is to say, that a fundamental normative proposition had 'the essential [normative or reason-giving] force of a law' not through its sanctions but merely through being true.[10] Several of Cumberland's most significant arguments for his position do and indeed must rely on theistic premises, as we shall see, but some—such as those involving the rationality of maximization—need not.

3. The Will of God

Natural laws, and our understanding of them, have their origin in God. But just as God has not implanted innate and certain knowledge of his existence in every human mind, so the same seems to be true of morality. In both cases, however, according to Cumberland, we can use our reason, along with the evidence of our senses, to demonstrate not only that there is a natural moral law, but what its content is.[11] It can be summed up as a requirement of universal benevolence 'to promote the common Good of the whole System of Rationals' (262; also e.g. 256, 292–3) (this requirement will be discussed in more detail in the following section).[12]

Cumberland offers several such arguments, often repeating them and running them together. The first argument we might call the *preservation argument* (540–1; also 272–3, 331–2). Since God willed our coming into existence, with a certain nature, it is only reasonable to think that he wills also our continuing existence in accordance with that nature. As we shall see shortly, Cumberland believes that the perfection of our

---

[10] It should not be forgotten, however, that behind Cumberland's own advocacy of benevolence is the thought of God's benevolence and his love for us (Schneewind 1995: 89).

[11] Cumberland was greatly influenced by Bacon's view that the laws of God were implicit in the universe, awaiting our discovery, but it is unclear whether Bacon's view extended to moral laws (Forsyth 1982: 33–5).

[12] The only liberty permitted to the agent arises when several actions conform to the principle of benevolence (517, 660–1).

nature consists in our exercising our rational faculties, and that will consist in recognizing and acting on the requirement to promote the common good.

The second argument—the *sanctions argument* (e.g. 333–4, 536–8, 542–3, 598–9)—
is given by far the greatest prominence by Cumberland, and involves his explaining the
rewards for obedience, and the punishments for disobedience, to the natural law.[13] It is
important to note that, though of course Cumberland is hopeful of persuading his
readers of these sanctions and thus motivating them morally, his primary aim is to use
the evidence of these sanctions to prove the existence of the law of nature and to elucidate its content. Just as the purpose of the sun is to provide light and that of rain to
provide moisture, so the purpose of natural laws is to regulate our actions: 'For that
Regulation is the *only* Effect they can have, and that they do *necessarily*, from their own
inward Nature' (500–1). And if there are natural laws, backed by divine authority, then
there must be sanctions attached to them (260). Without sanctions, except in the special case of God discussed above, there is no law. Genuine rewards and punishments
must all consist in benefits and harms to individuals, and so a vital element in
Cumberland's project is to show that virtue—that is, promoting the common good—
advances the self-interest or well-being of the virtuous agent, and vice harms that
agent.

Cumberland accepts the ancient view that virtue is good in itself (273–4, 508, 583,
597–9).[14] He supports this substantive claim with a detailed and sophisticated
explanation of *why* virtue is good. The central idea is that it perfects our nature through
the proper exercise of our cognitive and non-cognitive capacities in understanding
God and his law and willing actions in accordance with it (e.g. 261, 266, 269, 376, 508,
520–3). Living in such a way also instantiates a harmony between one's own mind and
that of God, and one's own practical principles and the correct principles (e.g. 256–7,
525–6, 531–2, 573, 594). Virtue also brings with it other important goods. Cumberland
is not a hedonist about well-being (523), but he does accept that even bodily pleasure is
good in itself, through its 'positive Agreement' (261) with our corporeal nature. There
are great pleasures in perfecting one's nature and in awareness that one is so doing (e.g.
372, 521, 527–8, 533–4), and in recollection of past virtuous actions (e.g. 525, 600).
Virtue provides a foundation for hope and expectation (e.g. 469, 534), in particular of
God's favour and eternal happiness in the afterlife (e.g. 268, 538). The virtuous person
takes pleasure in the prosperity of others (e.g. 296, 547), and the harmony in their life
brings them tranquillity and peace of mind (e.g. 296, 531). Human beings naturally
reward virtue (636); indeed even non-humans recognize the benefits of benevolence
(405–6). Benefiting others, that is to say, will be reciprocated (e.g. 534–5, 562). Virtue
requires adherence to the civil law, the purpose of which is the same as virtue—to

---

[13] Parkin (1999: 112) suggests that Cumberland's discussion of rewards and punishments was his most
important contribution to the natural law debate.
[14] Sidgwick says that this leads Cumberland into 'an obvious logical circle' (1906: 174). But Cumberland
is careful to exclude virtue from the common good which we are required by natural law to promote (516;
see main text below; also Albee 1902: 33; Irwin 2008: 228n34.).

promote the common good. The civil law grounds a variety of public goods, such as security, education, peace, wealth, many of which will follow individual obedience (e.g. 261–2, 266–7, 520, 591–2). Further, virtue will involve reason's governing the passions, which without such control can lead to great unhappiness (573, 642).

Cumberland's account of the evils of vice rests on his accepting the Augustinian view that evil is merely the privation of good (588–9; also 261, 297). This view may help one to avoid the problem of evil, but as an account of 'ill-being' it is quite implausible. Some alleged evils can indeed be understood in terms of privations, including those mentioned by Cumberland to illustrate his claim. Death is quite plausibly not bad in itself, for example, but merely in its depriving one of goods that would otherwise have been instantiated in one's life. But pain is not the mere absence of pleasure; it is bad in itself.

This metaethical view, however, can be detached from the full account Cumberland provides of the negative effects of vice on the agent's well-being. Just as virtue is a perfection, so vice is an imperfection (522), and so presumably an evil. Such imperfection is a form of mental disease or 'distemper', and is both physically and mentally harmful (e.g. 449, 563).Viciousness constitutes disharmony with the mind of God (547), and involves the agent in damaging practical contradiction (333, 563). Vice involves ignorance, ill will, envy, pride, fear, anxiety, and loneliness, all of which lead to misery and sorrow (e.g. 261, 296, 406, 528). The vicious are pained by their consciences and recollections of their past deeds (551, 563, 570). Their actions lead to habits which will make them more likely to act badly in future, as well as providing examples to others which if followed may harm the exemplar (578). The vicious risk the standard punishments of the civil law, such as death, pain, and expense (261, 552, 581–3, 636), as well as divine vengeance (334).

A third argument by Cumberland we might call the *human make-up argument* (431–58). According to this, our bodies and minds both provide evidence for the existence and content of natural law. Consider first our capacity for imagination. The fact that even non-sentient beings, such as trees, can preserve themselves suggests that our imaginations have a higher purpose. This is clearly connected with our brains, the size of which is greater in proportion to body-size than in any other animal (Cumberland says that he himself has compared the brains of humans with those of sheep and pigs). Also important here is blood, which is hotter and, again in proportion to body-size, more plentiful in human beings; this increases our animal spirits and enables us more effectively to perform our duties. We are also aided in our benevolence by our memories, which themselves benefit from our longer childhood and longer lives; we are thus able to learn more from experience. This grounds the decision-making virtue, prudence, the concern of which is how to observe the law of nature by promoting the common good.

Human beings also have an advanced ability to control their affections, and here Cumberland finds anatomical evidence from research on the nerves and the diaphragm. This research helps us understand both laughter, which facilitates socialization, and grief, which discourages socialization and has a physical basis such that it is of greater danger for humans to indulge in it than for other animals. He also mentions the human face. The fact that it reveals our emotions so well, through blushing for example, also encourages socialization, and the diversity of the human countenance enables a beneficiary to remember their benefactor and so to reciprocate. The hand is also an especially helpful tool for helping others. Of course, it is often not so used, but the world is such that—*pace* Hobbes—each of us, if we reason correctly, will recognize that co-operation is always the best strategy from the self-interested point of view.

Cumberland also places great weight on the influence of parent-child relationships in providing a basis for the extension of benevolence to the species as a whole. Human beings, who have no special 'mating season', are especially inclined to beget and to rear children, and the need for childcare over a long period leads to greater mutual affection.

4. Agreement and the Rationality of Maximization

Cumberland has two further, related arguments concerning the content rather than the existence of the law of nature, and neither of them depends importantly on claims about the will of God.

The first we might call the *argument from agreement*. We have already seen the role that harmony between an agent's practical principles and the correct principles, and between the mind of an agent and the mind of God, play in Cumberland's account of well-being and the sanctions of morality. Some statements of this argument are directed in particular against Hobbes (e.g. 356), and suggest that it is irrational for each agent to seek dominion over others, since it is as impossible for each to gain that dominion as it would be for a single body to move in a 'thousand *contrary* Directions'. Actions that are 'truly good' cannot be in opposition to one another, because the dictates of reason cannot themselves embody a contradiction (296, 529).

There is of course a natural response: the aim of each agent—that *they* have dominion over all—is not logically, physically, or conceptually impossible; it is merely unlikely to be achieved. And the claim that reason requires each person maximally to promote their own good can be employed by each agent without contradiction. Elsewhere, however, what Cumberland has in mind is clearer:

Whoever determines his Judgment and his Will by right Reason, must agree with all others, who judge according to right Reason in the same Matter. Whence it also follows *conditionally*...'If any right Reasoner, any wise Person, shall assign to each his proper Office, in order to the publick Good, all others who judge rightly, shall approve of the Distribution.'

The rational point of view, then, according to Cumberland is impartial. Consider a case in which I can bring about two outcomes. In A, my own good will be maximized at the expense of the common good; in B, the common good will be maximized at the expense of my own. If my judgement that A is preferable to B is rational, then it must be endorsed by all other rational agents. But some other agent may judge C, in which their good will be maximized, to be preferable to A. And here of course we do have a straightforward contradiction; whereas agents who embody impartial rationality may all agree that the best outcome is that in which the common good is maximized. Indeed that is the only outcome, Cumberland suggests, on which all rational beings (including God) can agree (537–8, 560). This is why Maxwell cites the second commandment— 'Thou shalt love thy Neighbour as thyself'—on the title page of his translation. According to Cumberland, from the rational point of view, the distinction between individuals is, in itself, irrelevant.

The second argument—the *maximization argument*—concerns the content of the judgement that will be made from the impartial point of view. Cumberland believes that the common or overall good can be seen as a whole constituted of various parts. These are the happiness in the lives of individual rational beings, and the honouring and gratifying of God (e.g. 262, 515, 611, 618, 651). (Because God requires us to promote happiness overall, these two components can never conflict.) These separate goods can be aggregated, and rational human beings have 'the power of collecting many Particulars (lesser good Things, for example) into one Sum, and comparing the same with one another, according to their *Difference* and mutual *Proportion*'; and this enables them to discover 'the chief Good, that is, the *Collection* of all good Things' (374; also 490–1, 514–15). Now recall Cumberland's view that rational beings, unless they are overcome by irrational passion, will necessarily pursue the greatest good. The goodness of actions itself correlates with the overall goodness of their outcomes, so the best actions are those that lead to the greatest good (263–4). This has the important implication that the weight any individual should attach to their own good is only proportional to its contribution to the overall good: 'The good of the Whole, is greater than the good of a Part', a proposition Cumberland claims to be as epistemically well founded as a mathematical axiom (356; also 369, 544, 610). As we saw above, Cumberland views the individual's relation to the society of rational agents as analogous to that between the parts of a body and the body as a whole: the role of each part is to contribute to the benefit not of itself, but that of the whole (663, 703, 705). Again we see the assumption of impartiality at work; but Cumberland's argument concerns not the necessity of agreement between rational beings, but the content of their judgements. Reason will always prescribe the best action, that is, the promotion of the greatest overall good, viewed impartially (517, 527). In this argument, we see expressed what Philippa Foot (1988: 227) later called 'the rather simple thought that it can never be right to prefer a worse state of affairs to a better'.

5. The Birth of Utilitarianism

Cumberland's view of the good and its relation to rationality is expressed in a form sufficiently coherent and comprehensive for it to be described as the first systematic statement of what later became known as utilitarianism.[15]

---

[15] Albee 1902: 14.

We have already noted his commitment to the overriding rationality of maximizing the overall good. If we leave aside the theological element of his view of the good—that it is in part constituted by the honouring of God through obedience to natural law— that view is welfarist: the good so understood consists only in the well-being of indi- vidual rational beings. Later, of course, the utilitarian tradition extended the scope of moral concern to cover all sentient beings. Cumberland's anthropocentrism is sup- ported by several arguments (310, 402–11, 513–14). First, human well-being is richer than that of non-humans, and because we are familiar with it we are in a better position to promote it, especially through our capacity for communication. Second, because other rational agents are more like us, our willing for them what we wish for ourselves 'Reason cannot but judge more agreeable to our inward Principles of action' than our willing those same things to very different beings. Third, other rational beings are more likely to reciprocate (and so, presumably, advance the overall good to a greater extent). Fourth, rational beings are, as the children of God, more similar to him and so of special concern to him. (We should assume that this argument merely adds a further reason to maximize the good overall, since it would be irrational of God to allow his special love for us to distort his judgement of the overall good.) Fifth, as we learn from studies in anatomy, zoology, and other sciences, God has so designed the world that members of each species tend naturally to care for other members of that species.

Maxwell, in one of the essays appended to his translation, plausibly suggests that 'the Author's Scheme would have been more compleat, had he included *Benevolence towards Brutes*' (647). This is not merely because kindness to non-humans strengthens a disposition to be kind to rational humans, but because God and any truly benevolent person will be concerned with the happiness of any sentient being. Cumberland's per- fectionism led him to exaggerate the significance of the happiness of 'the noble', and this view is itself in tension with his clear recognition of the important role of pleasure and pain in the happiness of rational beings. The motivation for extending the scope of ethics to non-rational beings, then, is already implicit in his position.[16]

Welfarists cannot admit the existence of 'impersonal' values. This raises a problem for a welfarist interpretation of Cumberland, given that he is willing to speak of wicked actions as deserving punishment (577). In fact, however, Cumberland's view is that such actions 'deserve' punishment only in the sense that such punishment serves to deter future wickedness (538). God himself both wills and distributes punishments with a view to promoting the common good, and we can infer that 'if any thing, neces- sary to this End, be wanting in this Life, it will be supplied by God in a Life to come'. (Here of course the deterrent effect depends on our using our God-given reason to recognize the existence of such posthumous punishment.)

The third chapter of Cumberland's book is on 'natural good', which he defines as 'that which preserves, or enlarges and perfects, the Faculties of any one Thing, or of

---

[16] As Sharp (1912: 372) notes, there is some textual evidence to suggest that Cumberland himself may have had misgivings about his exclusion of non-humans from the scope of morality.

several' (462; also 314–15). Our natural good, then, consists in what 'preserves or enlarges the Powers of the Mind and Body'. Cumberland goes on to distinguish natural good from 'moral good', which is attributed to the voluntary actions of rational agents in obedience to the law of nature or civil law. Natural good is clearly related to the happiness of individuals, which raises the questions of the relation of moral to natural good and of whether moral good can be understood in welfarist terms. Cumberland is clear that, *pace* the Stoics, virtue is not the only good (508). Virtue is good *because* it leads to natural good. At 463, Cumberland claims that moral good is 'ultimately resolv'd into the *natural common good*'. But there is little reason to think that Cumberland sees virtue as merely instrumentally good; that would not have required him to create the category of moral good independently from that of natural good. What he means by 'resolution' here is best understood in terms of the relation between moral and natural good, misunderstood by the Stoics. As Cumberland later puts it (516), we should not understand the notion of the common good as stated in the law of nature to include moral good, since 'it is absurd, to Define any thing, by what supposes the thing Defin'd already known'. In other words, though the common good itself (apart from the honouring of God) is to be understood in welfarist terms, Cumberland does accept that there is non-welfarist, moral value in acting in accordance with the law of nature. But this exception is, and remains, standard in the utilitarian tradition.

Most utilitarians have advocated the maximization of *subjective* utility, adjusting the value to be attached to various possible outcomes in the light of their probability, the agent's beliefs, or the evidence available. This is clearly Cumberland's position, though his understanding of probability in terms of the number of causes is somewhat peculiar:

[W]hereas we know not what shall hereafter happen, we may, nevertheless, know what is *possible*: And things *possible* may be *compar'd* among themselves; and it may be *certainly* known, not only, which of *two possible* Things will be of *greater* or *less Value*, when they do happen; but, also, which of them may be produc'd by *more*, which by *fewer*, *Causes*, that do now, or shall soon, exist. But that is *more probable*, which may happen *more ways*, and its *Chance* or Expectation is of *greater Value*. (492; also 270, 299–300, 551–2, 581–2, 643–4)

And, he suggests, '*right Reason* will *command* us, where greater Certainty cannot be obtained, to *chuse that way*, which … *most probably* leads to Happiness' (535).

Finally, consider Cumberland's view on the role of the principle of universal benevolence in decision-making. The vast majority of utilitarians have recognized that their theory may require agents not to attempt to apply it directly and immediately at every point of decision. Far more likely to promote the good will be a 'split-level' strategy based on many of the principles or virtues of our existing common-sense morality, which has developed over many centuries in the light of evidence about the effects on general happiness of certain forms of behaviour. Again, we find such a view in Cumberland. On some such views, the principle of universal benevolence is 'self-effacing', perhaps even to the extent—as in so-called 'Government House' utilitarianism

(Sen and Williams 1982: 16)—that it is entirely absent from the set of moral beliefs held by certain individuals. Cumberland's virtuous agent, however, will exemplify at all the times the virtue of 'prudence', under the guidance of the principles of piety and universal benevolence (275–6). But they will also exemplify certain intellectual virtues (656–7), and be fully aware of various subsidiary 'laws of nature' which are themselves derived from these ultimate principles, including the virtues of justice, fidelity, grati-tude, 'gentleness', temperance, obedience to the civil law, and so on (e.g. 279, 296, 394, 505, 659, 677–8, 695, 698–700, 708–12). So a prudent agent might, for example, keep some promise, and that will promote their 'immediate' aim (687). But they are entirely aware that such actions, though they advance some 'parts' of the good, are justified only in so far as promoting those parts promotes the good as a whole.

At times, Cumberland uses language that might be taken to imply that he believes there are certain 'side-constraints' on the promotion of the overall good (Nozick 1974: 28–33). For example, he claims that one must not hurt any innocent person (328), and is happy to speak of individual rights (e.g. 653). But it is clear that Cumberland does not see such constraints or rights as limits on the maximization of the overall good. Principles of individual rights are themselves mere rules of thumb. Cumberland is not unaware of cases in which, for example, innocents may have to be sacrificed for the overall good. Indeed he sees that one has to accept that this is a regrettable cost of judi-cial institutions (342). The subordinate laws of nature, that is to say, can be overridden by the ultimate law of universal benevolence:

[T]he *Law is not dispens'd with*, which, for the common Good, *prohibits the hurting Innocents*, if at any time an *innocent* Person is commanded (when the common Good requires it) to expose him self to *Danger*, or undergo even *Death*, if God clearly enough reveals his Will in the Affair: for by this means God, the Lord of All, receives his *due Honour;* and in the *properest manner*, because the *chief End is provided for*, according to his Judgment. Therefore in *this Case*, the *Safety* of a single Person is neither a *Part* nor a *Cause* of the *common Good*. (277)

Rights, that is to say, are grounded in, and extend only as far as, the common good (327–8). So there is no ultimate justification for an alleged right, say, to give priority to one's children, although such priority will often be required because of the con-tribution such relationships make to the common good (705–6). Cumberland's Aristotelianism even involves his reconstruing the doctrine of the mean in accordance with the principle of benevolence. The prudent person will hit the mean between pride and humility, for example, or excessive and deficient liberty of speech, but will do so in conformity with the good of all (e.g. 687–8, 691–2, 699–700).

Despite Cumberland's readiness to see the subsidiary laws of nature as violable in the name of benevolence, he is in fact relatively conservative, believing, for example, that ancient laws, even if not the best, ought to be retained because of the benefits of political stability (e.g. 365–6, 676–7), and that sovereigns are immune to prosecution (716–17). But this conservatism itself, of course, he attempts to justify in the name of the common good.

6. Deontology and Self-interest

How successful are Cumberland's arguments for his version of utilitarianism, as against rational egoism and deontology? The arguments from preservation, sanctions, and human make-up, if we grant Cumberland's theistic premise based on the first-cause argument, work against any form of rational egoism that recommends an entirely S-reason-based decision-procedure. But most forms of rational egoism will require agents not only to act in accordance with morality and to show concern for others, but to develop dispositions to do so of such a strength that they may in certain cases result in an agent's being moved by (fictional) M-reasons even when they are aware that they will suffer no external sanctions for ignoring morality or the interests of others. Of course, there may be exceptions, in which rational egoists claim that it is rational to violate morality or to harm others, so as to pursue one's own interest. The arguments from preservation and human make-up have little purchase here. And an argument from posthumous sanctions will not persuade a rational egoist who believes that God will punish agents only for deviation from the correct normative principles.

What about deontology? Because Cumberland accepts that the most plausible version of the principle of universal benevolence will require general adherence to common-sense morality, all three of these arguments provide at best equal support for deontology and utilitarianism. And the sanctions argument could be said to support deontology, if—as may well be the case—the vast majority support punishing individuals who violate common-sense moral principles for the sake of the common good. Further, it has to be admitted that it is hard to make the case for posthumous punishment purely on the grounds of deterrence, given the lack of clear evidence for it. In fact, the very existence of widespread wrong-doing counts against Cumberland's use of the sanctions argument. If God's intention were to deter human beings from such wrong-doing through the application of posthumous sanctions, his system of criminal justice appears somewhat inept.

The agreement and maximization arguments have greater plausibility, and not just because they can be formulated without theistic premises. The idea that rational agents should agree in their rankings of possible outcomes and actions, and not be swayed by their own personal perspective, has a long pedigree in philosophy and continuing appeal, as does the thought that agents have strongest reason to produce the best outcomes understood from some impartial point of view. But these ideas run into serious difficulties with so-called 'agent-relative' moral reasons and the appeal of partiality.

Consider first agent-relative reasons. Imagine that you have made a weighty promise to an old friend. Circumstances are such that, if you broke that promise, you would prevent some other person's breaking a similar promise. Many will believe that you have a special reason not to break your promise because *you* made it. From the impartial point of view, of course, it makes no difference whether you break the promise or not, since the upshot is the same in each case: the breaking of a promise.

Now consider the following case in the light of Cumberland's utilitarianism.

Status Quo

You   *Five other rational beings*

2   5

Outcome O

You   *Five other rational beings*

1   5.25

Each number represents a level of lifetime well-being. Assume that a life of 1 is barely worth living, while a life of 5 is happy and comfortable. If you are given the opportunity to bring about Outcome O, it seems that utilitarianism requires to do so, since you will bring about an increase in overall good of 0.25. But this requires you to halve the overall value of your life. And it is easy to see that there is no limit to the demands utilitarianism can make of you: you will be required voluntarily to submit to many years of agony followed by death, if this produces a better outcome overall. As Sidgwick famously put it:

> It would be contrary to Common Sense to deny that the distinction between any one individual and any other is real and fundamental, and that consequently 'I' am concerned with the quality of my existence as an individual in a sense, fundamentally important, in which I am not concerned with the quality of the existence of other individuals: and this being so, I do not see how it can be proved that this distinction is not to be taken as fundamental in determining the ultimate end of rational action for an individual. (1907: 498)

By accepting that we always pursue our own greatest happiness by nature (see above sect. 1), and by not clearly playing down the rationality of special egoistic concern,[17] Cumberland makes it harder for himself to argue for the rationality of impartial maximization of the good. But he would of course dispute my example, noting the relation between the good of an agent and the common or overall good. Causes which preserve wholes do so by preserving their parts (255), and this applies to the promotion of the happiness of the whole by the action of any one individual (e.g. 545–6, 616). The laws of nature, and indeed the civil law, as we have seen, are hugely beneficial to all, and to us as individuals. Further, co-operating with others in the project of obedience will itself lead to our benefiting from the reciprocity of others.

These claims on their own, however, seem insufficient to deal with the example, especially when modified to incorporate the requirement on one individual to undergo huge suffering to produce far less significant benefits to others who are already well off. Here Cumberland may appeal to his view that virtue will always maximize the virtuous agent's own well-being. That view, however, seems very hard to believe in cases where

---

[17] Cumberland does begin moving in this direction at e.g. 607–8. Again, his tendency to emphasize the rationality of impartiality rather than the irrationality of partiality remains characteristic of the utilitarian tradition.

maximizing the good will involve huge non-moral harms (such as agony for many years) or sacrifices of non-moral goods. Without this exaggerated conception of the value of virtue, and without a theological postulate, as Sidgwick so clearly recognized (1907: 503–8), the impartial and the partial points of view do not coincide, and universal benevolence conflicts with self-interest. Further, even if we assume the existence of God, Cumberland has to show that he is a utilitarian rather than a deontologist or a rational egoist, and as we have seen it is not clear that he has even the beginning of a case for that.

5

Locke:
The Sanctions of God

The influential empiricist philosopher John Locke (1632–1704), despite encouragement from his friends, and despite his brilliant and original work in political philosophy, did not write a comprehensive treatise on ethics. But the tenor of his thinking is resolutely practical, and a consistent theme in his work is the importance of basing one's judgements on one's own reasoning and the evidence available, rather than on authority. In the introduction to his most significant work, the *Essay Concerning Human Understanding* (1689), he says: 'Our Business here is not to know all things, but those which concern our Conduct' (1.1.6).[1] The *Essay* includes a good deal of discussion of ethics, broadly construed, as do several other works, including in particular the *Essays on the Law of Nature* (ELN), written over two decades before the *Essay*.[2]

One aspect of Locke's development is undisputed. In his earlier work, especially ELN, he focuses on developing a Grotian natural law theory. Then, in the 1676 essay 'Pleasure, Pain, the Passions', there appears to be something of a 'hedonic turn', in which Locke puts greater stress on the role of pleasure and pain in motivation and our understanding of happiness. Locke wrote a very great deal, and as with most major philosophers it is not easy to make all the pieces of the jigsaw fit together comfortably. In general I am inclined to think that we should not attribute a major change of mind to a philosopher without very strong evidence, preferably internal, and so I side with the 'compatibilists' among Lockean interpreters, who do not see the hedonic turn as indicating a major change in Locke's overall ethical position.[3] He is, then, like Hobbes in using hedonism to explicate his account of natural law. But, as we shall see, that account, and the conception of morality it supports, differ greatly from those found in Hobbes.

---

[1] Locke probably has in mind here Aristotle 1894: 1103b26–8. Unless otherwise unattributed, all references are to the *Essay*.

[2] References to the *Essays* are to the reprint of Von Leyden's translation in Locke 1997 (PE).

[3] Compatibilists include Colman (1983), Darwall (1995), and Sheridan (2016), incompatibilists Lamprecht (1918), Von Leyden (1954), Aaron (1955), Mabbott (1973), and Schneewind (1994). It is worth noting that psychological hedonism is implied at ELN 88, and that Locke refers in the *Essay* at 1.3.6 to the law of nature as grounded in the will of God.

1. The Response to Hobbes

According to Hobbes, morality is essentially an instrument for rational egoists to pursue their self-interest collectively. Any normativity it has is derivative from that of the rationality of self-interest. Locke rarely mentions Hobbes, and later claimed not to be sufficiently 'well read in Hobbes' to know his views on the immortality of the soul (PE 214n11). But, because of Hobbes's prominence, and the content of ELN, it is tempting to see these essays as at least in part a response to Hobbes. In the eighth essay (PE 127–33), Locke directly confronts the suggestion that the law of nature is based on self-interest.

He distinguishes his arguments into three, the first of which we might call the *derivation argument*. If some principle is the sole foundational natural law, then it must support any derivative natural laws. But none of our duties rests only on self-interest; indeed the most significant require us to benefit others at some cost to ourselves, as we can see from the list of those most admired throughout history for their heroic sacrifice.

One might be tempted here to object to Locke that his own views on the afterlife rule out any such sacrifice, since any losses in this life will be fully compensated for later. But Locke's response will be that, if natural law were, as far as this world goes, egoistic, then those who sacrifice their own good in this life will *not* be rewarded in the afterlife; indeed they will be punished: 'The very same people, in fact, whom we now admire as the best and the most eminent of men would have to be regarded not only as foolish but even as wicked and most pernicious' (PE 129–30; also 84–5). In other words, the pattern of rewards and punishments in the afterlife suggests that there are M-reasons for sacrificing one's own good in this world, even if in the long run one will gain overall.

Locke's second objection rests on two *impossibility arguments*. It cannot be that the foundational law of nature is such that it must be violated. But if it is grounded on self-interest, then it must be violated, since one cannot be concerned for the self-interest of all at the same time. Locke realizes that the view he is criticizing may be stated in a more straightforwardly egoistic form. But, he suggests, this postulates an unachievable end for each person, since my procuring the greatest number of useful objects for myself will leave the smallest possible number for you. This is, of course, a weak response, since the egoist will insist that, by so doing, I will have achieved my end. At this point, Locke goes on to assert that 'virtuous actions do not clash nor do they engage men in conflict', and that egoism implies that we are all in a state of war and mistrust (PE 132; also 'Morality', PE 168–9). There is no discussion of Hobbes's argument for doing one's duty even in cases in which it might appear egoistically rational not to do so. Hobbes can accept Locke's claim about the implication of egoism, but point out that he has provided a way out of the state of war through the establishment of morality and sovereignty. And once out of the state of war, harmony becomes a practical possibility.

Locke's presentation of his third argument begins with what is in effect a further denial of the rationality of conflict: no principle can be the basis of natural law if it implies that 'all justice, friendship, and generosity are taken away from life'. Locke might again here seem unaware of the possibility of grounding non-egoistic decision-procedures on the principle of rational egoism, claiming that it would not be possible for an egoist to help a friend at any cost to herself. But—surprisingly, given his claim about helping a friend—he is not. For he ends the essay by addressing the argument that, since rational egoism, properly applied, will produce peace, security, and so on, then self-interest must be the basis of natural law. Locke's answer—the *rightness-first argument*—is that 'utility is not the basis of the law or the ground of obligation, but the consequence of obedience to it'. This argument is close to being a sub-argument for a key premise of the derivation argument, since it concerns the nature of our moral obligations. Consider a case in which I am required to keep a promise at some cost to myself. In itself, that action is against my interests, though if there is a penalty for disobedience then I may have reason overall to perform it. But if the foundational natural law were egoistic, this penalty would not be due, and so rightness cannot depend on self-interest.

But the Hobbesian egoist may point out that the penalty they propose should be inflicted on promise-breakers is not for breaking the fundamental natural law itself, but for a derivative law which requires the keeping of promises. One can, then, speak of the 'right' action in two senses: what one has ultimate reason to do, and what is permitted by morality. Rightness in the first sense *does* depend directly on self-interest; in the second, it depends directly on morality, which in turn depends on self-interest. It is true that in such a case the egoist may, if they accept that God punishes us in the afterlife for violating natural law, also have to allow that *keeping* the promise when it would be possible to avoid any terrestrial punishment may be punished in the afterlife, as a violation of natural law. But that is just an implication of the egoistic account of natural law, only as counter-intuitive as the denial of M-reasons itself. And it is anyway not a difficulty for a Hobbesian who claims ignorance of the afterlife.

Locke's strongest move against the egoist is the appeal to M-reasons independent of self-interest, implicit in the derivation and rightness-first arguments. But it will not persuade those convinced of rational egoism who also believe that the fact that we have a morality grounded on egoism explains why it appears to some as if we have independent M-reasons. And as we shall see Locke's M-reasons are anyway not entirely self-standing, but depend in various ways on God and his commands.

2. The Law of Nature

In the first essay of ELN (PE 81–8), Locke had already provided several arguments for his own non-egoistic interpretation of the law of nature: (1) (a) As Aristotle rightly noted, the proper function of human beings is to act in conformity to reason; (b)

Aristotle also correctly distinguished between natural justice, which is the same every-where, and legal justice, which varies. There are certain moral principles accepted by all, and this implies that they are natural. This is shown also by the fact that there is a science of virtue, which there could not be were it merely a matter of convention.[4] It might be objected that many people who have reason appear to be ignorant of the law of nature. But we do not say that a law does not exist because a blind person cannot read the notice announcing it. And disagreement between rational beings about the content of the law of nature implies that there is such a law to disagree about. (2) The fact that our consciences condemn us for acting wrongly, even when we are not break-ing any positive law, suggests that there is a law of nature in the light of which we assess our own actions. (3) Everything in the world observes a fixed law and operates accord-ing to its nature. This seems particularly the case with humanity, in that we have been endowed with mind, intellect, and reason, the capacities that make us susceptible of law. (4) Human society requires a definite constitution, and this in turn requires a nat-ural law that restrains both those in power and their subjects. Also necessary is fidelity to contracts, and no one could expect someone to fulfil their promises if it does not benefit them, unless there is a natural obligation to do so. (5) Without natural law there would be no virtue or vice, no fault, no guilt, no duty. It would not be possible to do anything wrong.

Again it is tempting to see Hobbes as the main target of most if not all of these argu-ments. And it is clear enough what Hobbes's responses might have been. (1) (a) To act according to reason is to pursue one's own self-interest. (b) The universality of certain moral principles can be explained by all human beings having the same need to escape the state of nature. For these principles to function effectively requires that they be taught and viewed as objective and normatively independent of self-interest, even if they are in a sense fictional. This explains how a certain level of disagreement about them is possible. (2) Guilt is in large part fear of the consequences of punishment, by God, the sovereign, or other human beings, though it also involves belief in independ-ent moral law. (3) God's law will not go against reason, and we have reason only to pursue our own good. (4) The emergence of constitutions, and practices securing fidelity, can be fully explained in egoistic terms. (5) Once morality is in place, it is pos-sible for one to violate it. But its being in place is a matter of convention, not nature.

Questions also arise concerning the role of God in Locke's conception of natural law and morality.[5] Earlier in the essay, Locke equates the law of nature with the notions of moral good or virtue, and of right reason. This law is 'the decree of the divine will discernible by the light of nature and indicating what is and what is not in conformity

---

[4] Locke's moral epistemology was attacked during his lifetime, one of his earliest critics being Thomas Burnet. Burnet's arguments are reprinted in his 1989, along with Locke's somewhat dismissive responses. An extended defence of Locke, of which Locke himself strongly approved, was offered by Catharine Trotter Cockburn (1702).

[5] 'It is probably impossible to overestimate the primacy of Locke's theism for his whole account of the natural and the moral order' (Rogers 1981: 156).

with rational nature, and *for this very reason* commanding or prohibiting' (PE 82; my italics). God's authority to make these demands on us rests on our being his creation, and on his goodness and wisdom (2.28.8). Locke associates the idea of virtue with that of morality considered independently of divine law, seeing it as what is required by the 'Law of Opinion or Reputation' (2.28.10). But conceptions of virtue differ widely, and virtue is to be pursued only when that pursuit corresponds 'with the unchangeable Rule of Right and Wrong, which Law of God hath established' (2.28.11).

Locke was brought up as a Calvinist, and there are certainly strong voluntarist elements in his thought.[6] But the italicized phrase above is clear evidence that God's willing us to live by certain moral principles is not arbitrary on his part. God, 'according to his infinite and eternal wisdom,...has made man such that these duties of his necessarily follow from his very nature' (ELN, PE 126). Indeed 'God himself cannot choose what is not good; the Freedom of the Almighty hinders not his being determined by what is best' (2.21.49). We can distinguish between what morality essentially is, and what it requires: 'Virtue, as in its obligation it is the will of God, discovered by natural reason, and thus has the force of a law; so in the matter of it, it is nothing else but doing of good, either to oneself or to others' ('Virtue B', PE 297). The bond of obligation 'derives from the lordship and command which any superior has over us and our actions', and this superior must have both right *and* power over us (ELN, PE 116–17; 119–20; 'On Ethic in General', PE 320). Since God is superior to all, 'ultimately, all obligation leads back to God'.

The commands in the law of nature, then, emanate from God. But given that there are reasons within our nature for God to command us as he does, it may be tempting to think that we have reasons independent of God's command to act morally (see Irwin 2009: 279). Such a position would enable Locke to provide non-theistic versions of his argument for the law of nature: (1) (b)* The best explanation of the consensus that certain actions are wrong is that these actions are indeed objectively wrong. (5)* Certain actions, such as torturing a child for one's own gratification, are wrong. Locke himself occasionally might seem to be giving in to this temptation. In his first, Aristotelian argument for his view of natural law, for example, he claims that 'man must of necessity perform what reason prescribes' (PE 83). And elsewhere he speaks of the 'dictates' of reason or nature (PE 85, 97, 107). But it is clear that Locke sees such dictates as themselves derivative from the dictates of God. Reason does not ground the law of nature so much as enable us to discover it. It is 'not so much the maker of that law as its interpreter' (PE 82).

Locke suggests that it would violate God's dignity to make reason 'responsible' for the law of nature. But we might distinguish between an action's being required by a law, and our having a reason to perform it. If God has a reason, independent of his own will, to require us to act in conformity to our nature, it is not clear why we also do not have a

---

[6] This aspect of Locke's thought on natural law has become highly contested in the literature. See e.g. Oakley 1999: esp. 214–15n5.

reason to act in this way, a reason independent of God's willing. Locke himself occasionally speaks as if he accepts such independent moral normativity: '[A]ll obligation binds conscience and lays a bond on the mind itself, so that not fear of punishment, but a rational apprehension of what is right, puts us under an obligation' (ELN, PE 118). But this passage follows shortly after that in which all obligation is said to lead back to God, and Locke goes on to claim that the law of nature is binding because 'God, the author of this law, has willed it to be the rule of our moral life, and he has made it sufficiently known, so that anyone can understand it who is willing to apply diligent study'. That study will involve recognizing God's existence on the basis of empirical evidence used in support of arguments such as that to design (PE 102–3).

3. Morality and Self-interest

Why does Locke fail to allow for ultimate and independent moral normativity? The answer may be that, even if one were careful to express morality in terms of, say, reasons rather than laws or commands, and so avoid violating the dignity of God, Locke holds that such language would be empty. In the essay 'Of Ethic in General', intended for the *Essay* 4.21, and close in various ways to 2.28, Locke notes (PE 300; see also 302) that the 'common ethics of the schools' teaches us little in the way of virtue but how to use the moral terminology of the society within which we live. This is partly because of the widespread differences between societies on what counts as virtuous and vicious. But the more fundamental problem is that the schools 'do not show the inferments that may draw us to virtue and deter us from vice'. In other words, claiming that, for example, I ought to keep a promise just because it would be wrong or vicious to break it is a vacuous claim without any account of what might motivate me to do so. But could not mere recognition of such a moral reason motivate me? Here we must consider Locke's account of human nature and motivation.[7]

Locke is a psychological egoistic hedonist. EG begins: 'Happiness and misery are the two great springs of human action, and through the different ways we find men so busy in the world, they all aim at happiness, and desire to avoid misery'. Our desires for happiness and the avoidance of unhappiness are 'innate practical principles' (1.3.3), and were placed in us by God to move us: without them 'we should have no reason to preferr one Thought or Action, to another' and would live 'in a lazy lethargick Dream' (2.7.3). Now, since pleasure and pain are the 'hinges on which our *Passions* turn' (2.20.3), it may be tempting to think that strength of desire correlates with degree of expected pleasure over pain, so that the will is always determined by our greatest (expected) happiness. Locke admits that he himself once held this common view (2.21.35).[8] But he rejected it once he came to believe that the will is determined by the 'uneasiness' caused by a desire. Someone may sincerely believe that virtue will bring

---

[7] For a fascinating account of Locke's conception of moral agency, see LoLordo 2012.
[8] Indeed it is the view taken in the first edition of the *Essay*.

them the greatest happiness, but until they desire to be virtuous their actions will be influenced by other desires, that is, uneasiness at the lack of other perceived goods, such as an intemperate desire for yet another drink. Locke's explanations for weakness of will are, in effect, admissions of human irrationality (2.21.36–8; 44–6).[9] My desire for yet another drink causes me uneasiness, and I will see that uneasiness as incompatible with happiness and so seek to remove it. Further, I may know that tomorrow I shall have a headache, but the good of having a clear head tomorrow is 'absent' and so any uneasiness caused by a desire for it is weaker. Locke sees this form of irrational temporal bias in our response to the possibility of the 'infinite eternal Joys of Heaven'. If our will were determined by our greatest expected happiness, we would never pursue any worldly pleasure which would put at risk those eternal joys, even if they are less certain. As things are, once free of uneasiness, we tend to be contented with a moderate portion of good, even when we know we could achieve much more.

But despite Locke's amending his original psychological egoism to allow for weakness, it is clear that he cannot allow for self-standing moral motivation, independently of uneasiness, and that mere immorality cannot make me 'uneasy' except in so far as such behaviour promises to be painful or to result in pain.[10] Nevertheless, we might criticize Locke for linking justification and motivation—'right' and 'power'—so closely in his account of the divine source of natural law and moral requirements. As Locke allows (ELN, PE 85), civil laws can still apply to those who, perhaps negligently, have failed to recognize them. Similarly, we might suggest, I can have a moral reason to φ even if I have not recognized it, and even if, having recognized it, I fail to be motivated by it.[11]

At this point, it might be claimed that Locke's position rests on the plausible principle that 'ought implies can'. If I ought to φ, then it must be the case that I can φ. And, if I cannot be motivated to φ, then I cannot φ. This argument, however, though commonly accepted in contemporary ethics, is fallacious. Let us say that the reason for φ-ing is ψ. It may well be that I cannot be motivated to φ because ψ—that ψ fails to move me. But it does not follow that I cannot φ. For example, I may respond to some threat of punishment if I fail. Indeed this is exactly Locke's own account of moral motivation. God has authority to command me to act in conformity with my nature; but in so doing, I do not respond to God's authority or to the appropriateness of my so doing, even if I recognize both. I can respond only to pleasure and pain, but these, one might claim,

---

[9] At 2.21.58–68, Locke explains how we often make mistaken judgements about future pleasures and pains.

[10] A passage in 'Of Ethic in General' (sect. 8, PE 301n64), later deleted by Locke, suggests that 'moral goodness would be no reason to direct my action were there not really pleasure that would follow from the doing of it and pain avoided greater than is to be found in the action itself'. Locke then asks: 'Were there no loss of pleasure, no pain to follow for a man's satisfying his appetite as he could, would he not be fool to endure the pain of hunger, when his neighbour's barn or stall could furnish him, if no evil would follow from his taking what was not his but the danger of a surfeit?'. This passage could be read as implying rational egoism, rather than merely welfarism, which may explain Locke's decision to delete it.

[11] In modern philosophy, the most well-known attempt to establish a link between justification and motivation is Williams 1981.

may in at least some cases enable me, if I have certain ultimate M-reasons, if not actually to comply with at least to act in conformity with them. Talk of such reasons may
not, then, be empty, even if they cannot motivate us in themselves when recognized.

How can we grasp the content of the morality willed by God? By using both our
senses and our reason (ELN, Essay 4, PE 100–6). First, the argument to design enables
us to grasp the existence of 'a powerful and wise creator'. Second, since such wisdom
would act only for some purpose, we can conclude that God 'intends man to do something'. God's ultimate aim must be his own glory, which has the implication—though
Locke does not draw it explicitly—that we have obligations to worship him. Evidence
for such obligations lies also in our natural human faculties: sense and reason enable us
to grasp what God has created and his own wisdom and power, and this disposes us to
honour him. Further, we also feel an instinct to preserve ourselves and society itself,
using our capacity for language.

We are required by the law of nature to have certain sentiments, such as reverence
for God, affection for our parents, and love for our neighbours (ELN, Essay 7, 122–3).
And we must also perform certain actions: worshipping God, relieving others' distress,
and so on. We have some discretion over when to act in these ways; but some actions—
such as theft or murder—are always wrong. Here it might seem that Locke is clearly a
deontologist. But this is not so, since he later allows that what would otherwise be theft,
or some other forbidden action, can become permissible if God requires it (PE 126).

Some have claimed that Locke's view of morality is utilitarian (see e.g. Brogan 1959;
also Lamprecht 1918: 103–4). He certainly appears to hold a version of welfarism,
according to which our reasons for acting depend only on the promotion of well-being.
Locke is prepared to speak of 'moral goodness', but offers an evaluatively reductive
account of it as 'only the Conformity . . . of our voluntary Actions to some Law' (2.28.5;
also 2.28.8; 'Of ethic in general', PE 301 (incl. n64)), the result of which will be a genuine good—a self-interested reward. Ethics itself consists in seeking out 'those Rules,
and Measures of humane Actions, which lead to Happiness, and the Means to practise
them' (4.21.3). Virtue is 'nothing else but doing of good, either to oneself or others', the
bounds of justice and other requirements depend on the expected good they produce,
and 'the greatest vice . . . [is that] whose consequences draw after it the greatest harm'
('Virtue B', PE 287–8; also 1.3.6; 'Morality', PE 267; 'Virtue A', PE 271).

It seems plausible, then, that Locke would have rejected the claim that there are certain moral values—such as wrongdoers' receiving the punishment they deserve—
which are independent of the promotion of well-being, and may even result in harm to
individuals. The claim that degree of vice correlates with degree of harm might be
taken to imply a commitment to the impartial maximization of value overall. But welfarism does not imply impartiality. Locke's stated views are consistent with the claims,
for example, that promoting the well-being of certain individuals (e.g. the worse off) is
to be given special weight, or that there are rights protecting the well-being of certain
individuals against the demands of impartial maximization. Further, as Sidgwick
points out (1906: 177–8), the examples Locke gives of moral truths, such as 'where

WELL-BEING, MORALITY, AND PLEASURE 57

there is no property there is no injustice', have no obvious connection with the general happiness; and his own theory of property, set out in the second *Treatise of Government*, is based on the view that individuals have a right to the fruits of their labour, and also seems non-utilitarian.[12] Consider also the discretion noted above that he allows to agents to decide when and whom to help. Unlike utilitarianism, Locke's ethics is not, in that sense, demanding.

4. Well-being, Morality, and Pleasure

Given Locke's views about pleasure, pain, and motivation, it is no surprise to find that he is a hedonist about well-being (2.20.2; 2.21.41–2; 2.28.5; 'Morality', PE 268; 'Happiness B', PE 271; 'Ethica A', PE 318). Happiness consists in pleasure, and it is pleasure, or what causes pleasure, that we call good. Our only ultimate desires are for it, and the avoidance of pain (2.20.14). More pleasure is better than less, less pain better than more, and the two can be weighed against one another. Further, it is anyone's 'proper business' to maximize their own pleasure and minimize their own pain ('Thus I Think', PE 296). Indeed Locke is so wedded to hedonism that he seems to view the ancient debates on whether happiness consists in wealth, virtue, contemplation, or whatever, as analogous to an argument about whether apples, plums, or nuts are the 'best Relish' (2.21.55). As we might expect, given Locke's readiness to employ teleological argument, he is not a full hedonist at the explanatory level. Rather, happiness is 'the highest perfection of intellectual nature' (2.21.51): pleasantness is not the only good-making property.

Locke has a straightforward explanation available for action in pursuit of the agent's own pleasure. But what about moral motivation? We have already noted that he cannot accept that recognition of some moral requirement may in itself motivate an agent, even if they are fully rational. Consider the contrast drawn by Locke between a king and a pirate (ELN, Essay 6, PE 118). It is in discussing the former that Locke suggests that 'a rational apprehension of what is right...puts us under an obligation' (ELN, 118). And later he claims: 'we should not obey a king just out of fear...but for conscience' sake, because a king has command over us by right' (ELN, 120). In other words, Locke does believe that one has a normative reason to obey the command of a king, a reason derivative from the ultimate reason based on divine natural law. But if one is motivated to obey through recognition of that reason, the explanation of such motivation must be given in egoistic hedonistic terms.[13]

---

[12] Nevertheless, as Brogan (1959) points out, Locke has much in common with later utilitarians, e.g. in his account of sanctions.

[13] It is interesting to compare Locke's view of moral motivation with that of Damaris Cudworth Masham, in whose household Locke lived from 1691 until his death in 1704: 'Yet however certain it is, that the dictates of *Reason*, or *Nature*, discernable by our natural Faculties, are the commands of God to us, as rational Creatures; it is equally true that the love of happiness (which consists in pleasure) is the earliest, and strongest principle of Humane Nature; and therefore whatever measures Reason does,

Locke's strategy here is twofold: he plays down the value of bodily pleasure, and among non-bodily pleasures puts special weight on those associated with the performance of duty (2.28.5; 'Happiness A', PE 251–2; 'Thus I Think', PE 296–7; 'Ethica A', PE 318–19). Honour and wealth are empty, and sensual pleasures in general (presumably if taken to excess) are sordid, shameful, and unsatisfying. Bodily pleasures are short-lived. Even the most voluptuous individuals will find that they occupy a fraction, perhaps a very small fraction, of their lives. To support the conclusion that moral pleasures are lasting, Locke offers what we might call the *redoubling argument*:

The perfumes I smelt yesterday now no more affect me with any pleasure. But the good turn I did yesterday, a year, seven years since, continues still to please and delight me as often as I reflect on it. ('Thus I Think', PE 296; see 'Ethica A', PE 319)

Locke goes on in 'Thus I Think' to note the pleasure in anticipation of eternal rewards, and in 'Ethica A' to claim that the pleasure of acting morally outweighs any merely sensual pleasure: 'Whoever is so brutish as would not quit the greatest sensual pleasure to save a child's life whom he loved?... Love all the world as you do your child or self and make this universal, and how much short will it make the earth of heaven?'. Those who are unpersuaded should anyway remember that any apparently unjust losses or gains in this life will be compensated for in the afterlife. Indeed Locke held that the best way to motivate most people morally is through drawing their attention to the 'endless unspeakable joys of another Life' (Locke 2000: 163).[14] And this provides him with an answer for the person persuaded of the pleasantness of virtue in general, but who can see that in certain cases—where morality requires that one be tortured to death, for example—it is highly implausible that in this world the pleasures of virtue outweigh those of vice.

To conclude. Locke is the first of our authors who can be clearly understood to be combining psychological egoistic hedonism, as found in Hobbes, with the idea that in some sense there are non-egoistic M-reasons. But although he often speaks as if he holds such M-reasons to be entirely independent of God, he is reluctant to express such a view, because it may prejudice the dignity of God, through suggesting a source of normativity independent of divine law, and because such reasons can anyway not motivate us directly. But the main elements of self-standing moral normativity are there in Locke, and to that extent his reluctance can be seen as misplaced. Though obligation itself depends on divine will, the content of that law is not entirely arbitrary,

---

or might, prescribe, when particular occasions occur, the sentiment of what Men find pleasing, or displeasing to them, however contrary to those dictates of right Reason, is very apt to determine their choice' (Masham 1705: 71–2).

[14] Shortly afterwards, he claims: 'Upon this foundation, and upon this only, Morality stands firm, and may defy all competition'. Locke is also of course fully aware of the motivational power of pain, and the mere *possibility* of infinite misery (2.21.70; Colman (1983: 267n17) suggests Locke adopts this argument from Pascal).

and could plausibly be said to rest on M-reasons which apply to us, and can be under-stood, independently of divine law, even if, given our egoistic hedonistic psychology, we cannot be directly motivated by them. As we shall see, the combination of an egois-tic psychology with normative M-reasons is found also in several later writers, includ-ing Mandeville, Shaftesbury, and the utilitarians, and, unsurprisingly, different forms of at least some of the problems faced by Locke re-emerge.

6

Mandeville:
Morality After the Fall

The Anglo-Dutch philosopher and satirist Bernard Mandeville (1670–1733), who spent most of his life in England, became notorious in the first half of the eighteenth century for *The Fable of the Bees*, a book which many took to be as great a threat to morality as *Leviathan* in the previous century. Indeed the Grand Jury of Middlesex raised the same charges against him as those against Socrates: impiety and the corrupting of morals (1.383–4).[1] Mandeville is, however, very different from Hobbes. Though he is a psychological egoist, he advocates M-reasons in the form of an extreme Jansenist asceticism, and this constitutes an ideal at which we should aim within the constraints imposed on us by our fallen human nature.

The origin of the *Fable* was an anonymously published pamphlet of 1705, *The Grumbling Hive: or, Knaves Turn'd Honest*. This was republished in 1714 as *The Fable of the Bees: or, Private Vices, Publick Benefits*, which included a partly interpretative essay, 'An Enquiry into the Origin of Moral Virtue', and a large number of extended 'Remarks'. A further edition in 1723 added two more essays: 'An Essay on Charity and Charity-Schools' and 'A Search into the Nature of Society'. Then, in 1729, Mandeville published part II of the *Fable*, which consisted in a preface and six dialogues, involving a character, Cleomenes, with whom Mandeville explicitly identified himself (2.21).[2] Mandeville's thought developed after the original *Fable*, but, I believe, his later views are largely continuous with the earlier.[3]

Mandeville is not easy to interpret. The *Fable* itself is in essence an allegorical poem, most of the later additions to which consist in dialogues, and he is certainly aiming to

---

[1] All unattributed references are to Kaye's important two-volume edition (Mandeville 1924: xxxiii–vii).

[2] For more on the history of the text, see Tolonen 2013: ch. 3, which updates and corrects the information in Kaye. Other especially relevant works by Mandeville are *A Modest Defence of Publick Stews, or, An Essay upon Whoring, as it is now practis'd in these kingdoms* (1724) (M), *Free Thoughts on Religion, the Church, and National Happiness* (1729) (F), *An Enquiry into the Origin of Honour, and the Usefulness of Christianity in War* (1732) (E), and *A Letter to Dion, Occasion'd by his Book Call'd Alciphron, or* The Minute Philosopher (1732) (L).

[3] There are some obvious exceptions. For example, as Mandeville himself notes (E 13), his explicit distinction between self-love and self-liking led him to change his mind on whether pride and shame are affections of the same passion. For the view that the second part of the *Fable* represents a major change in Mandeville's position, as a response to criticism of the Hobbesianism of the original *Fable*, see the excellent discussion in Tolonen 2013: ch. 2. See also below nn. 6, 11.

provide satirical amusement for his readers. He is especially concerned to describe human nature rather than to issue direct prescriptions (1.40), and to expose inconsistency or hypocrisy in the views of others. But it would be a mistake to think that Mandeville's own normative views are entirely opaque (Selby-Bigge 1897: xvi; Edwards 1964: 203). Rather, he is seeking to make his case through satire, and his claims are often expressed directly, especially in the prose works and the interventions by Cleomenes. Nevertheless, his work is open to widely different interpretations (Hutcheson (1750: 41–3) describes five different possibilities, and there are many others; see also Monro 1975: 178). In general, the interpretative principle I shall adopt will be to take Mandeville at his word, except when he is clearly being ironic (as, for example, when Cleomenes is claiming to accept Shaftesbury's account of human nature (2.41–51)). Mandeville is undoubtedly out to expose hypocrisy, but he also wishes to promote a view of his own which rests on what he saw as a firm Christian foundation.

1. The *Fable* and Mandeville's Rigorism

Analogies between human society and a hive of bees have been common in literature for thousands of years. Plato, for example, compares his philosopher-kings to the leaders of a hive; and Mandeville would have been well aware of Milton's comparison of the devil's army to a swarm of bees in the first book of *Paradise Lost*, and Swift's analogy between ancient writers and bees in *The Battle of the Books*, published a year before the *Grumbling Hive*.

Mandeville describes a 'spacious Hive well stockt with Bees, That liv'd in Luxury and Ease' (1.17). Science and industry flourished under a constitutional monarchy. Millions of bees strove to satisfy each others' lust and vanity, and while some of them, because they engaged in activities such as picking pockets, were described as 'Knaves', 'bar the Name, The grave Industrious were the same' (1.19), since there were cheats in every trade or calling, including the law, medicine, the church, and the military. 'For there was not a Bee but would Get more, I won't say, than he should' (1.22). The result was that 'every Part was full of Vice, but the whole Mass a Paradise' (1.24), the vices in question including gluttony, avarice, prodigality, luxury, pride, envy, and fickleness (1.25). The bees, though contented, all complained about the vices of others, well aware of their own failings, crying *'Good Gods, Had we but Honesty!'*. This angered Jove, who made all the bees honest. The bees, now fully aware of their own vices, dramatically changed their behaviour: markets dropped, what would have been long legal disputes were decided quickly, doctors gave up prescribing quack medicines, superfluous clergymen resigned, forces were withdrawn from abroad, factories closed, and many bees left the hive. Those that remained were unable to defend the huge hive from attack, and 'to avoid Extravagance, . . . flew into a hollow Tree, Blest with Content and Honesty' (1.35). Mandeville ends with the moral of his story:

> Then leave Complaints: Fools only strive
> To Make a Great an Honest Hive
> T'enjoy the World's Conveniencies,
> Be fam'd in War, yet live in Ease,
> Without great Vices, is a vain
> EUTOPIA seated in the Brain . . .
> So Vice is beneficial found,
> When it's by Justice lopt and bound . . .
> Bare Virtue can't make Nations live
> In Splendor; they, that would revive
> A Golden Age, must be as free,
> For Acorns, as for Honesty. (1.36–7)

The reference to the Golden Age, in its Augustan context, would have made it clear to readers, if it was not so already, that Mandeville's hive is an allegory of contemporary Britain, and this explains a good deal of the offence immediately felt by those inclined to see their age as characterized by civic virtue rather than vice. But this response constitutes a failure to recognize that Mandeville's view of vice is to be be understood in the light of what has come to be called a 'rigoristic' conception of virtue (the term is Kaye's: 1.xlviii).

At E 1.48–9, Mandeville describes the emergence of the concepts of virtue and vice he uses in the *Fable*, claiming that in the past it was agreed to use 'vice' to refer to any action aimed at satisfying the agent's desires, if that action risked harm to others or making the agent less useful to others, and 'virtue' to actions in which the agent, contrary to natural impulse, aims at benefiting others[4] or conquering his own passions 'out of a Rational Ambition of being good'. Mandeville himself agrees with this definition of virtue (see 2.109), disagreeing with Aristotelians such as Shaftesbury who saw virtuous action as pleasurable in itself. Every virtue 'curbs, subdues, or regulates some Passion that is peculiar to Humane Nature' (E ix; also E vi).[5]

Mandeville's conception of virtue as self-denying is clearly influenced by the Jansenist thinking of his teacher Pierre Jurieu, as well as the arguments of other French intellectuals, including Pierre Bayle and Blaise Pascal (Cook 470). There is little reason to think that he ever rejected their view,[6] and Mandeville explicitly and frequently attests to his belief in Augustinian Christianity (Garrett 2013: 259). At E 26, through Cleomenes, Mandeville claims that belief in a single God, creator of heaven and earth, perfectly wise and good would have been rational even if it had not been revealed by reason and metaphysics, later defining a 'man of sense' as someone who has 'read the

---

[4] At 1.180–1, Mandeville appears ready to extend the scope of moral concern to non-humans.

[5] Mandeville allows that, once one has conquered one's passions through habit, one can go on to enjoy virtuous action without being 'sensible of self-denial' (E x–xi). But since all action is governed by passion (1.39, 184, 333; E 6), even action performed in the light of the dictates of reason (E 31), this turns out to be a case in which certain passions are conquered by others.

[6] See e.g. Lamprecht 1926: 577; Maurer 2009: 168. For the opposite view, see e.g. Harth 1969: 334; Colman 1972: 128–9; Monro 1975: 17, 176–7; Goldsmith 1985: 54–5.

Bible, and believes the Scripture to be the sole Rule of Faith' (E 116). There is nothing worse for a society than an atheist (E 154), for the Gospels teach us much more than we could discover through reason alone, and Christianity is such that 'there never had been a Doctrine or Philosophy from which it was so likely to expect, that it would produce Honesty, mutual Love, and Faithfulness in the Discharge of all Duties' (E 30–1). Mandeville's conception of Christianity was the Augustinian orthodoxy of his day (1.cxxi): after the Fall, human nature was corrupt, so that virtue could consist only in transcending it—and this is possible fully only through divine grace (2.264; E 38).[7] Nevertheless, such transcendence should be our ideal, and he is prepared to 'pay Adoration to Virtue' whenever he meets it (which will be rarely, if ever: 2.50, 336, 340) (1.152; see also 2.31, 102, 127, 356; F 16; D 3; E vii; 91). Although the *Fable* shows us how to make our nation a great one in the world, Mandeville claims that he has 'always without Hesitation preferr'd the Road that leads to Virtue' (1.231; also 1. 407). In his response to Berkeley, Mandeville states that 'the Kingdom of *Christ* is not of this World; and . . . the last-named is the very Thing a true Christian ought to renounce' (D 18), going on to claim that a 'Man's Salvation is the greatest Benefit he can receive or wish for' (D 38). Mandeville accepts that the practice of Christianity has deviated ever further from the ideal of self-denial (E 128–9, 167–8, 208), but he himself believes that a sincere Christian will be one who 'acknowledging the Difficulty he finds in obeying the Dictates of the Gospel, wishes with all his Heart, that he could practice the Self-denial that is required in it' (E 166; also D 63).[8]

This conception of self-denial is extreme. Cleomenes, we are told, was a 'Man of strict Morals', yet he claims to have no Christian virtue, since his actions are performed from a 'wrong Principle'—that is, vanity, consisting in a concern for his own reputation. Any worldly enjoyment is 'foreign to Religion', centred on the self, and 'accompanied by an Elevation of Mind, that seem'd to be inseparable from his Being'. Whatever 'principle' caused that 'elevation' (which Cleomenes admits is his highest pleasure), it is inconsistent with the 'Sacrifice of the Heart' required by the Gospel (2.18–19). This does not imply that Christians will find vice whenever any bodily desire is satisfied. If one satisfies thirst only because one believes that this will better enable one to love God and do his work, that is acceptable. Further, since vice consists in acting, there can be no objection to the mere enjoyment of drinking when thirsty. What matters is that one must not be motivated to drink by one's expected enjoyment. Whether that is possible or not, Cleomenes is clear that he is motivated only, or at least primarily, by such desires, and so frequently acts wrongly. The fact that Mandeville himself appears to have enjoyed worldly pleasures, then, is no reason to doubt his

---

[7] The subtitle of the later 1714 edition of the *Fable* suggests that it is intended to describe how 'Human Frailties, *during the degeneracy of MANKIND*' can replace moral virtues (see opp. 2.392).

[8] This requirement is an independent M-reason. When Mandeville claims that belief in the afterlife is necessary for obligation in this life (2.314), he is speaking of motivation ('Tyes'). It is worth noting also that this belief anyway has little effect, because of the attractions of this world and the futurity of the next: E 18, 35–6; L 19.

commitment to rigorist asceticism. Indeed he goes on to explain Cleomenes's—that is, his own—weakness of will, and his pessimism about the likelihood of reform: they arise from his continuing attachment to the opinion of 'worldly Men', and his strong disposition to take pride in certain objects, engendered in him from his earliest education (also 1.152).[9] He appears to have no hope of God's grace, or even of the power of his own reason to lead him in the direction of greater self-denial and 'real Virtues' (F 369).

2. Worldly Virtue and the Invention of Honour

On one form of rigorism, all wrong actions—that is, all actions motivated by worldly, self-centred desires—are morally equal. This is not Mandeville's view. The purpose of the earlier 'Enquiry' is to investigate how fallen humanity can still be taught to distinguish virtue from vice (1.40). First, it matters that one's actions are, if not motivated correctly, at least in conformity with morality. So Cleomenes, despite his self-centred motivation, does at least avoid 'Turpitude' (2.19). Second, the more self-denying one can be, the better. Even a small victory over one's passions is a victory (2.109). But mere mortification of the flesh for its own sake is pointless (1.260). Recall the definition of virtue, which requires self-denying action to benefit others or to become good (and so, presumably, be a person more likely to benefit others in the future).

The upshot of this is that one should seek to conform to the majority of the requirements of common-sense morality, except where they deviate from true Christian morality, and to resist, as far as one can, one's self-interested desires not to do so: 'I lay it down as a first Principle, that in all Societies, great or small, it is the Duty of every Member of it to be good' (1.229). The virtues Mandeville has in mind include industry, being a good parent, and usefulness to society (1.85), along of course with religious virtues such as sincerity and humility (2.17). As we might expect from the definition of virtue, benevolence is singled out as a virtue (2.121), but, as with all virtues, the value of the underlying motivation is limited by rational requirement. It is an 'unpardonable Weakness' to be excessively compassionate, educating children in Charity Schools, for example, with the result that they become worse off through the creation of desires which will remain unsatisfied (1.310).

What is the source of moral worth? Does Cleomenes deserve any praise for doing what is right, though for the wrong reason? According to Mandeville, 'Men are not to be judg'd by the Consequences that may succeed their Actions, but the Facts themselves, and the Motives which it shall appear they acted from' (1.87). He gives the example of the theft of money from a miser, which results in overall benefit through the circulation of his wealth in the economy: 'Justice and the Peace of the Society' require that the guilty be hanged. Mandeville is, then, ready to consider the value of

---

[9] Mandeville adds an incapacity to become an object of contempt or ridicule, but this is in essence an example of his first general reason.

consequences at the level of institutions, though not when it comes to assessing the moral worth of a particular action. What about Cleomenes? Because he is a fallen man, his actions are certainly defective and open to moral criticism. But, Mandeville will allow, he does the best he can in the circumstances, and is certainly not as blameworthy as those who violate common-sense morality and the law.

Moral perfection, then, consists in complete self-denial, acting out of love of God to benefit others. Such self-denial is achievable only through divine grace, but it constitutes an ideal nevertheless for fallen humans, that is, at least the vast majority. The central difficulty for us is the self-centredness of our passions. Humans are animals, and '[a]ll untaught Animals are only solicitous of pleasing themselves, and naturally follow the bent of their own Inclinations, without considering the good or harm that from their being pleased will accrue to others' (1.41). All passions 'center in Self-love' (1.75), and it is impossible that a fallen human 'should act with any other View but to please himself' (1.348).[10] What about apparent cases of weakness of will, in which a person appears to choose what they know is worse for themselves? In Mandeville's view, even if the person says that this is what they are doing, we should not believe them, unless their action is 'convulsive' and so not a matter of willing at all (2.179; also F 20). Given Mandeville's commitment to psychological egoism, it is not possible for a fallen human to have an ultimate desire to follow a moral requirement or to benefit others for their own sake. What are we to make, then, of what appears to be such action?

Part of Mandeville's answer here consists in a revival of Hobbes's cynical view of pity (1.56, 258). Pity is a mere emotion, like anger, and so not good in itself; indeed, as a natural emotion, it can produce bad consequences as well as good, for example by causing a judge to be unjustifiably partial. And it is self-centred. If I save an innocent baby from a fire, I deserve no praise, since I was motivated by a desire to avoid the pain of seeing the baby suffer. But Mandeville also has a sophisticated developmental story to tell about the origin of morality. The account begins in the earlier 'Enquiry' (1.42–9).[11] Mandeville claims that 'Lawgivers and other wise Men' have long sought to persuade people that it will be best for them to subdue their passions

---

[10] At 1.200, Mandeville allows for passions that tend to preserve the species as well as the individual; but there is no suggestion that such passions can conflict with those of self-love. Mandeville may, then, be read as a proponent of ego-restricted pluralism (see p. 7 above). Note also that Mandeville does not claim that these species-preserving passions are ultimate desires to preserve the species or to benefit others for their own sake.

[11] *Pace* Tolonen (2013: ch. 2), I see the differences between Mandeville's earlier and later views as of degree rather than of kind. He is himself tentative about the notion of intervention of politicians at 1.46 ('might have been'), and it is anyway used in the later *Fable* (2.319), although it is true that in the later *Fable* there is a greater emphasis on the gradual development of society itself rather than merely morality and on the role of the family in that development. The introduction of the notion of self-liking may indeed have been at least in part a reaction to Butlerian criticisms of the Hobbesian position on egoism, but it is important to note that the idea was standard in French thought at the time and Mandeville may be employing it as more neutral than the 'vice' of pride used in the earlier *Fable* (Colman 1972: 135). Nor is Mandeville's allowing that parents naturally love their children, to the point that they will even sacrifice their lives for them (2.199, 201, 240), clear evidence of his rejecting psychological egoism: see below n. 16.

and to promote the public interest. Noting how people enjoy the praise and dislike the contempt of others, they used the 'bewitching Engine' of flattery to link honour with self-denial and shame with the gratification of bodily desire and to encourage individuals to identify themselves with the self-denying 'higher' class. Further, even those in the lower class recognized that their superiors were aiming to benefit them, and that they were in competition with their superiors to a lesser degree than with fellow members of their own class. The result were the notions of virtue and vice noted above. The moral virtues, then, are 'the Political Offspring which Flattery begot upon Pride' (1.51).

So far, Mandeville's account rests on the idea of self-love and the desire for praise. In the second part of the *Fable*, he distinguishes between self-love and 'self-liking' (2.129–47). Self-liking is necessary for self-love, since no being can love what it does not like. It consists in an evaluation,[12] indeed an over-valuation, in which each individual values themselves at more than their true worth.[13] We should assume that this evaluation itself issues in motivation, since nature has provided creatures with self-liking to increase the degree of concern each has to preserve itself.[14] We human beings, unlike the other animals, are, in some sense, aware of our over-evaluation, and this leads us to be especially fond of and enjoy the approbation of others, since this confirms us in our evaluation. (Presumably we have to assume some mechanism of self-deceit here: see e.g. 2.78.)

It is self-liking that explains the origin of 'Politeness', which develops into common-sense morality more generally. Unshaped self-liking will lead human beings to become insufferable to one another. Gradually, practices of self-effacement develop, and people begin to conceal their own opinions of themselves, and even to pretend to believe themselves to be of greater value for others than for themselves. This process results in 'good manners', which involve individuals in praising the virtues, and acting in accordance with their requirements—at least externally (2.12).

Self-liking produces in us a desire for praise by others, which is in itself morally neutral as long as it remains within certain bounds. If it becomes excessive, it can lead to one's causing offence to others, and it will then be equivalent to the vice of pride (E 6–7). But pride in itself is not always bad. The good opinion of others, in agreement with one's own self-assessment, is *honour*, and produces pride, which can be deserved (E 8–9; 1.63). Its opposite is *shame*, the result of the tension between a person's evaluation of herself and the evaluation of that person by others. Honour in this sense is an 'invention' (1.198). Mandeville attributes that invention to 'Moralists and Politicians' (also E 30, 39), but elsewhere makes it clear that he means to include all

---

[12] We should not understand evaluation here in any heavily cognitivist way. Mandeville is speaking of a passion or attitude rather than a belief, shared by all sentient creatures (2.91).

[13] In Remark M (1.124), the over-valuation of oneself is said to be the result of pride.

[14] At E 68–9, self-liking is linked with the 'instinct for sovereignty', which may perhaps be understood as a natural inclination to act on one's own judgements on the ground that they are sounder than those of others.

those who over the ages have sought to civilize humanity (E 40).[15] Further, the good of honour to the agent, and the evil of shame, are 'imaginary', in the sense that they depend on our view of the opinions of others about us, unlike, say, the pain of a broken arm, which has a physical basis independent of the sufferer's opinion (2.95). But they are not imaginary in so far as the experience of them is real, as are the physical correlates of each (e.g. the dilation of the heart or blushing; 1.67).

Given human nature, honour is a much more effective motivator than virtue alone (1.222). Independently of honour, the only immediate recompense to me for denying the satisfaction of some bodily desire is the pleasure in that denial itself, 'which most People reckon but poor Pay'. Since my desire for honour is so strong, then the satisfaction of it may outweigh that of satisfying the bodily desire in question.[16] The 'Seeds' of most virtues lie in pride and shame (1. 67); hence the love of praise is 'commendable' and 'beneficial to the Publick' (2.90).

Hume later accepted that 'politicians' had a role in the development of the moral sentiments, but, probably with Mandeville in mind, objected that they could not be solely responsible for the distinction between virtue and vice. If we had no natural inclination to see certain actions or characters as honourable or dishonourable, praiseworthy or blameworthy, those notions would make no sense to us (T 3.2.2.25; 3.3.1.11). Mandeville might, given what he says about the experience of many generations (see above n. 15), just agree with Hume on the role of natural inclination in the process. But he need not. Mandeville points out how children enjoy praise and dislike blame even when they know it is undeserved (E 7–8), implying that this basic component of self-liking remains into adulthood. The point of praise, he goes on to suggest (E 9–11), is to express agreement with the agent's own self-evaluation, not to refer to any independent quality in the action in question as worthy of praise. Imagine a child does as they promised. They will think highly of themselves for having done so, because they think highly of themselves for acting in any way whatsoever. Their parent will then reinforce that judgement by praising them, thus strengthening their disposition to act in the same way in the future. Promise-keeping must be valuable, honourable, and praiseworthy, they will believe, because they themselves are.

Hume also objects (3.3.1.11) that there are virtues and vices other than those which tend to the public good, which could not explained by reference to the artifice of of politicians. He probably has in mind the 'monkish' virtues of self-denial, humility, and so on (E 9.3), and here Mandeville will disagree with him on the public good. The best thing for us, individually and collectively, is to retreat from the world.[17]

---

[15] See 2.142: 'we often ascribe to the Excellency of Man's Genius . . . what is in Reality owing to length of Time, and the Experience of many Generations'.

[16] Honour can even lead to one's sacrificing one's life (1.199): 'So silly a Creature is Man, as that, intoxicated with the Fumes of Vanity, he can feast on the thoughts of the Praises that shall be paid to his Memory in future Ages with so much ecstasy, as to neglect his present Life, nay, court and covet Death, if he but imagines it will add to the Glory he had acquired before' (1.213–14). But he 'that makes Death his choice, must look upon it as less terrible than what he shuns by it' (1.209).

[17] On Mandeville's Stoic conception of well-being, see below p. 70.

Overall, then, the development of the ideas of virtue and honour, and the changes in human attitudes and behaviour they have brought about, are welcome. But there is an obvious antipathy between honour, on the one hand, and self-denial, on the other, which emerges in what we might call, loosely, the *paradox of self-denial*. On the one hand, the virtuous person, or the person of honour, is self-denying, in so far as they resist the temptation to satisfy some bodily desire; but, on the other, they do so only to satisfy their desire for honour, that is, their self-centred pride. This tension explains Mandeville's remark that only a strict adherence to the Christian religion can curb pride, since that religion will limit the individual's focus on herself. There is, then, a 'dual use' problem with honour. It can help fallen humanity perform actions in conformity to the requirements of morality; but, as the vice of pride, it can also result in actions violating that morality. This damaging aspect of honour has been exacerbated by the development beginning in the sixteenth century among the superior classes of an 'ethic of honour', which is straightforwardly opposed to Christianity and designed to attract those on whom religion has no grip (E 14–15, 60–1, 73; 1.221–2). Honour encourages one to revenge, when any revenge should be left to God; religion forbids murder, whereas honour encourages it, for example in duelling (e.g. 2.82 E 76); humility is opposed to pride. The ethic of honour is attractive not just because of the pleasures of honour itself, but because of its latitude. A man of honour may not cheat, for example, but he may drink, swear, and owe money without any stain on his reputation. The underlying problem is that the ethic of honour appeals to an individual's love of herself, as opposed to Christianity, which requires genuine retreat from self-concern (E 84–5).

According to Mandeville, then, the earliest attempts to civilize human beings relied on the notion of virtue, supported by the theory of reward and punishment in the afterlife (Mandeville dates the emergence of the ideas of right and wrong prior to the decalogue: 2.272).[18] Then virtue was tied to honour and shame, which brought their own self-interested rewards. But in more recent times, the pride supporting virtue has extended beyond its remit, encouraging actions out of line with Christian morality. If one is a follower of the honour ethic, then even if one is not going to become truly virtuous (which requires divine grace) one should reject the ethics of honour for the standard virtues of common sense (E 82, 90). And those virtues themselves, properly understood, will require one also to reject the laxer interpretations of morality and Christianity currently widespread in contemporary society, which allow a good deal of indulgence in worldly pleasures.[19]

---

[18] Note that Mandeville's developmental account of the institution of morality is not debunking of belief in moral truth itself. The truths of morality are as necessary as those of mathematics (E vii–ix). Mandeville's 'trifling' example is: 'It is wrong to under-roast Mutton for People who love to have their Meat well done'. It may be that Mandeville provides this example because of the widespread disagreement on more substantive issues: 1.330–1. (He does not seem to recognize the possible implications of disagreement with his self-denying form of Christianity.)

[19] Mandeville blames the Catholic church for the decline in Christian practice (E 46, 92–3, 100).

3. Private Vices, Public Benefits

In Mandeville's time, as in ours, it was commonly thought that he was advocating vice, or at least the toleration of it, and there is no doubt that some passages—such as those focusing on the benefits flowing from what would have been widely accepted as vicious and criminal activity (e.g. 1.86–93)—could be taken to be implying such a view. But, as we have seen, that is far from Mandeville's true position. In the 'Preface' to the *Fable*, he makes quite clear how he thinks we should respond to vice and crime:

> When I assert, that Vices are inseparable from great and potent Societies, and that it is impossible their Wealth and Grandeur should subsist without, I do not say that the particular Members of them who are guilty of any should not be continually reprov'd, or not be punish'd for them when they grow into Crimes. (1.10; also L 33)

Mandeville's aim is to bring out the (to him) unpalatable fact that a nation can be strong and its economy flourishing only through the creation and satisfaction of worldly desires, in opposition to standard Christian teaching, and that any such nation is bound to include a good deal more of the kinds of activity condemned even by the less ascetic common-sense morality of his time (e.g. 1.4, 7). True virtue for an individual, and goodness for a society, consist in retreat from the world and its temptations.[20] For that reason, all, or nearly all, of us are vicious in the strict sense (e.g. 1.18, 22, 61, 80–1; F 8–9, 16; E 87–81). Our lust, vanity, envy, avarice, prodigality, pride, and luxury—'by Justice lopt and bound' (1.37) (that is, kept broadly within the limits imposed by common-sense morality and the law)—are necessary for the continuing wealth and power of our nation (e.g. 1.18; 2.106; L 21, 42). And even those of us who are virtuous by the lights of common-sense morality are often able to be so only through reliance on the vices of others: consider the wealthy brewer, whose conscience does not trouble him because he never reflects on the vice encouraged by alcohol (1.87; also 1.85).[21]

Mandeville's strict ethical position raises a question central to our enquiry: how does he see the relationship between S-reasons and M-reasons? In the *Fable* (1.26), Mandeville claims that industry in the hive, underpinned by vice, increases the 'real Pleasures' of the bees. Remark O (1.147–68) clarifies what is meant here by 'real', and also explains Mandeville's non-hedonist conception of well-being. He begins by

---

[20] Note also that, according to Mandeville, populations must decrease, as in the original *Fable* (1.104–5). Virtues such as honesty and frugality are 'only fit for small Societies of good peaceable Men, who are contented to be poor so they may be easy'. His argument is perhaps one of feasibility: the chance of converting a smaller number to a life of asceticism is greater than that of converting a larger, because it is impossible for certain individuals to reform (1.95). He could also have used the point from the *Fable* itself: any nation that converts en masse and independently will become a target for invasion.

[21] Mandeville is not always clear on whether he is talking about true Christian virtue, or common-sense virtue. That is in part because common sense will agree with Christianity on many virtues, differing only in how strictly they are construed. Consider, e.g., luxury, which for the Christian is the enjoying of *anything* superfluous (L 42). Many of Mandeville's readers failed to note that indulging in the 'vices' he saw as underlying national success would often not have been condemned by common-sense morality; see e.g. Hume's charge of inconsistency in his 'Of Refinement in the Arts' (1987: 280).

distancing himself from the long-standing debate whether Epicurus meant that the highest good consisted in the pleasures of virtue, or bodily pleasures. Whatever pleases one is a pleasure. Mandeville then describes at some length the life of worldly ambition, in which the morally worthless man of aspiration seeks to combine sensual pleasure with the pleasures of a reputation for genuine virtue: these are what the 'Vicious and Earthly-minded' will describe as 'real' pleasures (1.150). Mandeville contrasts this with the Stoic view, according to which true happiness lies in the subjugation of sensual appetites and the capacity to endure losses and pains with fortitude. He notes the objection to Stoicism that its standard is set too high, but claims that 'the generality of Wise Men that have liv'd ever since to this Day, agree with the Stoicks in the most material Points' (1.151; also E ii). On the plausible assumption that Mandeville would not describe the view as held by the wise if he did not himself agree with it, he is here committing himself to the position that (i) true happiness cannot depend on anything perishable, (ii) inner peace is the greatest good, (iii) conquering one's desires is the greatest victory, (iv) knowledge, temperance, fortitude, humility, and other 'Embellishments of the Mind' are the most valuable possessions, (v) no one is happy unless he is virtuous, and (vi) only the virtuous can enjoy 'real' pleasures. Of course, such a conception of well-being is what one would expect to be held by a Christian who believes both that God is benevolent and that he demands self-denial of us.

By 'real pleasures' in the *Fable*, Mandeville goes on to point out, he meant only the pleasures that people in reality enjoy. He cannot be claiming that bodily pleasures are not in fact pleasures, since he has already agreed to count as a pleasure whatever is enjoyed. Rather, he is best understood to be claiming that the pleasures of virtue are the only valuable pleasures. Having spoken of bodily pleasures as real in the *Fable*, Mandeville exclaims: 'How Vain is Mortal Happiness!'. We should not be misled, then, by claims of Mandeville's such as that the self-loving pleasure of reflecting on the praise one will receive from others is 'a superlative Felicity' (1.55). The agent virtuous only by the lights of common-sense morality, who sees the pleasure of honour as a good, and the self-denial for which it compensates as an evil, is mistaken on both counts. The true pleasure of virtue consists in the consciousness of one's own virtue, considered independently of one's own glory or the praise of others (2.127). And we should take Mandeville at his word when he claims that, in his view, for 'true Happiness' he would prefer:

a small peaceable Society, in which Men, neither envy'd nor esteem'd by Neighbours, should be contented to live upon the Natural Product of the Spot they inhabit, to a vast Multitude abounding in Wealth and Power, that should always be conquering others by their Arms Abroad, and debauching themselves by Foreign Luxury at Home.[22] (1.13)

Here we run again into the apparent paradox of self-denial. On the one hand, we are encouraged to admire the truly virtuous individual who sacrifices worldly pleasures

---

[22] Recall here the 'content' of the ascetic bees who migrate to the hollow tree (1.35). At L 22, Mandeville claims that if a reader of the *Fable* ('a Book of Exalted Morality' (L 24)) is converted to asceticism, all poison is removed from the book and all stings from the bees.

out of love for God, respect for moral principle, or concern for others; while, on the other, we learn that they are making no true sacrifice at all, since what they are giving up is of no value, and what they gain instead is of the greatest value to them, even if they are not motivated themselves by that self-centred thought.

The tension here could perhaps be resolved if Mandeville were to insist that what we are admiring in the virtuous individual is the fact that they choose the life of genuine virtue and value, or their selfless motivation. But there is nevertheless a point of serious strain in Mandeville's position that occurs in any view, Christian or not, which devalues, for the agent, the world and its desires while also requiring from that same agent concern for the worldly desires of others. Mandeville's account of the development of morality and virtue is in part an attempt to demonstrate its effectiveness in satisfying certain basic human needs and desires.

Indeed there are even broadly utilitarian elements in Mandeville's thought (see e.g. From 1944: 210; Colman 1972: 130; Monro 1975: 248). At M 89–91, Mandeville considers the objection to his argument for state-run brothels that he is advocating an evil means to a good end. His response is to claim that the role of government is to promote the public good:

[I]f a Publick Act, taking in all its Consequences, really produces a greater Quantity of Good, it must, and ought to be consider'd a good Act; altho' the bare Act, consider'd in itself, without the consequent Good, should be in the highest Degree wicked and unjust.

Mandeville goes on to give as an example a case in which a government orders that the surviving members of a crew from a shipwreck be shot so as to prevent the spread of infection to the population at large.

Immediately after this, Mandeville shows himself aware that his focus on temporal happiness may be seen by some Christians as inappropriate, given the weight attached in that religion to spiritual welfare. His response is exegetically correct, but unsatisfying: that Christianity concerns itself with both temporal and spiritual happiness. The question, then, is one for his brand of Christianity as a whole, but can be put to him specifically in the following terms: are the 'publick benefits' of vice truly benefits? If they are, then there is more to happiness than self-denial and the goods identified by the Stoics; if not, then why should government policy, and indeed individual behaviour, not be aimed at maximizing true self-denial through retreat from the world rather than the satisfaction of worldly desires?

The most plausible solution for Mandeville would be to allow for genuine worldly or bodily benefits, but to insist on the significantly greater value to be found in the rigorous life of asceticism and Stoicism. Even this, however, especially given the rewards of the afterlife (1.57; E 31–2), will not be enough for Mandeville to countenance genuine self-sacrifice. By distancing themselves from worldly goods of their own, and practising a life of religious virtue, benevolence, and contemplation, Mandeville's virtuous agent is guaranteeing for themselves the best life in this world, and the world to come.

Let me move towards a conclusion. In his own time and often since, Mandeville's ethics have been taken to be an egoistic and hedonistic paean to vice. That is far from the truth. He recognizes external M-reasons, grounded in a divine command, to love and actively to serve God and, in line with God's requirements, other sentient beings, in opposition to bodily desires. He recommends a life of humility, piety, and frugality, informed by a prelapsarian ideal of rational and complete self-transcendence and impartiality, and tailored to postlapsarian and corrupt human nature, in which all action flows from self-centred passions. We should, that is, do the truly virtuous thing—retreat from the world—from self-centred motives that are grounded in pride and hence wrong, but nevertheless as good as they can be. Our second-best available option is to follow common-sense morality, recognizing that on some matters—such as prostitution—it should be reformed for reasons of benevolence. The third-best option is to follow the code of honour, which, though it will often lead one to act wrongly by the lights of the true morality and common-sense morality, overlaps with those views in many situations. At all times, one should refrain from immoral action, and aim as far as one can at self-improvement, in the the light of the ideal of self-transcendence.

In this respect, then, Adam Smith's criticism of Mandeville that his 'licentious system' appears 'to take away altogether the distinction between vice and virtue' (TMS 7.2.4.6–14) is, though containing an element of truth, misleading (which is in fact exactly the point he himself makes about Mandeville's position). It ignores Mandeville's prelapsarian ideal, and the fact that this ideal makes it possible for Mandeville to distinguish morally between different *degrees* of vice, to the extent that they involve more or less self-denial (cf. Monro 1975: 191–2). Smith draws a clear distinction between love of virtue and love of justified honour, on the one hand, and mere vanity or love of praise on the other, and objects that Mandeville collapses the first two, which are good, into the third, which is bad. Again, there is some truth in this, since on Mandeville's view all human action is governed by passion, and those passions are corrupt. Smith is of course right to question that rigoristic Augustinian view of humanity, but arguing against it requires more than mere assertion of a more benign view. Smith fails to recognize that, though Mandeville cannot allow for genuine love of virtue, he can make room for motivation by honour *in the knowledge of moral truth*, and a desire to be honoured for doing what is right. This is indeed all 'vanity', but Mandeville recognizes degrees of vanity which correspond to Smith's own tripartite distinction.

Mandeville's ethics is significantly more complex than that of his immediate predecessors, and it is not clearly an exaggeration to describe his clarification of the problems central to ethics as the beginning of modern moral philosophy (Garrett 2020). He recognizes M-reasons, but as a psychological egoist believes that we fallen human beings cannot be appropriately motivated by them—and here we see a straightforward similarity with Locke's view of moral motivation. Mandeville's M-reasons are a blend of attractive benevolence (though some will object to Mandeville's utilitarian view of institutions), and a less attractive asceticism which emerges from his Jansenist theism.

Though Jansenists tended towards voluntarism, Mandeville says little about the relation between God's will and the contents of his commands, thus allowing for the possibility that he conceived of M-reasons as standing at least in part independently of God's will. His commitment to psychological egoism makes subjective self-sacrifice impossible, and his Stoic conception of well-being rules out objective sacrifice, though it represents a move away from the hedonism dominant in British moral philosophy since Hobbes. That egoism is again the result of his pessimistic Augustinian conception of fallen human nature, which plays a large part in explaining his cynicism about alleged virtue and his animus against more optimistic thinkers such as Shaftesbury. These thinkers were not just poor observers of humanity, but entirely misunderstood our relation to God.

Mandeville tells us that his aim 'is to make men penetrate into their own consciences, and by searching without flattery for the true motives of their actions, learn to know themselves' (F 11). His hope, though certainly not his expectation, is that by so doing he will have the same effect on his fellow citizens as that of Jove's intervention in the hive. Before that intervention, the bees criticize one another for vices they know they have themselves (1.26–7). The difference between them and Mandeville is that he admits to his own vices. But there is nevertheless something odd in criticizing others who one believes will share one's own incapacity for reform, and Mandeville is probably not being entirely disingenuous when he says: 'If you ask me, why I have done all this, *cui bono?* and what Good these Notions will produce? truly, besides the Reader's Diversion, I believe none at all' (1.8). Here, however, we need to remember his Stoic conception of well-being, according to which knowledge is one of the most important goods. Even if he could not change people's actions, he could improve their understanding of their own motives and hence themselves. And, for Mandeville, that would count as a genuine public benefit.

7

Shaftesbury:
Stoicism and the Art of Virtue

Anthony Ashley Cooper (1671–1713), 3rd Earl of Shaftesbury, was hugely influential on eighteenth-century thought, both philosophical and non-philosophical, in Britain and abroad. In philosophy, his impact on the sentimentalism of Hutcheson, Hume, and others is often noted, though his own metaethics was a version of rationalist realism. That metaethics itself emerged from a broadly Platonic metaphysics, in which the potential for conflict between self and others was resolved through the postulation of a divinely created, ordered, and governed universe, the mind of each individual being seen as part of a general mind or nature, divinely construed (e.g. 21; R 14–17, 138–9).[1]

Shaftesbury's early education was overseen by John Locke, who was a member of the 1st Earl's household. Shaftesbury remained deeply attached to Locke, but was critical of many of his views, including some of those in ethics and political theory.[2] Shaftesbury saw as deeply mistaken the attempt to understand society and social morality as developing out of a pre-social state of nature, since human beings are naturally social (e.g. 51). Shaftesbury also disliked the voluntarist and divine command elements in Locke's thought, and in particular the importance attributed to reward and punishment in the afterlife. In his earliest publication, a preface to an edition of sermons by the Cambridge Platonist Benjamin Whichcote, Shaftesbury allows that Christianity, partly because of the excellence of its precepts and its enforcement of moral duties, is the 'greatest Blessing imaginable' and that without it morality would

---

[1] Most of Shaftesbury's works were written in the five or six years leading up to their being published together in his *Characteristics of Men, Manners, Opinions, Times* in 1711 (Shaftesbury 1999); unattributed references are to this volume). Shaftesbury revised the work over the two remaining years of his life, and a new edition was published in 1714. The *Inquiry*, included in the *Characteristics*, has usually been seen as Shaftesbury's most significant contribution to philosophical ethics. As noted by Rivers (2000: 108; also 111), it is unwise to read the *Inquiry* independently of *The Moralists* (note esp. her quotation from Leibniz at 108n108). The *Characteristics*, which went through eleven editions between 1711 and 1790, will be my main focus, but it is also important to consider other writings, in particular the highly personal and revealing *Philosophical Regimen* (R), a collection of Shaftesbury's personal notebooks, apparently written only for himself and not published until 1900. That edition itself is problematic: see Voitle 1984: 354. An annotated version of the manuscripts is now available in Shaftesbury 2011.

[2] At SC 178, Locke and Hobbes are classed together—apparently as 'barbarians'—for their denial of ethical aestheticism.

collapse entirely (P iii–iv). But, as we shall see, he believed that virtue was a good in itself for the agent and that virtuous motivation did not need to, indeed could not, depend on goods or bads external to virtue itself, so that reference to divine punishment is required only when the non-instrumental arguments for virtue have failed (269; NL 11–12). Shaftesbury's theism is as rooted in ancient as in Christian thought, and his discomfort with the notion of a hell created by a benevolent and merciful God was clearly shared by Whichcote himself, who claims that, though God has indeed arranged matters so that vice leads to unhappiness, this punishment is inflicted internally and by the sinner himself, not by God (P xiii).[3]

1. Repression, Acceptance, and Badness

The *Characteristics* and the *Regimen* have several themes in common, but I shall begin with a short examination of some of the more extreme claims of the *Regimen* to bring out the depth of Shaftesbury's commitment to Stoicism.[4] Shaftesbury's notebooks contain many quotations from Epictetus and Marcus Aurelius, and the editor of the *Regimen* describes the trio of writers as 'the three great exponents of stoical philosophy' (R xii).

A central ethical question for the Stoics, as for the most significant ancient philosophers preceding them, was the nature of the self. Quoting Epictetus—'For who can be a good man if he knows not who he is?' (Epictetus 2014: 200)[5]—Shaftesbury adopts a dualist position, distinguishing the self as mental—including will, judgement, intellect, reason—from the body and its interests (R 129, 133–4, 137, 147). As is not uncommon in the Platonic tradition, Shaftesbury expresses a certain disgust for the body, 'an excrement in seed, already half being, half putrefaction, half corruption' (R 147). I should identify myself not with bodily matter, but with my 'self-knowing, ... self-remembering, ... self-determining part' (R 150). My reason should be 'self-commanding', giving me as an agent independence from the 'fancies' or 'appearances' that assail me, and controlling their influence on my action as a general controls his soldiers or a master his servants (R 170–1, 175, 177).

Because I am not to be identified with my body, Shaftesbury suggests, my well-being is entirely independent of the body (R 135–7, 150). You cannot murder *me*, only destroy the body which I have temporarily inhabited. That will free me to return to nature and the deity, from which I came (Shaftesbury appears to accept the Platonic view that the soul pre-exists the body). Bodily ill-health is likewise not to be feared

---

[3] Shaftesbury describes such punishment as 'inherent', which it is in so far as the painfulness is a property of the vicious action itself. But it is not clear—*pace* Gill (2006: 79)—that this conception of inherent punishment (and reward) entitles Whichcote or Shaftesbury to the claim that we should care about virtue for its own sake, rather than for its inherent benefits.

[4] On the Stoic view of the emotions in particular, see also Shaftesbury's important *Pathologia* (2013), with the very useful introduction and commentary by Maurer and Jaffro (2013).

[5] Shaftesbury knew Epictetus well and I assume the translations are his. My references are to the Oxford translation by Robin Hard.

(R 156). The only appropriate object of fear is 'loss of mind'—that is, one's no longer holding true metaphysical and ethical opinion. That is in effect equivalent to my ceasing to exist, since personal identity itself depends on the continuity of such opinions, and not on, say, memory (R 136, 162).[6] But such opinions are highly resilient, and can withstand more than false opinions. Pain, then, may be an object of fear, but only in so far as it may dislodge true opinion (so it may cause me to think that the pain I am feeling is genuinely bad for me, when what is really bad is my no longer holding the true opinion that it is not) (R 161–2). What I fear depends on my opinions, and these are a matter of my 'choice'. Shaftesbury need not be understood here to be advocating an extreme voluntarism about belief. What I believe depends on how matters appear to me. If I grasp the truth, I can grasp it as true, and voluntarily make efforts to retain that belief even when I am facing what might otherwise seem to be great evils, such as pain or death.[7]

Because Shaftesbury, like Plato, sees desire as closely related to the body, he is highly suspicious of it (see Voitle 1984: 152, 345). One must certainly 'suspend' it to enable contemplation of God and the order of the universe (R 24). But one must beware of a whole range of desires and their capacity to dislodge one from the true course: desires for revenge, sex, luxury, ease, power and position, goods in general, and even wishes that the past had gone differently (R. 270–1). Often these desires have to be entirely banished, sometimes only moderated (R 195).[8] One should not fight desire with desire. Rather, desire is to be combated by opinion or belief, grounded in rational reflection on true value (R 210). And the true value of most of the objects of human desire is significantly lower than commonly thought, so that the correct response to such desires is 'dejection and mortification . . . the depressing, extinguishing, killing that wrong sort of joy' and 'the introducing of a contrary disposition: the wearied, allayed, low, sunken; that which creates a mean and poor opinion of outward things, diminishes the objects and brings to view the viler but truer side of things' (R 157).

As one might expect, this view of desire significantly affects Shaftesbury's account of how we should relate to others, whose deepest concerns will of course often be as mistaken as our own prior to the process of repression. He instructs himself: 'cut off

[6] It may be that Shaftesbury is to be understood as rejecting the standard conception of the identity of persons over time; see Purviance 2004.

[7] In the *Characteristics*, Shaftesbury claims that the 'ill of [a] . . . private system [is] no real ill in itself', since what matters is the good of the whole (169; also 306, 315; on this passage, see Darwall 1995: 195n39). But he can be understood as relying on a distinction between pro tanto and overall goodness, since the example he mentions is the growing of teeth: one might think this is bad, but it is not because it leads to a good result overall (also R 9–10, where the good of a finger is set alongside that of the body as a whole, and R 20, where the 'distemper and ails of a few animals' are compared to the good of the universe as a whole). At R 32, Shaftesbury claims I must love e.g. hardship, if it is necessary for the good of the whole, but he may be claiming that I must love it as playing that instrumental role rather than as itself a good component of a general good. If a whole is perfect, he suggests, its parts must be perfect, probably meaning that they are unimprovable in the sense that no change to them could improve the good of the whole.

[8] Shaftesbury's view here is almost certainly influenced by Aristotle's 'doctrine of the mean', according to which some actions or feelings are always wrong, whereas others are in themselves neutral but can be performed or felt appropriately or inappropriately depending on the circumstances (Aristotle 1894: 2.6).

familiarity, and that sympathy of a wrong kind. Learn to be with self, to talk with self', adding the following requirements:

1. To take pleasure in nothing.
2. To do nothing with affection.
3. To promise well of nothing.
4. To engage for nothing. (R 144–5)

What about compassion for others (R 158–9)? Shaftesbury recognizes that in 'one order of life', this is only natural and appropriate. But this is the order of 'animals and men-animals'. At a higher level, that of rational beings, 'true affection' is for the world as a whole, nature, the deity. One should merely *express* sympathy, not feel it: 'when you see one weeping, have sympathy, but do not inwardly lament' (Epictetus 2014: 291).[9] Fortunately, perhaps, any attempts Shaftesbury may have made to suppress his concerns for others were not entirely successful, though he did at times withdraw from society for long periods. There is a sharp dichotomy here between his private thoughts and public statements, and if we assume that the latter were not entirely disingenuous then Shaftesbury's own mind seems divided against itself. He begins a letter to John, the son of his old friend Robert Molesworth, as follows: 'Amongst the many happinesses which heaven has afforded to mankind on no other condition, nor by other means than that of liberty alone, we ought, I think, to esteem friendship the most considerable' (R 520). Much of the *Regimen* consists in Shaftesbury's expressing regret, to the point of self-loathing, at his own failures to live up to Stoic principles.[10]

Shaftesbury's metaphysics is deeply teleological. We, like the rest of the universe, are the result of God's rationally willing our existence, for purposes of his own which we may be unable, and have no need, to understand—except that we do know it is for the best (R 19, 186–7). Divine design enables Shaftesbury to sidestep any accusation that when, for example, he defines 'natural' as 'orderly and good' (R 9), he is committing some version of the naturalistic fallacy or inferring an 'ought' from an 'is'. Nature is good—indeed the best—because it is the expression of the will of an omniscient and omnibenevolent creator, whose authority it would be unnatural and impious to disobey (R 8–9, 91–2). We are required to feel an affection for nature so understood that overrides all other affections, including what we might call 'ordinarily natural' affections for our children or friends (R 10).

Shaftesbury draws two surprising practical implications from this view of the place of humanity in the world. First, we must accept everything that happens, being as content with a short as with a long life, with no reputation as with a great one, with poverty as with wealth, with death as with life (R 218–19). Indeed our happiness, he suggests, can be identified with such contentment, consisting as it does in unity with the 'original

---

[9] This reference is to *Handbook* 16, cited by Shaftesbury as *Handbook* 26.
[10] See e.g. R 241. I shall return below to the issue of potential divisions in the mind in discussion of Shaftesbury's views on moral motivation.

mind' (R 257). Second, not only must we accept the inevitable, but we must will it (R 91–3). Failure to do so would be both impious and pointlessly foolish. Backward-looking emotions of regret are forbidden (R 10).

Several puzzles remain unresolved in Shaftesbury's broadly Epictetan position, of which he is not himself entirely unaware. If the course of nature is willed by God, then it is not clear what place there is for free and willed intervention by human beings who can be held accountable. Here we might appeal to some form of compatibilism, but Shaftesbury himself places an obstacle in our way through his suggestions that we should will what we know is inevitable and that all willing ultimate turns out to be for the best (R 41, 91). Imagine that my child is very ill with plague, and I know, on solid inductive grounds, that she will die; then I should will that, and not grieve before or after her death. The same implication might seem to follow for vicious action. Imagine that I am a serial killer, and have murdered a victim on each of the last ninety-nine Fridays. How should I reason on Thursday evening? Shaftesbury's view seems to be that I should aim to be virtuous as long as possible, and only switch to vice when there is no alternative. But the idea of switching to vice here is itself problematic, since my willing must be for the best and so, in effect, as virtuous as my willing before the switch. Shaftesbury's deterministic teleology seems to rule out the rationality of forward-looking as well as backward-looking emotions with any substantive content: I must accept, and will, whatever has happened, whatever is happening, and whatever will happen, and it remains unclear why I am entitled to vary my positive attitude to the particular constituents of these general states of affairs.[11]

2. Human Nature and Motivation

With the *Regimen* still in mind, let us now turn also to the *Characteristics*. There is no doubt that Shaftesbury holds some version of psychological egoism: 'We know that every creature has a private good and interest of his own, which nature has compelled him to seek by all the advantages afforded him within the compass of his make' (167; also R 30).[12] But he firmly rejects those versions of the view which cynically reinterpret apparently virtuous or other-regarding concern as an indirect expression of an ultimate concern only for oneself (54–5). The human 'machine' is complex, and involves natural and basic social affections. Having spoken approvingly of Epicurus's recommendation to avoid children and service to one's country, since it demonstrates Epicurus's recognition of the force of such natural affections, Shaftesbury goes on to to criticize those moderns who have reinterpreted those affections themselves as indirectly selfish.

---

[11] See Gill (2006: 155), who notes (287n14), with reference to Grean, Leibniz's positive view of Shaftesbury.

[12] At R 92, Shaftesbury claims that psychological egoism is true, necessarily, even of God.

Shaftesbury follows Aristotle in seeing human beings as fundamentally social in nature.[13] According to Theocles in *The Moralists*, a human being stripped imaginatively of his social affections is only as much a man as an egg or embryo: 'though his outward shape were human, his passions, appetites and organs must be wholly different' (285).[14] Human society, as is the case with other animals, begins with the natural affection of a parent for his or her offspring, and then develops directly into a household, an economy, a tribe, and finally a nation (287).

But if, as Shaftesbury asserts of himself in a letter to Robert Molesworth, 'it is possible to serve disinterestedly' (L 58), the question arises how this motivation can be consistent with psychological egoism. Again, Shaftesbury's account is Aristotelian. Aristotle begins his *Nicomachean Ethics* with the claim that 'every action and rational choice is thought to aim at some good', and he takes the proposition that happiness is the chief good—the good which includes all others worth aiming at—to be a platitude (2014: 1094a1–2; 1097b14–23). And yet he allows that a virtuous person aims at the noble (e.g. 1115b11–13), and, as a true friend, wishes good to his friend for that friend's own sake (1156b7–9). In 9.8, Aristotle seeks to resolve any apparent tension in his position by distinguishing two forms of self-love. The objectionable, 'selfish' kind consists in the pursuit of money, honours, and bodily pleasure. The virtuous person, however, recognizes that their good itself consists in virtuous activity, which will itself will involve direct concern for the good of others for their own sake. This view is essentially Shaftesbury's (56). Happiness is to be pursued in 'following nature and giving way to common affection'. Hence, '[i]t is the height of wisdom, no doubt, to be rightly selfish'.

This Aristotelian account of egoistic motivation resonates with Shaftesbury's view of moral motivation. Shaftesbury might seem unlike Aristotle in allowing for divine rewards and punishments in the afterlife; but the contrast is not as great as it might appear. According to Theocles (270), theists will infer the existence of posthumous justice through revelation of the nature of distributive justice in this world and of the providence of God. The unfairness of material rewards in this life can be explained as providing the 'theatre' for virtue: without risk or struggle against adversity, virtue would have been too easy: 'What merit except from hardship?'. Further, the standard

---

[13] I shall argue that Shaftesbury may have been more influenced by Aristotle than has been thought by most commentators, and perhaps by Shaftesbury himself: he contrasts the 'polite learning' of Aristotle to work on 'the deep and solid parts of philosophy', which includes ethics (115). Shaftesbury may have seen Aristotle as insufficiently focused on practice rather than theory; but see e.g. Aristotle's claim that the point of philosophical ethics is to become a better person (1894: 1103b26–9), and his rules of thumb for the agent seeking to improve their own character at 1894: 2.9. On Shaftesbury's readiness to keep some of his influences to himself, see Rivers 2000: 92, 95; also Sellars 2015: 2–3. I do not wish to deny other significant influences, including in addition to the Stoics (though it is worth remembering that here there will anyway be indirect Aristotelian influence), Plato and the Cambridge Platonists (see Cassirer 1970: ch. 6). Nor am I claiming that the influence of Aristotle is greater than, or even equal to, these others. It is worth mentioning also the possible influence of Cumberland's metaphysical and ethical views on Shaftesbury, though there is no evidence that Shaftesbury read the *Treatise of the Laws of Nature*.

[14] Like Taylor (1989: 252), Guyer (2004: 19), and others, I take Theocles to be, in general at least, 'spokesperson' for Shaftesbury in the dialogue.

Christian account of posthumous justice has its place in moral education. Many believe, mistakenly, that self-interest consists in power or wealth, and this was as true of the ancient Hebrews or Jews as of us (126). Further, reward and punishment can be understood not so much as providing incentives to virtue and vice, but as expressive of the view of these states as good or bad in themselves. They are in this respect an early stage in moral education, analogous to those used by a parent to instruct their children 'in virtue which afterwards they practise upon other grounds without thinking of a penalty or bribe' (187). Here, then, we can see an analogy with Aristotle, who insists that we become virtuous only by first doing virtuous actions not for their own sake but for some external good, thus creating a habit of virtue which provides the basis for an understanding of and a motivation towards the noble for its own sake (Aristotle 1894 2.1–40. Virtuous actions done for such instrumental reasons, however, do not have true moral worth. Those who have advocated virtue on the basis of posthumous reward have in fact made it hard to see what there is in virtue to be rewarded: 'For to be bribed only or terrified into an honest practice bespeaks little of real honesty or worth' (46). And the same goes for extraneous mundane rewards, such as reputation (20). God is not sufficiently 'weak, womanish and impotent' to care about his reputation among us, and we should follow his example. True moral worth requires the correct motivation, which leads to action based on the deliverances of the 'sense of right and wrong...a real antipathy or aversion to injustice or wrong and...a real affection or love towards equity and right for its own sake on the account of its own natural beauty and worth' (178; also 188), informed by love of God (269).

Kantian ethics has long been criticized for the 'alienation' involved in acting from a sense of duty.[15] A similar objection could be made to Aristotle's claim that the virtuous agent aims at the noble.[16] Should a virtuous person not be concerned, for example, with relieving the suffering of others? Defenders of Kant and Aristotle have often claimed that, properly understood, the notions of a sense of duty and the noble can themselves include genuine concern for the well-being of others. The same sort of dialectic can play itself out in interpretation of Shaftesbury. The social affections which ground morality are, as we have seen, natural, and 'the height of goodness' consists in loving the public, studying universal good, and promoting the interest of the whole world (20). The virtuous agent, then, is moved by recognition and love of God, duty, virtue, nature, and the well-being of others, as appropriate.

But what about their self-love? How is Shaftesbury's commitment to psychological egoism consistent with this account of motivation? As I have said, Shaftesbury's view can be read as Aristotelian. Recall that his conception of human motivation is pluralist, so that self-love can sit alongside other ultimate motivations. Self-love, to some degree, is natural, good, and fitting (170). But it has limits. A virtuous agent's natural social

---

[15] Recall Schiller's famous joke: 'Gladly I serve my friends, but alas I do it with pleasure' (Beiser 2005: 170); see also Williams 1981b.
[16] Hurka 2013: 20.

affections will lead them—at least sometimes—to act 'necessarily and without reflection' (60), and in particular without reflection on their own good. Here we see a split-level version of psychological egoism somewhat similar to that of Hobbes. The virtuous agent never stops believing that their virtue promotes their own good; but they recognize that a strategy of acting out of direct, non-self-interested concern will overall promote that good most effectively. In the case of Hobbes, of course, this strategy is itself grounded on rational egoism. But it is clear that Shaftesbury, and the virtuous agent as conceived of by him, see God, virtue, and so on as providing M-reasons.[17] These M-reasons, however, as a matter of necessity, never conflict with S-reasons. For Shaftesbury, this is true even in cases where the agent is motivated by the thought of the enjoyment they will receive from acting virtuously. For that motivation itself is strong evidence of their loving virtue for its own sake.[18] So even if a person is quite self-consciously aiming to advance their own enjoyment through acting virtuously, this need not detract from the moral worth of their action if they also love virtue for its own sake.

It remains unclear why Shaftesbury insisted so strongly on psychological egoism. At 126n57, he refers to passages in the bible in which Moses and Paul display a 'willingness to suffer without recompense for the sake of others, and...a desire to part even with life and being itself on account of what is generous and worthy'. Moses tells God that he is willing for his name to be entirely 'blotted out', and Paul appears to be making a similar offer. Both of them are motivated by concern for others, and there seems no obvious reason to think that they *must* have believed that their advancing the good of others by their own destruction would benefit them, presumably by making their lives as a whole more valuable for them than longer lives without sacrifice. This puzzle itself is again Aristotelian, since Aristotle makes it impossible for the virtuous person genuinely to sacrifice themselves. Even when they give their life in battle, they are assigning themselves the greater good of nobility (1894: 1169a25–b1). Psychological egoism, in various forms, was the standard view in ancient philosophy, and here we have another example of Shaftesbury's views lining up with those of Aristotle.

[17] If Darwall (1995: 219–20) is right to interpret Hutcheson as holding that Shaftesbury believed the only justification for virtue was egoistic, then Hutcheson seems to have misunderstood Shaftesbury quite significantly. But it is worth noting that the only text cited by Darwall which explicitly mentions Shaftesbury (E 186) does not commit Hutcheson to this interpretation (at IL 136–7, Hutcheson cites Shaftesbury as one of the proponents of the view that human nature is directly benevolent). Darwall himself suggests that Shaftesbury is a rational egoist, in that he held that the 'virtuous life is reasonable...because it is most in the agent's interest' (1995: 194). If we should understand 'solely' before 'because', then this again seems to misunderstand Shaftesbury (Darwall also claims that Butler read Hutcheson in this way). The beginning of the second book of the *Inquiry* suggests that Shaftesbury's aim is not to provide an egoistic justification of virtue, but to show how there is no 'plain and absolute Opposition' (193) between self-interest and virtue (a project entirely consistent with the view that it cannot be rational to sacrifice self-interest for virtue).
[18] 187. Shaftesbury uses a similar 'evidential' argument to explain why we admire virtue in adversity, even if it requires overcoming temptation. It cannot be good to be tempted; but to overcome temptation is strong evidence of the force of the agent's love for virtue: 'if there be no ill passions stirring, a person may be indeed more cheaply virtuous' (176).

3. Ethical Aestheticism

There is no sharp distinction between Shaftesbury's ethics and his aesthetics. Beauty is central to understanding the value of divinely created nature, and the enjoyment of beauty is crucial to understanding the human good (320, 327). At the heart of Shaftesbury's conception of beauty are the notions of order, proportionality, and appropriateness. It is through the idea of order that he approaches the analogy between the kind of beauty one finds in, say, gardens (R 247), and the moral beauty of virtue. Shaftesbury ends his sixth letter to Michael Ainsworth (the 'young man at the University') thus: 'Dwell with Honesty, and Beauty, and Order: Study and love what is of this kind' (NL 33). In the *Characteristics*, he claims that love of order of any kind can promote moral virtue (191), and that 'the most natural beauty in the world is honesty and moral truth', since 'all beauty is truth' (65; also e.g. 320). This truth is objective and independent: 'if the tree is known only by its fruits, my first endeavour must be to distinguish the true taste of fruits, refine my palate and establish a just relish in the kinds' (133; also 150, 466).[19]

The kind of order Shaftesbury has in mind is harmony. He compares the relation of the passions to one another to that between the strings of a musical instrument (199). Just as not all instruments are alike, the same is true of human beings, so that, for example, people who are especially prone to pleasure and pain may need counterbalancing passions such as compassion to ensure that they do not shrink from helping others when it is their duty to do so. But this is the only way in which such harmony depends on our own passions and sentiments: 'harmony is harmony by nature', in both art and ethics. The truly honest man 'instead of outward forms or symmetries, is struck with that of inward character, the harmony and numbers of the heart and beauty of the affections, which form the manners and conduct of a truly social life' (353).

But ethics is of course not solely a matter of the affections. It also involves doing what is right. For example, there is an obligation to keep one's promises, which does not depend on any prior agreement or contract (51). Moral worth requires knowledge of right and wrong as well as a rational capacity to 'secure a right application of the affections' (175). Again, in Shaftesbury's conception of virtue as involving moral understanding, harmony of the affections, and acting correctly, we find strong Aristotelian influence (see above n. 8). In outlining the doctrine of the mean, Aristotle compares the decision-making of the virtuous agent to the tuning of a lyre (1894: 1138b21–3; see Aristotle 1855, n. ad loc.). In the case of anger, for example, the virtue consists in feeling the right amount of anger, at the right time, for the right reason, and so on, while the excessive vice consists in feeling anger inappropriately—too much, at the wrong time, and so on—and the deficient in failing to feel it appropriately. Shaftesbury's account is strongly reminiscent of the doctrine of the mean. Consider again, for

---

[19] Voitle (1955: 37–8) suggests that objectivity was the main advantage Shaftesbury gained through the analogy between the moral and aesthetic senses, given early-eighteenth-century views on aesthetic value.

example, what he says about self-love, the 'affection towards self-good' (170–1). Excessive self-love is selfishness, while the lack of it is 'ill and unnatural'. The same is true of concern for others, which also can go to excess (172), so that happiness will consist in the correct balance or harmony between self-regard and other-regard (Albee 1896: 28). Likewise, there is a virtue in wit (see Aristotle 1894: 4.8). The virtu-ous person will be grave about what is truly serious, and ridicule the ridiculous (8, 59), and there will again be a pair of vices correlating with gravity and ridicule.

Aristotle's doctrine runs into serious difficulties with certain virtues, especially that of justice. For Aristotle's triadic account of each virtue to succeed, there must be a 'neu-tral' feeling (such as anger) or action (such as giving away money) which can be used to characterize the virtue and the vices of excess and defect in each case. In the case of justice, however, it is hard to identify any such neutral feeling or action. Aristotle him-self admits that his own attempt to use the notion of greed to explain justice requires us to understand the doctrine of the mean in a non-standard way (1894: 1133b32–1134a1). Because he puts less emphasis on the notions of excess and deficiency in every case, Shaftesbury can avoid these problems. The just person's passions and actions are in harmony, while those of the unjust are not. Shaftesbury also adds to Aristotle's account an explanation of our judgements of harmony themselves in terms of second-order passions or sentiments, felt in response to first-order passions or virtuous and vicious actions themselves (172). Further, Shaftesbury provides valuable resources for defence against charges of alienation or misfocus of attention by establishing an espe-cially close link between the morally beautiful and utility for the agent as well as for others (414–15).

But Shaftesbury presses the aesthetic analogy harder than Aristotle, and this leads in his theory to a regrettable blurring of the distinction between moral and aesthetic value. Some (e.g. Lear 2006) have read Aristotle as finding the same species of the 'kalon' (which can be translated as 'the beautiful', or 'the noble') in the character of the virtuous person as in a work of art. But kalos in Greek is in fact a much broader word than 'beautiful', similar in many respects to agathos ('good'). Aristotle does not specify any particular sense for 'the kalon' in his text, and therefore the audience of his lectures would not have heard him as drawing any close analogy between ethics and aesthetics. Aristotle's virtuous agent is aiming at the morally good or praiseworthy, not at any kind of harmony found equally in actions or characters on the one hand, and landscapes or poetry on the other (see Crisp 2014).

The distinction between ethics and aesthetics can be grasped most clearly via the notion of blame. Blame, as an emotion, is complex, but a central component is anger. When we feel blame—rather than when we are merely attributing some wrong action to an agent—we are feeling anger at some agent for violating an ethical norm. There is nothing analogous to this kind of anger in aesthetics, though of course it is not uncom-mon to find aesthetic criticism shading into moral alongside charges of, say, the degen-eracy of the object in question, or the deceitfulness of its maker. Blurring the aesthetic/ethical distinction also distorts Shaftesbury's account of moral education. The capacity to make good ethical judgements requires sensitivity to a quite different range of qualities from that required for good aesthetic judgements. History tells us of many cases in which aesthetic sensitivity sat alongside depravity and moral blindness, and it is not uncommon for aesthetic interests to distract attention from moral requirements and the needs of others.

4. Pleasure and Virtue

Shaftesbury frequently appears staunchly opposed to evaluative hedonism. He criticizes the philosophical and theological orthodoxy of his day, according to which we should 'rate life by the number and exquisiteness of the pleasing sensations' and so 'learn virtue by usury', valuing it for the pleasure it can produce (and presumably the pain it can prevent) (57; also NL 19). Shaftesbury also finds problems internal to hedonism itself. First, pleasure cannot be the foundation of a 'rule of good', since those who aim at unrestricted pleasure are constantly changing their minds about what is and is not pleasurable (138; also 151–2, 252–3, R 50). Consistency can be found only through aiming at virtue: 'if honesty be my delight, I know no other consequence from indulging such a passion than that of growing better natured, and enjoying more and more the pleasures of society' (138–9; also R 54–5). Second, and relatedly, any evaluative claim must be universally true (R 56–7). To be happy requires contentment, and one can be content without unrestricted pleasure, just as one can without fame or power. Further, pain cannot be said to be evil, since some people can tolerate it.

These arguments, it has to be admitted, are somewhat weak. If aiming at unrestricted pleasure and avoidance of pain produces a lower balance of pleasure over pain than some other strategy, then an evaluative hedonist can recommend that alternative. Further, even though it is true that hedonic value can diminish marginally, there seems no reason why an evaluative hedonist should not take this into account in their calculations, shifting to a new source at the optimum level to maximize the overall balance of pleasure over the pains of disappointment and boredom. Nor need the hedonist reject the universality claim. They can insist that the greatest balance of unrestricted pleasure over pain is universally good, and note that, since contentment is a kind of pleasure, Shaftesbury's own view can be understood as hedonist (see Sidgwick 1902: 185n1).

As we might expect, given his Stoic views on desire, Shaftesbury puts a very high value on contentment or tranquillity: one moment of it is more valuable than a lifetime of the 'tumultuous joy' of friendship (R 116). It is stable, does not lead to disgust, and is immune to the vicissitudes of fortune (R 151–2, 208). It is 'nothing else than the good ordering of the mind' (Marcus Aurelius 2013: 20), and Shaftesbury describes its absence, and indulgence in the passions, as 'near to real madness' (R 160).

Shaftesbury's main argument against unrestricted hedonism is again solidly Aristotelian. According to Aristotle, since all animals, including the intelligent ones, aim at pleasure, it would be absurd to claim that it is not a good (1894: 1172b35–1173a1).

But not all pleasures are worthy of choice, so unrestricted hedonism is mistaken (1174a8–11). The pleasure of virtuous actions is good, while that of vicious ones is bad, and the virtuous person is the touchstone of which pleasures are and are not valuable (1176a15–16). And these are primarily the pleasures really characteristic of a human being—that is, the pleasures of virtuous action itself (1176a22–9; see 1198a16–17). Shaftesbury is in broad agreement with Aristotle. Just as a man of 'breeding and politeness' will take care to develop his taste by focusing on the best architecture and paintings, so all of us should have 'the same regard to a right taste in life and manners' (150–1; also e.g. 335). Shaftesbury's objection, then, is not to hedonism, but to unrestricted hedonism (250–1).

This brings us to the question of how Shaftesbury views the value of virtue to the virtuous agent themselves. In his earliest publication, Shaftesbury drew a distinction between a justification of virtue grounded on the intrinsic 'Pleasure and Contentment in Works of Goodness and Bounty' (which were also experienced by God)[20] and one that appealed to 'some Advantage of a different Sort from what attends the Actions themselves' (P 10). Further, as one would expect, he accepts S-reasons: 'we should all agree—that happiness was to be pursued and in fact was always sought after' (56; also 170).

Shaftesbury is most plausibly understood as a substantive hedonist about well-being, in so far as he believes that happiness consists in pleasurable experiences arising from valuable objects, and in particular the state of mental contentment arising from virtue and virtuous activity.[21] Again, this position is close to that of Aristotle, though Aristotle is most plausibly read as claiming that happiness consists *only* in (pleasurable) excellent or virtuous activity (Crisp 1994), and, as we shall see, Shaftesbury reverses Aristotle's order of priority of intellectual activity over the exercise of the virtues of character (1894: 10.7–8). Shaftesbury is clearly not committed to explanatory hedonism, according to which the only good-making property is pleasantness. Pleasure in worthless objects is itself worthless. The fact that an experience is one of taking pleasure in a valuable object is itself good-making, but the explanatory account of goodness here is complex and must include reference to Shaftesbury's views on God, nature, and perfection.

Shaftesbury's view on the content of morality is, in many respects, close to that of common sense. He is committed to many standard virtues, and appears to accept

---

[20] Shaftesbury's point here is reminiscent of Aristotle's suggestion that we ought to 'take on immortality as much as possible, and do all that we can to live in accordance with the highest element within us' (1894: 1177b33–4).

[21] Shaftesbury's aim in pt. 2 of the *Inquiry* is to show that having the natural affections is to have '*the chief means and power of self-enjoyment*', and that having excessive private affections, or having unnatural affections, leads to misery; he notes that happiness is 'generally computed' from 'pleasures or satisfactions' (200–1, 216). Irwin (2008: 358; see Grean 1967: 229–32), referring to 250–1, claims that, according to Shaftesbury, the pleasant is merely what we think eligible. But Shaftesbury can be understood here to be objecting to a particular version of unrestricted hedonism. Seeing will and pleasure as 'synonymous' is equivalent to calling everything *which pleases us* 'pleasure'.

customary deontological views on justice, promising, and other issues. There is a strong welfarist element in Shaftesbury's thinking (e.g. virtue aims at 'the general good' (230) and 'the good of mankind' (244)), but his frequent mention of values such as justice alongside the promotion of overall good (e.g. R 71–2) suggests that we should not interpret him as any kind of utilitarian. When he says that making the most of life consists in doing the most good (R 346), he has in mind avoiding selfishness and living virtuously. Nevertheless, Shaftesbury's insistence on impartiality and the promotion of the good of the whole does introduce a consequentialist element into his normative ethics. It seems that he believes, like many pure consequentialists, that following the partial principles of common-sense morality will in most cases promote the overall good, though he may well accept that there are non-consequentialist reasons for so doing (e.g. 255–6). So the practical implications of his impartiality principle are relevant only in those probably rare cases in which one is required to sacrifice the interests of those close to one for the sake of the overall good (see e.g. 205–7; R 6, 97). Further, there is no hint in Shaftesbury of the idea that one adopt anything like Sidgwick's 'point of view of the universe', from which one's own good matters, as far as one's own practice is concerned, only as much as that of anyone else's. Some degree of partiality towards oneself is natural, and hence good and required. But there is no tension between the promotion of my good and the promotion of the overall good, since my good itself consists in the promotion of the overall good as Shaftesbury conceives it. The overall good, that is to say, does not consist in an overall sum of individual utilities, themselves calculated independently of that overall good. The overall good consists in the world's operating as it should, with each agent's following common-sense morality modified by the principle of impartiality.

Shaftesbury puts forward a series of suggestive and inter-related arguments to the conclusion that the life of the virtuous person is the happiest:[22]

(i) Natural Affections. To lack 'honesty', that is, virtue, would be to lack the natural social affections, a life without which is wretched (56). When we consider some creature void of such affections, we suppose it will feel little pleasure and be inclined to moroseness and distress (194–5, 215–16, 431–2). The reason for its state, though we tend not fully to recognize it, is disharmony. If we 'strain' some affection, or act on some wrong passion, this will upset the balance of our mind, causing deep and lasting distress. Our dependence on society is greater than that of any other animal, and we all strongly desire to be in friendly relations with others. Suppressing that desire will lead to disharmony, discontent, and unhappiness.

---

[22] Gill (2006: ch. 9) finds in Shaftesbury a separate teleological argument for virtue, independent of the 'mental enjoyment' account, and argues for tensions between the two. I read Shaftesbury's teleology as supporting the mental enjoyment account (if anything, Gill sees the relation running the other way: see 2011, sect. 4, penult. para.; also Albee 1896: 29). In outlining the teleological argument, Gill (2006: 120) quotes the question Shaftesbury suggests asking one of the 'sportly gentlemen' about a bitch who eats her puppies: 'whether he thinks the unnatural creature who acts thus, or the natural one who does otherwise, is best in its kind *and enjoys itself the most*' (430) (my italics).

Shaftesbury's focus here, like that of Plato's in the *Republic*, is on the life of the entirely vicious person. Confronted by, say, some gangster, who appears to have genuine love and concern for his family and friends, Shaftesbury can only doubt that genuineness, or insist that such partial concern anyway puts the individual into a position of conflict with the good of the whole which itself will result in discontent (the gangster's denial of that must again be taken to be disingenuous or the consequence of self-deceit) (194, 205–6; also Irwin 2008: 360).

(ii) Identity and Character. As we have seen (p. 76), in the *Regimen* Shaftesbury appears to believe that continuity of correct moral opinion is required for identity over time. In the *Characteristics*, he makes the weaker claim that what a person is—that is, we must assume, what kind of person he is—depends on his character and affections, so that if 'he loses what is manly and worthy in these, he is as much lost to himself as when he loses his memory and understanding' (56).

In both cases, Shaftesbury appears to be speaking of moral decline. It is not clear why someone whose opinions and character have been continuously villainous from the start should be denied the self of identity or of character required to ground any notion of self-interest.

(iii) Activity. It might be claimed that the highest pleasure is that of passive freedom from any kind of distress (142). But this life is equivalent to being asleep. True happiness consists in 'action and employment'.

In following Aristotle here, who also stressed the importance of activity as opposed to the mere possession of virtuous dispositions (2014: 1095b30–1096a2; 1098b18–20), Shaftesbury's position is plausible enough. But he fails to address the position of those who advocate a life of wakeful disengagement, and of course those who press the claims of the life of vice tend to be recommending the life of vicious activity. Shaftesbury will argue that luxury, like all vices, results in disharmony and hence discontent. But this is again an empirical claim, and it will be difficult for Shaftesbury plausibly to debunk apparent counter-examples. A more fruitful approach would be to accept the possibility of idle or vicious contentment but to question its value.

(iv) Perfectionism. Our own good or interest is itself the result of nature, and that good consists in fulfilling or perfecting our own nature (167, 205, 428; R 257; see Maurer 2009: 91–3). As we have seen, Shaftesbury views each individual as having a role to play in the promotion of cosmic order. Our playing that role itself constitutes our good; if we do not, our relation to the cosmos is like that of an unhealthy part of the body which grows unnaturally to the detriment of the body as a whole (R 49; 193). Our social affections are to promote not our own interest, but that of our species (R 3). But:

for a creature whose natural end is society, to operate as is by nature appointed him towards the good of such his society or whole is in reality to pursue his own natural and proper good. (432)

This order is clearly the result of design by a 'universal mind' (276), and this provides Shaftesbury with the material for a second perfectionist argument, independent of the claim that the good of an individual constituent consists in its fulfilling its natural role in promoting the good of the whole. For there to be a tension between the good of the part and the good of the whole, or between the self-interest of the individual and virtue, would itself be 'a blot and imperfection in the general constitution of things' (190).

Like most perfectionist arguments, Shaftesbury's can be accused of assuming what it is intended to prove. Shaftesbury himself accepts the naturalness of self-interest and the rationality of its pursuit, and so it is open to an egoist to argue that the perfection of any individual lies solely in promoting its own good. It is also possible to drive a wedge between the notions of perfection and well-being (see Glassen 1957). A rational egoist may accept that my living virtuously and so promoting the overall good will perfect my human nature, but deny that this will advance my own good. Now this will of course introduce the kind of tension into the cosmos which Shaftesbury's second argument denies. But competition between individuals is fairly obviously part of the natural order, and the claim that the hierarchical order that results from competition is any less the result of divine intention than that which arises through co-operation is not well grounded.

(v) Higher Pleasures. Shaftesbury claims that the pleasures (or perhaps rather 'enjoyments' (252)) of virtue are superior to bodily pleasures. His discussion, in part II of the *Inquiry* in particular (200–30), is sophisticated and wide-ranging, and further subsections may be helpful.

(a) Mind versus Body. Shaftesbury claims that most people will accept that the pleasures of the mind are greater than, and superior to, those of the body (200–2). As evidence, he cites the fact that those who have committed themselves to pursuing some mental pleasure cannot be diverted by bodily pleasures and pains. Even villains, on the basis of some principle of honour, will 'embrace any manner of hardship and defy torments and death'. In contrast, someone currently experiencing pleasures of the senses can easily be distracted by internal pain or distress.

These claims are, at the very least, somewhat hard to believe. But Shaftesbury also offers a dependency argument (211–12). Bodily pleasures depend on those of the mind—in particular, those of the natural affections. The pleasure of eating is insignificant without a table, company, and so on; prostitutes know that their clients wish to believe that the pleasure the clients are feeling is mutual.

Besides again relying on dubious empirical premises, this argument brings out two further problems lying behind Shaftesbury's overall position. The first is an equivocation on the notion of 'social affections'. On the one hand, it can refer to the pleasures of virtuous activity; on the other, to the pleasures of company. It is at least arguable that vicious people can enjoy the company of others, even if they have no moral concern for those others and treat them purely as a source of entertainment. The second problem is with the very distinction between pleasures of the mind and those of the body. It could be that there is some important difference between, say, the pleasures of working through some elegant mathematical proof, and those resulting from a massage. Here we might have a real contrast between the intellectual and the sensual or physical. But the pleasure of refined eating may involve a good deal of reflective thought on the nature and origin of the foods in question; and the pleasures taken in the company of others are sometimes sexual and to that extent bodily.

(b) The Informed Preference Test. As Mill was later to do (1998: 2.5), Shaftesbury revives one of Plato's arguments for the superiority of mental over bodily pleasures in the *Republic* (581e–583a) (202). Adequately to judge the relative value of two categories of pleasure requires experience of each. The virtuous person understands sensual pleasure, while the vicious person cannot grasp social pleasure.

One worry here is again whether there is empirical support for Shaftesbury's claim. Consider again the objection as raised by Alan Ryan against Mill's argument in favour of mental over bodily pleasures: 'The philosopher who is a half-hearted sensualist cannot estimate the attractions of a debauched existence, any more than the sensualist flicking through the pages of Hume can estimate the pleasures of philosophy' (1974: 111; see above p. 31). We might, however, allow Shaftesbury that at least some ordinarily virtuous people do seem capable of wholeheartedly enjoying sensual pleasures. A more serious problem is whether those virtuous people who, in certain circumstances, choose the pleasures of virtue over those of sensuality are doing so on the basis that the pleasures of virtue are *more pleasant* than those of the body. We might expect many of them to say that they prefer virtue, rather than the pleasures of virtue in particular, to bodily pleasure; that their own virtue would anyway decrease the amount of pleasure available to them from sensuality, if non-virtuous; and that their reasons for preferring virtue are moral rather than self-regarding. We can be sure that the judgements of some virtuous people would fit Shaftesbury's description; but there would be many that did not.

(c) Virtuous Activity versus Contemplation. Earlier in this chapter, we noted various ways in which Aristotle's ethics may have influenced Shaftesbury, either directly or through the development of his ideas by Hellenistic philosophers. Notoriously, at the end of the *Nicomachean Ethics*, Aristotle ranks the intellectual activity of contemplation above that of practically virtuous activity. Here Shaftesbury does not follow him (202–3). Shaftesbury is prepared to accept that intellectual pleasures are superior to those of sense. Those who apply their understanding of mathematical principles, for example, will experience an especially deep enjoyment resulting from 'love of truth, proportion, order and symmetry'. But even this pleasure is 'far surpassed by virtuous motion and the exercise of benignity and goodness...For where is there on earth a fairer matter of speculation, a goodlier view or contemplation, than that of a beautiful, proportioned and becoming action?'.

Shaftesbury's ethical aestheticism again seems to involve reliance on empirically doubtful premises. Compare, for example, the pleasure Archimedes felt when he discovered the relation between volume and displacement of water with that experienced by the person fulfilling a promise to a friend to post a letter for them on a rainy evening.

(d) Consequences. Shaftesbury is prepared to identify the natural affections with mental enjoyments. But he also argues that certain mental enjoyments flow from those

affections, in two ways (204–5). First, one is able sympathetically to experience a sec-ond-order enjoyment in the pleasure of others. Second, one can enjoy the admiration and esteem of others.

We have already seen the problems arising out of Shaftesbury's equivocation con-cerning the natural or social affections. A benevolent person will indeed take vicarious pleasure in the happiness of others, and may well enjoy their reputation. But the same will be true of at least some vicious people. The most that Shaftesbury can offer is an enticement to virtue for someone already attracted to it and the particular reputation that it will bring with it. It also has to be admitted that there is a tension between the argument from esteem and Shaftesbury's arguments elsewhere against attributing any great significance to reputation (see above pp. 77, 80).

(e) Self-review. According to Shaftesbury, anyone who introspects will find that the pleasures he experiences alone or with others are 'wholly founded in an easy temper, free of harshness, bitterness or distaste, and in a mind or reason well composed, quiet, easy within itself and such as can freely bear its own inspection and review' (206, 208–10). By 'anyone' here, Shaftesbury must mean 'anyone virtuous', since he goes on to insist that the pleasures he has in mind are the result of the natural affections.

Some will wish to object that such self-review exemplifies a form of vanity or self-indulgence; but against that it can plausibly be said that the absence of any kind of review is a sign of complacency. The problem is that many vicious people will also be able to bear or even enjoy this kind of self-review, in part because often the values against which they are assessing their own characters are themselves vicious (so while a virtuous person may be tormented by a single, uncharacteristically ruthless action, a vicious person may reflect on their ruthlessness with pride). Shaftesbury insists that all rational creatures will feel shame or regret at doing what is hateful (209). But, unless he is building a capacity to feel such emotions into his account of rationality itself, his confident generalization again seems open to doubt. Many psychopaths seem perfectly rational, in the procedural sense, and yet feel little or no shame. It is true, of course, that wrongdoers are often tormented by guilt, and one way to avoid that is to refrain from action one knows is likely to cause guilt. But another is to adopt strategies to weaken one's own proneness towards such negative emotions, as Nazis involved in the holo-caust were encouraged to do.

(f) Excessive Self-love and the Unnatural Affections. Shaftesbury analyses several self-regarding affections, including love of life (which can lead to miserable fear of death, for example), anger, luxury, sexual desire, love of wealth, pride, and love of ease, along with certain 'unnatural' affections such as sadism (216–29). He argues plausibly enough that such affections, especially if excessive, can cause distress to their subject.

But the truth is significantly more complex than Shaftesbury allows, and depends on the existing nature and situation of the person in question. Some vicious people appear to enjoy excessive indulgence in luxury, pride, or sadism, and even possibly intrinsically unpleasant emotions, such as anger, may have instrumental benefits for the vicious agent who can use them, for instance, to extort goods from others.

The upshot of the above is that we cannot accept that Shaftesbury has shown that *'every vicious action must be self-injurious and ill'*, on the ground that such actions encourage and strengthen vicious traits. In some cases, virtue will be more advantageous than vice in hedonistic terms; but in others it will not (e.g. in the case of the person morally required to allow themselves to be tortured). Further, Shaftesbury will face objections to his account of well-being from two opposed directions. On the one hand, unrestricted hedonists will insist that the contentment on which Shaftesbury places so much weight is only one kind of enjoyment among others, all of which should be brought into the discussion; on the other, non-hedonists may claim that Shaftesbury should have gone further in the direction of the ancient view that virtue, or virtuous activity, matters independently of its hedonic effects on the agent. Despite Aristotle's influence on him, his rejection of various Lockean views, his acceptance of M-reasons, and of course his own inventiveness, Shaftesbury seems unable to shake off the psychological egoism and substantive hedonism which dominated British moral philosophy after Hobbes.

8

Butler:

The Supremacy of Conscience

Joseph Butler (1692–1752) is often said to be one of the very greatest British moral philosophers of the eighteenth century, second only perhaps to Hume. His philosophy is largely limited to religion and ethics, though commitments to various positions in metaphysics, epistemology, philosophy of language, and other areas are implicit in his work. In ethics, he is best known for his *Fifteen Sermons* (1726), in particular the first three, on human nature, and the eleventh and twelfth, on the love of our neighbour, but also important are the second Dissertation *Of the Nature of Virtue* appended to the famous *Analogy of Religion* (1736), as well as passages in the *Analogy* itself and elsewhere.[1]

Butler was a cleric, appointed as Bishop of Durham shortly before his death, and his main aims were pastoral and protreptic. Though truth and precision were of great importance to him, he did not set out to write a comprehensive treatise on ethics. If necessary, he is prepared to construct arguments to what he saw as the correct conclusion on the basis of premises accepted by his audience but not himself. Partly because of that, but also partly because of his readiness to attach more than one meaning to some of his central terms, he is open to widely different interpretations. Against those who see him as a rational egoist (e.g. McPherson 1948) or as a dualist of the practical reason who would allow that in certain cases S-reasons trump M-reasons (e.g. Sidgwick 1907: 366), I shall argue that we should take seriously Butler's claim that conscience is primary. Butler is indeed a dualist in so far as there are S-reasons grounded in one's own well-being, and M-reasons grounded in the well-being of others and in morality.[2] But M-reasons, as grasped by our God-given faculty of conscience, are normatively prior to S-reasons in any conflict.

---

[1] I have used the most recent complete edition of Butler's works, by White, which is based on the second editions of the *Sermons* and the *Analogy*, with variations noted. (White's edition includes occasional mistranscriptions, which I have sought not to repeat.) I shall refer to the *Letters to Clarke* as 'C', to the Preface added to the second edition of the *Sermons* as 'P', to each sermon as 'S' followed by a number, to the *Analogy* as 'A', to the second 'Dissertation' as 'D', and to *The London Hospitals* as 'L'. References will be by paragraph number as in White, who rightly follows those in J.H. Bernard's 1900 edition. A reliable scholarly edition of Butler's complete works is yet to be produced: for criticism of existing editions, see Tennant 2011: 15–16. An excellent recent edition of the *Sermons* is that by McNaughton (2017).

[2] Not all moral reasons are other-regarding, according to Butler: prudence is a virtue (A 1.3.7; 1.4.4; D 6).

1. Human Nature and the Supremacy of Conscience

Butler outlines two starting points for—rather than general approaches to—ethical argument (P 12). The first begins with the abstract relations of things, the second with a 'matter of fact'—human nature. What does Butler have in mind here? Consider the obligation of gratitude. One might attempt an argument for that obligation by elucidating the relation of benefactor to beneficiary. No reference need be made to the nature of human beings in particular, since the obligation would be universal and hold wherever that relation was instantiated between two beings, human or not. Alternatively, one might begin with an account of human nature, and then attempt to show that gratitude is in conformity with that nature and ingratitude contrary to it.

Butler himself, as he implies,[3] is prepared to adopt either the abstract or the naturalist method, but notes, unsurprisingly given their title ('Upon Humane Nature'), that the first three sermons are naturalist. He suggests that the abstract method is more direct and (presumably partly because of that directness) less open to dispute; but the naturalist method is 'in a peculiar manner adapted to satisfie a fair mind; and is more easily applicable to the several particular relations and circumstances in life'. Butler's meaning here is not clear. As we shall see, his account of human nature centres around the supremacy of conscience. All human beings have a conscience and are aware of its supremacy (e.g. S 1.8), so anyone who denies it is perhaps exhibiting unfairness of mind. But since we all have a conscience, we all know what our obligations are (see e.g. S 3.4; 7.14), so a person who denies the abstract argument for gratitude seems to display the same epistemic vice.[4] Perhaps Butler believes that the supremacy of conscience is *especially* obvious. The second advantage he mentions is perhaps, if we emphasize 'several', the generality of the naturalist account. Rather than our having to provide an argument for each moral obligation in turn, by explicating the relevant relations, the supremacy of conscience provides us with a basis for all our obligations at once.

Note also that the abstract method does not rule out reference to human nature at later points in the argument, just as the naturalist method does not rule out appeal to a priori or abstract principles. Butler's remarks are about where to start one's argument, not about which considerations are relevant in that argument as a whole.

Butler sets out to explain and defend the view of the 'ancient moralists'[5] that virtue consists in 'following nature', to the extent that vice is more contrary to nature than torture or death (P 13). Most of us, he suggests, hold that view, but sometimes in a

---

[3] See the first sentence of P 13 ('The following discourses proceed chiefly in this method'). Butler mentions no third method here, and we can plausibly assume that he sees himself always as following some method or other. See Bernard's note (Butler 1900: 4n5).

[4] Butler's optimism about the clarity of our obligations under reflection may be deliberate overstatement, to encourage his audience to focus on those of their obligations they do take to be indubitable.

[5] Butler has in mind the Stoics; see esp. Cicero 1994: 3.5. For an account of the Stoic antecedents to Butler's position, see Irwin 2003; Long 2003.

mistaken or unclear form.[6] Once we do properly grasp human nature, we will understand the overriding nature of our moral obligations and be motivated to fulfil them
(S 2.1). Butler's appeal is to honest introspection: anyone who reflects on their own
capacity for shame, for example, will recognize that it was given them to prevent their
doing shameful actions (S 2.1).

What we must grasp first of all is the idea of human nature as a 'system' (P 14; also
S 3n1). To illustrate what he has in mind, Butler uses what had already become the
standard example of such a system: a watch. If someone is given the individual parts of
a watch, and yet has no idea how these parts relate to one another, they will lack the
idea of a watch. And they must understand those relations in the light of the purpose of
a watch—to tell the time. Human nature also has parts: '[a]ppetites, passions, affections, and the principle of reflection'. One of these parts or principles—'reflection or
conscience'—is in the relation of superiority to other principles, in that it has authority
over them analogous to that of a legitimate government over those it governs (P 24–5;
29; S 2.4, 8, 12–14; 3.1; see Shaftesbury 1999: 248). Hence, if an individual is function-
ing properly, their conscience will govern their decisions and ensure that they act virtuously; this is what it is for a human being to be a law unto herself. Our nature, as a
system, then, is adapted to virtue as the nature of a watch is to telling the time. Nor does
it matter, as far as adaptation to purpose is concerned, if most watches in the world are
broken, and so fail to tell the time, or if most human beings are vicious; both are failing
to achieve their purpose. But there is one important point of disanalogy here. Watches
are not responsible for failing; we, as responsible agents, are.

Watches are artefacts, and their purpose is to tell the time because that is the way we
designed them. Butler believes that God created everything, including us, and he is
claiming that our nature is to be virtuous because that is how God intended it (e.g.
S 2.15; 3.3, 5; 6.1, 7; A 1.3.1, 27–8). A watch is what it is—a device to tell the time—
because that is its function. Had we no interest in telling the time, but by some remarkable coincidence various pieces of metal came together in such a way that they were
physically identical to a watch, this would not be a watch. In the same way, human
beings are functional objects, and their purpose is to be virtuous. This explains the
ancient view that vice is more against our nature than torture: torture is inconsistent
with a single, lower principle (the desire to avoid pain), whereas vice is inconsistent
with the system as a whole (S 3.1).

Note that Butler's aim is to defend the view that virtue consists in following nature.
As part of that defence, he claims that conscience has authority—that is, that we have
an obligation to obey it. But he is not open to the objection that a mere function is

---

[6] Anscombe's criticism of Butler, that he 'exalts conscience, but appears ignorant that a man's conscience
may tell him to do the vilest things' (1997: 27), rests on a misunderstanding of the factive nature of conscience in Butler's thought. We all have the capacity to grasp moral truth, through exercising our consciences. But sometimes we fail to do that, e.g. because of immoral partiality to ourselves (S 3.4). If such
failures lead to incorrect moral judgements, these judgements do not issue from conscience. This is why
Butler finds it unproblematic to claim that we have an obligation to follow our consciences: S 3.5.

insufficient to ground normativity. Consider a world in which the Devil has designed individuals to be vicious, and to obey internal commands to harm others, commit injustice, and so on. The internal source of these commands, according to Butler, will have no authority, even if its possessors believe it does. Our consciences have authority partly because we are independently required to be virtuous. In other words, our reasons to be virtuous are in part self-standing M-reasons, rather than reasons grounded merely in God's purposes, intentions, or indeed our nature itself (the nature of the vicious individuals is to be vicious, but that does not give them any reason to be so). But this is not to say that God's having designed us does not add to our reasons to be virtuous, given God's nature as benevolent creator. We have obligations of piety and gratitude to him (S 1.2; 11.22), and his benevolence guarantees that the principles within us will be for our own good and the good of others.[7] But it is important to remember that Butler's ethics is not voluntarist: God's will itself is determined 'by what is fit, by the right and reason of the case' (A 1.6.12n9; also 2.8.11).

The 'principles' of which Butler speaks are principles *of action* (P 24), in the sense that they play a causal role in agency. He does not classify them using any distinction between the cognitive and non-cognitive. Appetites, for example, are non-cognitive, whereas conscience or reflection involves both cognition and motivation. But the principles can be ranked according to their reason-generating or reason-identifying capacities. Conscience's superiority or authority rests on its being a capacity for identifying our moral obligations, obligations we know—or should know—to be overriding and therefore conclusive. It is conscience that sets us apart from non-human animals (P 19–20). In its strict sense, conscience concerns only the agent's own 'propensions', passions, actions, and so on, but it can be used more broadly to include judgement of others (e.g. P 8; *pace* Akhtar 2006: 587). And like other principles it has motivational power of its own, enabling a parent to continue caring for their children, for example, when their natural love for them might have been insufficient. The judgement of conscience, as Butler conceives of it, is direct and immediate; in particular, it does not rest on an evaluation of consequences, either for the agent or others (D 2).

Butler claims, then, that virtue—obedience to one's conscience—is to follow nature. But, someone may object (S 2.3), this is very odd. We all know how often people act wrongly. Why should we not allow vice to be as natural to humanity as virtue, and understand following nature to consist in action in accordance with whatever is the strongest principle within us?

Butler's immediate response to this objection is that, if it is true, St Paul's claim that human beings are a law unto themselves is false. He goes on to define three different senses of 'nature'. The first in effect is equivalent to 'human': any human principle counts as natural; the second is that of the objector; and the third is obedience to conscience. He argues for the third conception by developing an analogy between

---

[7] Hence the question behind Sermon 8, on resentment: given God's benevolence, how is it that our nature appears to include a malevolent principle?

conscience and another central human principle: self-love (S 2.10–15). If some animal is tempted to enter a trap by the bait inside, we will see its action as corresponding to its nature. But if a human being does the same, knowing they will be made much worse off, their action is disproportionate to their nature, whereas if they had resisted their action would have been natural. This shows that the principle of self-love itself is superior to particular passions, such as the desire for the bait. If we now consider conscience we can see that it stands in the same relation of superiority to *all* other principles. Indeed, Butler suggests, it is a conceptual truth that conscience has overriding authority.

If conscience is understood as our capacity for making final decisions on how to act, this conceptual claim is plausible. But if it is understood, as it seems to be in Butler, as our capacity for understanding moral obligation, then it is less plausible. It is not a conceptual matter whether moral obligations can be overridden. Imagine I have made a promise, and realize that keeping it will be extremely costly. It may be morally wrong, but it is not incoherent, to claim that I have strongest reason to break this promise.

Butler concludes his second Sermon with a thought-experiment (S 2.17). Imagine that there is no natural supremacy of conscience, and that the only distinction to be made between one principle and another is that of strength. What would follow from this? Impious actions or parricide, for example, would be as appropriate to the nature of human beings as actions of reverence and filial duty.

Note that Butler is not asking us to imagine a world in which human beings lack consciences entirely. In such a world, humans would be like non-humans, and Butler clearly has no moral objection to a non-human animal's killing its parent. In this world, then, we have to assume that these men's consciences tell them that actions of impiety and parricide are wrong. But their conscience has no natural authority. Butler concludes that we ourselves, 'in our coolest hours must approve or disapprove' equally of parricide and filial duty as committed by these humans, and that this is the greatest absurdity.

Sturgeon (1976: 328) suggests that Butler's argument implies the 'Full Naturalistic Thesis', according to which judgements of conscience always depend on judgements of naturalness. The actions of these human beings are equally natural, and this, Sturgeon suggests, is why conscience must approve or disapprove them equally (1976: 322–3). But elsewhere Butler implies that conscience judges actions on the basis of properties such as justice, veracity, or charity (e.g. A 1.3.14). So why should we not, in our coolest hours, judge the actions of parricide by these human beings to be, say, unjust, and therefore to be disapproved of more than those of filial duty? This would imply that these men should not have performed these actions—that is, that their consciences had authority. But we have been assuming that those consciences have no authority; and this undermines our disapproval.

Butler's example is a peculiar one, since it requires us to imagine a world in which natural facts remain the same, but moral properties (in particular the authority of conscience) change. But his argument need not rely on it. He could point out merely that those who deny the authority of conscience (in our world) are also committed to approving or disapproving equally of all actions.

2. Self-love and Benevolence

(i) Self-love

The distinction between my self and other selves is central to Butler's ethics. Butler finds unhelpful the analogy between the relation of the body to its parts and that of society to the individual (S 1.4). But he is prepared to compare 'the nature of man as respecting self, and tending to private good...and the nature of man as having respect to society, and tending to promote publick good'. The central self-regarding principle is self-love (S 11.5). As its name and its being a principle of action suggest, it has an important motivational or affective component: a general desire for one's own happiness.[8] But such a desire itself depends on the subject's being sufficiently rational and reflective to possess the concept of their own happiness (so Butler often describes self-love as 'cool'). This general desire is to be distinguished from particular passions for particular objects. And again it can be understood teleologically. It is obvious that we are strongly motivated to protect our own lives, health, and private good, and since this is often entirely appropriate, indeed required, we can safely assume that this principle is itself part of God's design (S 1.5, 15).

The objects of particular passions Butler describes as 'external', while the object of self-love—our own happiness, that is, enjoyment (e.g. S 13.6) —is 'somewhat internal'. External objects will be sought by self-love, but only as means to happiness, while particular passions aim at those external objects as ends in themselves. This distinction is multiply problematic, so it is fortunate that it is not essential to Butler's argument. First, a desire for my overall well-being is not the same as a desire for my own enjoyment.[9] Even a hedonist will seek enjoyment not entirely for its own sake, but as constitutive of their own well-being. Second, there can anyway be particular passions for particular internal states, such as the thrill of a roller-coaster, or the euphoria from a certain drug (see e.g. Duncan-Jones 1952: 49). Butler himself can be more precise (especially if we, quite reasonably, take the 'or' in the following as epexegetic): '[P]rivate happiness or good is all which self-love can make us desire' (S 11.8). Actions done from self-love so construed are 'interested', while those done from particular passions are— by definition—not.

---

[8] Butler allows that we may claim that this general desire 'proceeds from' self-love, rather than constituting it. He is best understood as permitting a strict use of 'self-love' as a pure affection for oneself. Distinctions can be drawn between Butler's use of 'passion', 'appetite', 'desire', 'affection', and so on, but they are not, as he doubtless recognized, crucial for his main arguments.

[9] We see the same blurring of the boundary between self-love and particular passions in Butler's case of the man who works very hard for some great reward without knowing what it will be (S 1n3). According to Butler, this action is solely the result of self-love, and not any particular passions. But without some conception of one's own good, the principle of self-love is inert, as Butler elsewhere points out (P 37). This individual has a passion for great rewards.

Butler seeks to support his claim that particular passions are for external objects in one of his most famous arguments:

That all particular appetites and passions are towards external *things themselves,* distinct from the *pleasure arising from them,* is manifested from hence; that there could not be this pleasure, were it not for that prior suitableness between the object and the passion: there could be no enjoyment or delight from one thing more than another, from eating food more than from swallowing a stone, if there were not an affection or appetite to one thing more than another. (S 11.6)

Butler might, then, attempt to deal with the roller-coaster counter-example by claiming that, if I enjoy it, this can only be because I already had a desire for something other than pleasure (e.g. roller-coasting, thrilling and new experiences, constrained danger, or whatever). But even if my having such a desire is a necessary condition for my enjoyment, I may still have a particular passion for that enjoyment. Further, even if Butler is right about enjoyment's depending on such a prior desire, his argument can be deployed only against strong versions of psychological hedonism, according to which all ultimate desire is for pleasure. More plausible versions, restricted to conscious aims, remain untouched. We might allow, for example, that a baby can find pleasure only in bodily contact with its mother because it has an instinctive desire for such contact, and yet claim that as soon as the baby is able to make decisions it will aim ultimately at pleasure and the avoidance of suffering.

Butler has a more successful argument against the suggestion that all action is prompted by self-love because all action is motivated by one's own desires and the pleasure one gains from the satisfaction of those desires is one's own pleasure (P 35; S 11.7). As Butler points out, there may still be a difference between self-regarding and other-regarding objects of a person's desires. The question, then, is not the absurd one, whether all my desires are my own or not, but whether all my ultimate desires are for my own good. Again, however, this version of psychological egoism is weak. More commonly, a psychological egoist—Hobbes for example—will seek to explain apparently non-self-regarding ultimate desires as in fact self-regarding, and here Butler will need other arguments (see Sober 1992).

Conscience, as we have seen, is factive for Butler. If I believe that my conscience is telling me to φ, and yet it is the case that φ-ing is wrong, then I am mistaken: this is not the voice of my conscience (God does not lie) (see e.g. Brownsey 1995: 77). This is not so with the principle of self-love (e.g. S 9.20). This brings out a further problem with the internal/external distinction, since I may (falsely, according to Butler) believe my good consists in certain external states, such as, say, the flourishing of my children, or the success of certain projects after my death. But Butler clearly sees that my own good does not itself consist in self-love, its phenomenal manifestations, or the actions to which it leads: 'People might love themselves with the most entire and unbounded affection, and yet be extremely miserable' (S 11.9). Our happiness, Butler believes, 'consists in the gratification of particular passions', and excessive self-love can actually distract one from such gratification.

Self-love can not only lead us astray, but fail to keep us on the right path. This explains Butler's initially surprising claim that '[t]he thing to be lamented is not that men have so great regard to their own good or interest in the present world, for they have not enough' (P 40; also S 1.15). This is one of the reasons it is absurd to claim that self-love lies behind all human action: weakness of will is rife, and we continually sacrifice what we know to be our best interests to 'any vagrant inclination'. Self-love, that is to say, sets limits for passion, which without it will be entirely unconstrained (S 1.41; also e.g. A 1.5.n1).

(ii) Benevolence, Compassion, and Love of our Neighbour

Butler also finds in human nature a natural principle of benevolence, 'which is in some degree to *society*, what *self-love* is to the *individual*' (S 1.6; also P 21; 5.1). This is benevolence as a 'settled reasonable principle', a principle of 'reason', analogous to 'reasonable and cool self-love' (S 5.10; see e.g. Mackinnon 1957: 190–1). But just as cool self-love is insufficient to advance the good of the individual and needs the support of particular appetites and passions, such as hunger, so benevolence requires the affections of joy in the happiness of others, and compassion for their suffering, affections which arise particularly in actual contact with others (S 1.10; 5.2–3; 10–11). Reason does motivate, but weakly. Nor—*pace* the Stoics—is there anything regrettable in these affections, or the affections generally (S 2.3; 5.11). It is true that God does not feel them, but they are natural to us in our imperfection and perform the vital function of motivating us to promote the well-being of others.

We have already seen Butler as prepared to use the term 'self-love' to refer to a desire for enjoyment, which should be construed within his framework as a particular passion. So it is no surprise to find him using the term 'benevolence' both for the rational principle, strictly understood, and for the affections: a passing feeling of compassion, for example, or 'momentary love' is described as benevolence. And in neither the general nor the particular case should we accept radical redescriptions or reductions of the phenomenon: Hobbes's suggestions that benevolence is in fact the love of power, or compassion towards the suffering of another fear of one's experiencing that suffering oneself, are patently absurd (S 1n2; 5 n1). No one with 'plain common sense' could accept them (S 5.15).

Benevolence leads people to do good to others. But are there not also principles that lead to the doing of evil (S 1.11–13; also S 2.2)? This Butler will prefer not to allow, given the benevolence of our designer. There are indeed particular passions which can lead people to do what is against the interests of others, and indeed themselves. But there is no pure ill-will in human nature analogous to general benevolence, just as there is no pure self-hatred analogous to self-love. Butler's excessive optimism here is unnecessary. It is true that basic self-destructive or malevolent desires are hard to explain, if we were created by a benevolent designer. But their existence is very hard to deny, and the task of explaining them adds only slightly to the difficulty of explaining the existence of passions that result in evil, and indeed the existence of evil in general.

Compassion at the suffering of others, Butler claims, is much more significant than positive joy in their happiness; indeed we hardly have a word for the latter (S 5.2–3). Here again we see Butler inferring to the best teleological explanation. People who are happy need no help, since they already have what they want. Human beings are especially susceptible to suffering (S 6.2). It can last much longer than periods of happiness; and it is much easier to make people miserable, and to relieve people's misery, than to make them happy. Further, any good we provide diminishes marginally in value (S 6.6–7). The worse off someone is, the more they are likely to benefit from our help, other things being equal. An agent's compassion can prevent them from committing an injustice (S 6.4), and even when that constraint is lacking the resentment which would be prompted by the compassion of others for the victim can serve as a deterrent (S 5.10). Nor is compassion merely a useful human quality. 'Pain and sorrow and misery have a right to our assistance', and we owe that assistance to ourselves (since it is a demand of our nature) as well as to those who suffer.

There is little doubt that Butler sees general benevolence as of less significance than self-love as well as conscience. This is partly because of the smaller role it plays in human motivation and action, which is itself indicative of God's intentions for it (Penelhum 1985: 35). The most significant principles in our nature are self-love and conscience (S 1.15; 3.9), and though there certainly will be cases where benevolence, broadly construed, leads to action against one's conscience, this will occur much more frequently as the result of self-love and self-regarding passions.[10]

Benevolence receives especially close attention in Butler's twelfth sermon, the second on the love of our neighbour, the text for both being Romans xiii.9: 'And if there be any other commandment, it is briefly comprehended in this saying, namely, Thou shalt love thy neighbour as thyself'. Butler discusses three issues: who counts as our neighbour; what constitutes loving our neighbour; and how this commandment includes all others. The final issue I shall postpone until the following section.

Who is our neighbour (S 12.2–4)? Unlike God, we cannot love the entire universe, since our capacity for love is limited, we have influence over only a small part of creation, and we tend not to think on such a large scale. Butler's argument here is weak, if we take him to be speaking only of the sentient universe. Our capacity for love is unlimited, in the sense that each of us might be disposed at least to benefit any sentient being at no cost, or only trivial cost, to ourselves. Butler goes on to consider whether

[10]   At S 3.9, Butler claims that reasonable self-love and conscience are the superior principles in human nature, and that an action becomes unsuitable if either of these principles are violated. Broad (1930: 80) appears to take this to contradict Butler's assertion of the superiority of conscience (he does not provide a precise reference to the passage he has in mind). But what Butler goes on to say in this paragraph shows that he is speaking of the operation of these principles in a world in which duty and self-interest are always consistent, because of the afterlife. Any action against self-interest may anyway be forbidden by morality even in the absence of other moral constraints, because prudence is a virtue; but even if it is not, it is unnatural through its being in violation of the principle of self-love. Nothing Butler says in this paragraph commits him to allowing it to be natural to act against conscience in a world in which self-interest and morality diverge.

we should be said to love all mankind—which he again finds too general—or one's country or community—which are too general for most people. Our neighbour, he claims, is 'that part of the universe... which comes under our immediate notice, acquaintance, and influence, and with which we have to do'. Butler's exegesis of the passage from Romans is not unreasonable; but it is pessimistic, and the text—perhaps interpreted in light of the parable of the Good Samaritan—could be read more generously. Further, Butler will have been quite aware of the fact that his fellow citizens had long been giving money to help poor individuals unknown to and unconnected with them. It is tempting to think that his narrowing of the scope of benevolence is pragmatic, and based on a low view of the moral capacities of his audience.

What is meant by loving one's neighbour as oneself (S 12.5–19)? Butler offers three possibilities.

On the *kindness* interpretation, the love one should have for one's neighbour is of the same kind as the love one has for oneself. This interpretation itself may contain two elements: (i) one should promote the good of others *to some extent*; (ii) one should consider oneself as sharing in the happiness of others, in the sense that, for example, one takes joy oneself in the joy of others. The second element will lead to our putting ourselves in the position of others, recognizing harms and injustices to them, and so following the golden rule and acting towards others as one would wish them to act towards oneself.

This interpretation is more plausible than the second, the *proportionality* interpretation. Here Butler notes that one's moral character depends not on the absolute strength of any particular principle, but on the relation of these principles to one another. Consider two individuals who feel equal concern for the suffering of others, and who would—other things equal—be led by that concern to assist others to the same extent. This would not be enough for us to describe these individuals as equally compassionate, since one may be resentful to the point that they help others less. In other words, what is required is that our love of our neighbour is proportionate to our self-love.

What are the practical implications of this interpretation? Butler is keen to note that he is not imagining there to be any upper limit on benevolence. If one is doing all one should for oneself, then the more one does for others the closer one comes to obeying the commandment. But, plausible as that may be, the initial proportional reading is strained, as Butler himself admits (S 12.12). Further, it is not clear why Butler allows it, given his view that our inner principles can be judged to be appropriate or inappropriate in themselves, even if only within certain ranges. The inappropriate obsessiveness of a narcissist's concern for themselves, for example, cannot be cancelled by an equally obsessive concern with the happiness of others; and the same goes for the case of someone who cares very little either for themselves or for others. And this is so even if both the narcissist and the apathetic do what they should.

The final, *equality*, interpretation is more plausible than the second, though again less plausible than the first. On this view, one's affection for others should be equal to one's affection for oneself. What does Butler have in mind? He elucidates the state of equality as follows: 'Suppose a person to have the same settled regard to others as to himself; that in every deliberate scheme or pursuit he took their interest into the account in the same degree as his own, so far as an equality of affection would produce this' (S 12.15). On one reading, Butler has in mind something like impartiality of concern, in which no extra weight will be given by the agent to any interest purely on the ground that it is hers. But this interpretation also looks unlikely, given what Butler goes on to claim. He suggests that, even if a person has equality of affection, they will also have particular affections, passions, and appetites which could not be felt in common with others. And these will tip the balance of their concern overall towards themselves and their own interests. What Butler has in mind, then, seems to be equality of weight of the general principles of self-love and benevolence, such that in any decision, leaving particular affections out of it, one might choose by tossing a coin.

A somewhat hydraulic conception of principles seems to be at work here, but what seems most bizarre is Butler's idea that the weight of each of the general principles in any real situation could be entirely independent of the particular passions, and the number of others, concerned. Imagine some case in which I can hugely advance my own good or advance the good of another only a tiny amount; or a case in which I can hugely advance the good of another or advance my own good only a tiny amount; or indeed a case in which I can hugely advance the good of millions of others or advance my own good only a tiny amount. We can imagine a person neutral between each option in every case; but this is not how we would naturally understand 'equality of affection'. Our desire to promote our own happiness, and to promote the happiness of others, is in both cases to promote happiness maximally, other things being equal. So, although Butler's point that my own hunger will have a *direct* motivational force on me which the hunger of others cannot have is important and significant, it is hard to see why a person with *genuine equality of affection* should not be moved indirectly by the hunger of others to the same extent.

At S 12.18, Butler notes, in effect, that 'ought' implies 'can'. Since we have an awareness of our own interests the salience of which could not be replicated by awareness of the interests of others, we cannot help but give special priority to ourselves. As an empirical point, this seems right, and the proponent of impartiality is likely to require that we be only as impartial as possible. But against this can be set Butler's point in the previous paragraph, that we have a special obligation to promote our own interests. As Butler sees, this is quite consistent with his own conception of equality of affection, and unproblematic since the special force of our own particular perceptions will ensure that we will indeed give extra weight to our own interests. But it is of course inconsistent with equality of affection understood as impartiality, unless each principle is allowed to take its place in a pluralistic view in which the agent must weigh the overall good against their own good in deciding how to act.[11]

---

[11] I have defended such a form of the 'dualism of practical reason' in Crisp 2006: 5.2.

Butler goes on to explain what traits of character would develop out of one's loving one's neighbour as one should: meekness, compassion, trust, readiness to think well of others, friendliness, appropriate respect and obedience, inoffensiveness, and so on (S 12.20–4). The general relation between benevolence and other virtues or good characteristics will be discussed in the following section.

3. Butler's Ethics

To return now to the final issue discussed in Sermon 12, on how the commandment to love one's neighbour includes all the other commandments (S 12.25–33). Butler's first point is that, when benevolence is spoken of as comprehensive, it is not as a mere undirected feeling, but as a principle directed by reason (S 12.27, 29). Reason enables us to grasp not only the relevance for happiness of distant consequences, but also that we have special obligations, to children, friends, benefactors, and so on. Reason will also lead to modesty about our own capacities for prediction and impartiality, and hence to reliance on common sense and the law.

Butler is here distancing himself from any utilitarian conception of benevolence.[12] I am benevolent only in so far as my disposition to advance the good of others is bounded by rational recognition of non-utilitarian duties,[13] and even when acting within those boundaries I should not seek to work out for myself which of my actions will produce the best overall outcome. But he is also ready to find common ground with utilitarianism. He is a welfarist: 'It is manifest that nothing can be of consequence to mankind or any creature but happiness' (S 12.28). So we can owe nothing to anyone except to promote their happiness, as required by morality.[14] This bounded notion of welfarist benevolence explains how love of our neighbour involves not only special obligations, but any actions that affect the happiness of others. Intemperance, for example, often harms others, and so is against benevolence.

Does his welfarism make Butler a consequentialist? Consequentialism is itself open to several different definitions. Some would claim, for example, that the attachment of weight to the relations in which the agent stands to others is non-consequentialist or deontological. But given that my duties to such individuals are always conditional on, and could plausibly be said to be grounded in, my bringing about positive consequences for their well-being, any such duty can always be described in terms of such consequences. But consequentialists are sometimes said not to put moral weight on an agent's motive, and of course this is central for Butler (e.g. C 7.3).[15] What is perhaps

---

[12] In the later discussion of the limits of benevolence at D 8–11, Butler probably had Hutcheson in mind. See e.g. Garrett 2012: 182n31.

[13] Foot makes essentially the same point in her 1988.

[14] Note that Butler is not identifying moral properties with properties of promoting happiness (P 39). Rather, he is making the criteria of rightness and wrongness depend on the promotion of happiness.

[15] Butler is also clear that the focus of morality is an agent's will or intentions: D 2.

more important than placing Butler within some broad category or other is to grasp the specific details of his ethics.

It might be thought that welfarism limits some of the obligations we might have taken ourselves to have. Consider, say, a promise to someone who one knows will remain entirely unaware of whether or not it has been performed. Butler is characteristically careful to ward off any implications of moral laxity (S 12.n3). He cannot of course claim that promises are binding in themselves, independently of happiness. But he grounds the obligations of common-sense morality on a practically non-welfarist basis through stressing our poor capacity for predictions on what will most promote happiness. To remedy that, God imposes particular obligations on us which we recognize as independent of their consequences—to refrain from treachery, indecency, meanness, for example, and to be faithful, honourable, and just. Are virtues such as justice, then, identical with benevolence; or non-moral useful qualities, like natural beauty; or exceptions to the general rule of benevolence? Butler sees no need to answer this question. What matters is that our lives and actions should instantiate these virtues.

Butler's strategy here is highly reminiscent of the split-level theories standardly employed by utilitarians (e.g. Mill 1998: 2.24; Hare 1981: chs 2–3). Though he describes it as 'presumptuous' to claim that divine punishment is for the purposes of deterrence (P 29), it is certainly a view he is prepared to take seriously (A 1.3.8).[16] Though ultimately his reasons are beyond our understanding (A 1.2.3; 1.7.3; 2.5.3, 7, 20), God may be a utilitarian (Louden 1995: 270). His aim after all is the happiness of his creation. But we must remember: '[W]ere the author of nature to propose nothing to himself as an end but the production of happiness [which, we should presume, he would not do unless there were no other worthy end], were his moral character merely that of benevolence; yet ours is not so' (D 8). If God is a utilitarian, then utilitarianism would be the ultimate truth about morality. But human obligations are non-utilitarian, and there is no need for us to inquire into whether, if their source is the pure utilitarian benevolence of God, they are in some sense merely instrumental. We are bound by them, recognize them, and should live by them. And our conscience will itself frame our conception of God as 'a righteous governor' (A 1.3.3), rewarding and punishing us appropriately for our actions.

Butler goes on to provide a second 'more general' argument to the conclusion that benevolence is morally comprehensive. If we abstract from the particular nature and circumstances of any creature, including God and any moral agent, benevolence seems to include all that is good. What Butler is seeking to bring out here is the welfarist basis of moral principles. All reasons for action are ultimately welfarist. God will indeed be just; but his justice is for the good of his creation. Butler never confronts head on the

---

[16]   Butler's view of human civil punishment is distinctly forward-looking: '[T]he only purposes of punishment less than capital are to reform the offenders themselves, and warn the innocent by their example' (L 331). And he takes the same view of the passion of resentment (S 8.8).

SELF-LOVE AND VIRTUE   105

question whether God would, at the last judgement, when considerations of deterrence are no longer relevant, punish wrongdoers. And doubtless if asked he might have claimed ignorance. Nevertheless, given his welfarism and his conception of God's benevolence, it is hard to believe that he would have not have predicted mercy rather than retribution.

What about piety? Is this not independent of the promotion of happiness? The point of piety, Butler suggests, is not itself to promote happiness; but it is not independent of such promotion, consisting rather in a love of it and of goodness in general: 'Thus morality and religion, virtue and piety, will at last necessarily coincide, run up into one and the same point, and *love* will be in all senses *the end of the commandment*' (S 12.33).

4. Self-love and Virtue

Our nature was shaped by God, and, though we can certainly distinguish between private and public good, every principle within us, including self-love and benevolence, promotes both, albeit in differing degrees (S 1.6–7). We can nevertheless speak of certain passions as private, and others as public, depending on whether their 'primary intention and design' is the good of the individual, or of society (S 1.7; 5.1; also P18). Hunger, for example, is private, whereas the desire of esteem is public, since its purpose is to regulate our behaviour towards others (S 1.7n4). Anyone can see, Butler suggests, that, given our nature and circumstances, private and public passions 'perfectly coincide, and mutually carry on each other' (S 5.1; also 1.4). Butler's claim is, of course, elliptical: the harmony between private and public depends on our principles operating as they should. As we have seen, Butler is fully aware of the potential conflicts between self-love and particular passions. But the tension here is 'meerly accidental', and is much more common than that between an agent's own interest and benevolence (S11.18–19). Further, the latter tension more often concerns the means to one's good or enjoyment than that enjoyment itself. So I may be tempted to keep my money for myself; but in fact I can give a great deal of it away without any cost to myself, because I have more than enough of it.

Butler's main argument for harmony between the principles of self-love and benevolence depends on the distinction between general self-love and the particular passions (P 36, 38, 42; S 5.1; 6.11; 11.11–13, 16). Self-love and the particular passions can each serve on their own as ultimate motivations for action, though as we have seen for self-love to issue in action requires some particular passion or other. Further, there is nothing to prevent an agent's having a particular passion to promote the good of others; indeed, as we have seen, such benevolence is a natural principle in human nature. The good of others—like virtue itself (P 42)—can be pursued disinterestedly and for itself: 'Love of our neighbour then has just the same respect to, is no more distant from, self-love, than hatred of our neighbour, or than love or hatred of anything else' (S 11.11). In other words, there is nothing to prevent my reflecting upon my own good and deciding that the best way to promote it is through benevolent or virtuous action; nor to prevent my acting unreflectively on my passions for the good of others or for virtue, either as an unreflective element in a strategy chosen reflectively, or in their own right. Nor should we think of self-love as amoral, or even immoral, and benevolence as virtuous (P 39). Appropriate self-love is a virtue—prudence—and inappropriate benevolence is a vice. This explains the superiority of conscience as the faculty that enables us to judge the appropriateness of self-love, benevolence, and all other principles, in the circumstances in which we find ourselves (S 3.8).

Butler's case against psychological egoism is a strong one. The idea that all our other-regarding desires are instrumental to our only ultimate desire—that for our own good—will strike many as a distortion of everyday phenomenology. But what about rational egoism? Might this not justify our distancing ourselves from benevolence or virtue? Consider compassion, for example. It might seem rational to seek to extirpate it, as a form of sorrow, or to avoid its objects (S 5.3). But joy in the prosperity of others is a good, and the capacity for compassion is not independent of that (S 5.5–6). Further, compassion not only helps others (if only through their knowing someone cares about them), but the capacity is itself a source of positive good for its possessor (S 5.7–8; 6.10–13).[17] It can, if not extreme or excessive (see S 6.9), bring a 'peculiar calm kind of satisfaction', through awareness of one's virtue and of the fact that one is not oneself experiencing the other's misery (Butler does not object to the latter—it is really the same as the pleasure one feels e.g. when taking off a tight pair of shoes). Our greatest happiness lies in this kind of tranquillity, as opposed to anxiously and vainly seeking the pleasures of the moment. Callousness also makes it hard to experience most other kinds of pleasure, except the grossest (see S 5.12). Suffering itself can be to our advantage, making us more temperate and reasonable, and by 'voluntary resort to the house of mourning' we can achieve the same benefit at a lower cost. We will be less open to temptation by the life of pleasure, and more inclined to recognize that this life is 'a foreign country', a temporary stage leading to a 'higher and better state'.

Similar points carry across to benevolence and virtue in general (e.g. S 3.6–8; 11.12–16; A 1.3.5). Why should it be thought odd that certain people enjoy helping others? Even the pleasure of a good deal of vice depends on a certain regard for others, such as that involved in the pursuit of honour, status, or wealth (in so far as one wishes to avoid the shame of poverty), and even the vicious have to accept that some restraint on particular passions is rationally required. Imagining his opponents retreat to the view that the rational agent will resist regard to others only when it promises less satisfaction, Butler responds: 'You have changed sides then'. The emotional life of the vicious person—with its envy, rage, and so on—should not be assumed to be more pleasurable than that of the compassionate virtuous person, who enjoys benefiting others and their good reputation, and of course greater tranquillity. Virtue is not difficult, especially when it becomes habitual. Love of our neighbour as a 'virtuous' principle is gratified by

---

[17] At S 6.5, Butler suggests that the fact that we can become inured to suffering is itself evidence of 'nature's compassion'—that is, God's (non-affective) benevolence or compassion.

a mere awareness that one is seeking to benefit others, while as a 'natural' affection, it is gratified only by success in that endeavour (S 11.16).[18] Indeed that is partly how virtue can be its own reward: the vicious person who fails in their aims has no gratification at all (S 11.13).

Even if we accept Butler's claim that conflicts between duty and interest are rare and unnatural (e.g. A 1.3.15), we might wonder about the really hard cases, in which benefiting others appropriately, or virtue, will cause huge suffering to the agent, perhaps to be followed by death. Some have read the most famous passage in Butler as suggesting that, if such a case were possible, reason would require us to side with or own good against duty. Butler begins S 11.20 by pointing out that religion does not set itself against self-love, and indeed often appeals to it, 'and always to the mind in that state when reason presides, and there can no access be had to the understanding, but by convincing men that the course of life we would persuade them to is not contrary to their interest'. Note that Butler is not here committing himself to an egoistic veto, that is, to ego-restricted pluralism: he is describing how religion (of which the 'we' suggests he sees himself as a part) appeals to veto egoists. They are, then, his audience, not a group with which he is identifying himself. He continues:

Let it be allowed, though virtue or moral rectitude does indeed consist in affection to and pursuit of what is right and good, as such, yet, that when we sit down in a cool hour, we can neither justify to ourselves this or any other pursuit, till we are convinced that it will be for our happiness, or at least not contrary to it.

As noted by others (e.g. Grave 1952: 83n18; Penelhum 1985: 73; Irwin 2008: 533; Maurer 2009: 315; McNaughton 2013: 382; pace e.g. Kyle 1929: 260; McPherson 1948: 327; Kleinig 1969: 406; Leites 1975: 45), Butler nowhere in this passage expresses his own acceptance of egoism or even an egoistic veto. Were he to do so, it would contravene one of his most fundamental views: that conscience is supreme. Rather, he is pointing out that virtue can be justified even to those who do accept the veto. Why is that? Because, as he says, happiness and duty always coincide. But what about the hard cases? Here again religion has nothing to fear. Conscience, having condemned some action in itself, 'naturally and always goes on to anticipate a higher and more effectual sentence, which shall hereafter second and affirm its own' (S 3.8). This is of course the afterlife. As Butler says of the virtuous: 'God himself will in the end justify their taste' (S 11.15; also P 44; A 1.2; 3; 1.Conclusion).[19]

Butler's view on conflicts between duty and interest also emerges in another well-known passage in the Preface. Having stressed that our nature requires us to 'enforce upon ourselves' the authority of conscience (P 25), Butler criticizes Shaftesbury for failing to incorporate the authority of conscience into his ethics. Confronted by the

---

[18] Butler probably means that true natural benevolence involves desiring that others actually do well, though this is consistent also with one's wishing to be the kind of person who tries to bring it about that they do.

[19] Butler does not object to one's being motivated by a concern for the afterlife: P 44.

case of a moral sceptic, Shaftesbury claims it to be 'without remedy' (1999: 189). Indeed, without the authority of the agent's own moral approbation, they would have to be said to be under an obligation to act viciously, since there is clearly an obligation to promote one's own happiness. Butler imagines someone's suggesting that even allowing for the authority of conscience does not help, since one will still be left with the obligation to advance one's own interest. Taking the obligations in question to be overall rather than pro tanto, and ignoring the possibility of moral dilemmas, Butler responds that claiming that someone is under two contrary obligations is to say they are under no obligation. But, he continues, it is a mistake in such a conflict to think that the self-interested obligation remains:

> For the natural authority of the principle of reflection, is an obligation the most near and intimate, the most certain and known: whereas the contrary obligation can at the utmost appear no more than probable; since no man can be certain in any circumstances, that vice is his interest in the present world, much less can he be certain against another: and thus the certain obligation would entirely supersede and destroy the uncertain one; which yet would have been of real force without the former. (P 26)

In other words, were the agent to be as certain that their self-interest lies in vice as that they have an obligation to virtue, the two 'obligations' would cancel one another out—they would have to suspend judgement on both (see Sidgwick 1907: 341–2). If by 'certainty' here, Butler believes wholehearted commitment to the truth of the proposition in question, it is not clear how he can allow alongside that a belief in the probability of the self-interested obligation. Either the agent must accept that the self-interested obligation's appearing to them is an illusion, or they must weaken their credence in the moral obligation. Butler's argument is best understood as an anticipation of a Bayesian account of subjective degrees of belief. In any imaginable case of possible conflict between duty and interest, the agent's credence in duty will be greater than that in interest, and therefore it will be rational for them act in line with duty.

Butler's claim about the present world is highly questionable, unless morality is much weaker than most people believe it to be. Imagine a case in which an evil sadist captures me, and offers me a choice, which I know to be genuine. Either he will torture me for two minutes, then erasing all memory of the torture, or he will torture ten thousand children, in some distant country, for six months, erasing any memory I have of the choice I have made. It is hard not to believe both that it is my duty to allow him to torture me, and that this torture will make me worse off, in this life. What about the possibility of the afterlife? Here matters are more complicated, because the afterlife for the vicious is usually thought to be not only extremely unpleasant, but also of infinite duration. So even if the agent faced with conflict believes that the possibility of the afterlife is extremely small, it is not implausible to claim that the best understanding of expected utility and rational choice under certainty requires one to choose virtue, accepting the cost of virtue in this world to avoid any possibility of the cost of vice in the next. But it is also possible, of course, that the afterlife is run by the Devil, who will inflict eternal suffering on the virtuous. The force of Butler's argument, then, depends on views about God and epistemic rationality. If it can be rational to believe that the probability of the afterlife as understood by Christians is greater than that of any similar scenario which will inflict infinite cost on the virtuous, then it may be rational to choose virtue over vice in any conflict.

To conclude. Butler's view on the relation of self-interest and morality is complex, but we can see it as part of the move away from Hobbesian psychological egoism we find in Cumberland, More (probably), Hutcheson, and Clarke, who all like Butler allow for self-standing M-reasons. And, like More and Hutcheson, who deny not only rational egoism but veto egoism, Butler allows that these M-reasons can, at least in the abstract, be taken to override S-reasons. Such overriding is made less likely by virtue's (ultimately hedonistic)[20] contribution to the agent's well-being, but since Butler, like all his predecessors in the tradition we are considering, believed in posthumous reward in the afterlife, overall objective sacrifice remains impossible on his account. But that is something he would almost certainly have welcomed: a perfectly rational and good God would surely not create a world in which virtue would ultimately conflict with self-interest?

---

[20] On Butler's hedonism, see Frey 1992: 246–9.

9

Hutcheson:
Impartial Pleasures

Francis Hutcheson (1694–1746) was born in Northern Ireland and educated at the University of Glasgow, where he took up the chair of Moral Philosophy in 1729. His work played a significant role in the Scottish Enlightenment, influencing Hume, Smith, and Reid, as well as many thinkers beyond Scotland (See e.g. Campbell 1982: 167–8). Hutcheson himself was modest about his own originality (S 1.xlvii): '*All who have looked into such subjects know that the general doctrine and foundation of morals may be found in the antients...* [Plato, Aristotle, Xenophon, Cicero], *and in Dr. Cumberland, and in Lord Shaftesbury*' (SI 5). It is true that his views in general have a good deal in common with these predecessors, but also that the detailed and powerful statement of those views, including not only his theory of moral sense but also his position on morality and self-interest, is imaginative, historically significant, and highly suggestive. Given our focus on the morality question, it is worth noting that Hutcheson sees more deeply than Cumberland into the true nature of broadly utilitarian impartiality, while usually avoiding Shaftesbury's equivocation between genuine impartiality and the pleasures of partial friendship. Further, although he is a devout Christian, and his ethics is theistic in certain important respects, unlike More and Shaftesbury he tends to maintain a clear distinction between religious and moral experience. Hutcheson is in this respect strongly committed to the idea of natural law, seeing the aim of moral philosophy as to demonstrate to each person, with reference to nature rather than the supernatural, that their individual greatest happiness lies in virtue (I 179; E 174–5; S 1.1).[1]

---

[1] Hutcheson's central ethical texts fall into three broad groups. The fundamentals of his ethics were stated in the four influential treatises in the *Inquiry into the Original of Our Ideas of Beauty and Virtue* (I) and the *Essay on the Nature and Conduct of the Passions and Affections* (E). Twenty or so years later the *Institutio* appeared, to be translated into English as *A Short Introduction to Moral Philosophy* (SI) in 1747. In the meantime, Hutcheson had been working on the *System of Moral Philosophy* (S), which was published posthumously by his son. His views did change, but in general on the nature of morality and self-interest they remained largely consistent (see Stephen 1876: 2.57). For helpful discussions of the development, or lack of it, in Hutcheson's views, see Scott 1900: chs 9, 10, 11 (1), 12; Moore 1990; Darwall 1995: ch. 8; Bishop 1996. Note that the Liberty Fund prints, in a revised edition, the second edition of I but with complete textual notes of variations in the other three significant editions.

1. God, Morality, and the Will

It is reliance on revelation that Hutcheson is rejecting for his philosophy, not theism, since belief in God can itself be justified through evidence from nature (S 1.170–5; see also LM 3.1). For example, the complexity of the system in which heat from the sun combines with water and soil to produce nutrition and growth in plants and animals is such that we can infer from it an 'original designing wisdom and power'. The happiness we gain from the pleasure of self-approbation in the exercise of our moral sense trained on our own impartial benevolence gives us insight into the moral character of God. It would be absurd for an omnipotent God to deprive himself of the pleasures of virtue and rely solely on those of self-interest or self-love, given that the pleasures from each source are consistent with one another. God is, then, impartially benevolent.

Here, of course, Hutcheson must face the problem of evil. First, he claims, we must recognize the clear prevalence of good over evil in the world. Hutcheson tends to focus on the good of humans rather than non-humans. Any 'separated Spirit', he claims, would prefer the chance of embodiment in some infant to complete annihilation (E 122). The pleasures of sense are far more frequent than the corresponding pains, while there are hardly any pains at all to set against the pleasures of imagination and knowledge (S 1.190; 194–8). The pains of sympathy are exceeded by the pleasures we take in the alleviation of others' suffering and their prosperity. Virtue, with its pleasures, is much more common than vice, with its pains. The pains that do exist are either necessary for, or unavoidable consequences of, greater goods (S 1.178–88). In particular, they are required for the highest pleasures—those of beneficence. (Hutcheson thinks the pleasures of relieving suffering are much more significant than those taken in the happiness of others. He even claims (182) that happy beings cannot benefit one another.) Natural laws are such that the innocent do sometimes suffer, but these laws themselves provide the basis for beneficent action. Pain provides a contrast against which we can experience and appreciate the goodness of pleasure, and also directs us away from threats. Even our failures in virtue have the advantage of making it possible for us to intend to improve ourselves in the light of an ideal of perfection, which we might hope will be realized in some future state (S 1.192–3) And moral evil makes forgiveness and the return of good for evil possible (E 123). Hutcheson does admit that some non-humans appear designed to suit the interests of those of superior species which predate upon them. But even their deaths are often more painless than they would be otherwise.

Some will wonder here whether losses for one being can appropriately be compensated for by benefits for another. And it has to be admitted that the sheer number of sentient non-humans, and the shortness and painfulness of many of their lives, threaten Hutcheson's optimism, as does the possibility that certain pains, or some quantity of them, are discontinuously bad to the point that they cannot be counterbalanced by any amount of pleasure, human or non-human, whether in a single life or across the lives of different individuals. Hutcheson explicitly denies any such discontinuity, claiming that any finite mundane evils can be justified if they are necessary for an infinite amount of good in the afterlife (E 123). Further, he cannot see how the misery of a virtuous person can be necessary to a good end, so virtuous people are the most likely to prosper in any afterlife (E 129). As we shall see, a virtuous person should not be motivated by any thought of benefit in the afterlife, but Hutcheson notes the usefulness of such thoughts in combatting false views about the ultimate value of goods to be gained through vice (CS 103; E 186), in enabling virtuous people to feel satisfied with their current lot, whatever that has turned out to be (R 48), and in alleviating our distress at the apparent misfortunes of the virtuous or of those we love (S 1.202, 130) (see Harris 2008). Further, punishment of the wicked in the afterlife may even deter any potentially vicious rational spectators in the universe who may be influenced by what they see of human life (S 1.204).[2]

The afterlife, then, provides Hutcheson with no more than a back-up to his main arguments for virtue, which are based on the idea of independent M-reasons acting upon which will advance the happiness of the agent. Indeed, Hutcheson argues, the very fact that God does reward virtue and punish vice suggests that there is 'natural' merit and demerit in each respectively, which we can ascertain through our natural moral sense (SI 37). The moral sense is 'that Determination to be pleas'd with the Contemplation of those Affections, Actions, or Characters of Rational Agents, which we call virtuous' (I 9). Moral goodness is that quality perceived in actions which results in pleasurable approbation of the agent independently of any natural advantage to that agent, moral goodness being an entirely different category of value from mere natural goodness, just as the pleasure of moral approbation itself is different from merely natural pleasure (I. 85, 88–9). That pleasure in our very perception of these qualities is especially great when we have performed the actions in question ourselves. In being perceptual, the moral sense is independent of reason as Hutcheson understands it, though reason may correct it (E 149–50). I may initially see the punishment of some child as cruel, but on reflection recognize that it promotes the overall good and hence see it as morally good: 'all justifying reasons, or such as shew an action to be good, will at last lead us to some original sense or power of perception' (S 57).[3]

Hutcheson's ethics are somewhat complex. There is little doubt that he accepts M-reasons, in the form of obligations to benevolence which are not be understood as self-interested constraints (I 181–3). The notion of moral obligation is itself elucidated by reference to the moral sense. To say that someone is under such an obligation is to say '[t]hat every Spectator, or he himself upon Reflection, must approve his Action, and disapprove his omitting it, if he considers fully all its Circumstances' (E 146). Hutcheson is certainly a consequentialist of some form, though he holds that the moral value of any action lies not in its actual or probable good consequences, but in the agent's

---

[2] Hutcheson was probably driven into this position by his view that the primary reason for punishment is deterrence; see below p. 119.

[3] For an argument that Hutcheson's sentimentalism is consistent with talk of reasons for action, see Radcliffe 2013: esp. 12.

intention to bring them about (e.g. I 189; E 36; SI 125).[4] And the best intention is that
to produce the best consequences. To the virtuous person, that is to say, 'that Action
is best, which procures the greatest Happiness for the greatest Numbers' (I 125).[5]
Hutcheson's position here rests in part on the notion that, other things equal, more
good must be preferable to less: 'In the *calm publick Desires*..., where there are no
opposite Desires, the greater Good of another is always preferred to the less: And in the
calm universal Benevolence, the Choice is determined by the *Moment* of the Good,
and the *Number* of those who shall enjoy it' (E 34). Further, the more good there is at
stake in my willing some action, the stronger the obligation to perform it, and the less
laudable the action (SI 122). An agent who wills a certain good outcome and succeeds
deserves no greater praise than a similar agent who fails.[6] Hutcheson here anticipates
Hume's view (T 3.3.1.4–5) that in praising some action we are in effect praising the
agent, not for willing this particular action but for their character as a whole:
'duties...as are done deliberately, and from steddy purpose of heart, are more lovely
than those which proceed from sudden gusts of kind passions' (SI 120). Nor is blame
appropriate only for bad, or less than the best, intentions; those who are culpably
negligent when they could have acted with benevolent intentions are also blameworthy (e.g. I 101).

Of course, though my acting morally well consists in my intending the greatest
good, my aim is not the having of that intention itself, but the greatest good. This central kind of moral goodness Hutcheson calls 'formal' goodness (S 1.252–3). He allows
that we can call an action that turns out to advance the public good 'materially good',
noting that formal goodness consists in the attempt to instantiate material goodness in
one's actions. Formal rightness also requires that probabilities are taken reasonably
into account: the intention has to be that of a 'diligent' agent (S 1.230; also I 126; R 50–1;
E 38; S 1.245–6). Further, Hutcheson is best understood not to be requiring that, if one
does not have benevolent affections, one should act out of such affections, which
would of course be impossible.[7] One is required to intend the greatest good, and the
ideal moral agent—the one who acts rightly as well as doing what is right—will be
benevolent.

Hutcheson tends to think of motivation in somewhat hydraulic terms. Consider a
case in which I will some maximally good outcome, but am also motivated by self-
interest. If I would not have acted without that self-interested motivation, or if I would
have intended less good, then this detracts from the moral value of my action (I 129;

[4] Strasser (1990: 130) aptly classifies Hutcheson as a '*motivational* utilitarian' (my italics). As such, Hutcheson would not be impressed by Strasser's objection (1990: 170) that he should have attached moral value to motivation by a sense of duty; see also Blair 1755: 19.
[5] Hutcheson appears to be echoing here a phrase of Leibniz: see Hruschka 1991. As noted by Scott (1900: 274–5), the idea is at least implicit in the writings of several Stoics.
[6] Hutcheson does not discuss the fact that our actual sentiments of approbation and condemnation vary according to outcome and not merely intention (see below pp. 163–4, 174–6; Williams 1981c). Doubtless his view would have been that such variation constitutes a defective response to the facts.
[7] See on this e.g. Jensen 1971: 92, 109.

SI 123).[8] As this claim suggests, Hutcheson allows for degrees of moral goodness, the best action being that intended to produce the best overall outcome on the basis of a rational assessment of probabilities. Hutcheson claims that the degree of goodness here depends on the agent's abilities (e.g. I 128; S 1.238; SI 124).[9] Imagine that we both will to benefit others, and do so to the same extent, the only difference being that I have less ability to benefit others. My action then has greater moral worth, presumably because it is closer to the moral ideal. This may be one of the several places in which Hutcheson appears to blur the distinction between formal and material goodness. Assume that, although our abilities are indeed different, we in fact have the same view about what our abilities are. In that case, it seems that our actions, from the formal point of view, are equally good. But if I believe my abilities are less than yours (even if my belief is false), then I am willing an outcome closer to the best possible and so can plausibly be said to be more virtuous.

Hutcheson also attributes an important role to difficulty (e.g. I 129; S 1.241). If it is more difficult for you than for me to will some outcome, then to that extent, other things equal, your willing or action is morally better, presumably because it is evidence of your greater benevolence. The agent's attitude to God is also relevant (E 199–200). On the one hand, Hutcheson suggests, seeking to express gratitude to God by doing what is virtuous is, like attention to one's self-interest, likely to detract from the moral value of one's action, which should depend on one's benevolent affections (there is no moral value in willing some good outcome through desire for reward or to avoid punishment (e.g. S. 1.272)); on the other, if one aims to thank God or indeed advance one's self-interest on the ground that acting on such motivations will itself increase one's benevolent affections, this increases one's virtue. And if they do *not* in fact increase one's level of beneficence, then they detract from one's virtue for the reasons mentioned above.

It may seem that there is a significant gap in Hutcheson's account, in that he fails to discuss the possibility that benevolent intentions might fail to align with the goodness of outcomes. Imagine a person, for example, whose capacities for ethical calculation are such that they would produce a better outcome by following the deontological rules of common-sense morality without any intention to benefit or affection for others in general. Should they, persuaded by Hutcheson's view of formal rightness, seek to change themselves, increasing their affection for others in general and trying to benefit them? Hutcheson is not, however, committed to the view that they should. If they know that they will produce more good by staying as they are, then their intending to do that will itself be consistent with their intending to do what is best. What if they believe that change will be for the best? If, and only if, that view is a reasonable one, then Hutcheson, it seems, must advocate change, even if it is for the worse. In this

[8] Hutcheson in fact here speaks of *producing* rather than intending less good. In general, he is not always consistent on this matter, though it is clear enough that he sees morality as concerned primarily with intention rather than outcomes. See Scott 1900: 190–1.
[9] For some problems with Hutcheson's calculus, see Strasser 1990: 107–9.

respect, then, Hutcheson's ethics prioritizes moral value over the natural value of well-being.[10]

2. Impartial Beneficence and Subordinate Virtues

Hutcheson at times appears to characterize the moral sense partly through the positive and negative moral emotions it evokes: love and hate, admiration and blame, and so on. So understood, it is easy to make sense of the views of those who make moral judgements—concerning, say, retributive punishment—independent of benevolent affections. They are using their moral sense, but it is in error. Their moral 'taste' requires improvement, as does the palate of a person who cannot distinguish a fine burgundy from jug wine (S 1.59–60). At other times, Hutcheson's conception of the moral sense may seem narrower, such that it is exercised only in approval of benevolence.[11] The most charitable interpretation is that the narrower conception concerns the moral sense correctly applied (see Strasser 1990: 31), though it remains possible that Hutcheson was too ready to see the immediate contrast with self-love as love of others and then to link that latter form of love to the moral sense (e.g. E 54).[12]

The moral sense, then, when operating properly is a response to benevolent affections, or to affections connected with benevolence (I 177; S 24). Hutcheson believes that some degree of benevolence is part of human nature (E 188; SI 130). Relationships with friends and family are all but universal, but there is a human disposition to extend that benevolence to one's country, other nations, or even beings on distant planets (I 114–15; SI 121–2). That disposition, however, is rarely exercised by most human beings (E 140), and this may be unobjectionable, since most human beings have the opportunity only to benefit those close to them and in doing so are in effect maximally promoting the good (S 1.158; SI 82–3, 122). But our circle of concern should be as wide as possible, and we can often extend it through calm reflection on our different possible beneficiaries (E 175; S 1.10, 168–9; SI 81–2). On such reflection, we will recognize that our feelings for our friends and others close to us tend to be 'turbulent' and to that extent irrational. Hutcheson sees here an analogy between self-interest and morality:

[T]here is deeply rooted in the soul a steddy propensity or impulse towards its own highest happiness, which every one upon a little reflection will find, by means whereof he can repress and govern all the particular selfish passions, when they are any way opposite to it; so whosoever in a calm hour takes a full view of human nature ... will find a like general propension of soul to wish the universal prosperity and happiness of the whole system (SI 31–2; also S 1.50; 2.118).

---

[10] For discussion of Hutcheson's notion of moral goodness, see Maurer 2009: 198–201.
[11] As Irwin implies (2008: 432–3), this commits Hutcheson to the view that the 'normal moral observer' will be utilitarian. The two different conceptions are stated together at e.g. E 173–4. On the increasing role of benevolence in Hutcheson's ethics, see Scott 1900: 203–7.
[12] See Frankena (1955: 358–9), who sees the problem as arising especially in the arguments of I.

Lack of conflict between partial and impartial benevolent affections not only can be found in those unable to promote the public good more generally, but is also possible for human beings generally to the extent that their relationships with others can be calm rather than turbulent (E 188). That is, those who are both calm and, say, disposed to gratitude or to help their friends are also likely to be those most capable of promoting the good impartially, in part because their relationships with others will assist them in projects to advance the public good (SI 83). But what is the attraction of impartiality in the first place? Why is calmness preferable to turbulence? Here the influence of Shaftesbury's (and hence, as I have suggested, Aristotle's) ethical aestheticism on Hutcheson begins to emerge. Impartiality has a certain dignity or nobility, which can be explicated in analogy with architecture: 'the most perfect Rules of Architecture condemn an excessive Profusion of Ornament on one Part, above the Proportion of the Whole' (I 127; also S. 1.255–6). And again Hutcheson's theism is in the background: in being impartially benevolent, we are imitating the Deity in his attitude to his creation (CS 98).

If (unusually, according to Hutcheson) a conflict arises between the demands of impartial and partial benevolence, the former must be given priority (E 32–3; S. 1.158, 255–6; 2.242–3; SI 85–6). We must 'pursue our own interests, or those of our friends, or kinsmen, no further than the more extensive interests will allow' (SI 50), though in general aiming not to limit our more partial affections but to focus as required on those who would benefit from our allowing priority to impartiality over partiality (SI 86).

Just as he is more aware than Cumberland of the potential conflict between the principle of impartial beneficence and attachments to particular individuals or groups, so Hutcheson recognizes that other moral principles must also be based on and limited by that principle. True distributive justice, for example, consists in that distribution of goods and bads which maximizes the universal good, impartially construed. In the case of God, for example, '[n]o unworthy favourites shall find in him a partial tenderness inconsistent with the general good', and '['t]is no injust partiality that the lot of some should have many advantages above that of others', if it is required for 'the best order and harmony of the whole' (S 1.208). Hutcheson's conception of justice can be seen to rest on his observation that the innocent suffer natural evils, and the fact that God allows this suggests that he is acting out of benevolence rather than any concern for a conception of distributive fairness independent of the maximum good of his creation (S. 1.197–8).

Benevolence is indeed the 'Foundation of all apprehended Excellence in social Virtues' (I 118), and for that reason Hutcheson is open to the objection standardly made against utilitarians that they fail to give sufficient weight to moral principles other than that of benevolence. The highest subordinate virtue is the sense of, and consequent desire for, moral excellence itself (S 1.67–8). Veracity is called for because of the benefits of being able to rely on information from others (S 1.66–7; 2.28–9). Gratitude is required because of the pleasure it gives to benefactors, the prospect of which is itself an incentive to giving (I 117, 149–50; IL 138–9; S 1.307–8). There is one obvious exception to this: our pious gratitude to God (S 1.210–17). First, we should note that the aim of the grateful is to express their gratitude for benefits received, not to benefit others. If it were the latter, and known to be the latter, the benefit in question would not itself arise. For that reason, the moral sense cannot approve of fine-tuned dispositions to gratitude which attempt to discriminate between recipients on the ground of whether or not they can benefit. Second, expressing gratitude to God, through worship, living virtuously, and so on, bring us our greatest joys, as well as providing us with a sense of security for the future lacking to the impious and a consolation for those evils inflicted on those close to us, grounded in a faith in God's providence (S 1.153–4). Indeed pious obedience to God is itself justified on the basis of its promoting the overall good, as is God's own right to issue commands (S 1.265–6). But Hutcheson is clear that the dispositions underlying certain subordinate virtues—such as fortitude, veracity, or piety—can become excessively strong (S 1.109). Just as the virtue of these dispositions depends on their promoting the public good, so their underlying dispositions must be limited by awareness of that good.

Hutcheson takes care to ensure that in placing limits on the subordinate principles of morality he is not advocating immorality (S 2.120–40). Consider a case in which it is clear that I can promote the good by cheating some innocent person. What we must not say is that this is a case in which injustice is required. Rather, we must claim that the behaviour in question is virtuous, though ordinarily it would be vicious. The subordinate moral principles, or laws, that is to say, allow for exceptions. But only in very unusual cases should we stop to consider whether some proposed action of ours is an exception. Ordinarily, we should follow the subordinate moral rules, since the general following of such rules is what will best promote the public good. Exactly when we should deviate from them is a difficult matter, to be decided according to something like Aristotelian practical wisdom.

The same account of subordination to benevolence applies to the notion of rights, which receive a great deal of detailed discussion in Hutcheson's work (e.g. I 177–98; S 1: bk. 2, chs 3–6; 2: bk. 2, chs 14–17; SI 2.2, 4–5, 16).[13] Often rights are merely the shadows of utility. Each of us has certain 'natural' rights, which, unlike 'adventitious' rights, do not depend on such human institutions as contract (e.g. S 1.253–4, 293–9; SI 111–12, 128–30). Nor do they depend directly on the principle of impartial benevolence. Imagine some individual in a state of nature, gathering fruit for themselves and their family, leaving plenty for others. We will naturally approve of what they are doing to advance their own good and that of those close to them, and object to any interference: this is sufficient for us to say that they have a 'private' right. But such rights, to the extent that they are genuine, must line up with universal benevolence (e.g. I 183; SI 110–12; also Blackstone 1965: 35–7). In this weak sense, then, I have a right to act in

---

[13] Hutcheson's views on the relationship between rights and the costs of their protection or enforcement, and on how principles of rights can serve a role in everyday morality, clearly had significant influence on later utilitarian thinkers, especially Mill (see e.g. 1998: chs 2, 5).

some way, or to gain some object, if my acting in that way, or my possessing that object, will maximize the overall good.

But Hutcheson realizes that there are important questions about what level of protection should be afforded such rights, and distinguishes three categories of rights with that in mind (e.g. I 183–6; S 257–9; SI 113, 129–32; also CS 105–6). He further recognizes that, given that ethics is grounded on benevolence, the relevant question to ask about any such protection is not whether it is intuitively right or wrong in itself, but whether it promotes the overall good; and that the notion of rights has a role to play in our everyday or lived morality, that role itself to be justified by appeal to the overall good.[14] In other words, the relevant question to ask about whether some right should be protected is whether it would promote the good were it to be generally accepted in society that it should.

Perfect rights, then, are so central to the public good that they must be protected, if necessary by violence. For example, we might force a person who has harmed another to compensate her. Perfect rights tend to be negative, i.e. rights not to be harmed in some way or other. *Imperfect* rights are such that respecting them will promote the good, but failure to do so will not cause huge misery. They are not to be enforced through coercion, partly because of the harms of such coercion itself but also because such coercion may prevent the pleasures associated with freely benefiting others: a key example of an imperfect right is that of the poor to the assistance of the wealthy. Hutcheson's distinction between perfect and imperfect rights, then, does not depend on whether the duty-holder has a duty to some specific individual. Every poor person has an imperfect right to assistance from every rich person. Further, he introduces a third category: *external* rights. These are in a sense the mirror of imperfect rights, since they are to acting in some way, or to possessing some good, which is both detrimental to the public good but also such that attempts to coerce the possessor into doing what they should would itself do more harm than good. A rich person, then, has an external right to their wealth, even though they would do more good were they to transfer some of it to the poor.

Hutcheson distinguishes also between alienable and inalienable rights. The latter include those we are unable to surrender (e.g. a right to private judgement) and those it would do overall harm to surrender (e.g. our right to serve God). He suggests, plausibly, that property rights are justified partly because of their incentive effects, and that the rights of those in government are both justified and limited by impartial benevolence. He also ascribes rights to non-humans (e.g. S 1.314; see Garrett 2007), and to groups—in particular that of the most extensive 'system' of all sentient beings (though he clearly has humans especially in mind) (S 2.105–16; SI 210–11). An example of the latter is our collective right to prevent suicide, on the ground that a general unwillingness to do so would lead to many who would otherwise go on to live happy lives, and to contribute to

---

[14]   It has to be admitted that Hutcheson does not always clearly separate the issues of whether e.g. some action harmful to another falls into a category of actions which are *always* inconsistent with universal benevolence, or a category of actions the overall *tendency* of which is inconsistent with universal benevolence.

the well-being of others, killing themselves to avoid some temporary misery. This may seem harsh, but it is worth noting Hutcheson's claim that we are entitled to interfere in cases of '*unreasonable* dejection' (SI 2.106; my italics). He may well have allowed a right to suicide, for example, at the conclusion of an agonizing terminal illness.

Rights and justice concern the distribution of harms or bads as well as goods, in particular that of punishment. Hutcheson offers what amounts to a debunking account of deontological views of punishment (E 59, 96; S 1.137–8, 256–7). He admits that we often feel very strongly that someone who has committed some wrong should be punished. But such views are the result of anger, an unpleasant emotion which is relieved (and replaced by a temporary 'turbulent joy' (S 1.137)) through harm's being inflicted on the wrongdoer (or the wrongdoer's showing remorse, which is in itself harmful because unpleasant). But this anger itself has been implanted in us by God with a view to our acting so as to prevent future such behaviour on the part of wrongdoers (I 183–4; S 1.108; 3.331–6). To a calm person, 'the *Misery of another* is only grateful as it allays, or secures us against a furious Pain; and cannot be the Occasion, by itself, of any Satisfaction' (E 96). In general, the turbulent passions are regrettable, and it would be better if they were replaced with a calm concern for the public good: 'Superior orders of beings may want these passions altogether' (S 1.257). Here we see the influence on Hutcheson of Shaftesburian Stoic doubt about the passions.

3. Two (or Three?) Grand Determinations

Hutcheson, as we have seen, is happy to think of God as at least in part self-interested, and it is unsurprising to find that he frequently allows the same to be true of human beings. We have a sense of self-interest which, for example, causes a particular kind of joy when we become aware of some advantage coming to us (I 25–6). But this is not our only sense. For example, we also have the capacity to take pleasure in beauty. It may be said that we seek beauty—in architecture, gardening, or whatever—just because it advances our own self-interest. But this gets things in reverse. Had we no sense of beauty, we might desire a house because it would be, say, warm; but we could not want it for the pleasure of its beauty.

But the sense of beauty in itself is not an ultimate source of motivation. All desires and intentions, whether derivative or ultimate, are either self- or other-regarding:

The acts of the will may be again divided into two classes, according as one is pursuing good for himself, and repelling the contrary, or pursuing good for others and repelling evils which threaten them. The former we may call *selfish*, the later *benevolent*. (S 1.8)

Many of our desires are turbulent and unreflective. But the self- and other-interested aspects of our nature are such that, when undisturbed by irrational passion, two 'grand determinations' of human action become apparent:[15]

---

[15] Darwall (1995: 244n1) rightly points out that Sidgwick's later 'dualism of the practical reason' owes much more to Hutcheson than to Butler; cf. Sidgwick 1907: xviii–xix.

As there is found in the human mind, when it recollects itself, a calm general determination towards personal happiness of the highest kind it has any notion of; so we may find a like principle of a generous kind. When upon reflection we present to our minds the notion of the greatest possible system of sensitive beings, and the highest happiness it can enjoy, there is also a calm determination to desire it, abstracting from any connection with or subserviency to our private enjoyment. We shall find these two grand determinations, one toward our own greatest happiness, the other toward the greatest general good, each independent on the other, each capable of such strength as to restrain all the particular affections of its kind, and keep them subordinate to itself. (S 1.50; also S.9–10; I 104; E 22, 58).

Hutcheson is not claiming that all human action is in fact the result of one or both of the two grand determinations themselves. People are often weak-willed or immoral, or act unreflectively on the basis of passion or appetite. Rather, a calm, reflective, and rational individual will base their actions ultimately on these determinations, because we have both a reason to promote our own good maximally, and a reason to promote the good of all sentient beings.[16] Our passions often leave us unable to recognize 'the Importance of every Action or Event' (E 47). But if we try in the proper way, we may able to discern, using our God-given faculty of reason (IL 141), 'that just *Ballance* and *Oeconomy*, which would constitute the most happy State of each Person, and promote the greatest Good in the whole' (E 47).

Like Shaftesbury, Hutcheson is attracted to the view that any discrepancy between the deliverances of the two principles would indicate a 'blemish' in the design of the world (S 1.149; see above pp. 74, 88). But Hutcheson takes this view only in relation to the higher species, or 'more noble systems', in particular, of course, human beings. The interests of a lower species may be subordinate to that of a higher. But if there were an 'established inconsistence' between the two principles governing any rational being, and consequently between the affections required to satisfy those principles, this would be a defect. Does this suggest that there is no possible case in which the self-interest of any rational being can conflict with their advancing the overall good? Or does an occasional such conflict allow that, in general, such consistency is 'established'?

Let us first consider Hutcheson's views of human nature. It is clear that he denies an extreme form of psychological egoism, according to which each agent consciously aims at all times to promote their own self-interest (E 24–30; also LM 135).[17] In particular, Hutcheson objects to the 'Epicurean' view according to which our desire to

---

[16] For a good defence of the view that Hutcheson is offering a theory of ultimate normative justification, see Blackstone 1965: 17–19. That we have these reasons depends on our affective nature. Hutcheson is without doubt what Williams (1981a) has called an 'internalist' about reasons: 'He acts *reasonably*, who considers the various Actions in his Power, and forms *true Opinions* of their *Tendencies*; and then chuses to do that which will obtain the highest Degree of *that*, to which the *Instincts* of his Nature incline him, with the smallest Degree of those things to which the *Affections* in his Nature make him averse' (E 143; also L 18–19). On Hutcheson's view, then, a purely self-interested being would have no M-reasons.

[17] For helpful discussions of Hutcheson's arguments against psychological egoism, see Jensen 1971: 13–19; Mautner 2002: 42–7; Gill 2006: ch. 11; Tilley 2016.

benefit others arises from our desire to benefit ourselves. First, though we may enjoy benefiting others, that enjoyment cannot itself be the object of the desire in question, since if it were then we might strongly desire some trivial object—such as the 'turning of a Straw'—or indeed the misery of others, to obtain the pleasure in question. Second, we cannot understand our desire that others are happy as based on the desire for our own good along with the belief that our having that desire will benefit us. That would result merely in a desire to have that desire. Third, we can often recognize in ourselves an ultimate desire that others are happy, and it is this ultimate desire which we consider morally valuable. Imagine that you believe that you will soon die, that your mind will die with your body, and that you have the power to make your children and fellow citizens either happy or unhappy (see IL 139–40).[18] Would you not choose to benefit them at the very moment of your death?

Hutcheson also explicitly denies split-level psychological egoism, according to which agents recognize the self-interested advantages to themselves of acting out of concern for others rather than concern for themselves, and so develop virtuous dispositions for strategic reasons (S 1.140). Rather, Hutcheson insists:

That we have not only *Self-Love,* but *benevolent Affections* also toward others, in various Degrees, making us desire their Happiness as an *ultimate End,* without any view to private Happiness: That we have a *moral Sense* or Determination of our Mind, to *approve* every *kind Affection* either in our selves or others, and all publicly useful Actions which we imagined do flow from such Affection, without our having a view to our *private Happiness,* in our Approbation of these Actions.(E 136; also I 110–12; S 149)

Further, we see virtue, rightly, as disinterested. The virtuous agent is praiseworthy for acting out of concern for others, not for herself (e.g. I 112; S 1.55, 141), except to the extent that they see themselves as just one among others whose good constitutes the public good (I 122–3).

Are human beings capable of subjective sacrifice for others, that is, of acting in a way that they believe will be better for others but worse for themselves? Perhaps because of his insistence on disinterest in virtuous motivation, Hutcheson rarely discusses cases in which an agent acts benevolently while explicitly thinking to themselves that they are acting against their own interests. But consider the following passage:

[I]n many cases…the kind heart acts from its generous impulse, not thinking of its own interest. Nay all its own interests have sometimes appeared to it as opposite to, and inconsistent with the generous part in which it persisted. (S 1.75).

Here Hutcheson does appear to allow for genuine subjective sacrifice. This, then, raises the question which of the two principles of practical reason should I follow in a situation of conflict? Should I advance my own happiness, or that of all? Hutcheson is

---

[18] For the history of this argument in Hutcheson's texts, see Mautner 2002: 74. As pointed out by Stewart (1982: 277), it is important that the decision to benefit one's children be such that, because one's death will follow immediately upon its being taken, it cannot itself increase the balance of one's pleasure over pain.

in no doubt that the moral sense here has priority over an individual's sense of their own good. Following Butler, in his inaugural lecture Hutcheson claims that the moral sense, or conscience, is naturally fitted to govern our lives as to hēgemonikon—the ruling element (IL 131–2). 'This dignity and commanding nature we are immediately conscious of, as we are conscious of the power itself' (S 1.61). The moral sense, that is to say, is the capacity to grasp the weights of all reasons, including those of self-interest (S 1.101). Our calm desires arise from our beliefs about the goodness or badness of their objects, and will conform themselves to the results of a rational comparison of the values of different objects. In the case of a 'kind' desire for some good to someone close to us, for example, which we can fulfil only by failing to promote the overall good, which we also desire, we will, if rational, act on the impartial desire, 'since where a greater good is discerned, the calm desire of it is stronger than that toward a smaller inconsistent good, whether pursued for ourselves or others'. Here, then, the basis of Hutcheson's account of practical reason is revealed. Our reasons are based on, and only on, value; and strength of reason necessarily tracks degree of value. Hence the rational agent will always maximize the overall good, since the value of that outcome is greater than that of any other, including any outcome in which they themselves do better than in the overall best outcome (E 143). We are, then, in all cases required to promote the greatest good overall (S 1.281).

According to Sidgwick (1907: 420), a rational egoist at this point may refuse to accept that the action required by impartial benevolence is indeed the most valuable. They may, however, admit it, yet deny that reasons must track overall value. They may claim, for example, that the fact that some good is going to be instantiated in *their* life gives them a reason to promote that good independently of reason to promote it captured by the principle of impartial benevolence (Crisp 2015a: 198–9). Hutcheson is not unaware of the power of self-interest to undermine morality. The pull to benefit ourselves will be strong even in those with an active moral sense, and it may well give rise to doubts about the rationality of impartial beneficence. In closing the first book of the *System*, Hutcheson explains his reason for going on to examine the pleasures of virtue, and the pains of vice, in such great detail: 'to remove, as much as may be, all opposition arising from the selfish principles' (S 1.99; also S 1.62). He will argue that, though we may be required by morality to sacrifice '*worldly*' interests (S 1.240; my italics), it is in fact always in our interest to follow the demands of impartial benevolence (e.g. S 1.287). It is to those arguments I shall turn in the final section of this chapter.

Before that we must briefly consider whether Hutcheson is not in fact committed to a 'triplism', rather than a dualism, of the practical reason.[19] Hutcheson does require that we are grateful to God, and his standard account of the reasons for gratitude is stated in terms of its benefits to benefactor and beneficiary. But God must already be perfectly happy, and it would be an obvious imperfection in him were his happiness dependent on our contingent attitudes or behaviour. Further, we are required to obey

---

[19] Virtue itself might ground yet another principle: see below n. 20; see also Jensen 1971: 88–9.

God's commands, and Hutcheson speaks of such piety as a principle alongside that of impartial beneficence (e.g. R 53; S 1.228, 274; 2.120). Since God is impartially benefi-cent, he will require impartial beneficence of us, and so the two principles are practically consistent. Hutcheson does suggest that benevolence 'may include even our duties toward God' (S 1.222), and claims that God's right to command itself rests on his pro-motion of universal happiness: 'the ultimate notion of right is *that which tends to the universal good*' (S 1.266). But there is here a tension in his position (see McCosh 1875: 81); and his frequent mention of the two principles as independent, along with the implausibility of the claim that our obeying God *in itself* promotes happiness, suggest that if pressed he would commit to a triplism rather than a dualism of the practical reason.

4. The Highest Pleasures

Hutcheson was, for most intents and purposes, an evaluative hedonist, at least at the substantive level, and held also that pleasure is the sole object of the will (LM 126).[20] The happiness of any individual is identical with 'pleasant perceptions', and public hap-piness is merely the aggregate of such perceptions (R 42). These perceptions give us our first idea of natural goodness, and we attribute immediate goodness to those objects likely to produce such perceptions, such as drink or harmony, and mediate goodness to objects instrumental to immediate goodness, such as wealth (I 86). The same rela-tions hold between pain and badness, and lead to aversion rather than positive desire (e.g. S 1.4; I 26). Hutcheson's definitions of happiness are less precise than those of his successors in the hedonist tradition. For example, he defines happiness as 'a state wherein there is plenty of such things as excite these general sensations or one kind or another, and we are free from pain', and misery as 'frequent and lasting sensations of the painful and disagreeable sorts, excluding all grateful sensations'. Nor, like Mill (1998: 2.2), did he retain a clear distinction between happiness as pleasure, and happi-ness as the greatest balance of pleasure over pain within a life. But he clearly recognizes that pleasures and pains can be weighed against one another, and his advocacy of maximization at both the intra- and interpersonal levels suggests that he would have accepted a conception of well-being according to which it consists in the greatest bal-ance of pleasure over pain. Degrees of pleasantness and painfulness depend entirely on their intensity and duration (e.g. E 37).

Often (e.g. E 9), Hutcheson appears to mean by 'intensity' degree of pleasurableness. At times he appears to distinguish between intensity and dignity. For example, the earlier statement of the 7th axiom of calm desire at E 37 is: 'In computing the *Quantities* of Good or Evil, which we pursue or shun, either for our selves or others, when the *Durations* are equal, the Moment is as the *Intenseness*'. Hutcheson later added

---

[20] In his later writings (e.g. SI 48), Hutcheson spoke of the love of virtue itself, which may be taken as a source of non-hedonic motivation independent of both self-interest and morality: see Bishop 1996: 289–91.

', or Dignity of the Enjoyment' (E 210). Indeed he allows that the dignity of certain individuals can justify choosing an outcome in which they benefit over another of equal hedonic value (E 39). At SI 9, he claims that we should compare enjoyments according to their dignity and duration, making no mention of intensity. And at SI 54, dignity appears to be equivalent to value at a time: the dignity of the sensual pleasures consists only in the 'intenseness of the pleasure in the sensation'; the superior pleasures have their own 'excellence'. Hutcheson does believes that dignity—understood as something like 'excellence'—can increase pleasurableness, because of the pleasure taken in dignity, claiming: 'These moral Pleasures do some way more nearly affect us than any other: They make us delight in our *selves*, and relish our very *Nature*. By these we perceive an *internal Dignity* and *Worth;* and seem to have a Pleasure like to that ascribed often to the Deity, by which we enjoy our own *Perfection*, and that of every other Being' (E 107; also S 1.132). But it is tempting to think that, again like Mill, Hutcheson at least comes close to allowing that non-hedonic properties of experiences can increase a person's well-being directly, as well as indirectly through increasing pleasurableness. In other words, Hutcheson is a substantive but not an explanatory hedonist. The moral pleasures are best for us, but not merely because of their greater pleasurableness: their dignity also matters. Consider also S 1.117: 'By this intimate feeling of dignity, enjoyments and exercises of some kinds, tho' not of the highest degree of those kinds, are incomparably more excellent and beatifick than the most intense and lasting enjoyments of the lower kinds' (also I 4, 77; E 94–5; S 1.29, 117, 129, 2.380; SI 40, 56–7).[21] And, of course, there is a corresponding indignity in vice, which makes it the greatest evil (S 1.139–40). Nevertheless, it would certainly be fair to say that the dominant idea emerging from Hutcheson's ethics is that the balance of pleasure over pain should be maximized at both individual and social levels, and that pleasantness and painfulness are the most significant good- and bad-making properties respectively.

As is standard in philosophical discussions of pleasures and pains, Hutcheson divides each into various different categories (SI 55–62, 70; also S 1.116–39). The most basic are bodily or sensual pleasures, which are felt when we satisfy those appetites we share with non-human animals. They have 'none of that dignity which is the object of praise'. Next are those pleasures that emerge from the 'elegance and grandeur of life', as

---

[21] For an interpretation of Hutcheson as a purely 'quantitative' hedonist, see Dorsey (2010). By quantitative hedonism, Dorsey means the view that the welfare value of a pleasure is simply a function of its pleasurableness (446). He later cites the link made by Hutcheson at S 100 between 'supreme happiness' and 'the most intense and durable pleasures' as evidence for a quantitative interpretation (Dorsey in fact says 'qualitative' but he has confirmed to me that this is a typographical error). But if by 'intensity' Hutcheson means degree of pleasurableness-at-a-time, the passage seems consistent with forms of qualitative hedonism according to which pleasurableness depends partly on dignity, and/or welfare consists in the greatest pleasures, the welfare value of which depends at least partly on dignity as well as pleasurableness. Strasser (1987: 521–2) suggests that Hutcheson is not open to Moore's objection to Mill that allowing quality as well as quantity of pleasure to count commits Mill to a non-hedonist position, because 'Hutcheson does not believe in the instrinsic moral worth of happiness or pleasure'. But, as Strasser himself notes, Hutcheson does believe in the intrinsic natural value of pleasure, and Moore's argument—for what is it is worth—could be directed against that position.

well as those of the arts, sciences, and intellectual activity in general. These pleasures are 'purer... more honourable and joyful', and yet not absolutely the highest. The next highest are those of sympathy, as we can see from the fact that we will not envy a person with profuse bodily and intellectual pleasures, but no social pleasures. Unlike Shaftesbury, Hutcheson distinguishes clearly between these pleasures and those of the conscience or moral sense, which arise through reflection on one's own character and actions. And it is in the pleasures of virtue—in particular, acting virtuously—that we find the 'highest happiness'. Hutcheson's detailed arguments for this broadly hedonistic view are perhaps the most developed in the history of philosophy, though as with Shaftesbury some of them depend on dubious empirical claims.

Hutcheson takes care to reject those versions of Stoicism according to which what is central is making oneself immune to contingent harms (E 83). That would involve a failure of compassion for the suffering of others, an excessive focus on the self rather than others, and a move towards passive retreat from the world rather than active engagement with it (also S 1.132). Such a position is in effect inconsistent with true human nature, which reveals itself when the agent is calm—and hence impartially benevolent (I 164). Our benevolent nature is of course the result of benevolent design (R 53; E 8; S 1.1.75; SI 23, 40), and so we should not be surprised to find that our moral sense is itself designed to give its possessors pleasure (I 100).[22] Hutcheson also locates himself within the perfectionist Aristotelian tradition, according to which happiness itself consists in the perfection of one's nature (S 1.29). This general position resonates with his revival of the Shaftesburian argument that, since the self is independent of the body, the bodily pleasures are in that sense alien and inferior (E 107; S 1.147).

As we have seen, pleasures are of different kinds. How should we compare them? Referring appropriately to Plato and Shaftesbury (see above p. 89), and anticipating Mill (1998: 2.5–8), Hutcheson advocates reliance on the verdicts of a competent judge, rather than on each individual's position (rather than a pig, Hutcheson imagines a fly or maggot judging its pleasures to be superior to all others) (E 88–9; also S 1.120–1; SI 57). According to such a judge, there is no doubt that the pleasures of virtue are the highest. These include the pleasures of benevolence (I 134; S 1.140–1, 147), but also those of piety, which Hutcheson tends to classify independently and as the very highest (S 1.222, 234; SI 87).

As far as benevolence is concerned, pleasantness increases with impartiality (S 1.132). As we might expect (see above p. 116), this pleasantness is at least to some extent aesthetic: 'in some extensive Principles of Action', as in certain theorems, we perceive a beauty analogous to that in sensible objects (I 24).[23] The approving awareness of

---

[22] This teleological element in Hutcheson's thought is a problem for any account of the role of the moral sense in the origin of our moral distinctions which rules out teleology (e.g. Gill 2006: 177–8).

[23] Hutcheson almost certainly has impartial benevolence in mind here. See e.g. the reference to 'extensive affections' at S 1.59–60. In a later edition, Hutcheson stated that the purpose of geometry is to show how what is true of one figure is also true of others; from the practical perspective, he may have in mind the extension of the scope of practical principles from egoism, through partial benevolence, to impartial benevolence.

one's own virtue is a great joy (SI 40–1), while vice brings with it the pains of guilt, regret, and remorse (SI 40, 66, 145, 147), and of reproach by others (SI 148). These pains are themselves distracting, making it impossible for the subject to focus on the sources of external, or bodily, pleasure (SI 63). Remorse also often arises after indulgence in the bodily or sensual pleasures (SI 56, 126), whereas reflection on past virtuous deeds is deeply pleasurable (R 45; SI 61) and the development of a virtuous habit increases pleasure even further (S 1.133). Even in the absence of such remorse, reflection on past external pleasures is hedonically neutral, and such pleasures are brief and transient, producing nauseous satiety and languor (I 164; E 105–8; S 1.124, 132, SI 56, 88–9). Just as the pleasures of virtue have the greatest duration, the same is true of those of vice (E 108; SI 66): unlike Mill, Hutcheson allows for different qualities of pain as well as pleasure (SI 100, 139).

The pleasures of virtue, unlike even those of the imagination, are a support in difficult times (E 105–6), and the virtuous can even rise above physical pain (R 46; S 1.151–2). Further, if the pain is an obstacle to a virtuous action, that of course only increases its value (I 165). The virtuous can enjoy the external pleasures, and do not need them in excess: a simple life is sufficient (I 1.106; S 1.127). In general, 'external' goods such as wealth are required for 'complete' happiness (SI 64, 222), but the virtuous gain more from them (E 104). Their moderation increases pleasures from such sources (SI 58), while unmoderated indulgence itself causes vexation. Further the virtuous, because others will feel affection for them, are more likely to be beneficiaries as well as benefactors.

The emotions of the vicious—anger, malice, and so on—make them miserable even when opportunities for external pleasure are open to them (I 164). In response to the objection that the vicious clearly do experience some valuable external pleasures, Hutcheson can respond that this is true only of the majority of the vicious who are in a way partly virtuous (S 1.153, 191–2). Virtue consists in benevolent affections, and most of the vicious have some social affections, which are valuable in themselves and may make it possible for the vicious to gain some value also from external pleasures (SI 57).

These points are part of the explanation why virtue is necessary for other goods to be valuable (I 165–7; S 1.126). But there is another component. There was a good deal of discussion in the eighteenth century of the story of the Roman general, Marcus Atilius Regulus (see below pp. 191, 193–5). According to this story, Regulus, having been taken prisoner by the Carthaginians, was sent back to Rome on parole, to offer terms of peace. Regulus is said to have advised the Senate to reject these terms, and then to have returned to Carthage as he had promised, where he was tortured to death. We might, Hutcheson suggests, wish that he had not been tortured; but none of us would wish, for his sake, that he had broken his promise. This is a very clear example of the work being done by dignity in Hutcheson's account. Only pleasures are valuable, but their value depends not only on their being pleasant, but on their dignity. In this respect, then, Hutcheson, is again, like Mill, moving away from a pure explanatory hedonism to allow in non-hedonic good-making properties. Many have wondered why Mill did not go the whole way, and move beyond substantive hedonism altogether, perhaps even allowing happiness to consist in more than subjective states—in particular, in virtuous actions. The same question arises for Hutcheson, as does the question whether the approval we feel for Regulus's behaviour may be grounded on our view of the morality of his actions rather than whether he himself benefited from them.

We can now grasp the main outlines of Hutcheson's conception of the role of virtue in happiness. In general his view is that the pleasures of impartial benevolence, combined with piety, are discontinuously more valuable than others, and for that reason virtue guarantees the best outcome for the agent, usually in positive happiness but sometimes only in diminution of misery (S 1.178; SI 78, 249). In certain passages, however, Hutcheson appears to accept weaker views. He allows that death may be preferable for a person 'under grievous bodily pain' (SI 65), implying that the exercise of courage in such circumstances is insufficient for happiness. At E 97–8, his argument for the superiority of virtue over the avoidance of bodily pain explicitly appeals to actions of great virtue, when his stated position elsewhere appears to be that all virtuous pleasure is superior to avoidance of bodily pain of any kind. At E 143, he claims that the reasonable person will examine the *tendencies* of the various types of action they consider doing, and that the pursuit of the public good is the *most probable* route to the greatest happiness. These and other passages, though in a minority, suggest a certain—quite justifiable—reluctance on Hutcheson's part to accept the strong Stoic thesis that virtue guarantees the greatest happiness and hence immunity to fortune. That reluctance may be explained partly by his commitment to substantive hedonism. It may be somewhat implausible to claim that the virtuous person who chooses to die in agony on the rack has lived the happiest or even the best life possible for them; but to claim that they have experienced the most pleasurable life is even harder to believe.

Hutcheson, then, goes as far as he can in defending the view that, even on a substantively hedonist view, there is nothing to be lost by choosing the truly virtuous option on every occasion. But there is some evidence that he recognized the plausibility of the view that at least sometimes the best option, from the self-interested point of view, is not that of virtue. In that respect, then, there is a dualism (if not a triplism—see above pp. 122–3) of the practical reason in Hutcheson's position, and, since he denies psychological egoism, the possibility of both subjective and objective sacrifice. But that sacrifice will be merely mundane, or short-term, because of the more than compensatory divine rewards in the afterlife. In the next chapter, we shall see some of the same hesitations, and some analogous positions, in the work of Samuel Clarke.

10

Clarke:
Virtue and the Life Hereafter

Samuel Clarke (1675–1729) was the most important Newtonian philosopher of his day, and a prominent defender of natural religion whose work brought him to the attention of Queen Anne. His defence of a rationalist metaethics put him strongly at odds with Hutcheson, and, though he sees the attractions of utilitarianism, his norma-tive ethics is best seen as a form of pluralism. But his views on the relation between virtue and self-interest, and on the role of the afterlife, are closer to those of Hutcheson in his less Stoic moods, and also demonstrate a wavering on the role of the afterlife in ethics.[1]

According to Clarke (D 111–14, 121, 174–7), certain things, and relations between things, are fitting or unfitting, and this is as obvious as simple mathematical or geo-metrical truths to all intelligent beings who consider them appropriately. All will agree, for example, that it is unfitting that an innocent being should be extremely and eter-nally unhappy, or, given his superiority, that we do not honour and worship God. Such fitness is the ground of moral reasons for God and for us. These reasons are autono-mous, in that they are independent of, and prior to, any reasons we might have based on the authority of God or the self-interested benefits and harms correlated respectively with virtue and vice (D 148, 174, 189, 215–18). A virtuous person, if they could gain all their neighbour's wealth with the flick of a finger without the knowledge of anyone, including (*per impossibile*) God, would not do so (D 219–20). Indeed, were human beings not corrupted by false opinions and evil habits, they would all act in accordance with rational moral principles (D 200–1).

Like Hutcheson, Clarke finds it plausible that, in some sense, reasons track value: 'that which is Good is fit and reasonable... and that which is the greatest Good, is that which is always the *most* fit and reasonable to be chosen' (D 204; also 120). But there is more to Clarke's normative ethics than just the principle of beneficence (P 65–6, 81, 118–20; D 120, 148, 167, 186, 197–211). There are three 'great branches' of duty, each of

---

[1] Clarke's *Sermons* contain interesting material on individual virtues, but the main sources for his views on ethics in general are the *Practical Essays* (P), first published in 1699, and the *Discourse* (D). The latter consists of Clarke's two sets of eight Boyle lectures, themselves given as sermons in 1704–5. Each set was initially published separately. I have used the last editions of P and D published in Clarke's lifetime.

which is a natural law as well as a law of God. First, *piety* requires us to honour, worship, serve, pray to, and thank God. The primary aim of religion is to recommend and enforce morality (P 89), and our service to God itself consists primarily in the furthering of *righteousness*, which is the second great branch. Righteousness itself has two components: equity, and love. Equity can be elucidated in terms of a universalizability principle: if I treat you in some way in which I myself would want not to be treated, such as by cheating you out of some money, then I have violated equity and justice. Love is equivalent to benevolence, and, though partiality is natural and permissible, impartiality is its highest form. Every human being is 'born to promote the publick good and welfare of all his Fellow-creatures' (D 206). The final branch is that of *sobriety*, which involves temperance, moderation, and, most importantly, self-preservation. One is required to preserve oneself because of one's duties of righteousness, but sobriety is best understood as not merely a 'meta-' or 'enabling' virtue. Clarke's distinction between the duties of righteousness and those of sobriety itself rests on the distinction between self and others, which also emerges in his recognition of self-interested reasons to promote one's own good. Indeed at D 207 Clarke describes sobriety as a self-regarding duty of righteousness.

Clarke's ethics is broadly welfarist. Even justice is chosen by God with a view 'to the welfare of the whole Universe' (D 148; also 174, 176, 180). But some things are by nature absolutely evil, such as breaking faith, refusing to perform just contracts, or cruelty (D 181). But what about the possibility of conflict between equity and love, justice and beneficence? Because of the welfarist grounding of justice, Clarke claims that 'the *Good of the Universal Creation*, does always *coincide* with the *necessary Truth and Reason of Things*' (D 223; also 245–6).[2] Clarke will not allow exceptions to the principle of equity for utilitarian reasons. Justice is more valuable than life and all the enjoyments of the world, and injustice the greatest corruption of God's creation. But this is not to give up on the idea of maximal promotion of the impartial good. Consider some typical counter-example to utilitarianism, such as the 'sheriff case', in which a sheriff, by hanging an innocent person, can prevent a riot which would otherwise produce a greater balance of harm over benefit than the hanging. If the riot takes place, those who are killed, maimed, or otherwise harmed might appear to have lost out. In fact, however, they have not: they can be compensated in the afterlife. By refusing to commit an injustice, the sheriff is also promoting the greatest good. Any mundane injustice, then, can be put right in the afterlife (D 115, 254–7). Clarke does offer consequentialist arguments against the breaking of the rules of righteousness (D 224), but again he should not be seen as a utilitarian or any kind of consequentialist. God's purpose in creating the world, and promoting justice within it, is to advance the well-being

---

[2] Clarke says this is true 'in the whole'; but it is not clear how he could allow any exceptions. He probably intends to contrast the claim with more specific, and doubtful, claims involving particular conceptions of the good.

of his creatures; but he himself recognizes the independent normative weight of justice.

The afterlife allows Clarke to avoid conflicts not only within his pluralistic ethics, but between that ethics and self-interest. Clarke's claims about well-being strongly suggest he was a substantive hedonist. Even God's own happiness is to be understood as the eternal enjoyment of his own infinite perfections (D 113). We ourselves can share that enjoyment in the afterlife, along with the pleasurable awareness of God's favour, which of course requires virtue on earth (P 85–7; also 165). But God's reason for establishing the afterlife is not purely one of benevolence. It is only fitting that the virtuous be rewarded, and the vicious punished (D 148–50, 244). And manifest mundane injustices, in which the virtuous do worse than they should, and the vicious better, are themselves evidence of the afterlife: God would not leave his creation so disordered (vice indeed constitutes such disordering (D 244), and posthumous rewards and punishments are required for his commands to constitute proper laws (D 151, 248–52, 260).

Unlike Hutcheson, Clarke does not insist that truly virtuous motivation will be purely other-regarding. Clarke allows that the Christian view of the afterlife will inspire human beings happily to surrender earthly enjoyments for the sake of the pleasures of the afterlife gained through virtue (P 46). In a perfect world, virtue would always be the chief good, consisting as it does in the enjoyment and imitation of God (D 258–9). But in our corrupted world, virtue only *tends* to make people as happy as possible (D 150). So it can only be a means to the chief good, and morality requires the assistance of the supernatural (D 303). Realizing, presumably, that it makes the afterlife morally unnecessary, Clarke explicitly rejects outright the Stoic view that virtue and happiness are bound to coincide in this life (D 221, 223, 258).[3] He does claim at certain points that mundane pleasures are worthless (138–9, 171), suggesting that on our deathbeds we shall correctly judge that the only pleasures are to be found in virtue. But this must be exaggeration, since again it would make the afterlife unnecessary for moral motivation. Clarke's reflective view incorporates an egoistic veto: it is not reasonable to expect people to give up their life and current pleasures for no later reward. Virtue is indeed the most direct route to the primary and necessary component in happiness that consists in inner peace and satisfaction (D 253), and that satisfaction is greater than that to be found in sensual enjoyment; but sometimes virtue is not enough. The afterlife, then, is required for the defence and enforcement of moral principles, and for reliable moral motivation in the case of each of us (P 79–80; D172–3, 306, 332).

As Sidgwick notes (1902: 181–3; see also Shaver 1999: 112–14), the role Clarke gives to self-interest introduces a tension into his position. Consider a world like ours, except without an afterlife. What would a rational agent do in such a world? On the one hand, as we have seen, Clarke believes that immoral behaviour is irrational, and arises

---

[3] As noted by Irwin (2008: 474), Clarke appears to reject the Stoic view on hedonist grounds, failing to discuss the view that happiness is to be identified with virtue itself.

through false belief and bad habits; on the other, he claims that in certain unusual circumstances, absent an afterlife, virtue would be unreasonable. Clarke wishes morality to be autonomous and normatively overriding, and he also recognizes the hedonic costs of virtue in some cases. But he cannot bring himself to give up psychological and probably also the egoistic veto in ego-restricted pluralism (see Shaver 1992: 2, 111).[4]

[4] Le Rossignol (1892: 80) argues against Sidgwick that the afterlife removes any tension in Clarke's position. But Clarke's claims about the rationality of ethics, and his mathematical analogy, strongly suggest that ethical principles as conceived by him are overriding independently of the afterlife.

11

Reid:

The Goodness of Virtue, and its Limits

The Scottish 'common-sense' philosopher Thomas Reid (1710–96) began his career as a Minister of the Church of Scotland, but resigned this position to take up a professorship at King's College, Aberdeen. In 1764 he succeeded Adam Smith as Professor of Moral Philosophy at the University of Glasgow. Like Butler, Reid is hard to characterize as either a 'rationalist' or a 'sentimentalist'. There is evidence that his moral philosophy developed throughout his philosophical career, and it culminated in some important chapters in his final work, *Essays on the Active Powers of Man*, published in 1788.[1] As the editors note (ix), Reid saw Butler as especially significant, along with Socrates and Cicero, and the similarities between their positions are often striking.[2] Reid believes that human nature itself provides evidence of God's intentions, and that virtue consists in following those intentions ('Introduction' 5; 3.3.6.178; 3.5.1.273). Reid uses the watch analogy (4.1.191), and argues that conscience—the faculty which gives us access to moral truth—clearly has a divine origin (3.3.7.185; 4.1.192) and that its deliverances take priority over other principles of action (3.5.1.271). Reid understands reason as 'calm' (3.3.2.157); but he believes also that the motivational power of reason is insufficient, and requires the support of benevolent sentiments (3.2.3.107–8), understanding benevolence as consisting largely in various 'partial' concerns (3.2.4). These benevolent passions are themselves 'ultimate', and should not be reduced to disguised self-interest (3.2.3.110). There is easily enough here to make it appropriate to describe Reid's ethics as 'Butlerian'. But he does not agree on everything with Butler, accepting, for example, the existence of genuinely malevolent affection (3.2.5), along with a non-hedonist conception of well-being (see below). Further, Reid's variations on Butlerian themes are penetrating and original, and had important influences on later philosophers, and so clearly require our attention.

---

[1] Unattributed references are to this work, where appropriate by essay, part (if appropriate), chapter, and page numbers. Page numbers are omitted when the reference is to a whole chapter. Another important source for Reid's ethics is Reid 2007: esp. I–IX.

[2] See also Sidgwick 1902: 227; Schneewind 1977: 64; Davis 2006: 28; the editorial introduction to Reid's *Practical Ethics* (2007: xvi–vii, xxii); Irwin 2008: 754.

In the third essay, Reid describes three types of principles of action. *Mechanical* principles, which include both instinct and habit (3.1.2–3), involve neither will nor intention (3.3.1.152). *Animal* principles, such as desire or affection (3.2), involve will and intention, as well as belief or 'opinion', but not rational decision or 'judgement'. Again, like Butler, Reid follows the standard philosophical line in characterizing human beings as rational in opposition to non-rational animals, who can act only on their strongest desire at the time of action. Only human beings are capable of self-government by reason, and so of moral virtue (4.1.190). The *rational* principles, then, are those involving the exercise of practical reason. One of these principles is that which concerns our 'good on the whole' (3.3.2). Unlike animals and young children, we have the capacity to consider our possible actions from a temporally extended point of view. Imagine that my strongest desire is currently to φ, but I know from past experience that φ-ing is almost certain to do me more harm than good. It is clear, Reid plausibly claims, that the principle concerned with my good on the whole should rationally take priority, and that I would by φ-ing open myself to justified criticism.

The claim that this principle is the sole rational principle is rational egoism, against which Reid offers several objections (3.3.4). First, most human beings are unable to adopt the extended point of view required by the principle. We tend to be ignorant of what is best for us, and even when we do know—perhaps even through our own philosophizing—we often fail to act in the light of that knowledge, being overcome in the moment by our animal passions. A sense of duty, along with guilt and its other sanctions, will prove a much better motivator than 'a dubious view of distant good'.

Reid is here making an empirical point about human capacities. If he were right, then a rational egoist could agree that rational agents should adopt some action-guiding principle other than rational egoism itself. Further, lying behind Reid's argument is his position on well-being, which as we shall see admits virtue as a significant component. On this account, our moral failures only compound the hedonic effects of weakness of will on our own well-being. At the very least, it is less clear on a hedonist account of well-being that a strict application of rational egoism is self-defeating.

Reid's position on virtue as a component of well-being emerges explicitly in his second argument. An enlightened egoist will recognize that their greatest good requires them to be virtuous. But this motivation will not allow them to exemplify the 'noblest kind of virtue', which involves love of virtue or the common good for its own sake: 'it is the image of this divine attribute in the human character, that is the glory of man'.

Again, however, Reid's argument concerns decision-procedures rather than normative principles. Rational egoism is quite consistent with the view that pursuit of virtue for its own sake will maximize the agent's own good. The only problem is the technical one of how to bring such motivation about. If one is lucky, one may have been brought up to love virtue for itself, perhaps through the associationist route described by John Gay (SR 15.1). Otherwise, one should seek to change one's own habits of attention, perhaps through spending time with others who love virtue. One might anyway question the moral value placed by Reid on lack of self-regard. Consider, for example, the virtuous person—

perhaps as described by Aristotle (1894: 9.8)—who combines genuine concern for others with full awareness of the truth that their own good provides them with reasons to act.

Reid states his third argument elsewhere with an explicit reference to Butler (3.3.4.166n86). The concern for one's own good, he suggests, is not in itself enjoyable to exercise, and brings with it unpleasant emotions such as fear and anxiety. As does Butler himself, Reid seems to be running together general and particular principles. It may be true that the principle of self-concern is itself practically empty without some substantive conception of well-being. But just as it can bring no good on its own, it can bring no harm either. If all I know is that I should pursue my own good, but I have no idea what is good or harmful, I can have nothing to fear or be anxious about. It could be said that I might fear just not attaining my maximum good; but then it is not clear why I should not enjoy the prospect of attaining that good. But the fear and anxiety Reid is thinking of is almost certainly that concerning harms, and there seems no reason why someone, with some substantive conception of good, might not take pleasure in the prospect of attaining future goods.

Reid goes on to claim that the pursuit of virtue for the sake of self-interest is more painful than that for its own sake. This again is an empirical claim, which provides at most a technical challenge for the rational egoist. And again it can be questioned. Given our natural benevolence, the egoist may argue, it is not unlikely that the agent who allows herself to follow those inclinations purely in order to advance their own good will in fact find such a course of action as enjoyable as that of the agent pursuing virtue for its own sake. There are ways, then, in which the rational egoist can themselves exploit the resources of a Butlerian moral psychology.

At this point we should also note that Reid is another of those who appeal to the pleasures of virtue and the pains of vice (e.g. 3.3.7.183–6). The 'testimony of conscience', he claims, is 'the purest, the most noble and valuable of all human enjoyments'. This is because of its intrinsic dignity and intensity, and also because of its stability, duration, its being under our control, and its immunity to bad luck. Remorse, on the other hand, is full of pain and self-hate.

Reid's claims seem as questionable as those by Hutcheson (SR 8.4.penultimate paragraph). Mundane virtuous actions, or virtue in certain dire circumstances, seem often more painful than pleasurable, and at least some vicious individuals seem truly unconcerned about the moral status of their actions and characters. Further, as we shall see below, Reid, like many of his predecessors, is forced to appeal to the afterlife to justify virtue in all circumstances, and like some of his predecessors faces the difficulty of explaining how a Christian believer can act purely for the sake of virtue fully aware of the fact that they will be maximally rewarded for so doing in the afterlife if not before.

Reid's arguments against rational egoism suffer in general from a failure to distinguish clearly between normative theory and accounts of decision-procedures.[3] He is

---

[3] Cuneo (2010: 246–7) claims that Reid believed that a moral theory has to be transparent. But there is no evidence that Reid clearly identified the contradictory view, or that he offers arguments for transparency.

on far stronger ground in his suggestion that the egoistic principle does not stand alone: 'The ends of human actions I have in view, are two, to wit, What is good for us upon the whole, and what appears to be our duty' (3.3.1.154; also e.g. 3.3.5.169). Reid is careful to point out that, though these ends are entirely consistent, they are—contrary to the views of those many philosophers who have identified them—to be distinguished conceptually (3.3.1.159). Reid is, then, like Hutcheson, a dualist of the practical reason.[4] But, unlike Hutcheson, and again like Butler, he is a deontologist. In criticizing Hume's account of justice, Reid claims (correctly) that utility is not itself a moral notion (3.5.5.302), and continues: 'when men come to the exercise of their moral faculty, they perceive a turpitude in injustice, as they do in other crimes, and consequently an obligation to justice, abstracting from the consideration of its utility' (3.5.5.306; also 3.5.5.327).[5]

What is the relation between Reid's two principles? They are in complete harmony: 'They are very strictly connected, lead to the same course of conduct, and cooperate with each other' (3.3.1.154; also 3.3.3.159; 3.3.5.173). For that reason, there is no need for Reid to assert the normative priority of duty over self-interest: our faculty of reason comprehends both (3.3.5.173). But Reid follows Butler in asserting the priority of conscience. He emphasizes the greater value of the principle that we should obey our conscience and do what is right *because* it is right: it is both more noble than the principle of self-interest, and in many cases a clearer guide to action (3.3.5.169–72). And this noble principle 'ought never to stoop to any other', being intended by nature and hence God 'to be the immediate guide and director of our conduct' (3.3.8.194, 191; also 3.5.1.271).

Reid follows Butler also, then, in his view that vice is unnatural (3.5.1.273), but, as we have seen, narrows the potential gap between his two principles by claiming also that virtue itself is a constituent of well-being (3.3.3.160–3). Consider what you would wish as the greatest good for a close relative or friend: a life of honour, rather than a life of sensual pleasure (or, presumably, though Reid does not say this, a vicious life containing sensual and other kinds of pleasure). Further, my affections for others in effect make the good of others part of my own (3.3.4.164). But virtue is not the only good: the view that even eternal misery does not matter is 'the extravagance of some Mystics' (3.3.8.193). But this of course raises the question of whether there may not be cases in which the degree of misery is such that the value of virtue is outweighed. Here Reid

---

[4] Note that Hutcheson can also be read as accepting a 'triplism' of the practical reason, in which a duty of piety sits alongside reasons or duties of benevolence to oneself and to others (see above pp. 122–3). At 3.5.2.282, Reid speaks approvingly of the Christian triad of duties to God, self, and neighbour; but he would see all these as distinct from the principle of self-concern. In a manuscript (see 3.3.1.159n79; 3.5.1.271–2n1), Reid describes himself as taking a 'Middle way' between Epicureanism and Stoicism, probably having in mind, respectively, egoistic hedonism and the view that well-being consists only in virtue. The Stoic 'wise man' was one in whom a regard to the *honestum* swallowed up every other principle of action' (3.3.8.192; also 3.3.3.16). In other words, Reid's view allows for reasons grounded in self-interest and reasons grounded in duty.

[5] Reid does accept a principle of benevolence (3.5.1.273, item (3)). His point is that its status as a duty is not itself a matter of utility.

might have insisted that virtue is always more valuable than the avoidance of any amount of suffering. But, plausibly enough, he would probably have seen this view as more extravagant mysticism. Rather, again like many of his predecessors, he seems to appeal to the afterlife to ensure a necessary overlap between duty and self-interest (3.3.8.193–4):[6]

While the world is under a wise and benevolent administration, it is impossible, that any man should, in the issue, be a loser by doing his duty.

The atheist, by contrast, is, as Shaftesbury puts it, 'without remedy':

He must either sacrifice his happiness to virtue, or virtue to happiness; and is reduced to this miserable dilemma, whether it be best to be a fool or a knave.[7]

---

[6] The reference to the afterlife is here, as elsewhere in the *Essays*, somewhat veiled. Wolterstorff (2010: 201) sees Reid's argument as purely mundane, grounded on the hedonic value of the testimony of conscience. But if Reid does indeed see that value as always outweighing the hedonic costs of virtue, then it is not clear why the atheist faces any difficulty, since the pleasure of virtue is equally open to them (except for the pleasure of piety, and there is no evidence that Reid is putting special weight on that virtue in this text). Note also Reid's lectures on the soul, where he claims that there is the 'greatest probability' that in this life virtue is not always rewarded and vice punished, and that reason could not approve of an administration of the world which did not remedy this injustice (2002: 622–3). As Cuneo notes (2010: 256), Reid goes on to accept that it is not unreasonable to doubt his claims about God and the afterlife (2002: 629). His view, that is to say, is a matter of probability rather than certainty (630).

[7] As Irwin notes (2008: 806), Reid seems to exaggerate the practical implications of atheism here, since someone who accepts both principles might follow each of them at many points.

12

Hume:
Morality as Utility

We have already seen the full spectrum of views on the rationality of partiality represented in the period of British moral philosophy under discussion. We began with one
extreme, Hobbesian egoism, and then found Cumberland shortly after Hobbes advocating action to promote the overall good, entirely impartially. And between these
extremes, we have seen a consequentialist or utilitarian form of the dualism of practical
reason in Hutcheson, and a deontological form in several other philosophers. The
question of where to place David Hume (1711–76) on this spectrum is not
straightforward.

Hume was an important essayist and historian, but he is now best known for his
philosophy, which is one of the key statements of empiricism. Hume was also broadly
naturalist, and was certainly committed to some form of scepticism, though exactly
which remains a matter of much debate. Hume attended the University of Edinburgh
while still a child, and began work on his *Treatise of Human Nature* (1739–40) when he
was twenty-three. His scepticism and suspected atheism led to the failure of his application for a chair at Edinburgh in 1745. In 1751, he published the *Enquiry concerning
the Principles of Morals*, a development of the third book of the *Treatise*.[1]

Hume is a remarkably deep thinker, but also something of an indirect writer. He is
certainly no egoist; but whether he is a utilitarian has been a matter of much debate.[2]

[1] The so-called 'second *Enquiry*' (E) is the main source for Hume's normative ethics, since the *Treatise*
(T) focuses primarily on the epistemology and metaphysics of ethics. Also significant are his collected
Essays. References to T will locate passages according to book, part, section, and paragraph, respectively,
except for the 'Introduction', to which reference will be by paragraph alone. Those to E will be by section or
to the appendix ('App.') or to 'A Dialogue' (D), and by paragraph, and to the *Essays* by part, number, and
page (I treat 'Essays Withdrawn and Unpublished' as part 3), except in the case of 'My Own Life', which is
included in the front matter of the *Essays*). Hume himself regretted publishing the *Treatise* at such a young
age, at one point even recommending that his views be judged solely on the basis of later work (Norton and
Norton 2007: 586–7). In his autobiography he famously describes the second *Enquiry* as 'incomparably the
best' of all his writings (*Essays*, 'My Own Life': xxxii). I shall again assume that Hume's thought can be
treated as continuous, at least on the topics I discuss, in the absence of strong evidence to the contrary.
[2] For the view that in some sense he is, see e.g. Stephen 1876: 2.86–7; Laird 1932: 236; MacIntyre 1959:
457–8; Broiles 1964: 25, 94; Plamenatz 1966: 22, 28; Glossop 1967: 535–6; Rawls 1999: 20n9; Harrison 1981:
33, 88; Rosen 1996: lxiii; Sobel 1997: 58; 2009: chs 5–6; Rosen 2003: ch. 3; Ashford 2005; Hardin 2007: 231.
Utilitarian interpretations are denied in e.g. Wand 1962: 193–6; Botwinick 1977; Mackie 1980: 151–4;

According to standard act utilitarianism, right actions are those which maximize over-all utility, and they are right just because they have this property. Hume is not an act utilitarian, allowing that it is sometimes right to act in ways that fail to maximize—and are known by the relevant agents to to fail to maximize—utility. So Hume might be described as a deontologist, who believes, for example, that the keeping of a promise is right (when it is right) because of its being what it is—the fulfilling of a promise. But this description would be somewhat misleading, since the deontic right-making prop-erties are not explanatorily ultimate. We can ask what it is that makes a property a right-making property, and here Hume's answer is utilitarian. His first-order view on actions, then, is analogous to those forms of rule utilitarianism, according to which the right action is that consistent with the ideal set of rules, viz., that set of rules which, if followed by all, or a majority, would maximize utility; but Hume's indirect form of utilitarianism must be stated with reference not to the ideal set of rules, but the ideal set of motives, or *character*.[3] The right action is that which would be performed by (or perhaps advised by; see Sobel 2009: 164–5) the agent with the ideal character, that character being the type that would in general maximize utility.

One might, then, describe Hume then as a 'character-utilitarian'. But there are sev-eral further complications. First, Hume does not engage in the ethics of action in the standard way. He believes that when we praise an action as, say, right, what we are really seeking to praise is the character of the person who performs it. Second, he does not engage in the ethics of character in the usual way either, and would probably have rejected the attribution to him of character-utilitarianism above as itself explanatorily lacking. On the standard view, two individuals might both adopt the moral point of view or perspective, and then disagree over whether, for example, the morally ideal character is that which maximizes utility overall or that which results in performing independently right actions (such as keeping promises) or feeling independently admirable feelings (such as compassion). But Hume understands the moral point of view itself as essentially involving the kind of impartiality between oneself and others found in standard forms of act utilitarianism. For him, there cannot be a fully deonto-logical form of moral theory. Finally, Hume does not see morality, grounded as it is in extreme impartiality, as overriding. He allows for forms of partiality to self and others which can conflict with, and in some cases, outweigh moral considerations.

In this chapter, I shall defend and elucidate this interpretation, aiming to bring out some of the power and subtlety of Hume's position, and to show how in his work the

Capaldi 1989: 303–5; Long 1990: 12–13, 23, 26; Baier, A. 1991: 250; 2013: 415; Sayre-McCord 1996: 280; Baillie 2000: 146–7; Lecaldano 2008: 269; O'Brien 2012: 301n13; Cléro 2013; Swanton 2015: ch. 5; Garrett 2015: 326; Reichlin 2016. There is more consensus on the view that Hume's position in the *Enquiry* is closer to utilitarianism than that in the *Treatise*; see e.g. Rosen 2003: 29; Cohon 2006: esp. 273; see also Mackie 1980: 153.
[3] At T 3.3.3.9, Hume claims that the 'ultimate test of merit and virtue' rests on whether a person's char-acter is 'as little wanting to himself as to others'. If it is, that character 'must so far be allow'd to be entirely perfect'.

possibility of genuine, full-blooded sacrifice, both subjective and objective, is finally regained.[4]

1. Hume, the Moral Anthropologist?

Before proceeding with any examination of that position, I must first deal with the objection that Hume is best seen merely as a philosophical anthropologist out to discover the nature of the morality, rather than to justify or recommend it or any particular moral theory.[5]

There is no doubt that much of Hume's ethics is descriptive. His broad-brush portrait of morality, as well as the detailed sketches of individual virtues and character traits, rank as among the most significant since Aristotle. Further, Hume himself seems to characterize his project as entirely descriptive. He introduces the *Treatise* with the claim: 'The sole end of logic is to explain the principles and operations of our reasoning faculty, and the nature of our ideas: morals and criticism regard our tastes and sentiments' (T Intro. 5). And he closes it by drawing an analogy between himself and an anatomist, saying:

The anatomist ought never to emulate the painter; nor in his accurate dissections and portraitures of the smaller parts of the human body, pretend to give his figures any graceful and engaging attitude or expression...An anatomist, however, is admirably fitted to give advice to a painter...[T]he most abstract speculations concerning human nature, however cold and unentertaining, become subservient to *practical morality*; and may render this latter science more correct in its precepts, and more perswasive in its exhortations.[6]

We must not lose sight of the fact that a central aim of Hume in his ethical writings is to *explain* morality: to offer an 'anatomical' account of its origin, its nature, and its content. But even here he is suggesting that just as the painter can learn from the anatomist, so the moral agent can learn from abstract philosophy. And in his later writings Hume came to state more clearly that the very distinction between abstract speculation and practical morality was not as sharp as these passages from the *Treatise* might suggest, and that the moral philosopher might have a directly normative contribution to make to practical ethics.[7] In an essay published before the *Enquiry*, Hume is indeed wary of seeing it as part of the role of philosophy to offer advice on the ends to be sought in life.

---

[4] This full-blooded notion of sacrifice has, I presume, been part of common sense for millennia; in the western philosophical tradition before Hume it is rare, but as I have suggested (see above p. 4n6) may be found at least in Plato's *Republic*.

[5] For this common view, see e.g. Mackie 1980: 5–6, 152; Darwall 1994: 61. See also the many references in Shaver 1995: 317; Shaver's paper provides further arguments against a purely descriptive interpretation of Hume. See also e.g. Cohon 2008: 9.1–2.

[6] T 3.3.6.6; see also Hume 1975: sect. 1, para. 5. For an interesting reading of the quoted passage, which sees it as drawing the engaging/accurate distinction rather than the prescriptive/descriptive distinction, see Shaver 1992: 319.

[7] See Sayre-McCord 1994: 203–4. It is likely that Hume was, to some extent, stung by Hutcheson's complaint that the *Treatise* lacked 'a certain Warmth in the Cause of Virtue' (Hume 1932: letter 13 [1739]).

But, he says, 'to satisfy you, I shall deliver my opinion upon the matter, and shall only desire you to esteem it of as little consequence as I do myself. By that means you will neither think it worthy of your ridicule nor your anger'.[8] Hume goes on to argue that 'the happiest disposition of mind is the *virtuous*', and notes that one role of philosophy is that '[it] insensibly refines the temper, and it points out to us those dispositions which we should endeavour to attain, by a consistent bent of mind, and by repeated habit' (*Essays* 1.18.168, 171). This, presumably, is what he sees himself as doing in the *Enquiry*, when he describes the several qualities of Cleanthes, noting: 'A philosopher might select this character as a model of perfect virtue' (E.9.2; also Shaver 1992: 320).

In the *Enquiry* itself, we find strong implications of normative positions. In the first section, for example, Hume suggests that no one can avoid making moral judgements: 'Let a man's insensibility be ever so great, he must often be touched with the images of RIGHT and WRONG' (E 1.2; cf. 5.39). It is pretty easy, he claims, to enumerate 'estimable or blameable' human qualities, and:

> The only object of reasoning is to discover the circumstances on both sides, which are common to these qualities; to observe that particular in which the estimable qualities agree on the one hand, and the blameable on the other; and thence to reach the foundation of ethics, and find those universal principles, from which all censure or approbation is ultimately derived. (E 1.10)

We can deduce, then, that Hume to some degree accepted the morality he describes, and that he would have seen his own praise and blame for the qualities he describes as resting on the principles he outlines. The philosophical anthropologist arrives, one might suggest, at some of their conclusions through introspection of their own commitments: If this is right, then the morality Hume describes is likely to be, in large part, his own practical morality.

It is true that in the *Enquiry* Hume continues to see the aim of his project as 'being more the speculative, than the practical part of morals' (E 2.5). But note the comparative nature of his remark here, and the fact that he makes it after admitting that, having 'forgotten' this fact, he has provided various considerations in favour of the view that the social virtues are 'estimable'. He continues:

> [N]o qualities are more entitled to the general good-will and approbation of mankind, than beneficence and humanity, friendship and gratitude, natural affection and public spirit, or whatever proceeds from a tender sympathy with others, and a generous concern for our kind and species.

The end of the *Enquiry*, moreover, is a clear admission by Hume that he saw the respective analytic and commendatory aims of abstract speculation and of practical morality as both within his purview:

---

[8] 'The Sceptic', E 18.161–2. I take it that, unlike the three essays preceding it ('The Epicurean', 'The Stoic', and 'The Platonist'), this essay contains ethical views at least close to those of Hume himself. See e.g. Green and Grose 1889: 47; Fogelin 1985: 117–22. For a dissenting view, see Immerwahr 1989.

Having explained the moral *approbation* attending merit or virtue, there remains nothing, but briefly to consider our interested *obligation* to it, and to enquire, whether every man, who has any regard to his own happiness and welfare, will not find his account in the practice of every moral duty. If this can be clearly ascertained from the foregoing theory, we shall have the satis-faction to reflect, that we have advanced principles, which not only, it is hoped, will stand the test of reasoning and enquiry, but may contribute to the amendment of men's lives, and their improvement in morality and social virtue. (E 9.14)

Hume goes on to suggest that his philosophical account of morality has represented virtue 'in all her genuine and most engaging charms', thus recognizing that a descrip-tion can itself attract people to its object (E 9.15). The conclusion of the *Enquiry* is a famous paean to virtue, closing with the Platonic view of virtue as a superior pleasure: 'These natural pleasures, indeed, are really without price; both because they are below all price in their attainment, and above it in their enjoyment'.[9]

Nor—despite what the 'anatomical analogy' may in isolation suggest—is Hume's view in the *Enquiry* a change of mind as opposed to a change of emphasis. If we look back, we shall find in the *Treatise* the same recognition that descriptions can engage or attract:

Were it proper in such a subject to bribe the readers assent, or employ any thing but solid argu-ment, we are here abundantly supply'd with topics to engage the affections. All lovers of virtue (and such we all are in speculation, however we may degenerate in practice) must certainly be pleas'd to see moral distinctions deriv'd from so noble a source, which gives us a just notion both of the *generosity* and *capacity* of our nature. (T 3.3.6.3)

In recent years, it has become common to attribute to Hume a form of practical scep-ticism, based on his view of motivation, which would also threaten my interpretative project. Christine Korsgaard, for example, suggests that 'Hume's view is that there is no such thing as practical reason at all' (1997: 222), and Garrett Cullity and Berys Gaut ascribe to Hume the position that 'there are no normative practical reasons' (1997: 7).

Anything approaching a full discussion of this issue is beyond the scope of this chapter, but it does seem to me that the case for such a strong form of scepticism is far from proven. Consider, for example, the fact that Hume is 'contented with saying, that reason requires' certain conduct (T 3.3.1.18). Of course, he believes that what we think of as the reason that *opposes* passion is in fact itself a 'determination' of a passion, a calm one. But this is a view about what practical reason is: Hume's scepticism is about not practical reason as such, but a particular conception of it. And it is important to remember also that this determination is itself 'founded on some distant view or reflexion', and that it 'correct[s]' the (violent) passions.[10] It has, that is, a cognitive

---

[9] E 9.25. See Plato, *Republic*, 580d3–588a11; see also above pp. 88–90, 125.
[10] T 3.3.1.18; see also T 3.3.1.21. These calm passions can also be 'corroborated by reflection' (T 2.3.8.13). For a plausible explanation of how these claims can be fitted into Hume's subjectivist framework, see Cohon 1997: 835–9.

grounding,[11] and Hume provides us with the resources for claiming, if not reasonableness, then 'correctness' for certain calm passions. More on this below.

Hume is contented to speak also of normative reasons. He asks, for example, if I have borrowed some money, '*What reason or motive have I restore [it]?*'.[12] It is worth recalling as well that Hume thought that his view that virtue and vice lie 'in the senses' had no implications for the 'reality' of these qualities, or for moral practice or first-order ethical theory.[13] Even if the most plausible interpretation of Hume is as some kind of sceptic about practical reason, he innoculates normative ethics against any potentially paralyzing implications of metaethics.

So, though Hume is not sanguine about the effectiveness of philosophy as a normative enterprise,[14] we can conclude that not only did he attribute this role to it, but he was prepared to allow his own philosophy to play that role. We are, therefore, entitled to ask normative questions of Hume.

2. Ethics of Action, Ethics of Motive

First-order philosophical ethics usually focuses on actions. The act utilitarian will claim that the right action is that which maximizes utility, the Kantian that which is performed on the basis of the Categorical Imperative, and so on. Hume is certainly prepared to make judgements about actions. It is clear, for example, that he thinks I have a duty to repay a debt (T 3.2.1.9). This obligation is, in part at least, one of justice. In order to understand Hume's view of the rightness of actions, then, let me begin by considering his account of the virtue of justice (T 3.2.2; E 3).

Hume suggests that human beings are driven to a great extent by self-interest, and by love of those close to them (see T 3.2.5.8; 3.3.2.10).[15] Unregulated, these passions would be destructive of society, and harmful to all, so the institution of justice develops to solve this problem. It is not itself consciously instituted, but develops as a convention in the way that two people rowing a boat fall into a certain rhythm without agreeing beforehand. So justice is artificial, a device to deal with two important features of the human situation: our limited generosity, and the scarcity of goods. Were we not

---

[11] See Kydd 1946: 137; Stroud 1977: 192; Norton 1982: 120, 129.

[12] T 3.2.1.9. It is true that Hume does not, in this passage or elsewhere, distinguish as clearly as he might between motivating and normative reasons. But the context here suggests that he is implying that he himself would be motivated to return the loan by his concern for justice, and that his being motivated would itself consist partly in his taking justice to be a 'sufficient [normative] reason for' him to make the return.

[13] *Essays* 1.18.166 n. 3; see also T. 3.1.1.2.

[14] The final paragraph of 'The Sceptic' (*Essays* 1.18.180) claims that 'human life is more governed by fortune than by reason', and concludes that its value is so low that even reasoning about it would be to overvalue it, were it not that 'this occupation is one of the most amusing, in which life could possibly be employed'.

[15] I take at face value Hume's frequent mentions of 'self-interest', seeing the question of how his conception of self-interest relates to his view of the self as a 'bundle of perceptions' (T 1.4.6.4) as extraneous to my discussion.

partial, or were the goods with which justice is concerned not scarce, the institution of justice would be unnecessary.

As yet, the moral sentiments have not entered the story.[16] They do so through the operation of a remarkable human faculty: sympathy. By 'sympathy' Hume means not some specific feeling or emotion, but the capacity we have to take on the sentiments of others. Once the institution of justice is in place—protecting our property, for example—I shall feel an unpleasant sensation if I see you about to break some principle of justice protecting some of my property. But because of my capacity to sympathize, I shall feel the same 'uneasiness' if I see you about to threaten someone else, or even hear of some breach of justice long ago, to someone not known to me. This uneasiness is a moral sentiment, and a natural one, and it is impartial in the sense that it does not vary in proportion to the intensity of my concern for the threatened individual. The institution of justice has to work, so it cannot repeat the biases towards self and near and dear which it is its function to counteract. It has to operate as a system of communication between all people, so it rests on 'the general survey',[17] an impartial point of view from which each person should, as it were, see and feel things the same way. This natural sentiment is also 'augmented by a new *artifice*, and...the public instructions of politicians, and the private education of parents, contribute to the giving us a sense of honour and duty' (T 3.2.6.11). 'Thus *self-interest* is the original motive to the *establishment* of justice: But a sympathy with *public* interest is the source of the *moral* approbation, which attends that virtue.'[18]

Hume's account of the virtue of justice seems, on the face of it, to be broadly utilitarian:

[J]ustice is a moral virtue, merely because it has that tendency to the good of mankind; and, indeed, is nothing but an artificial invention to that purpose. The same may be said of allegiance, of the laws of nations, of modesty, and of good-manners. All these are mere human contrivances for the interest of society.[19]

---

[16] Hume believes they arise after the laws of justice have been established on the basis of self-interest: T. 3.2.6.11. Note that it is not only sympathy which explains the moral sentiments. Reason also plays a central role: 'Men are superior to beasts principally by the superiority of their reason' (T 3.3.4.5), and it is on account of their inferior 'knowledge and understanding' that animals 'have little or no sense of virtue or vice...and are incapable of' participating in institutions such as those of 'right and property' (T 2.1.12.5). See Tranöy 1959: 100.
[17] T 3.2.2.24. I discuss this notion further below in sect. 4.
[18] T 3.2.2.24; see also 3.2.5.15 (on the utilitarian foundation of promising); 3.2.6.6; E 3.22 (on the foundation of law); E 4.20 (on the foundation of the laws of war and conflict).
[19] T 3.3.1.9; see also 3.2.6.1. Sayre-McCord (1996: 280, 289–90) has objected to a utilitarian interpretation of Hume's conception of justice that Hume is concerned with not the good of all, but the good of each. Hume is quite prepared, however, as we see in this passage, to speak of the good of society as a whole, and because he believed justice to be in the interest of all (T 3.2.2.2) he had no reason to draw any distinction between the good of all and the good of each such as might be necessary for one considering, in the light of the 'separateness of persons' (see Findlay 1961: 235–6; Rawls 1999: 24), whether the overall good might justify the sacrifice of the good of a particular individual. Further, since the normative significance of the separateness of persons almost without exception is made to depend on considerations of justice independent

A somewhat similar story may be told regarding the 'natural' virtues, such as ben-evolence.[20] If you are my sister, a mere natural desire to help you is not sufficient to ground my sentiment as a moral one. Moral sentiments are based on impartiality, so that I shall view my helping you, and some stranger's helping another stranger, as mor-ally equivalent, and worthy of the same praise or admiration. And, just as the institu-tion of justice emerges to provide various social benefits, so do the natural virtues:

The necessity of justice to the support of society is the SOLE foundation of that virtue; and since no moral excellence is more highly esteemed, we may conclude, that this circumstance of usefulness has, in general, the strongest energy, and most entire command over our sentiments. It must, therefore, be the source of a considerable part of the merit ascribed to humanity, benevolence, friendship, public spirit, and other social virtues of that stamp.[21]

According to act utilitarianism, the right action is that which maximizes utility, or expected utility. Given Hume's grounding of a virtue-centred, common-sense moral-ity on its utility, it may be tempting to offer a split-level act utilitarian interpretation of Hume, according to which the right action is that which maximizes utility, and the best way to decide how to act is to follow the norms of common-sense morality.[22]

Hume is not an act utilitarian. This can be seen clearly in those cases of artificial vir-tue in which we are required to act in accordance with the virtue, and not to override it in order to bring about a greater good. A split-level act utilitarian interpreter of Hume may well argue that we should be loath to override the rules of common-sense moral-ity because of the difficulty of predicting consequences reliably. And they may point, for example, to Hume's allowing that, in the several cases that come before a judge, '['t] is impossible to separate the good from the ill' (T 3.2.2.22). But Hume in fact thinks that we should praise an action emerging from a virtuous trait of character even when we *know* that that action is unproductive of utility: 'When a man of merit, of a benefi-cent disposition, restores a great fortune to a miser, or a seditious bigot, he has acted justly and laudably, but the public is a real sufferer' (T 3.3.2.22).

Nor, it is clear, is Hume any kind of rule utilitarian, who appeals to the consequences of the following of moral rules in some imagined situation, such as that in which the majority accepts those rules (see Brandt 1979: ch. 15; Hooker 2000). Justice is a good because it is actually in the public interest, not because it would be so in some imaginary circumstances.

---

of utility, it is hard to see how Hume even has the conceptual space to ascribe independent significance to the each/all distinction.

[20] The natural virtues, according to Hume (T 3.3.1.11–12), do not require artificial institutions, being based on sentiments which human beings will feel naturally and without acculturation. Further, every exercise of a natural virtue will do good, while in the case of the artificial virtues it is only the *system* as a whole that has utilitarian value.

[21] E 3. What Hume means by the claim that 'usefulness' is a source merely of a part of the merit ascribed to the social virtues here will be discussed in the following section.

[22] For the most well-known modern version of such a split-level position, see Hare 1981: ch. 2.

At the level of the rightness of actions, then, Hume is best understood as not *any* kind of utilitarian at all, but as a virtue-centred, common-sense, even deontological moralist, who will praise and blame actions in accordance with his best understanding of that common-sense morality the tenets of which are to a large extent agreed upon.

But—and this is further to justify my use of 'virtue-centred' to describe Hume's version of common-sense morality—Hume's focus in ethics is not *primarily* upon actions at all:

'Tis evident, that when we praise any actions, we regard only the motives that produc'd them, and consider the actions as signs or indications of certain principles in the mind and temper. The external performance has no merit. We must look within to find the moral quality. This we cannot do directly; and therefore fix our attention on actions, as on external signs. But these actions are still consider'd as signs; and the ultimate object of our praise and approbation is the motive, that produc'd them.[23]

It is tempting to assume that Hume is here making a somewhat proto-Kantian point, that what we are concerned about in ethics is not the action as an 'external event', but the agent's intentions. For these, it may be suggested, are what we are, and may be held, responsible for.

This, however, is certainly not Hume's view. He sees no clear or significant distinction between mere natural abilities and moral virtues, and refuses to distinguish between them on the ground of whether a person possesses them voluntarily or not (T 3.3.4.3). First, many moral virtues, such as fortitude, are involuntary. Second, virtue and vice *could* be entirely involuntary, since the notion of vice emerges from the pain or pleasure we feel from the 'general consideration of any quality or character', and qualities can produce pleasure and pain (and hence praise and blame (E App. 4.21)) even when they are involuntary. Third, there is anyway no such thing as free will.

This is not to say that Hume fails to recognize the significance of intention (T 2.2.3.3–10). If you cause me some injury, and I blame you for it, I shall withdraw my criticism if I find that the injury was accidental. But this is not to say that if it were not accidental I should be blaming you because you have performed, voluntarily, a wicked action for which you are morally responsible:

'Tis not enough, that the action arise from the person, and have him for its immediate cause and author. This relation alone is too feeble and inconstant to be a foundation for these passions. It reaches not the sensible and thinking part, and neither proceeds from any thing *durable* in him, nor leaves anything behind it; but passes in a moment, and is as if it had never been. On the other hand, an intention shows certain qualities, which remaining after the action is perform'd, connect it with the person, and facilitate the transition of ideas from one to the other. (T 2.2.3.4; also 3.3.1.5)

It is, then, the durability or the steadiness of moral qualities that leads to their being the primary concern of ethical judgements (see E D 37). As we have seen, Hume is

---

[23] T 3.2.1.2. For objections based on this passage to a utilitarian interpretation of Hume, see Wand 1962: 193; Mackie 1980: 152; Sayre-McCord 1996: 287; see also Darwall 1994: 59–60. Sobel (1997: 56) ascribes to Hume a utilitarian theory of right action based on his utilitarian view of motives. But this seems to me to miss the force of Hume's redirecting our reflective consideration from actions to motives.

prepared to make common-sense moral judgements about actions. But he interprets those judgements as themselves referring to certain moral qualities—virtues—in the agent. We may, then, ask not, 'Which actions should one perform?', but, 'Which qualities should one possess?'. And here Hume's answer is utilitarian: Qualities are justified to the extent that they promote utility.

In this respect, Hume's view may be seen as similar to what Robert Adams has called 'motive utilitarianism'.[24] As Adams characterizes it, this view is that 'the morally perfect person... would have the most useful desires, and have them in exactly the most useful strengths; they would have the most useful among the patterns of motivation that are... possible for human beings'.[25] The best set of motives for me, then, is not those that would, *in my special circumstances*, maximize utility, but those which are most useful in general for human beings to have. Compare Hume:

[T]he tendencies of actions and characters, not their real accidental consequences, are alone regarded in our moral determinations or general judgments... Why is this peach-tree said to be better than that other; but because it produces more or better fruit? And would not the same praise be given it, though snails or vermin had destroyed the peaches, before they came to full maturity? (E 5.41n24)

Now it is important to note that Adams himself distinguishes motives from, for example, traits of character.[26] Hume speaks of motives, qualities of character, virtues, and so on, without drawing clear distinctions between them. If we take 'motive' in its broad Humean sense, Hume's view appears to be a form of motive utilitarianism. But, as I shall suggest in section 4, Hume's motive utilitarianism, though it is indeed a first-order view in the ethics of character (as opposed to the ethics of action, in which, as I have shown, Hume is best understood as a virtue-centred, common-sense moralist), emerges from a utilitarian understanding of the very phenomenon of morality itself. His first-order utilitarianism, that is to say, rests on what one might call 'utilitarian metaethics'. But before discussing this, I must first deal with two common objections to any kind of utilitarian interpretation of Hume.

3. *Maximandum* and Maximization: Two Objections

According to the first objection, if Hume were a utilitarian, he would have to claim that the virtues are based on utility alone. In fact, he says that, in the case of the social

---

[24]   Adams 1976. See Raphael 1972–3: 102; Harrison 1981: 33, 88; Ashford 2005: 69–70.
[25]   Adams 1976: 470. The language of maximization and implicit precision here is alien to Hume, as I shall show in the following section. But the essence of the position—that motives are to be judged in accordance with the principle of utility alone—is entirely Humean.
[26]   Adams 1976: 467. Note also that I do not wish to attribute to Hume the view that there is a *single* set of motives for *every* human to have, as opposed to the view that the list of virtues and vices at any time and place to some extent depends on the circumstances then prevalent. But it may be that Adams would allow his motive utilitarian also to adopt this latter view.

virtues, 'the public utility of these virtues is the *chief* circumstance, whence they derive their merit'.[27]

Hume does indeed state that, in addition to conduciveness to public utility, there are three further classes of quality which serve as the foundation for our esteem of the virtues: (a) qualities useful to ourselves, such as discretion, industry, or frugality (E 6); (b) qualities immediately agreeable to ourselves, such as cheerfulness, greatness of mind, and courage (E 7); (c) qualities immediately agreeable to others, such as good manners, wit, or decency.[28] But in fact he is merely distinguishing between what may be seen as different sources of utility, construed hedonistically. Hume insists that pleasure and pain constitute the 'chief...actuating principle of the human mind' (T 3.3.1.2), and that the 'right enjoyment' of the 'common occurrences of life' is 'the chief part of our happiness' (Essays 1.1.4).[29]

A quality, such as discretion, recommended for its usefulness to oneself is still being recommended on the basis of its promotion of happiness. My own good is part of the social good (see Glossop 1967: 535). It might be objected that these qualities could be being recommended purely on the basis of self-interest. But, in fact, though Hume may allow such recommendation, he also stresses that these virtues are esteemed for the sake of utility, and from the same impartial moral point of view as those virtues conducive to the good of society as a whole (E 6.2–3).

But what about the 'agreeableness' of classes (b) and (c)? Is this not something independent of utility? Not really (*pace* Baier 1991: 204–5). Hume is merely distinguishing between qualities which produce pleasure indirectly, and those which do so directly, as soon as they are confronted.[30] If I am discreet, that will be to my long-term advantage.

---

[27] E 5.4 (italics added); see also E 3.48 quoted in the text above. For the objection, see e.g. Mackie 1980: 151–2; Sayre-McCord 1996: 280; Capaldi 1989: 304; Baier 1991: 205, 250; Beauchamp, 'Editor's Introduction' to Hume's *Enquiry*: 40. Long (1990: 26) argues that Hume's notion of utility is primarily aesthetic, and not to be understood in terms of expedience. In fact exactly the opposite is the case: Hume's aesthetics is itself utilitarian; see e.g. T 2.1.8.2–3; 3.3.1.8.

[28] E 8. The categories are not mutually exclusive. Courage e.g., as well as being agreeable, is of clear utility 'both to the public and to the person possessed of it' (E 7.11).

[29] At T 2.1.1.4, Hume seems to elucidate goodness and badness in terms of pleasure and pain. See also T 2.3.9.1; 2.3.9.8; Karlsson 2006: 246; Baier 2013: 417. Swanton (2015: 60) takes Hume's suggestion (Essays 2.2.269) that happiness 'according to the most received notions, seems to consist in three ingredients: action, pleasure, and indolence' as an expression of a non-hedonist position on well-being. But in the rest of the paragraph Hume goes on to explain the value of both indolence and action in terms of satisfaction, enjoyment, and 'relish'. By 'pleasure', here, Hume seems to have in mind 'passive' pleasures, such as the enjoying of some object one has produced rather than that of the production itself.

[30] See Kemp Smith 1941: 164; Wand 1962: 193; Glossop 1967: 535. Reichlin (2016: 7–8) objects to my collapsing of the distinction between utility and agreeableness on the ground that Hume allows for conflicts between utility and agreeableness (e.g. T 3.3.2.14). But these conflicts are between different sources of utility, as Hume makes clear in the passage just cited e.g. by explaining agreeableness in terms of one's own immediate satisfaction (see Baier 2009: 252). (Similarly, *pace* Gill (2014a: 23), one cannot base a non-utilitarian interpretation of Hume on his claim at T 3.3.34 that our approbation may arise from considerations other than utility.) Reichlin also claims that agreeableness can be understood purely aesthetically, independently of pleasure and pain, citing the example of excessive benevolence (E 7.22). But earlier in the same section, Hume explains the source of our approval of such qualities: 'Their immediate sensation, to the person possessed of them, is agreeable: Others enter into the same humour, and catch the sentiment, by a contagion or

My discretion here can be seen purely instrumentally, but it comes to be admired as a virtue because of its usefulness in the long term in the production of pleasure. In the case of qualities such as cheerfulness, however, the pleasure 'which they communicate to the person possessed of them' is 'immediate' (E 7.29):

No views of utility or of future beneficial consequences enter into this sentiment of approbation; yet it is of a kind similar to that other sentiment, which arises from views of a public or private utility.

The same contrast between immediate and non-immediate pleasure, of course, also underlies the category of 'qualities immediately agreeable to others'. As Hume puts it in the *Treatise*: 'The very essence of virtue...is to produce pleasure, and that of vice to give pain.'[31] The four categories of the virtues merely distinguish between who feels the pleasure and pain as a result of the quality in question, and whether it is felt immediately or not.

A second common objection to any utilitarian interpretation of Hume concerns the notion of maximization. According to a utilitarian theory, the rightness or moral goodness of whatever is the focus of that theory depends on its producing the greatest balance of happiness over unhappiness (see e.g. Mill 1998: 2.2). Hume, however, never speaks in such terms, and the technical apparatus of aggregation, calculation, cost/benefit analysis, and so on, is entirely absent from his writings.[32]

This objection is, as far as it goes, largely correct. Hume does suggest that even common-sense morality demands 'just calculation, and a steady preference of the greater happiness' (E 9.15). But the apparent difference between Hume's position and that of modern, technical utilitarians is indeed striking.

We should not, however, expect a technical version of utilitarianism in Hume. His project begins with everyday morality as it is, seeking justification for those rules we have as opposed to having no rules at all (see Beauchamp 1998: 40). Once he has demonstrated the huge amount of good produced by institutions such as justice, a question may arise about whether these are the *best* institutions, or the best forms of such

---

natural sympathy: And as we cannot forbear loving whatever pleases, a kindly emotion arises towards the person, who communicates so much satisfaction. He is a more animating spectacle: His presence diffuses over us more serene complacency and enjoyment: Our imagination, entering into his feelings and disposition, is affected in a more agreeable manner, than if a melancholy, dejected, sullen, anxious temper were presented to us' (E 7.2). The 'monkish virtues'—celibacy, fasting, and so on—are rejected because they produce no pleasure for others or for the agent, not because they neither produce pleasure nor have some positive aesthetic quality independent of pleasure (E 9.3). I am not here (*pace* Swanton 2015: 91) confusing the criteria for virtue with the pleasures of the moral sentiments: the latter might indeed be seen as partly constitutive of the value of the virtues, but depend on prior and more significant pleasures independent of those of the moral sentiments.

[31] T 2.1.7.4. This seems the clearest evidence that Hume does not hold what Sayre-McCord (1996: 287) calls a 'Bauhaus' theory, which avoids 'any commitment to there being a single overarching standard for evaluating all solutions to problems'; see also T 3.3.1.12. For the claim that right and obligation both have their origin in public utility, see T 3.2.6.8.

[32] For the objection, see Botwinick 1977: 429, 431, 435; Mackie 1980: 152; Sayre-McCord 1996: 280; Beauchamp 1998: 40. Note that Hume is prepared to speak of prudence as aiming at one's 'greatest possible good' (T 2.3.3.10).

institutions, that we might have. Here, however, Hume believes there is an undeniable degree of vagueness in calculating utilities:

That there be a separation or distinction of possessions, and that this separation be steady and constant; this is absolutely required by the interests of society, and hence the origin of justice and property. What possessions are assigned to particular persons; this is, generally speaking, pretty indifferent; and is often determined by very frivolous views and considerations.[33]

Hume believes that attempts to calculate the different utilities of individual components of some moral institution will generally be a waste of time: 'To reduce life to exact rule and method, is commonly a painful, oft a fruitless occupation.'[34] So, since individual moral agents are not being charged with maximizing utility, and since there is little hope of improving the moral institutions we have, any talk of 'maximization' or its equivalent would be otiose. This is not, of course, to say that Hume is entirely conservative. When the overall harms of some element of common-sense morality, or some version of it, are salient, he recommends its abandonment, as in the case of the monkish virtues (E 9.3). But, here again, talk of maximization would be pointless.

The lack of any notion of maximization in Hume is, then, entirely explicable. Nor is the spirit of maximization absent, though doubtless Hume would have found the technical calculations of Bentham and his followers somewhat barbarous. When disagreements arise about what common-sense morality requires, Hume recommends reference to the principle of utility:

[W]herever disputes arise, either in philosophy or common life, concerning the bounds of duty, the question cannot, by any means, be decided with greater certainty, than by ascertaining, on any side, the true interests of mankind.[35]

There seems no reason to think that Hume would deny that one should choose the best option from the point of view of overall utility. But he would stress that exactly what that option is may well be undecideable. '[Q]ualities are approv'd of, in proportion to the advantage, which results from them' (T 3.3.4.11). Or, as he might have put it, 'roughly in proportion'.

But if Hume is so vague about the calculation of utility, should we continue to call him a utilitarian? We should, since other central figures in the utilitarian tradition, including J.S. Mill, have been equally pessimistic about maximization, saying little or nothing about it, and concentrating their attentions on elements of common-sense morality which they saw as clearly pernicious rather than on delicate balancing

---

[33] E App. 3.10n65; see also the text of E App. 3.10 itself. Note that Hume believes that such rules of justice are adopted as 'best serve the . . . end of public utility' (E App. 3.6; italics added).
[34] Essays 1.18.180. Cf. Griffin 1996: 105; see also Mackie 1980: 152: 'Hume repeatedly deprecates any enquiry about what would be the best way of distributing property or the best form of government or the best choice of rulers; though it is true that his argument in each case is that the public interest would actually be harmed by attempts to promote it in such detailed ways, because of the disputes and conflicts and insecurity that would result'.
[35] E 2.17. This passage should not be taken to commit Hume to utilitarianism in the ethics of action.

between principles or virtues whose presence was more beneficial than their absence. A weighty commitment to a theoretical or practical role for maximization is not an essential element of utilitarianism.

A central component, however, of any utilitarian view must be impartiality from the moral point of view between amounts of utility. This notion is central not only to Hume's motive utilitarianism, but also to his understanding of the nature of morality itself, which itself grounds his motive utilitarianism and explains his unreadiness to propose anything like act utilitarianism. This topic will be the subject of the next section.

4. Utilitarian Impartiality and the General Point of View

We have seen that Hume is a kind of motive utilitarian. When asked how people ought to act, Hume will answer as a virtue-centred, common-sense moralist (albeit one whose common-sense morality is itself shaped by utilitarian considerations). But when asked about the motives, or qualities of character, that people ought to have, he will claim that they should possess those qualities that, in general, are productive of overall utility. But there is a very important difference between his form of the theory, and that offered by contemporary moral theorists such as Adams. Ordinarily, motive utilitarianism is a view *within* morality. That is, the motive utilitarian will see herself as in disagreement with, say, a deontologist, about what makes a motive right, good, or justified. But Hume's motive utilitarianism is a view not merely within morality, but *about* morality itself. As Hume sees it, the very institution of morality is to be understood in motive utilitarian terms (see e.g. E 6.5). In other words, Hume is answering not just the question, 'Morally speaking, which motives ought I to have?', as if there were already some kind of agreement on what morality consists in; but he is attempting initially to deal with a quite different question: 'What is morality?'. And here is one of the points where he might hope that his description, based as it is on social utility, might prove an 'engaging' one.

Hume, as we have seen, accepts that human beings are concerned primarily for themselves and those close to them. He explains this in terms of the effects of 'contiguity' on the vivacity of our impressions and hence on our will: 'When I am a few miles from home, whatever relates to it touches me more nearly than when I am two hundred leagues distant' (T 1.3.8.5). We care most for ourselves, then for our friends and relatives, and finally for strangers, and this partiality affects our ideas of vice and virtue. We find ourselves blaming someone who pays all his attentions to his family and likewise someone who pays them no attention and prefers the interests of strangers:

From all of which it follows, that our natural uncultivated ideas of morality, instead of providing a remedy for the partiality of our affections, do rather conform themselves to that partiality, and give it an additional force and influence.[36]

---

[36] T 3.2.2.8. This passage makes it clear that it is uncultivated morality that Hume has in mind at T 3.2.2.18 when he says that 'we always consider the *natural* and *usual* force of the passions, when we determine concerning vice and virtue'.

Further, Hume notes, this partiality in our sympathies might seem to pose a problem for the view that morality, which is impartial and does not so fluctuate, rests on our sympathies (T 3.3.1.14–15). His explanation of the development of morality and of the moral point of view turns out also to be a series of arguments in favour of morality. The first argument—which I shall call the *conflict-resolution argument*—is implicit in the quotation just above: The practice of cultivated, or impartial, morality provides a 'remedy' for the problems of partiality, a remedy which we have seen is of benefit to all.

Relatedly, the adoption of a 'common point of view' makes possible the expression of our natural and impartial sentiments of 'humanity' (E 9.5–8). According to the *communication-enabling argument*, then, impartial morality not only provides a motivational counter to our partial affections, but enables us to express our impartial sentiments of sympathy. And this, of course, makes possible the whole enterprise of evaluation, with all its potential for informing and guiding (T 3.3.1.18; 3.3.3.2; E 5.42). We learn by experience what to expect from a person described as 'cruel', for example, just as we learn from experience what a piece of gold will buy us in the market (T 3.2.2.10). If we were merely to express our sentiments from our own partial, and constantly changing, points of view, there could be no 'intercourse of sentiments'.

Hume's third argument in favour of the impartial common point of view is the *veridical argument*. The common point of view is the *correct* point of view, and represents things as they are, 'real and intrinsic value' (T 3.2.72) as opposed to appearance. Consider an aesthetic analogy (3.3.1.15). If I find pleasure in a beautiful face, and the owner of it moves away from me, it will from a distance appear like any other face. But I shall not judge the face in the light of that appearance, preferring to correct it in the light of my knowledge that, were I to approach it, I should feel the same pleasure at its beauty as I did previously. Similarly, we correct appearances of size via an understanding of perspective (E 5.41). The same goes for morality. Moral sympathy consists in an impartial concern for the happiness of all sentient creatures (T 3.3.1.25). From the common point of view, we judge the value of a character trait by its actual effects on the person who possesses it and on others: "'Tis only when a character is consider'd in general, without reference to our particular interest, that it causes such a feeling or sentiment, as denominates it morally good or evil'.[37]

When we adopt the moral point of view, we must be entirely impartial between ourselves, those close to us, and strangers.[38] This is not merely a requirement to imagine ourselves in the positions of others before returning to our own, partial, perspective. If

---

[37] T 3.1.2.4; see also T.3.3.1.9. Note further: 'tho' sympathy be much fainter than our concern for ourselves, and a sympathy with persons remote from us much fainter than that with persons near and contiguous; yet we neglect all these differences in our calm judgments concerning the characters of men' (T 3.3.3.2; see also E 5.42).

[38] See Laird 1932: 220; MacNabb 1951: 195; Stewart 1963: 94. On the similarity between Hume's view and Adam Smith's Impartial Spectator model, see e.g. Glossop 1967: 530; Harrison 1976: 114; Mackie 1980: 67. Pure impartiality is of course an ideal. Hume is fully aware that it is not always achieved, and that actual moralities have developed on the basis of less than fully impartial attempts to adopt the common point of view.

we were not impartial, the moral point of view would not be one which all could adopt in common. One must 'forget' his own interests, and 'depart from his private and particular situation'.[39] But what kind of impartiality does Hume have in mind? For there are conceptions of impartiality other than the utilitarian one, according to which equal moral weight attaches to equal amounts of utility. Indeed, it may be urged that Hume nowhere explicitly says that 'forgetting' one's own interests is equivalent to utilitarian impartiality, with its insensitivity to the separateness of persons.

It is indeed true that Hume nowhere explicitly advocates utilitarian impartiality. But one can judge his conception of the impartiality implicit in the common point of view by what is delivered from that point of view. And since what emerges from that point of view, in the ethics of character, is motive utilitarian, we should conclude that the common point of view is itself utilitarian. If it were not, it would produce a different first-order morality. Imagine that the common point of view required partiality towards, say, one's family and friends. Then, when describing the basis of virtues such as justice and benevolence, Hume would mention the special weight to be attached to the interests of those individuals. But he does not. Rather, the virtues are such because of their tendency to the good of 'mankind', or 'society', as a whole. Further, given the foundation of justice and indeed the moral point of view itself in impartial utilitarianism, it is hard to see how Hume could be thinking of anything other than straightforward utilitarian impartiality. Other conceptions of impartiality will rely on the notion of the separateness of persons, which is absent from the foundations of Hume's position.

Why did Hume not consider a less stringent conception of impartiality, one which would perhaps even allow some of the natural bias towards persons that is exemplified in all human beings? The answer lies primarily, I suggest, in the nature of his arguments. As the quotation above suggests, Hume would have seen the inclusion of any kind of partiality within the common point of view as a diminution of its effectiveness. If the problem is partiality, then partiality cannot be part of the solution. When it comes to communication-enabling, it is important that we attach the same sense to evaluative terms. If 'kind' means 'kind-from-my-perspective', you can learn nothing useful from my attributions of kindness, since you do not occupy the same perspective, and may know nothing of my situation. Finally, for the perspectival analogy to go through for the veridical argument, there must be only one answer to the question of how valuable something is, just as there is only one answer to the question how large some object is.

One further reason for Hume's adopting a utilitarian conception of impartiality may have been an analogy between the temporal impartiality of prudence, and the 'spatial' impartiality of morality.[40] Prudence—'what in an improper sense we call *reason*'—requires me to be entirely impartial between different times in my life, and it is an easy

---

[39]   T 3.3.1.591; E 9.6; see also T 1.4.2.22; E 9.5.
[40]   T 3.2.7.5. I owe this point to Elizabeth Ashford.

step to the notion that morality consists in complete impartiality between people (see Rawls 1999: 23–4).

These reasons explain rather than justify Hume's conception of impartiality, since it is not clear why a conception that allowed for partiality, but on the agent-neutral or universalizable assumption that everyone's reasons for partiality are the same, would not do what he requires of the common point of view (see Cohon 1997). Consider a conception of impartiality, for example, which allowed, first, that each person has reason to give himself and those close to him *some* priority, and, secondly, that *some* priority be given to the worst off. This conception would presumably give rise to a first-order ethics of character which, though it included the virtues of friendship and justice, would surely nevertheless serve as well to provide a moral motivation to counter excessive partiality. Further, given that each person would view the moral world in the same way, communication would not be prevented. Again, there seems no reason to deny that this conception of impartiality might not be said to be veridical. It is, after all, a single conception, and one with independent attractions. Finally, the problems arising from the separateness of persons with the direct extension of prudential principles into morality are, of course, well known.

It is true that Hume's impartial, motive utilitarian conception of morality may permit partiality in practice. Indeed, as we have seen, Hume claims that pure impartiality in practice would be beyond human capacity, and that encouraging it would lead not to an increase in the overall good so much as to the drying up of more partial, but nevertheless productive, moral concern:

[W]hile every man consults the good of his own community, we are sensible, that the general interest of mankind is better promoted, than by any loose indeterminate views to the good of a species, whence no beneficial action could ever result, for want of a duly limited object, on which they could exert themselves.[41]

But this, of course, will not be enough to satisfy those who deny that morality itself is to be understood in terms of strict utilitarian impartiality. Indeed, they may use Hume's plausible claims about the limitations of the human will against his own conception of morality. Given those limitations, is it not more likely that the common point of view itself would have incorporated some of that partiality human beings find it so difficult to expunge from their everyday lives?

To conclude our discussion of Hume's moral position. We have seen that his views on virtue, utility, impartiality, and the nature of morality are surprisingly complex. At the level of right action, Hume is best understood as a virtue-centred, common-sense

---

[41] E 5.38n22; see also E 5.42n 25. Note in addition the passages discussed above concerning the sources of justice in self-interest and those concerning different sources of utility. At T 3.3.3.2, Hume suggests that, though we are quite aware of the partiality of human beings towards their friends and family, we approve of such partiality from an impartial perspective of sympathy which takes all into account. In general, Hume is a lot more pessimistic about the possibility of first-order impartiality than, say, William Godwin, J.S. Mill, or Peter Singer.

moralist who will recommend those actions that are in line with his own conception of common-sense morality. But he sees praise or blame of actions as directed ultimately at qualities of their agents—virtues—and these qualities are themselves justified, from the moral point of view, by their promoting overall utility. Finally, the moral point of view itself is to be characterized in impartial utilitarian terms. The institution of morality itself emerges only because of its utility value: 'Common interest and utility beget infallibly a standard of right and wrong'.⁴² It might be argued, then, that Hume has removed the ground from beneath the feet of non-utilitarian or deontological positions in the ethics of character. Since the phenomenon of *morality itself* is utilitarian, a non-utilitarian moral position on which character or virtues we should have turns out to be, for him, a conceptual impossibility. Even if his non-utilitarian opponents remain unpersuaded, it is, I suggest, incumbent on them to reflect, as Hume did so carefully, upon the origin and nature of morality, and the implications of that reflection for first-order ethics.

5. Hume's Dualism of the Practical Reason

On what is now seen as 'standard' utilitarianism, ultimate reasons for action are entirely impartial. According to act utilitarianism, for example, an agent's strongest, and indeed only, reason is to perform that act with the overall greatest utility or expected utility. The distribution of that utility is irrelevant: all that matters is aggregation—the overall total (see e.g. Rawls 1999: 32–3). But reflection on the earlier utilitarian tradition illuminates various different possible views on the relation of the overall good, or morality, to an agent's self-interest.

A utilitarian can just avoid talk of self-interest altogether: one is required to maximize the overall good, and that is the end of it. We might call this a position of *pure impartiality*. On this view, the only role that the term 'self-interest' might play is to refer to that portion of the overall good, available to some particular agent, instantiated in their own life. On a less impartial, *dual source* position, reasons are grounded not only in the overall good, but in the good of the particular agent. Such positions may vary in the status accorded to reasons from each source. On the *necessary harmony* view, reasons of self-interest and reasons to promote the overall good necessarily cannot conflict. This may be because, in all possible worlds, an agent's mundane self-interest always consists in promoting the overall good, or because, in all possible worlds, God

---

⁴² E 4.20; see also E 9.8, cited above; Mill 1961–91: 8.849–50. I discuss the tendency in the utilitarian tradition to 'instrumentalize' morality in Crisp 1999: 95–7. 'Utilitarian metaethics'—the view that the actual institution of morality is founded on utility—is commonly found in the empiricist tradition. Locke e.g. offers a theistic version: 'For God, having, by an inseparable connexion, joined *Virtue* and publick Happiness together; and made, the Practice thereof, necessary to the preservation of Society, and visibly *beneficial* to all, with whom the Virtuous Man has to do; it is no wonder, that every one should, not only allow, but recommend, and magnifie those Rules to others, from whose observance of them, he is sure to reap Advantage to himself' (1975: 1.3.6).

exists and will ensure that an agent's overall self-interest, both mundane and posthumous, is maximized by their promoting the overall mundane good. On the *contingent harmony* view, there are possible worlds in which self-interest and the overall good can conflict, but this world is not such a world, perhaps because we have developed in such a way that maximizing the overall good always happens to maximize our own self-interest. On the *contingent actual disharmony* view, conflict in this world is possible, and several further positions may be taken on such conflict. One is the *incommensurability* view, on which self-interested reasons and reasons grounded on the overall good cannot be weighed or compared. According to *overriding egoism*, self-interest always trumps the overall good, while according to its opposite, *overriding moralism*, the overall good always trumps self-interest. On the *variable* view, whether self-interest or the overall good has greater weight in any case depends on what is at stake in that case.

As we have seen, Hutcheson, for example, accepts the necessary harmony version of the dual source view, while Butler and Clarke, if we allow for the possibility of actual disharmony, advocate overriding moralism. What about Hume? As far as human nature is concerned, he is anxious to reject the 'selfish hypothesis'—that is, psychological egoism—on the ground that we should accept the appearance of dispositions such as benevolence as veridical until there is a strong philosophical case to the contrary, which there is not (E App. 2.6; see also Essays 1.11.84; E 5.17). Further, when it comes to normative reasons, Hume is clearly no rational egoist, and allows for the existence of M-reasons. Like many of his predecessors, Hume is keen to stress the hedonic advantages of virtue over vice. In particular, he revives Butler's argument that self-love requires an object, and there is 'none more fit for this purpose than benevolence or humanity' (E 9. 20). Consciousness and memory of virtue are pleasant, and a reputation for virtue makes its possessor an object of the goodwill of others (E 9.21). Knaves are frequently at some point caught out (E 9.24), and knavery anyway rests on a mistaken evaluation of pleasures:

[I]n a view to *pleasure*, what comparison between the unbought satisfaction of conversation, society, study, even health and the common beauties of nature, but above all the peaceful reflection on one's own conduct: What comparison, I say, between these, and the feverish, empty amusements of luxury and expence? These natural pleasures, indeed, are really without price; both because they are below all price in their attainment, and above it in their enjoyment. (E 9.25)

These rousing closing words of the *Enquiry* do not discuss whether the pleasures of virtue are worth the price of any pain. Hume never appeals to the pains and pleasures of the afterlife to justify virtue in this world: 'By what arguments or analogies can we prove any state of existence, which no one ever saw, and which no wise resembles any that ever was seen?' (Essays 3.10.598). In 'The Sceptic', an essay published nearly a decade before the *Enquiry*, Hume is prepared to insist that virtue is 'undoubtedly the best choice, when it is attainable', though he accepts that some virtuous people are nevertheless unhappier than some of the vicious (Essays 1.18.178–9). Does this suggest that choosing virtue will always make one happier? It seems not. Hume goes on to note that the remorse of a villain who has the capacity to feel shame (a virtue) makes him more unhappy than an entirely 'abandoned villain'. In other words, Hume appears to allow that the virtuous choice (not seeking to undermine one's own sense of shame, for example) is best, but potentially costly: it can be a genuine sacrifice.

Does Hume allow that there can be cases in which S-reasons outweigh M-reasons? Consider a society in a state of economic collapse such that many will die. Here Hume allows that the 'strict laws of justice are suspended,...and give place to the stronger motives of necessity and self-preservation' (E 3.8). But Hume insists on the moral limits of humanity; even *in extremis* it is not the case that anything goes, morally speaking. But what of a case in which someone can gain some large benefit through an act of injustice which could not plausibly be said to be inhumane, such as defrauding some large and flourishing company? Here Hume admits that a 'sensible knave' may decide to cheat: 'he, it may perhaps be thought, conducts himself with most wisdom, who observes the general rule, and takes advantage of all the exceptions' (E 9. 22). No argument is required to persuade a virtuous person to reject the sensible knave's position: their antipathy to vice will lead them to reject it out of hand (E 9.23). But, Hume confesses, it will be difficult to find an argument that will persuade someone without that antipathy.

Hume's admission is standardly taken to imply that he believes that there is no argument to be had against the knave, even one that would not persuade the knave himself (see e.g. Darwall 1995: 309–10; Pigden 2012). But Hume's points are carefully restricted to the rhetorical force of arguments for virtue, not their intrinsic plausibility. He says that justice is 'perhaps' an exception to the principle that virtue coincides with self-interest, and that a virtuous person may '*seem* to be a loser by his integrity' (E 9.22; my italics). Hume does say: 'That *honesty is the best policy*, may be a good general rule; but is liable to many exceptions'; but given the context this view is best read as that of the sensible knave, not of Hume himself. Hume himself does not say that the knave 'conducts himself with most wisdom'; rather, he says that this 'may, perhaps, be thought'.

Most importantly, Hume himself provides an argument against the knave: 'Inward peace of mind, consciousness of integrity, a satisfactory review of our own conduct; these are circumstances very requisite to happiness' (E 9.23; see Baillie 2000: 187; Sobel 2009: 352–5).[43] He goes on immediately to point out that it is only the honest man who will pursue these goods, but that is again a point about rhetorical force. It is only the honest man who can understand the value of virtue:

---

[43] Baier (2013: 403) suggests that Hume's 'sermon' on the sensible knave may be ironic. Elsewhere (2008: 312), she says that the response 'begins in candid calculation of interest, but ends in rather unconvincing edifying rhetoric'. As I shall suggest below, I think the sermon can be read as in line with Hume's earlier views on the limits of morality. The rhetoric may be unconvincing, but his position is stated not so much ironically as somewhat indirectly.

But were they [i.e. the knaves] ever so secret and successful, the honest man, if he has any tincture of philosophy, or even common observation and reflection, will discover that they themselves are, in the end, the greatest dupes, and have sacrificed the invaluable enjoyment of a character, with themselves at least, for the acquisition of worthless toys and gewgaws. (E 9.25)

There is a case, then, for taking Hume's version of the dualism of practical reason to be a harmony view, in its contingent form, given the lack of any theistic backing for the harmony across all possible worlds. As we have seen with previous writers, that argument would be severely weakened by his failure to weigh the pleasures of virtue against the pains that could in certain circumstances be avoided through vice.[44]

But perhaps the most plausible interpretation is indeed that Hume believes he has no argument against the knave. Remember first that Hume allows that justice will *in extremis* give way to self-interest. Again, in the essay 'Of the Origin of Government', Hume admits that '[s]ome extraordinary circumstances may happen, in which a man finds his interests to be more promoted by fraud or rapine, than hurt by the breach which his injustice makes in the social union' (Essays 1.5.38). And in 'The Sceptic' (Essays 1.18.169–70), he accepts that a person with no 'relish for virtue' can plausibly claim that his dispositions are such that he cannot enjoy moral pleasures.

In what way, then, are sensible knaves 'dupes'? Note that the mistake they have made is now in the past: they have sacrificed the chance of a virtuous character. Now, given their tastes and preferences, it may well be too late for them to enjoy the pleasures of virtue. In other words, despite his wishing to be warmer in the cause of virtue, Hume is unwilling to adopt a harmony view. Rather, his position is one of actual disharmony. And the version of that position he holds is variabilism. Sometimes, morality trumps self-interest, and genuine sacrifice is the reasonable option; at others, morality is trumped by self-interest, either because of what is at stake or because one has vicious tastes and preferences. The knave, then, may be not only sensible, but reasonable. To deny that would require Hume to argue that the knave has M-reasons which do not answer to any of their own passions; and that position is ruled out by the Hume's own sentimentalist conception of normativity.[45]

---

[44] It may be objected that Hume is under no obligation to consider such problem cases, given his restriction of ethics, strictly speaking, to characters rather than actions. But he clearly is willing to discuss the morality of actions; consider e.g. his discussion of justice, in usual and extreme situations. Further, one may ask whether one is best advised to possess, or perhaps rather to cultivate, a character that would make it more likely that one would commit, in extreme circumstances, actions that would usually be described as immoral or 'inhumane'.

[45] For a modern statement of the Humean position, see Williams 1981a.

13
Smith:
The Delusions of Self-love

Adam Smith (1723–90), a slightly younger contemporary of Hume, was also a key figure in the Scottish Enlightenment, known for his moral philosophy and moral psychology, but also particularly for his foundational work in political economy. He was appointed to the chair of Moral Philosophy at the University of Glasgow in 1752. Smith developed his own version of sentimentalist ethics, and, again like Hume, attaches great weight to utility, though, following Butler and other predecessors, Smith also incorporates utility into his account of the benevolence of God, and includes a particular non-utilitarian conception of 'propriety' at the foundation of his ethics. His ethics is also Butlerian in its involving a sharp distinction, at the human level, between benevolence and justice, with a proto-Kantian emphasis on the 'awful' virtues of self-command.[1] Smith's most influential contribution to normative ethics has been his notion of the 'impartial spectator'.[2] Though God is an impartial spectator of human activity, the spectator Smith has in mind is—as is only appropriate for a morality designed for human beings—a partly idealized human, imagined from the point of view of the moral agent themselves and indeed partly constitutive of that agent. Here we find another link to Butler: the voice of the impartial spectator is that of conscience. And, while it is free of the excessive partiality to self characteristic of flawed beings like us, it is also based on a recognition of the reasonableness of some such partiality, and hence of independent S-reasons as well as M-reasons.

1. Sympathy

With Hobbes and Mandeville clearly in mind, Smith begins his most significant work in ethics, *The Theory of Moral Sentiments* (1759),[3] with a commitment to a natural human 'interest' in the well-being of others:

[1] For insightful discussions of Kantian themes in Smith, see Fleischacker 1991; Haakonssen 1996: 148–53. On the virtues of self-command, see Montes 2016.
[2] What is original in Smith is the substance of his account; the notion of elucidating the moral point of view in terms of spectatorship is found earlier, in e.g. Hutcheson (I 221–2) and Hume (see SR 12.4).
[3] All unattributed references are to Smith 1979, which is based on the 6th edition of 1790. The book was first published in 1759, but Smith's ethical views remained largely consistent through the several editions; see

How selfish soever man be supposed, there are evidently some principles in his nature, which interest him in the fortune of others, and render their happiness necessary to him, though he derives nothing from it except the pleasure of seeing it. (1.1.1.1)

Any such interest in the well-being of others arises solely through our imagining ourselves in the situation of another (1.1.1.2).[4] Smith describes the resulting 'fellow-feeling' with any passion of another as 'sympathy' (1.1.1.5), noting that we take immediate pleasure in being its object, whether it is with our own joy or sorrow (1.1.2.1, 4).[5] The scope of our concern is universal, extending to any 'innocent and sensible being' (6.2.3.1). Nor can sympathy be seen as 'in any sense, . . . a selfish principle' (7.3.1.4). If I am sympathizing with your grief over the death of your son, I am imagining not what I should suffer were my own son to die, but what I should suffer were I you. In other words, I am imagining your grief, and sympathizing with you directly:

That whole account of human nature . . . which deduces all sentiments and affections from self-love, which has made so much noise in the world, but which, so far as I know, has never yet been fully and distinctly explained, seems to me to have arisen from some confused misapprehension of sympathy.

Sympathizing, even with the unhappy, though of course sometimes painful, is agreeable to us (1.1.2.6), and our natural liking of harmonious fellow-feeling and dislike of discord are also manifested in a basic desire for the approval, and absence of disapproval, of others (3.2.6–7), a desire not only to *be* approved of, but—at least in the case of most of us—to be *worthy* of approval as truly admirable or virtuous.

Calling such desires 'natural' is, for Smith, equivalent to describing them as divinely created. God's purpose in creating rational creatures seems to have been their happiness (3.5.7; see also 2.1.5.10; 2.2.3.5; 2.3.3.3; 6.2.3.2; 7.2.3.18).[6] No other purpose would be worthy of his wisdom and benevolence, and one can see it behind all works of nature, which seem designed to promote happiness and to protect us from unhappiness.

Griswold 1999: 28. References are to part, section (if appropriate), chapter or 'introduction' or 'conclusion' (if appropriate), and paragraph.

[4] Raphael (2007: 13) suggests that Smith's example of 'instantaneous transfusion' of an emotion to another does not involve imagination. But Smith's point is that the transfusion occurs in the absence of knowledge of what is causing the emotion, not of what it is like to be feeling that emotion. Your sad expression will cause me pain, even if I am ignorant of why you are sad, because I can imagine myself as sad. It is true (see main text below) that sympathy involves one's imagining oneself in the *situation* of another, and in this case all one knows or believes of the other's situation is that they are sad; but that can be sufficient for sympathy in these non-standard cases. Norton and Stewart-Robertson (1980: 396–7) find in Reid the objection to Smith that genuine sympathy is 'prior to reflection'. But, as his discussion of transfusion shows, Smith does not claim that sympathy arises only after some period of deliberate and conscious exercise of the imagination.

[5] Montes (2004: 51–4) notes that Smith also uses 'sympathy' to refer to the 'process' of coming to sympathize as an end. For very helpful discussions of Smith's views on sympathy and other key notions in the *Theory*, see Debes 2016; Montes 2016; Schliesser 2016. Smith is insightfully contrasted with Hume in Sayre-McCord 2015.

[6] In recent years, it has been argued that Smith rejected teleological explanations (e.g. Haakonssen 1981: 77). For a persuasive defence of the traditional interpretation, see Kleer 1995.

Consider, for example, the compassionate sharing of the sorrows of others: nature requires us to do this only to the extent necessary for us to be prompted into helping (1.3.1.12); or the fact that our beneficent desires vary in strength according to the value of acting on them (6.2.introd.3), though occasionally they require checking through the authority of the impartial spectator (7.2.1.44) (who will be discussed further below).

Our sympathy, exercised through imagination, does not merely mimic the sentiments of others, but corresponds to what we think those sentiments *should* be (1.1.1.4). Sympathy arises, then, not so much from our recognizing another's sentiments, but from our understanding their situation.[7] For example, we can feel embarrassed at another's rudeness, imagining what we would feel, and what should be felt, in their situation, even if the rude person is quite unaware of having done anything wrong (1.1.1.10). The object of our sympathy may even be unable to appreciate their situation. When we feel compassion for a person who is demented, though apparently content, Smith suggests, it is the result of our imagining how we would feel in their situation (which is of course severe distress) if we were also—*per impossibile*—able to consider it rationally (1.1.1.11; see also 2.1.2.5).

The correspondence of our sentiments with those of others, when sympathizing, is limited not only by what we believe appropriate, but also by the fact that we cannot help but be aware that the person with whom we are sympathizing is not ourselves (1.1.4.7–10). The object of our sympathy will of course themselves recognize that, and because they desire harmony between us will seek to 'flatten' their own affections or emotions as far as they can, imagining themselves in the position of the spectator just as the spectator seeks to imagine themselves in the object's situation.[8]

In general, the judgements of the appropriately informed are preferable (1.1.4.3). And in standard cases I will assess another's judgement according to whether, by my lights, it is in accordance with 'truth and reality' (1.1.4.4)—and my lights themselves depend on my own sentiments. But the sentiments of the judge should also be in good order. Indeed when we know that our own are out of line, we can correct our own judgements. If I know I am in a gloomy mood, I can appreciate the excellence of a joke even though I am not currently amused by it, aware that it is the kind of remark that in normal circumstances would make me laugh (1.1.3.3–4). Equally, I will criticize those who laugh louder at a joke than it deserves (1.1.2.6).

2. Normative Standards and the Impartial Spectator

Smith's philosophical ethics, like that of Hume, is sometimes interpreted as purely descriptive. But the sentiments Smith is describing are his own, so when he describes

---

[7] It is probably a mistake, then, to see Smith's account of sympathy as 'proto-simulationist': see previous note; Nanay 2010.
[8] Otteson (2013: 428) plausibly sees this process as analogous to that of aiming at an Aristotelian mean.

standards of appropriateness for those sentiments, and speaks in favour of normative principles corresponding to them, it is most plausible to understand him as expressing his own moral views rather than as attempting merely to articulate them in a confessional or positivist spirit.

The standard by which we judge affections, and the actions they produce, is one of *propriety* (1.1.3.5–6), which Smith elucidates as an Aristotelian mean between excess and deficiency (1.2.introd.1). If your laughter is appropriate, then I will approve; if is too soft or loud, or lasts for too long or short a time, I will disapprove. The standard of 'exact' propriety is perfection (6.3.23–4). So I can judge my own character and actions against those of a perfect agent in my situation, and, even if I am among the wisest and best, the result of that cannot fail to be humility and regret. But I can also judge myself against the common standards of my day, which may—or of course may not—lead to a more positive assessment.[9]

Propriety is a matter of the pure 'fittingness' of some affection or action, and in clearly distinguishing the standard of fittingness from that of utility Smith in effect seeks to distance himself from Hume: 'it seems impossible... that we should have no other reason for praising a man than that for which we commend a chest of drawers' (4.2.4; see also 7.2.3.15).[10] But he does not deny an important role for utility in ethics, thus also distancing himself from Clarke and Shaftesbury (7.2.1.48). Indeed the virtues have a beauty grounded in their utility, which itself makes our approbation of them appropriate (4.2.1–5), and, as we have seen, their promoting happiness is the reason God instantiated them in our nature (3.5.7).

The *merit* and *demerit* of actions consists in the good or bad results which the affection that led to the action aims at or tends to produce, and it is these qualities that ground deserved reward or punishment (1.1.3.5–7; 2.1.introd.).[11] The approval of others is desirable, and disapproval undesirable, and they may in that way be seen as rewards and punishments. But Smith's position must be that we should never approve or disapprove, or adopt some strategy for such approval or disapproval, for pragmatic or consequentialist reasons. That would be to ignore the distinction between propriety and utility, and so itself unfitting and inappropriate. And in particular there is a set of

---

[9] 1.1.5.9. See the discussion in the main text below of virtue that falls short of propriety.

[10] At 7.2.3.21, Smith allows that the 'system which places virtue in utility'—and presumably he sees Hume's view as one such system—is in fact a system based on propriety. So, properly understood, utilitarian moral views imply notions of moral value independent of the value of happiness. In this passage, Smith tells us that the only difference between his view and that of the utilitarians is that his standard is that of the impartial spectator, while that of the utilitarians is utility. But why should a utilitarian not incorporate into their position the notion of an impartial spectator? There is no reason, as long as the sympathy of the spectator is with the motives of agents and the gratitude of beneficiaries of actions, and not with the mere happiness of those affected (7.3.3.17). And the utilitarian might then appeal to the notion of propriety to justify assessing moral agents and furniture in different ways.

[11] Nature, or God, has designed us to 'correct' the standard distributions of goods and bads resulting from virtue and vice (3.5.9). Industry standardly produces benefits for the industrious, which provides an incentive to work. But we may seek to deprive the 'industrious knave' of such benefits, and that will provide an incentive to virtue in general. The rules of both nature and humanity, however, 'are calculated to promote the same great end, the order of the world, and the perfection and happiness of human nature'.

attitudes which themselves are appropriate to actions that deserve reward and punishment. The most important of these are gratitude and resentment, respectively (2.1.1.1–4), each of which we find ourselves able to sympathize with in others (2.1.2.4–5).[12]

Both propriety and utility, then, justify our approbation of the virtues, but it is always propriety that lies behind our immediate and unreflective responses (4.2.5–12). And propriety has a beauty of its own, independent of utility, as we can see in the case of the capacity to control fear or anger (6.3.4). It is in the virtues of prudence, justice, and beneficence that utility plays the more significant role in grounding our approval (6.concl.6). Smith is, then, a pluralist about the grounds of approbation. But he is a pluralist also about the focus of moral judgement itself. Standard moral theories concern the rightness and wrongness of actions, and here Smith allows a role for both propriety and utility. But Smith is also fully aware that we often judge actions by their motives, and here the same two factors play a role. When it comes to my own moral agency, I should aim to be virtuous, preferably with an awareness of both propriety and utility. What if they conflict? Rather oddly, instead of suggesting that one weigh each consideration against the other, Smith seems to assert that one should always come down in favour of the 'welfare of society' (7.2.3.17).

Let me return to the question of normativity. As we have seen, Smith believes that our capacity for sympathy itself involves an assessment of the appropriateness of the relevant feelings, or indeed lack of them, on the part of the object of our sympathy. I sympathize not merely with another's sorrow, but with another's sorrow only in so far as it is justified; and I will sympathize with them even if they are unaware of the sorrowful nature of their circumstances. Given that some perspectives on a person's situation are better than others (my perspective e.g. has greater weight than that of the demented but contented person with whom I am sympathizing), we should now examine how Smith characterizes *the* correct point of view.

Correctness itself Smith elucidates using an analogy with visual perspective informed by the Berkeleyan theory of vision (3.3.1.2–3). From where I sit, the landscape I see outside my window seems out of proportion to the room I am in. I can properly understand the size of each only by occupying, in reality or imagination, a point of view equally distant from each. Likewise, if there is some conflict between my own interest and that of another, I should compare those interests not from my point of view, or from the point of view of the other, but from the point of view of an impartial judge with no connection to either of us. And just as distance is objective, so is morality.[13] Smith often allows that in fact people seek objectivity through imagining

---

[12] As Darwall nicely brings out (1999: 145), central to the idea of resentment in Smith is the thought that the wrongdoer has treated one in a way one does not deserve—that is, without proper respect for one's dignity as a person: 2.3.1.4–5. The potential significance of dignity in Smith's account is discussed also in e.g. Darwall 2004; Debes 2012; Nussbaum 2019; see also Griswold 1999: 235–9. For an interesting comparative discussion of Butler and Smith on resentment, see MacLachlan 2010.

[13] As Campbell points out (1971: 233), Smith's confidence in divine design sits alongside a confidence in the universal authority of morality.

how they would appear to those in their own culture. But cultures themselves can be mistaken as a whole, as was that of the later Greeks, who allowed infanticide (5.2.15). Less significant differences between cultures, such as that between the somewhat disordered hospitality of the Poles and the frugality of the Dutch, may be acceptable, but only because 'the style of manners which takes place in any nation, may commonly upon the whole be said to be that which is most suitable to its situation' (5.2.13; see also 5.2.7–8; Shaver 2006: 193–4). Further, the fact that others can be mistaken explains how what really matters to us, when we are confident of our own moral opinions, is our being praiseworthy, not actually being praised (3.1.5; see below n. 17).

This is what Smith means by the *indifference* of the spectator. Our sentiments, and the judgements lying behind or emerging from them, are excessively biased towards our own interests and concerns. A European, Smith suggests (3.3.4), having heard that the whole of China had disappeared in an earthquake, would express various humane sentiments, but then return to his own activities as if nothing had happened. Likewise, we can put excessive weight on what concerns us in particular. Consider resentment (1.1.5.2; see also 2.2.1.2). If you do me some non-trivial wrong, I am likely to be extremely angry and resentful. But the kind of resentment we admire is that 'noble and generous' kind, which mirrors that which would be felt by the impartial spectator and involves a desire to inflict no more punishment 'than what every indifferent person would rejoice to see executed'. The kind of indifference Smith has in mind, then, is not lack of concern, but unbiased concern.

Echoing Plato's metaphor of individual reason as an internal human being (Plato 2003: 588c–e), Smith describes the impartial spectator as 'the ideal man within the breast' (3.3.28; see also 38), the ideal consisting not only in impartiality, but also in being appropriately informed of the relevant facts (7.2.1.49). In that sense, then, the position of the impartial spectator is ideal both in its perfection, and in its constituting a goal which we can strive to approach in the knowledge that it may be ultimately unattainable. Impartiality is likely to be especially difficult when I am examining my own conduct, and my self divides into judge and person judged (3.1.6).

It is significant that the impartial spectator is seen as a human being. His perspective is not that of God, as we learn for example from Smith's discussion of what is now called 'moral luck'.[14] Smith describes as the 'equitable maxim' the view that we should praise or blame others solely for what they intend, independently of how their actions turn out (2.3.introd.), noting that while everyone will agree with it 'in abstract and general terms', in practice our sentiments are influenced by how things turn out. This 'irregularity of sentiment' has, as one might expect, a beneficent purpose (2.3.3; 6.3.30). Without it, we would persecute others constantly for mere intentions or suspected intentions, we would be less concerned to avoid negligence, and so on. Now one might expect the impartial spectator's sentiments to be 'equitable' and 'regular', perhaps as

---

[14] At 3.2.32, the spectator is described as a 'demigod...partly of immortal, yet partly too of mortal extraction', and Smith admits that the spectator is hesitant in the face of significant criticism from others.

antidote to this further bias within our natural sentiments. But this would defeat the purpose of the irregularity itself. So we find, for example, that the spectator will 'feel some indulgence for what may be regarded as the unjust resentment' of someone who has been injured in an accident by someone else without fault on either side (2.3.2.10). One has to accept that there is a tension in Smith's position at this point. The correct point of view is that of God, and to that extent in cases of moral luck the view of the spectator is distorted. But Smith can at least allow that there is room for reflection on the equitable maxim, which may moderate our sentiments in accordance with whatever rule is in fact optimum for humanity as a whole (2.3.3.6).

It is clear that what Smith is personifying in the spectator is conscience (3.2.32), and that his conception of conscience owes much to Butler (3.5.6). To advance human happiness on the whole, conscience is placed within us to direct our conduct, and its authority over our passions and other elements within us is self-evident: 'What is agreeable to our moral faculties, is fit, and right, and proper to be done'. In cases of internal conflict, such as that between beneficent affections towards different individuals, the spectator is the ever-reliable arbiter, and 'if we *really* view ourselves with his eyes..., his voice will never deceive us' (6.2.1.22; my italics). Here it is essentially playing the role of Aristotelian *phronesis*, or 'practical wisdom', grounding decisions on a proper understanding of the significance of salient features of situations rather than merely on the application of 'casuistic rules', and judging propriety as a mean between extremes (3.6.8–11; 6.3.14; Aristotle 1894: 1143b–1145a).[15]

3. Smith's Ethics

How should we characterize Smith's normative ethical theory? At what we might call the human level, it is a form of deontology, and its requirements emerge through Smith's general account of the structure of the virtues themselves. At T 3.3.4.2, Hume says:

Each of the virtues, even benevolence, justice, gratitude, integrity, excites a different sentiment or feeling in the spectator. The characters of *Cæsar* and *Cato*, as drawn by *Sallust*, are both of them virtuous, in the strictest sense of the word; but in a different way: Nor are the sentiments entirely the same, which arise from them. The one produces love; the other esteem: The one is amiable; the other awful.

---

[15] Smith does not find the impartial spectator only in the virtuous person. The spectator often e.g. plays a role in moderating excessive passions (e.g. 6.concl.2–6). Further, Smith insists that the sphere of justice is not vague or indeterminate (3.6.10–11; cf. Aristotle 1894: 1098a). It is worth noting another Aristotelian analogy: we can judge what is right only by becoming *phronimoi* or impartial spectators, not by attempting to 'apply' some theory couched in terms of the spectator to our circumstances. In that respect, then, the spectator is not a heuristic procedure (Griswold 1999: 145). But (*pace* Griswold) this is not to suggest that 'the spectator's responses are themselves constitutive of what is and what is not morally appropriate' (Nussbaum 1990: 344–45; cf. Griswold 1999: 185). The right way to understand the spatial relation between my room and the landscape outside is to occupy a position from which one can grasp that relation; likewise, the spectator is in the right place to grasp the appropriateness of actions.

Smith draws the same distinction between the amiable virtues of 'candid condescension and indulgent humanity', on the one hand, and the awful virtues of 'self-denial, of self-government, of…command of the passions', on the other (1.1.5.1), and describes the perfectly virtuous person as in full possession of both (3.3.35). And, as one might expect, given the weight placed on both types, Smith is prepared to say that, though the sense of duty should be our ruling principle, actions prompted by beneficent motivation should depend as much on our passions as on a regard for duty (3.6.1–4).

Virtues, for Smith, are *excellences*: the virtuous person's qualities will exceed those of 'the rude vulgar of mankind' (1.1.5.6–8). In that respect, then, virtue goes beyond run-of-the-mill propriety. The latter calls for approval, the former admiration. So, according to Smith, virtue is supererogatory (see 2.2.1.6). One should be celebrated for possessing it, but not blamed for lacking it. Smith even allows that in certain cases there can be virtue in actions which fall short of *perfect* propriety, where the difficulties of acting rightly are such that even the virtuous fall short but nevertheless do considerably better than an ordinary person would.

This claim about virtue, however, is not universal. There is one virtue that correlates entirely with propriety: justice (2.2.1.5). Injustice consists in positive harm to another, which always justifies resentment or punishment, whereas failure to benefit cannot, among equals, be 'extorted by force' (2.1.2.3, 7; see also 6.2.introd.2). We can disapprove of the ingrate, but not resent him, because 'he does no positive hurt to anybody'. But ordinary gratitude is not supererogatory: the ingrate *ought* to recompense his benefactor. So there are two classes of wrongs in Smith: those that consist in positively harming others, which may deserve resentment or punishment, that is, acts of injustice; and those that consist in a failure to benefit others when such benefit is morally required (see also 3.3.4; 3.5.2). It has to be admitted that, though this is an interesting suggestion, it exemplifies either an unusual lack of psychological sensitivity on his part or an unusual willingness to redescribe a common moral notion (i.e. resentment). It is a plain fact that benefactors snubbed by their beneficiaries usually feel resentment, and will even seek to 'punish' them, perhaps by making known their failures to others who might have been inclined to benefit them.

Smith explains the origin of this aspect of the distinction between justice and beneficence by emphasizing the necessity of constraints on harmful actions (2.2.3.2–9). Justice is foundational to society, whereas beneficence is a mere ornament. But his explanation (which is also an attempted justification of God's designs) is problematic. First, the claim seems implausible in cases of minor injustices. Even if all were disposed to engage in minor acts of cheating or fraud, society would continue. Second, we do not know what the effects would be of everyone's lacking any concern for others beyond their near and dear. Most people are incapable of ignoring the serious distress of someone close to them, for example, and it may well be that were this no longer the case society would break down (partly through the injustices that we might then feel able to commit against others). Finally, given that God's aim is our happiness, and, as Smith is fully aware, beneficence promotes happiness, even given the costs of resentment and punishment to all concerned, it is far from obvious that a regime of resentment and punishment for failures to benefit—at least in certain cases—would not be more effective than the system Smith describes. There is also an apparent tension internal to Smith's position, since he allows that superiors—magistrates or sovereigns—can for good reason coerce inferiors into performing good offices (2.2.1.8). Why should we accept that equals, perhaps in groups, can never find themselves in a situation in which coercing others to perform such offices is justified?

Above I described Smith's moral theory as deontological at the human level. But because he sees God's aim as purely to promote happiness, it may be that Smith's God, like Hutcheson's, is a utilitarian.[16] In that respect, then, it could that our deontological M-reasons are derivative from God's non-deontological ultimate M-reasons. But Smith does not recommend the solution of conflicts between moral principles by appeal to the principle of utility (except for the somewhat aberrant passage on motives at 7.2.3.17 mentioned above). For us, the primary virtue is piety. The moral rules, when understood as the laws of God enforced by posthumous sanctions, take on a special sacredness, and any theist must accept that our primary aim should be to conform to God's will (3.5.12–13). Not to do so would be vain, absurd, unnatural, ungrateful, and imprudent, unless one's religion has been 'corrupted by the factious and party zeal of some worthless cabal'. But, just as we should not always be motivated primarily by a sense of duty, so, though obedience to God should govern our lives, it would be quite mistaken to think that Christianity allows no room for motives such as natural affection (3.6.1). The second requirement of that religion is that we should love our neighbours as ourselves, and we 'love ourselves surely for our own sakes, and not merely because we are commanded to'.

4. Smith's Dualism

Like Hutcheson, Butler, and others, Smith is fully aware of the motivational and normative weight of self-love and self-interest. The self/other distinction is central, for example, to his analysis of the virtues. When we consider an individual's character, we 'naturally view it under two different aspects; first as it may affect his own happiness; and secondly, as it may affect that of other people' (6.introd.1). The self/other distinction is mirrored in Smith's emphasis on what we might call the individual/group distinction in his discussion of punishment (2.2.3.8). Our concern for others is in standard cases a concern for particular individuals, not 'society': 'our regard for the multitude is compounded and made up of the particular regards which we feel for

---

[16] As Irwin notes (2008: 707n78), Smith's God seems to be concerned with posthumous retributive justice as an end in itself (2.2.3.12). Smith says here that 'Nature' teaches us to hope for, and religion authorizes us to expect, divine justice. It may be that this hope itself has a utilitarian justification, and will not in fact be realized, perhaps because of God's mercy. But then one must wonder why God does not prevent our thinking of him as a utilitarian, since this seems to undermine any such hope and expectation. Whether Smith was in fact a theist is contested in the literature: see e.g. Graham 2016.

the different individuals of which it is composed'. It may be, as suggested above, that the ultimate justification of punishing someone is the good of society; what motivates us to do so, however, will be concern for the individual person who has been wronged.

Smith sees morality as a limit on self-interest, and sometimes appears to suggest an extreme form of impartiality:

[I]t is the great precept of nature to love ourselves only as we love our neighbour, or what comes to the same thing, as our neighbour is capable of loving us. (1.1.5.5)

But it is clear that Smith accepts as reasonable the 'natural preference which every man has for his own happiness above that of other people' (2.2.2.1). Since each of us is best able to look after ourselves, 'it is fit and right that it should be so'. We are justified, that is to say, in giving priority to promoting our own interests over those of others. What we cannot do is positively harm them. Each individual, 'in his own breast', prefers himself to all others. But he can also view himself as others do, and:

If he would act so as that the impartial spectator may enter into the principles of his conduct, which is what of all things he has the greatest desire to do, he must, upon this, as upon all other occasions, humble the arrogance of his self-love, and bring it down to something which other men can go along with. They will indulge it so far as to allow him to be more anxious about, and to pursue with more earnest assiduity, his own happiness than that of any other person…But if he should justle, or throw down any of them, the indulgence of the spectators is entirely at an end. It is a violation of fair play, which they cannot admit of.

Further, the spectator will recognize the weight of our special obligations to others, such as our own children, though the limits of these are also important (3.3.13).

Smith's dualism, then, differs from Sidgwick's later version (1907: 382, 506–9). Both accept that, from the individual's point of view, their own good alone is what matters (3.3.3). But Sidgwick's 'impartial spectator'—that is, the individual taking 'the point of view of the universe'—puts no weight at all on the distinction between persons. In that respect, their voice is indeed that of a purely benevolent God. Further, Smith sees no tension between the individual and the impartial points of view. We should act in the way approved by the impartial spectator, and the 'wise and just man' 'almost becomes that impartial spectator' (3.3.25; see also 29). But from that spectator's point of view we will accept that it is reasonable for the individual to give some priority to their own interests, and indeed a person who fails to advance their interests appropriately—for example, by being biased towards the near future—is open to criticism as imprudent (6.1.11). But that priority is limited by the demands of morality, including not only requirements not to harm, but requirements to benefit certain others, such as our own children or benefactors.

In a sense, self-love is more basic than morality, for Smith (3.3.4, 21; 3.4.1–12). Morality, captured in the point of view of the impartial spectator, is nature's 'remedy' for the 'delusions of self-love' (3.4.7; see also 3.1.5; 3.3.3–5, 31; 3.4.6, 12; Heath 2013: 250–3). We have a natural sense for the 'deformity' of vicious actions, borne out by the opinions of others, and adopt general rules not to engage in them ourselves. Reverence for those rules then enables us 'to correct the too partial views which self-love might otherwise suggest, of what is proper to be done'. But it is important to remember that, in many cases, acting out of such reverence—that is, a sense of duty—is merely second-best (3.5.1). Moral perfection also involves feeling the appropriate sentiments of affection. Nor will the virtuous person see the general rules of morality negatively, as mere constraints on the pursuit of self-interest. He will of course avoid the horrors of shame, remorse, and blame (2.2.2.3; 3.2.29; 3.3.31), and even a knave who avoids those on certain occasions will be caught out (3.5.8). But they will love virtue for its own sake (7.2.4.8).

Further, it is highly significant for Smith that the 'chief part of human happiness arises from the consciousness of being beloved' (1.2.5.1; see also 3.2.17; 3.5.8; 7.2.2.12–13), and the virtuous person can look forward to the esteem and gratitude of others as well as enjoy the self-approbation in taking the perspective of the impartial spectator on his actions, proportioning that self-approbation to the degree of self-command he has shown (2.2.2.4; 3.3.26–7; see also 3.2.8).

By not giving my own interests sufficient priority in certain cases, I will be acting imprudently and hence unreasonably. But Smith also allows that there can be occasions on which I am required to sacrifice important interests of my own for the sake of others (6.2.3–4; 7.2.1.45). Indeed the virtuous person should be willing that:

all those inferior interests should be sacrificed to the greater interest of the universe, to the interest of that great society of all sensible and intelligent beings, of which God himself is the immediate administrator and director. If he is deeply impressed with the habitual and thorough conviction that this benevolent and all-wise Being can admit into the system of his government, no partial evil which is not necessary for the universal good, he must consider all the misfortunes which may befal himself, his friends, his society, or his country, as necessary for the prosperity of the universe, and therefore as what he ought, not only to submit to with resignation, but as what he himself, if he had known all the connexions and dependencies of things, ought sincerely and devoutly to have wished for. (See above pp. 77–8.)

Such subjective sacrifice is possible: we see it in the case of soldiers marching cheerfully to what they know is likely to be their own deaths. It is true that it will be rewarded in the afterlife (2.2.3.12; 3.2.12, 33; 3.5.3, 10, 12; see also 7.2.3.20). But their motivation, as is that of the just person's sacrificing themselves for the greater good, is not a desire for posthumous rewards, but 'the love of what is honourable and noble, of the grandeur, and dignity, and superiority of our own characters' (3.3.4).[17]

Smith recognizes the role of the impartial spectator in the internal struggle prior to virtuous sacrifice (3.3.26–8; see also 3.3.4; 6.3.4; 7.2.1.47).[18] The virtuous man's natural feelings, when his leg has been shot off by a cannon, mean that he does not 'perfectly

---

[17] As Schliesser points out (2016: 39–40), this love of the honourable explains the virtuous person's concern with praiseworthiness rather than praise.
[18] On the role of inner debate in Smith's conception of the impartial spectator, see Brown 1994: ch. 3.

identify himself with the ideal man within the breast'. Here, then, are two further points where Smith differs from Aristotle: his virtue is, for Aristotle, mere continence; and his virtuous person does not 'assign himself the greater good' (1894: 1145a–b, 1169a). The virtuous person will indeed be compensated to some degree by self-approbation and that of others, or by its anticipation (3.2.5; see Griswold 1999: 119), but it would not be 'fit' for nature to allow that compensation to make their 'sacrifice' worthwhile, since they would have no motivation to avoid it. And without a leg they will be of less use in future to themselves and others.

This seems mistaken, however, once we recognize that one can be praised for prudent self-command. Nature must build into us strong motivations to avoid bodily harm, motivations which cannot be squashed at will. Even if we and the virtuous person believe that bravely dealing with the loss of a leg in battle will be best for them in the long run, we can approve strongly of their capacity not to give in to short-term desires to panic or express distress. And given that we and the virtuous person *should* believe that, according to Smith, it is not clear what the object of their and our approbation can be independently of prudence, unless we are forgetting the rewards of the afterlife. Indeed Smith himself seems to forget them, as in the passage just discussed concerning the war hero or 7.2.2.13, where virtue's advantageousness to the agent is limited to 'all ordinary occasions'. And in his famous explanation of why we sympathize with the dead (1.1.1.13), he suggests that we overlook 'what is of real importance in their situation, that awful futurity which awaits them'.

If we take seriously the idea that God is a utilitarian, however, no room can plausibly be made for posthumous justice. The virtuous cannot be rewarded, nor the vicious punished, and this may explain Smith's amnesia concerning the afterlife. If posthumous reward is left out of the story, then Smith, like Hume, makes room not only for subjective but for objective sacrifice grounded in M-reasons. But Smith will not allow that it can ever be rational to act against moral requirements. Morality—as expressed in the voice of conscience—permits me to give some special weight to my own interests in my practical reasoning, but I am never permitted to go beyond that limit. It can never be rational for me to disobey my conscience, even if I benefit greatly by so doing.

14

Price:

Morality as God

Richard Price (1723–91), a Welsh dissenting minister, theologian, probability theorist, and philosopher, set out clearly and forcefully an intuitionist epistemology and deontological ethics which provided the foundations for later work by W.D. Ross and others. His main work in ethics—*A Review of the Principal Questions in Morals* (1758)—was not unreasonably described by Hastings Rashdall as 'the best work published on Ethics till quite recent times' (1907: 1.81n1).[1] Price emphasizes the mundane goods available to the virtuous, but he also recognizes that virtue is not always the best choice in this world, from the point of view of self-interest. There are, however, overriding M-reasons always to do one's duty, and virtue itself consists in doing what one believes to be one's duty *because* it is one's duty. And because the truths of morality are, in some sense, constitutive of God, loving duty turns out to be equivalent to loving God, and piety the highest virtue. Further, because God is just, he will ensure the appropriate rewards and punishments in the afterlife, though the virtuous person will never allow those rewards to motivate them to act.

1. Price's Deontological Pluralism

Price speaks broadly of the 'obligations of virtue' (11), seeing virtue as in effect equivalent to morality, obligation, or what is morally right (15; 105–6; 110).[2] So an examination of his views on virtue will provide us with an overview of his first-order or normative ethics as a whole.

The seventh chapter of the *Review* includes Price's discussion of what he calls the 'heads' of virtue—that is, of particular virtues. He lists six: piety, self-love, beneficence,

---

[1] Unattributed references throughout are to Raphael's edn., itself based on the 3rd edn. of 1787. In his 'Editor's Preface' (vii), Raphael plausibly suggests that Rashdall had Sidgwick's *Methods of Ethics* (1874) in mind as the work that surpassed Price's. Åqvist (1960: 9) takes a view similar to that of Rashdall.

[2] Note that Price distinguishes 'the virtue of the action' from 'the virtue of the agent', the former being equivalent to what is 'objectively right', independently of the intention of the agent, and the latter to the agent's willing what they believe to be right (184; see below sects. 2 and 3). As he points out, this distinction allows him to claim that doing what is objectively wrong (as far as the virtue of the action is concerned) can be virtuous (since the agent's motivation is correct).

gratitude, veracity, and justice. Interestingly, he excludes courage and other executive virtues. This is perhaps because his moral ideal is 'saintly' rather than 'heroic'.[3] On the standard conception of courage, it is required for overcoming recalcitrant fears. Price's ideal moral agent will presumably feel fear when appropriate; but there will no temptation to give in to such fear. Nor does he speak of humility, but perhaps he would see this as falling under the head of piety. Price would doubtless have held that the pious person, properly understanding the status of God, would see herself as nearly worthless in comparison.

Price is, then, an ethical pluralist. He is well aware of the utilitarian view that morality is to be understood as consisting solely in a principle of impartial beneficence. His immediate response, with liberal quotation from Butler, tends to involve counterexamples.[4] We think that the virtuous deserve to be happy, and the vicious unhappy, and would choose to bring these states of affairs about even if the opposite distribution produced no less happiness overall (79–80). Gratitude and promise-keeping are good, and stealing the fruits of someone's labour bad, independently of consequences (131–2). We think that lying is wrong even if it has no bad effects, and must conclude that there is '*intrinsick rectitude*' in veracity (133). And, in a thought-experiment reminiscent of later work on future generations by Sidgwick (1907: 414–16) and Parfit (1984: part 4), Price notes that on the utilitarian view:

any number of innocent beings might be placed in a state of absolute and eternal misery, provided amends is made for their misery by producing at the same time a greater number of beings in a greater degree happy (159–60).[5]

Price does not wish to play down the significance of beneficence. He admits that it is 'the most general and leading consideration in all our enquiries concerning *right*', and even that in extreme cases it can override all other obligations, including justice (153). The promotion of happiness, he suggests, is God's only reason for creating and sustaining the world, though he pursues that end under the (genuine) constraints of justice, veracity, and other principles of rectitude (249–52).

In his conception of beneficence, then, Price anticipates Ross, whose conception of beneficence is essentially equivalent to the utilitarian principle, but whose ethics also contains other principles in possible tension with beneficence. One can imagine Philippa Foot, for example, asking Price whether he really believed that bringing about the scenario in which innocent suffering is outweighed by the creation of happy beings is an exercise of beneficence (Foot 1988: 236–7; see above p. 103). (And imagining this brings out how Foot's question is really just raising in a secular context the problem of

---

[3] David Brink suggested to me that Price's neglect of the executive virtues might be thought to reflect his strong internalism about moral motivation (59, 186, 213). But, as Brink himself noted, Price's internalism seems to amount to the view that moral belief is sufficient only for pro tanto, not overall, motivation.

[4] See also his criticism of rational egoism at 105–6 (discussed below in sect. 5).

[5] Here Price is also anticipating John Findlay's claim (1961: 235–6) that 'the separateness of persons...is...the basic fact for morals'; see above pp. 143–4n19.

natural evil.) There is also here in Price an implicit response to those who claim that any ethical theory can be 'consequentialized' (e.g. Dreier 1993). Justice, for example, is not itself an end or a good that can ground teleological reasons. Of course, one could describe a consequentialist view according to which justice was such a good and which had the same practical conclusions as Price's view. But the reasons for those conclusions would be quite different in each case, and so therefore would the underlying moral theories.

Price is fully aware of the split-level consequentialist strategy, according to which the apparently non-consequentialist judgements we make in the cases he describes are:

owing to the idea of a plan or system of common utility established by custom in the mind with which these vices are apprehended to be inconsistent; or to a habit acquired of considering them as of general pernicious tendency, by which we are insensibly influenced, when, in any particular circumstances or instances, we contemplate them (134–5).

Price's subtle response to this strategy is essentially twofold. First, he objects to the pressure for normative monism within consequentialism (137–8; see Irwin 2008: 750). Why, for example, should truth or gratitude not matter independently of happiness, and ground their own independent principles? This is a powerful point. Of course, as Price fully accepts, some principle of parsimony must operate within ethical theory as elsewhere. But there is no reason a priori to assume that ethics must rest on a single principle. Nevertheless, it must be admitted that by making the promotion of happiness so central within his own account, Price provides something of a hostage to consequentialism. If happiness is really the only reason for our being on this earth, should we not take very seriously the idea that other things we think important are so only because of their relation to happiness?

The idea that our judgements themselves rest on the recognition of such a relation Price dismisses by describing cases in which consequences are no longer relevant, and in which the inclination to object to ingratitude or injustice remains (135). He also suggests (136) that children make such deontological judgements at an early age, when they cannot plausibly be assumed to have a conception of the long-term consequences of such actions on human happiness.[6] Further, when we introspect, we shall find that we—even though we ourselves may be aware of these consequences and see them as significant—disapprove of ingratitude, injustice, and so on in their own right.

But what about the second split-level position, according to which we are 'insensibly influenced' by our habit of disapproval of certain actions on the ground of their consequences? Here it emerges that Price has offered another hostage to the consequentialist

---

[6] Here I cannot resist quoting Hudson (1970: 99): 'This is a very debatable theory. Children frequently lie, or at least romance, without showing any signs of aversion to their own action. On the contrary, they seem to derive positive satisfaction from it, and their parents have to discourage such conduct by impressing upon them the unfortunate consequences of telling tall stories'. Hudson may speak from experience: he dedicates his book on Price to his own children.

through his recognition of the utilitarian case for deontological principles. Given that God's only reason for creating us is one of beneficence, and that 'there is the greatest occasion for [deontological principles] to secure the general welfare,...therefore it might antecedently be expected that a good Being would give them to us' (137).

This position seems to ascribe to God 'pragmatic' reasons for bringing it about that we believe deontological principles (see Butler S 12.31n13; above p. 166). These reasons, the consequentialist might claim, could conflict with our epistemic reasons, and this would raise the question of how a God committed to veracity could cause us to believe what is false for the sake of the overall good. But perhaps even in the case of God the principle of beneficence can override all other principles. And if that is so, since our believing deontological principles appears to produce so much good and prevent so much harm, the consequentialist might argue that God would ensure that we believed them *anyway*, thus undercutting any epistemic case for them based on our own judgements.[7]

2. Moral Motivation and Moral Worth

Consider a case in which some one individual has committed a crime, and two people A and B have each been charged. A judge is making a decision on whom if either to punish, and finds a great deal of persuasive evidence that A is guilty, and little evidence against B; so A is punished. In this case, according to Price, the judge does what is *practically* virtuous, this notion being equivalent to what many would later call *subjectively right* (see Russell 1970: 10–15). If B is in fact guilty, however, the judge's action is *abstractly* (or 'objectively') vicious or wrong. Abstract virtue denotes what an agent, 'if he judged truly,...would judge that he ought to do' (177).[8]

One might claim that the practically virtuous action could be described as, to some extent, abstractly virtuous, since any agent is required—independently of their beliefs about such a requirement—to do what they sincerely believe to be right. But what Price has in mind by abstract virtue is presumably the action a virtuous and *fully informed* agent would do in the circumstances.

Which notion of virtue is the basis of moral assessment? Price is clear that it is practical virtue (184). Our judge is certainly not to be blamed for the decision they came to; indeed they would have been blameworthy for punishing B rather than A. This seems plausible, though it might perhaps have been wiser for Price to avoid talk of 'virtue' at all in connection with what he has in mind by 'abstract virtue'. The actions he has in mind could be described as the 'correct' rather than the 'morally right' actions, the concept of morality being so closely connected to those of blame and praise.

---

[7] There are analogies here with Sharon Street's (2006) argument that the case for moral realism is undercut by evolutionary explanations of our moral beliefs.

[8] Hudson (1970: 132) suggests that Price was developing Hutcheson's use of the material-formal distinction. For helpful discussion of the abstract-practical distinction, see Thomas 1977: ch. 4.

Price also accepts *volitionalism*, making it clear that, strictly speaking, morality concerns not actions as external events, but the intentions or 'willings' behind those events (184–5; see 200–1; 207).[9] If someone intends something,

[w]hat arises beyond or contrary to his intention, however it may eventually happen, or be derived, by the connexion of natural causes, from his determination, should not be imputed to him.

Among other things, in defending volitionalism Price is accepting Smith's 'equitable maxim' (see above pp. 163–4). Further, reflection on cases of moral luck show that he is right to do so (see Crisp 2017). Consider the following well-known case, adapted from Thomas Nagel (1979: 25):

The reckless drivers. Two drivers, through culpable lack of attention, fail to notice a red traffic light. The unlucky driver kills a pedestrian who has started to cross the road. The lucky driver does not, but only because there is no pedestrian for them to hit. All else is equal.

As Smith implies, in this case the unlucky driver would in fact be blamed a good deal more than the lucky one, and this blame would represent itself as appropriate and deserved. Since in general degree of blame tracks degree of wrongness, it seems that our sentiments incline us to the view that the unlucky driver has committed a significantly greater wrong than the lucky one. And of course we expect that it is only reasonable that the unlucky driver be wracked with guilt, while the lucky one—if they become aware of what they have done—will feel if anything only a twinge of guilt, mixed with relief. But our sentiments are at odds with the equitable maxim, and Price is correct that we should reject the beliefs they imply. We have to revise our everyday moral judgements not only about negligence, but also, for example, about attempts which fail for reasons independent of the agent, or about cases in which decisions are made under uncertainty and turn out one way or the other.

Price has seen that morality represents itself to us as set of norms governing the wills of rational agents. And he sees further than Smith, who allows moral status to depend not only on intention, but also on the 'affection of the heart'.[10] Price's argument here is reminiscent of Kant's view of moral worth (2002: 4: 398):

Wherever the influence of mere natural temper or inclination appears, and a particular conduct is known to proceed from hence, we may, it is true, love the person, as we commonly do the inferior creatures when they discover mildness and tractableness of disposition; but no regard to him as a *virtuous* agent will arise within us. (191)

---

[9] Price occasionally appears to deny volitionalism. See e.g. the weight he puts on what I do rather than what I intend in his discussion of veracity (155–6); here I suggest we should understand him, strictly, to be distinguishing my intention now to fulfil my promise from an intention (that is, an intentional attempt) to fulfil my promise when appropriate.

[10] Price occasionally slips, allowing at 140 e.g. that affections can be 'owed' (see also 143).

Our passions, Price believes, as opposed to our affections, depend on our rational deficiencies (76). If, for example, parents were fully aware of their reasons for acting in certain ways towards their children, there would be no need for parental love.[11] Rational benevolence is in effect equivalent to respect for duty; natural benevolence may be amiable, but it cannot ground moral worth. This comes from rational moral judgement, and that is primarily a 'perception of the understanding' (62).

Price also holds that rational volitionalism leads directly to a strictly rationalist conception of moral worth. An action's being virtuous and praiseworthy consists in its being done from 'a regard to goodness and right' (123; also 188–92). And this regard is a matter of degree, and it is the degree of regard for rectitude which determines the degree of moral worth (200). It may seem as if Price also agrees with Kant that moral worth is exemplified in the overcoming of the passions by reason:

[T]he more remote a good is, and the more temptations we have to forego our own interest, the greater is our virtue in maintaining a proper regard to it. In these cases, reason is necessarily more called forth to interpose and decide; our passions concur less with its dictates; and our determinations are more derived from its authority. (194)

But it becomes clear from other passages that Price sees moral worth in the exercise of reason itself, not in the conquering of the passions by reason:

How unreasonable then is it to affirm, that human virtue exceeds that of angels, because of the opposition it encounters; or to regard it as a question of difficulty, whether the excellence of the moral character of the Deity would not be encreased, if he had within him some dispositions contrary to goodness?—Can the very circumstances which argue *imperfection in virtue*, add to the *merit* of it? (205)

God is morally perfect, in that he always wills what is right and is incapable of temptation otherwise, and the closer we come to God the more virtuous we are—though of course we will never achieve perfection itself (221–2).

Price seems to offer two quite different pictures of an agent's virtue. On one, which we might call the *actualist* position, an agent's degree of virtue over their life depends on the degree to which they in fact will what is right during that life. This allows for 'good' moral luck, since the more opportunities an agent has for willing rightly, the more virtuous they will be. The actualist view is primary in Price's account. But he also, in discussing the significance of overcoming passions, suggests what we might call the *potentialist* account:

As long as the degree of virtuous attachment is the same, it matters not whether or no any opposition is subdued: The character remains equally worthy. The man, who in a course of goodness, meets with less hindrance than another from his passions and temper, may be equally virtuous, if he has in him that affection to goodness, which would engage him, if he had

---

[11] Price speaks of 'parental affection', but he is best understood as failing to respect the distinction he drew two pages earlier.

the same opportunities and trials with another, equally to master the same hindrances. Difficulties and inconveniencies attending virtue are the means of shewing to others, who cannot see immediately into our hearts, what is in us, and what our moral temper is. (203)

The reference here to 'opportunities', the use of the subjunctive in 'would engage', and the reference to 'moral temper' might be taken as the claim that what matters in virtue is not actual willing but the *power* to will, which may remain unexercised.[12] Price should perhaps have made it clearer that there are in fact two ways of morally assessing an agent, and that these are not mutually exclusive. As far as actualist virtue is concerned, the highest degree of this will be achieved by always willing what is right. And if one agent is given more opportunity to perform morally admirable actions than another, they will, from the actualist perspective, have lived a more virtuous life. But this is not, the potentialist will point out, to say that they are a less virtuous *person*. A maximally virtuous person has the power always to will what is right in every circumstance. Someone who is morally lucky in actualist terms is not thereby a more virtuous person. So the focus of volitionalist morality is twofold: on the willing of actions, and the will itself. Which conception is relevant to the assessment of desert of posthumous reward? It might be said that God will accept the equitable maxim, so he is a potentialist. It would be quite unjust if the morally lucky person were to do better than the morally unlucky, given that neither lucky nor unlucky is responsible for the circumstances in which they find themselves. On the other hand, it might also be argued that the equitable maxim applies only 'within' morality, and that opportunities to be benefited or harmed through it may be unequal (Crisp 2017: 17–18).

Also important in understanding Price's evaluation and assessment of virtue in particular individuals are what he says about piety and about the unity of virtue.

Price has very little time for atheists: 'as long as men continue void of religion and piety, there is great reason to apprehend they are destitute of the genuine principle of virtue' (144). He goes on to suggest that the virtuous action of such people is probably the result of 'instinct and natural temper', and is of little moral value. On the face of it, this seems somewhat unfair. Let us assume that Price is an 'intellectualist' about virtue, who believes that the virtuous agent must be aware of their reasons for acting (see e.g. Hills 2015: 7–8). If he were a divine command theorist, who saw all moral reasons as resting ultimately on the will of God, his harsh judgement of the atheist would have some justification. But Price explicitly rejects the divine command theory: will 'implies nothing of a *rule, direction*, or *motive*, but is entirely ministerial to these, and supposes them' (148). Morality, then, is prior to God's will. So why should we obey God? Because he is God—our 'universal and almighty Parent, benefactor, and ruler', and because his will is 'in necessary union with perfect rectitude'.

The second, epistemic reason given here does not justify Price's harsh judgement of atheists, since all they are doing is ignoring one, admittedly significant, source of moral

---

[12] See 206n†. Here Price suggests substituting 'power' for 'virtue' and continues: 'The *power* of a being is the same, whether it meets with any opposition or not'.

knowledge or understanding. The first reason is substantive, and explains Price's claim that those who merely pretend to piety for their own advantage are 'the most inexcusable and wicked' (145). But two serious problems with Price's position remain. First, his claim that atheists are motivated by 'instinct' seems unfounded. It is not clear why an atheist should be in any worse a position than a theist to recognize fundamental moral principles, such as that gratitude is appropriate to a benefactor. Second, his weighting of impiety against other vices is disproportional. How can it plausibly be claimed that the deceit of a Tartuffe is more vicious than, say, the actions of a sadistic serial murderer? Price appears to believe that a pious belief in the infinite goodness of God implies such a moral ranking, but in the *Review* itself he offers little justification for this position.

In 'A Dissertation on the Being and Attributes of the Deity', however, which Price included as part of the Appendix in the 3rd edition of the *Review*, saying he had omitted it previously only on grounds of its difficulty, Price argues that truth is not itself independent of God; rather, he constitutes it (290).[13] This may be thought to explain Price's ranking of virtue and vice. If I violate some non-religious moral rule, then I am violating God, and this is a form of impiety. The most wicked are those who violate moral rules to the greatest degree, so it follows analytically that the most wicked will be the most impious, and vice versa.[14]

Having discussed the various heads of virtue, Price notes (164–5) that he has covered only 'the main and leading branches of virtue' and claims that it may not be possible to 'comprehend' all the particular instances of virtue within any number of heads. What Price seems to mean is not that there is some endless list of virtues, but that any list will be not be sufficient to provide guidance in individual cases, because of the huge variety of circumstances in which agents find themselves. This leads Price to suggest that the various heads of virtue all 'run up to one general idea' and are all modifications of a single universal rational law (see 252–3). He then claims that '[n]o part of [virtue] can be separated from another'.[15] In the sense just explained, this is unobjectionable: virtue in relation to God and virtue in relation to one's own well-being are both virtue. But Price's claim is significantly more substantive than just this. He suggests that any degree of 'partial virtue' is morally equivalent to any other, and that any agent who neglects any single virtue is 'an apostate from righteousness and order, as if he neglected them all'. Again, there are weaker and stronger interpretations available. Perhaps Price is merely claiming that the neglect of a single virtue cannot be morally cancelled out by action in accordance with the others. Neglecting a single virtue is

---

[13] The difficulties of this position, internal and external to Price's position, are outlined by Thomas (1977: 24–6).

[14] The discussion of piety and impiety in the *Review* itself is restricted to the sphere of religious belief and observance.

[15] For critical discussion of Price on inseparability, see Irwin 2008: 753. I take it that Price cannot be understood as committing himself to a strong identity claim, according to which, say, benevolence and justice are identical in all significant respects. This is ruled out by, among other things, his clear distinctions between the heads of virtue.

blameworthy just as clearly as neglecting all virtues is blameworthy. But what Price goes on to say suggests a much stronger interpretation:

To transgress...in one point...is to throw off effectually our allegiance, and to trample on the whole authority of the law....As long as any evil habit is retained,...we continue under the curse of guilt...and unqualified for bliss. (165–6)

On the face of it, Price's position seems implausibly harsh: a person who lives in accordance with all the virtues except, say, gratitude is morally as bad as a sadistic serial murderer. As Price himself later says: 'He that is just, kind, meek, and humble, but at the same time an habitual drunkard, can have no pretence to genuine virtue' (220). But he then goes on to offer a further argument (220–1). The habitual breach of one moral law shows that, if the agent had equally strong temptation to do wrong in other areas, he would do so. As far as virtue is concerned: 'He then loves her not at all, who loves her not *first*'.

Price's reliance here on counterfactuals is problematic for at least two related reasons. First, it ignores the distinction between action and character, central to voli-tionalism properly construed. According to Price's own volitionalism, morality con-sists in a certain set of rational requirements on an agent's will. If any agent, properly motivated by concern for the moral law, acts correctly in any case, then their action is maximally morally worthy—that is, they themselves are praiseworthy to a certain degree for acting in that way on that occasion. No agent in similar circumstances who acted similarly, from similar motivation, could deserve more praise. Of course, they may deserve blame for *not* acting rightly on other occasions, which means that their life will have been lived less morally well than that of some other agent who always acted rightly. But equally if their lapses are not universal their life will be more morally worthy than that of some other agent who always acts wrongly, even if the circum-stances they find themselves in are similar to those of our partially virtuous agent.

This is all a matter of the moral worth of one's actual actions. One's moral character, however, can be understood dispositionally, as a matter of what one *would* do in cer-tain circumstances. Here, then, we may claim that the character of an agent who would act wrongly if the temptation to do so increased is morally less valuable than the char-acter of an agent who would resist. And Price is right to say that acting wrongly in one sphere might be taken as *some* evidence that, under greater temptation, one would be more prepared to act wrongly in other spheres. But this raises a second problem for Price: he appears to have raised the bar so high that not only those with partial virtue, but also many, and perhaps all, of those with apparently full virtue—that is, those who always act rightly—are unqualified for bliss. For it is not implausible that there is *some* degree of temptation—which may of course be to avoid some bad outcome, such as severe suffering—sufficient to motivate any agent in any circumstances to act wrongly. So the only individual with true moral worth would be God himself.

Price himself may have recognized this problem, for he goes on to reassure us that he does not mean that we must be *perfect*:

A work of any kind may have all its essentials, and be complete in all its parts, when yet it may be unfinished…Some infirmities will cleave to the best, and it is impossible at present always to hold our passions under such strict discipline, as that they shall *never* surprize or hurry us into any thing which our hearts shall disapprove. But whenever this happens, it is essential to the character of a good man, that it is his *greatest* trouble, and that he is put by it upon more future vigilance. His settled *prevailing* regard in heart and life is to truth, piety, and goodness. (221–2)

In effect, Price is retreating in the face of the second objection raised above, and allowing that partial virtue—as long as the agent greatly regrets their lapses and tries harder to avoid them in future—is sufficient for virtue and a place in heaven.[16] But the reference to the agent's regret may also provide a clue as to why he was initially tempted to such a harsh judgement of partial virtue. An agent who violates a duty is violating the moral law, going against God's will, and in a sense violating God himself. But their regret shows that their 'prevailing' attitude to God is one of respect. The sin of disrespect to God is not one that Price is ready to see as a matter of degree (presumably above some fairly low threshold). Any significant disrespect at any time damages one's moral character to the point that only sincere repentance provides hope of saving it, and hence oneself.

3. Virtue as Law, and Supererogation

Price says of rectitude that it is 'a law as well as a rule to us' (108). A rule merely directs, and a moral rule certainly does that; but it also binds us, in the sense of having ultimate and primary authority (108–10). Further, morality is all-encompassing and overriding: any other alleged rule of action can only assist in our discovering what it is right to me. And when one judges that some action is 'fit to be done', one is

tied in the most strict and absolute manner, in bonds that no power can dissolve, and from which he can at no time, or in any single instance, break loose, without offering the most unnatural violence to himself; without making an inroad into his own soul, and immediately pronouncing his own sentence.

This seems an especially clear expression of what I have elsewhere (Crisp 2006: 35) called 'the myth of bindingness', the idea that something normatively significant is achieved through adding to the claim that one has overall reason to ø the further claim that one is 'bound' to ø, where the notion of bindingness is not being used merely to point to the existence of sanctions for non-ø-ing. The passage also enables us to anticipate the problem Price is going to have with supererogation. Standard cases of supererogation seem to involve the agent in going *beyond* the demands of reason and morality, and it is not clear why this will not involve their doing the most unnatural violence to themselves.

---

[16] On Price's view of repentance, see Thomas 1977: 34; 37–40.

As one might expect from a writer with the insight and integrity of Price, the general problem is recognized a few pages later, with a reference to Lord Kames's *Essays* (119– 24). The first form of the objection is put in terms of rightness. How can the right be what we are bound to do, if there are actions that are right, and even more praiseworthy than if they had been our duty, and yet we are not bound to perform them?

Price here draws a distinction between two senses of 'right'. One is the sense he has been using, which is opposed to 'wrong' and means 'such that one is obliged'. The right action is that which one is rationally required to perform. But there is another, broader sense in which what is right is what is merely *permitted*. The right action will, of course, always be a right action; but there will be actions that are right but not required.

This allows Price to draw a distinction between perfect and imperfect duties, though he does not use this Kantian terminology (120–1). His example is beneficence. We may say of someone who does something kind that they were not obliged to do this particu- lar act. Beneficence in general is a duty, and so the person who never helps others will be blamed, but we have a certain amount of discretion to decide whom we benefit and how.

Further, echoing Aristotle (1894: 1098a20–33), Price suggests that ethics is some- what indeterminate. No one can tell, for example, *exactly* how much of their wealth they should donate to charity, though there is clarity at the extremes: giving a few pence will be insufficient, while giving everything (if they have duties to their children, for example) is excessive. But, as Price has already insisted, everyone is obligated 'to do all the good he can for his fellow-creatures' (120), and in general 'whenever any behav- iour...appear[s], *all things considered*, BEST', it becomes obligatory (122). So any par- ticular action, Price claims, will be either right (in the sense of 'obligatory'), wrong, or indifferent. And a particular action, such as helping someone in need, may be indiffer- ent, although there may be a duty to perform such actions in general.

But allowing for imperfect duties is of course not yet to allow for supererogation, as Price again sees, asking how it can be that certain indifferent actions are more 'amiable'. The answer, he says, is 'very easy'. As we have seen, Price's view is that the virtuous agent is motivated by concern for the good and the right. He first notes that this motivation can arise even in cases of indifference. So, when helping someone, I may be motivated by an argument along the following lines: 'There is a general duty to help people. This action is a case of helping someone. So I will help this person.'

Price then asks how it is that we often see '*greater* merit' in actions of this kind. I take him not to be implying that we generally find beneficent actions more meritorious than, say, just actions. Rather, he is referring to the apparent phenomenon of supererogation. I say this because of his own response to the problem:

As every action of an agent is *in him* so far virtuous, as he was determined to it by a regard to virtue; so the more of this regard it discovers, the more we must admire it. And it is plain, it is more discovered, and a stronger virtuous principle proved, by fixing (in cases where the limits of duty are not exactly defined) upon the greater rather than the less. (123)

This *discovery* argument shows that Price's position is in fact inimical to the idea of supererogation. He allows for indifference only in cases of discretion within the limits of imperfect duty. In the case of a person who appears to be going *beyond* duty, Price will insist—if the person is acting rationally—that this is in fact a case of doing what is best, and so required rather than optional. As he puts it, 'acting *beyond* obligation' is equivalent to 'acting *contrary* to obligation' (124).

But there is a further problem, internal to his own strictly deontological position. Consider a case in which I know that I am required to help someone financially. I know that I am required to give them £90–100 or so, but cannot be more precise. According to Price, if I give £100 then this proves a 'stronger virtuous principle' in me, and so I am to that extent more praiseworthy. But then it is not clear why any agent in a similar position is not *required* to give £100. Why would we not blame someone for—meanly— giving only £90 when they could have given £100?

Now Price does note here the distinction between the virtue of the *action* and the virtue of the *agent*. So his thought could be the following. It is permissible for any agent, when it is required of them to give £90–100, to decide that any amount within that range is *required* of them. So the person who gives £90 is doing what they believe is right, and so cannot be blamed. But because their action is less demanding it is evidence of a 'weaker virtuous principle' and their action is therefore less 'amiable' than that of the person who gives £100. This seems problematic in two ways. First, Price seems to be allowing that a virtuous agent—even the most virtuous agent in such circumstances—is not only ignorant of the true normative circumstances, but ignorant in a way that allows them to do something morally more admirable. Second, it remains unclear why we are not required to act on the strongest virtuous principle in every case—that is, how it can be morally permissible to do less than the morally best. As Sidgwick later put it (1907: 220), this notion will seem to common sense an 'immoral paradox'. On Price's view, it seems that it will be significantly easier for the naturally stingy person, for example, to avoid wrongdoing than a person with abundant natural generosity.

4. Virtue and Egoism

The sixth chapter of the *Review* begins with an explanation of the close relationship between the concepts of fitness, rightness, moral goodness, reasonableness, obliga- tion, ought, should, duty, and virtue. Price then considers the view that we are not obligated to refrain from anything, even if it is wrong, unless it advances our own self- interest or is commanded by a superior power (105–6). He charges the view with self- contradiction, on the ground that wrongness just is what we obligated to avoid independently of self-interest or the will of any higher power. The charge of self- contradiction is an odd one, however, since Price's opponent will of course deny that they are using wrongness in Price's sense. Nor does their usage seem to involve any kind of conceptual error.

Price goes on to claim that:

those who maintain that all obligation is to be deduced from...self-love, assert what...implies, that the words *right* and *just* stand for no real and distinct characters of actions; but signify merely what is...conducive to private advantage, whatever that may be...; and any the most pernicious effects will become just...if but the smallest degree of clear advantage or pleasure may result to him from them.

Price's argument here is not straightforward. On one interpretation, he is once more assuming a conceptual truth: that rightness cannot be identical with what maximally promotes the agent's self-interest. This may be because he accepts the Kantian view that duty must provide reasons in at least potential competition with self-interest (Kant 2002: 4: 414). But this again is certainly not a conceptual truth, and further argument is required. On the face of it, there is nothing incoherent about a form of ethical egoism, according to which each agent is morally required only to do what most advances their self-interest. Nor does there seem to be anything to prevent such an egoist from adopting Price's realist metaethics, and arguing that the real property of rightness is in fact identical with the real property of maximizing the agent's good.

Another interpretation puts more weight on Price's reference to 'deduction'. It may be that he has in mind a form of normative egoism stated in non-moral terms, from which position are then 'deduced' various claims about moral obligation. One way to make such a deduction valid, of course, will be to include a further premise, such as ethical egoism. But Price may be thinking of a position according to which the word 'right' is used just to *mean* what is in the agent's self-interest. If so, one might have expected him to point out that this position relies on a clear misuse of language, rather than that it leads to morally unacceptable conclusions.

The 'unacceptable conclusions' argument also seems to rely on something close to a hedonist conception of the good. Price fails to consider the possibility of an egoistic veto of the kind found in ego-restricted pluralism, according to which no agent ever has reason to do anything which does not maximally promote their own good. The good may then be said to be identical with doing what is required by morality. (These requirements may themselves be reason-giving, but need not come into conflict with the egoistic principle. Indeed it may be a necessary truth that the agent's good will be maximally promoted by acting in conformity with morality. Equally, however, the requirements may not be reason-giving, and then some other account of them will be required, such perhaps as a divine command view.)

Nevertheless, Price's point about the implausibility of the implications of ethical egoism is a strong one, and he later uses an analogous argument against consequentialism (131–8; see below sect. 4). Both egoism and utilitarianism are strongly counterintuitive, and Price rightly puts the onus of justification at this point on proponents of either.

Price's conceptual claims appear to commit him to what some have called 'moral rationalism', the view that moral reasons are always overriding. That position emerges also in a further *revaluation* argument against egoism (107–8). Consider a case in which what morality requires is against my self-interest. According to the egoist, I have here no reason to obey morality. This, Price claims, implies not only 'that virtue itself would cease', but it 'would be changed into vice'. This is because, on the egoist position, my obligation must be to do what is best for myself; so going against that obligation would itself be vicious.

Again, to respond to this argument the egoist may insist on a distinction between rationality and morality, that is, between what one has a reason to do and what is required by morality. According to the most plausible form of normative egoism, my only reason is to advance my own self-interest, and this reason is not itself an 'ethical' or 'moral' reason. This allows for a conception of morality as a set of demands or requirements that are not in themselves normative, that is, do not constitute practical reasons. On this view, the requirements of morality may be seen as analogous in certain ways to the requirements of logic or epistemic rationality. So they may be genuine requirements, but the question of whether they ground practical reasons remains open, a possibility ruled out within Price's somewhat narrow conceptual scheme.

5. Virtue and Happiness

Price is convinced that, in general, choosing a life of virtue over one of vice will advance the agent's own happiness. This is in large part because '[s]elf-approbation and self-reproach are the chief sources of private happiness and misery' (59). The virtuous person loves virtue more than anything else, and pursuing and engaging with the objects one values most highly will produce the greatest pleasures (222). Nor is it any objection to this claim that making virtue one's primary goal will be self-defeating, since virtue requires disinterestedness (222–3). The virtuous person aims not at his own happiness, but to act rightly; pleasure is not a *cause* of his desires, but an *effect* (74–6; see Butler S 11.6–7; Irwin 2008: 716). Vice, however, if its possessor is not entirely evil, will produce in the agent a state of 'constant intestine war' (259), in which the agent is torn between rational and irrational desire.

But what if the agent *is* entirely evil? Price admits that such a person may be happier than the partially virtuous agent (258–9). Further, as far as happiness or pleasure are concerned, in the present state of the world these vicious individuals—and, presumably on the occasion the conflicted individuals—are the happiest. Price does not say explicitly that these vicious individuals could not have been even happier had they chosen virtue, but this is clearly what he means: 'A person who sacrifices his life, rather than violate his conscience, or betray his country, gives up all possibility of any present reward, and loses the more in proportion as his virtue is more glorious' (258).

Price's view here contrasts strongly with Aristotle's:

It is true also of the good person that he does a great deal for his friends and his country, and will die for them if he must; he will sacrifice money, honours, and in general the goods for which people compete, procuring for himself what is noble...he gets what is noble, and therefore assigns himself the greater good. (1894: 1169a18–29)

On Aristotle's view, virtue is always the best choice to make as far as the *eudaimonia*—the happiness, or good—of the virtuous agent is concerned. It cannot guarantee happiness—as in case of Priam (1894: 1101a7–8)—but even when it does not result in happiness it still produces the best outcome for the agent, since the alternative would be vicious and hence unhappy rather than 'non-happy'.

Price sometimes uses language which suggests the Aristotelian position. Having mentioned the 'tranquility and bliss' consequent on virtue (229), he goes on—with explicit reference to Plato's *Republic*—to praise the comparison of the mind of the virtuous person to a well-governed and harmonious state, asking: 'Is there any thing that deserves ambition, besides acquiring *such* a mind? In what else can the true blessedness and perfection of a man consist?'. A virtuous mind is the 'first and highest good'.

Later, however, having allowed that virtue should always be chosen in preference to vice, whatever one's circumstances, Price makes it clear that this is *not* because virtue is 'more *profitable* than vice (or attended with more pleasure)', but because it is of '*intrinsick* excellence and obligation' and 'is to be chosen for itself, independently of its utility' (257–8; also e.g. 119).

The contrast here between, on the one hand, what is 'profitable' (presumably either in itself or for its consequences) and, on the other, what is intrinsically good independently of any such profit or utility suggests that we must interpret Price in the earlier passage to be implying that a person's highest good is not always identical with what is best *for them*. This is another place, then, where he parts company with Aristotle, denying the central and unstated premise of the 'function' argument of *Nicomachean Ethics* 1.7 (1894: 1097b–1098a).[17]

Price might appear, then, to be attracted towards a hedonistic account of the good, such that consistency with the view that virtue always benefits the agent could be achieved only through the adoption of some extremely implausible claims about the pleasantness of acting virtuously. But in fact he has an independent reason for denying the Aristotelian position. On Price's view, we have a great deal of evidence for the existence of God. In the *Dissertation*, Price claims that 'this visible universe, of which we are a part, is, *self-evidently*, an exhibition of the power and wisdom of a powerful and wise cause' (285). This allows him to use the fact that the wicked prosper in this world as itself an argument for an afterlife, in which all will receive their just deserts:

Can it be conceived, that the wisdom and equity of providence should fail only in the instance of virtue? That here, where we should expect the exactest order, there should be the least?...'Tis of little consequence, how much at any time virtue suffers and vice triumphs *here*, if *hereafter* there is to be a just distinction between them, and every inequality is to be set right. (260–1; also 83, 166)

---

[17] Irwin (2008: 717) suggests that Price seems not to have understood what Aristotle had in mind.

But what is to prevent God's always immediately rewarding the virtuous and punishing the vicious in *this* world? This, Price suggests (261), would make it impossible for
him properly to test our characters, since we would always choose virtue for 'mercenary' reasons. Here, however, we can see how close to the wind Price is sailing. On
the one hand, as we have seen, he wishes to claim that moral obligations are overriding, and should be acted on whatever the consequences for one's happiness; on the
other, his theology involves the idea that virtue will always be rewarded and vice
punished, perhaps to an infinite degree: virtue, that is to say, is not only ultimately
cost-free, but also ultimately maximally beneficial to the agent. But if I perform the
virtuous action now with an eye on heavenly reward perhaps many years hence, why
is that any less mercenary than my doing so for an immediate reward? Price's
response would doubtless to return to the Butlerian distinction between pleasure as
cause and pleasure as effect. But again it is not clear why a clear grasp of that distinction would not allow God to create a system in which immediate reward follows only
on virtuous actions motivated independently of any desire for that reward itself. Our
dispositions and motivational make-up are as much God's handiwork as anything
else in the world.

I have just mentioned the possibility that rewards and punishments in the afterlife
may be infinite. Price was a brilliant probability theorist, and in the *Review*'s conclusion he attempts a further happiness-based, Pascalian argument for virtue grounded
on the implications of infinite goods and bads for expected utility theory: 'when the
good is infinite the value of any chance for it must be likewise infinite' (271).

This argument is problematic in at least two ways. First, it is dangerous pragmatically
for the sorts of reasons discussed above. If Price persuades me that I will be punished
for eternity for vice, how can I avoid being motivated, to some degree, by that belief,
which may itself put me at risk of that very punishment for failing to act in the morally
correct way? Second, there is a possibility (it does not matter how small) that God
admires those self-reliant individuals who pursue their own good at any cost to that of
others. That possibility cancels out that of Price's God, and Price will have to rely on
non-probability-based arguments to make his case (see Mackie 1982: 203).

When it comes to motivation, it is clear that Price's ideal agent will care, ultimately,
for nothing but virtue: 'nothing else deserves one anxious thought or wish' (267). This
explains why Price can see no reason why we should not praise the person who, on the
basis of their religious principles and knowledge of divine reward and punishment,
always chooses virtue on the basis of self-love. Such a person is *not* motivated by
S-reasons, or their beliefs about S-reasons. Self-love is a *duty*, and the virtuous person
will therefore be prudent for the same reason that they are benevolent or just.[18] It is
true that self-love is rational, since our desire for happiness is not merely instinctual
(71). It is an affection, rather than a mere passion. But it is not, as rational, practically
ultimate. The virtuous person's motivation, we must presume, is focused on duty, and

[18] As Barnes says (1942: 170), this is 'a difficult doctrine'.

the duty of self-love regulates the degree to which we should act on our affection for ourselves. The virtuous agent's actions are determined, that is to say, by their reason. Their love for themselves is, though reasonable, from the motivational point of view a mere fact about themselves taken into account in their practical thought.

Does all this imply that Price's view of reasons somehow transcends the distinction between persons entirely, so that there are no S-reasons? Not at all. There is no reason to believe that Price would deny that, say, severe and undeserved suffering is bad for a person, and that this badness gives them a reason to avoid it. They should not, however, be motivated by or concerned to any degree about that reason. This allows for the possibility of unproblematic subjective sacrifice as far as the goods of this world are concerned. But Price's account certainly strongly suggests that he would admit the possibility of subjective sacrifice when any thought of posthumous reward is absent from the agent's mind at the time of acting. (He may not have allowed such sacrifice in the case of atheists, since their actions are 'instinctual'.) What is ruled out, of course, is any possibility of overall objective sacrifice.

Price's virtuous person, then, is concerned for little or nothing other than duty. But does Price not allow for an area of life in which we are free from the requirements of morality, and can act on S-reasons? His denial of supererogation, and his view that self-love is a duty, as well as his explicit claim that we should care about nothing other than virtue, rule out any such space for S-reasons to feature in normative justification or rational motivation. We do have a reason to promote our own good, but that reason is duty-based, and requires us to promote that good as far as possible within the constraints of duties other than prudence. Here, then, is another place in which Price moves beyond Aristotle's already highly moralistic account of value and practical reasoning. Aristotle's virtuous person will be motivated by nobility, but he will be fully aware that acquiring such nobility will advance his own happiness. And nothing Aristotle says suggests that this awareness should not play any part in his being moved to act virtuously. Indeed, it may be that his motivation is entirely egoistic, and that he aims ultimately only at promoting his own good. Price's virtuous agent, however, ultimately loves only duty. And since the truth about duty is identical to God, his loving duty is close to his loving God. But he must love God ultimately for his intrinsic goodness, not for the goods he bestows, here and in the afterlife. To do what is best for oneself, then, involves the complete renunciation of self-love in favour of love of virtue.

15
Gay, Tucker, Paley, and Bentham:
Variations on the Theme of Happiness

Jeremy Bentham (1748–1842) is often described as the first 'classical utilitarian', a title used to refer also to J.S. Mill and, sometimes, Henry Sidgwick. This description, as we have already seen, is somewhat misleading: Cumberland, Hutcheson, and Hume can all be described as utilitarians, and Hutcheson's position in particular is not only close to Bentham's and to utilitarianism as it is currently understood, but significantly more developed as a normative ethics than Bentham's. In this chapter, with the topic of the relation of self-interest and morality in mind, and in order to provide a fuller picture of the road to Bentham, I shall discuss three other important writers who can plausibly be categorized as utilitarians: John Gay, Abraham Tucker, and William Paley.

1. Gay: Virtue and its Associations

John Gay (1699–1745), not to be confused with his older cousin, author of *The Beggar's Opera*, was educated at Cambridge, and briefly taught Hebrew, Greek, and ecclesiastical history there. He had a serious interest in philosophy, and was well known as an authority on Locke. In 1731, Edmund Law published an English translation of William King's *Essay on the Origin of Evil*, including as an anonymous introduction Gay's *Preliminary Dissertation concerning the Fundamental Principle of Virtue or Morality*.[1] Gay was acknowledged as author in the 4th edition of 1758.[2] The work is indeed Lockean in certain respects, but is often seen as one of the earliest statements of utilitarian ethics, influencing, among others, Tucker, Paley, and Bentham.[3] Gay's essay is worth studying also for his unusual attempt to explain moral motivation from an

---

[1] The title page of the volume uses the name '*Dissertation concerning the Fundamental Principle and Immediate Criterion of Virtue*'.

[2] Unattributed references are to pages of the first edition. Much of the essay is reprinted in Schneewind 1990: vol. 2, 400–13. Schneewind uses the 1781 5th edn., which contains minor revisions, apparently by Law. Some ellipses are not marked in Schneewind's version.

[3] Also worthy of mention here is Daniel Waterland (1683–1740). In his work on the Christian sacraments, published the year before Gay's *Dissertation*, Waterland draws a distinction between material and moral goodness, the former consisting in an action's tendency towards 'the general Good of Mankind', the latter in the action's being chosen in conformity with divine law (1730: 13).

egoistic psychological hedonist perspective, using associationist ideas which them-selves were to influence the work of David Hartley, and James and J.S. Mill.

Gay begins (xi–xii) by noting the apparent widespread disagreement among philosophers concerning the 'criterion' of virtue—the property the possession of which by some action entitles us to describe that action as virtuous—and suggests that, since these philosophers tend to agree on the substantive issue of which actions are in fact virtuous, they may well be using different terms for what is in fact the same criterion. He goes on (xiii–xv) to note, with reference to Hutcheson, that the egoistic psychological hedonist claim that the actions of rational beings are all aimed only at the happiness of the agent seems inconsistent with the facts that many approve of vir-tue without being able to give any further reason for their approval, and may pursue virtue even when it seems 'destructive of their Happiness'. Gay admires Hutcheson's notion of the moral sense, but objects that it is close to a doctrine of 'occult qualities'. Rather, we can use the notion of the association of ideas to explain morality in psychologically egoistic terms.

Gay then proceeds to inquire further into the criterion of virtue (xv–xviii). That requires him to define virtue itself:

Virtue is the Conformity to a Rule of Life, directing the Actions of all rational Creatures with respect to each other's Happiness; to which Conformity every one in all Cases is obliged: and every one that does so conform, is or ought to be approved of, esteemed and loved for so doing.

So to ascertain the criterion we have to find which rule of life we are obliged to conform to, and this requires Gay to examine the notion of obligation itself (xviii–xxi). Gay's conception of obligation is shaped by his psychological egoism: obligation is '*the neces-sity of doing or omitting any Action in order to be happy*'. He does not consider the pos-sibility of moral obligations independent of the agent's happiness, which an agent understood in terms of psychological egoism might nevertheless fulfil were virtuous actions to be in her self-interest. Gay would almost certainly have denied that any such alleged moral requirements could count as 'obligations': the only thing that can ultimately bind the will of a rational agent is the promotion of her own happiness and the means to it.

Gay sees obligations as falling into four categories: *natural* obligations rest on our perception of natural consequences; *virtuous* obligations arise from merit and 'demerit', which result in the esteem or disfavour of others; *civil* obligations arise from the authority of the magistrate; and *religious* obligations from the authority of God.[4]

Gay claims that the only universal obligation is religious, since only God can in every case make someone happy or unhappy. Since moral obligation is itself universal, then, its criterion must be the will of God. (Once again, we see the notion of divine reward and punishment's being used to ensure an overlap between self-interest and morality.) But what does God will? His only end in creating humanity is its happiness;

---

[4] Cf. Bentham's 'sanctions': see below pp. 200–1.

so my own actions should aim at promoting the pleasure and avoiding or alleviating the pain of humanity. It is this, Gay suggests, that those who speak of the 'fitness' of certain actions have in mind; he does not consider that certain actions might be fitting independently of any promotion of happiness, revealingly claiming: 'Fitness without relation to some *End*, is scarce intelligible'.[5] 'Right reason' likewise consists entirely in the foresight of hedonic consequences. It is these claims, blind as they are to the possibilities of deontological ethics, that ground Gay's title as one of the founders of utilitarianism.[6]

Even if we accept Gay's account of the relation of virtue and self-interest, he continues, the problem remains of explaining how it can be that agents appear to pursue virtue for its own sake, independently of their own happiness. This requires an examination of 'approbation and affection' (xxii–iii), which Gay finds to be entirely based on anticipated pleasure. The prospect of future pleasure—'passion'—is *itself* pleasurable, and leads to desire ('affection'). All other desires and conative states have their source in such anticipations of pleasure and pain, and so Gay believes he now has the material to explain moral motivation itself (xxiii–xxxiii). Since my happiness is dependent on the wills of others, I must approve of whatever, through constituting the happiness of another, will motivate that other to promote my own happiness. Further, because we desire what we approve, we will desire the happiness of any agent who has benefited us.

Gay moves too quickly here from the claim that I will desire that *element* in another's happiness that leads to happiness for me to the claim that I will desire another's happiness in itself. He goes on to introduce the idea of *merit* as the entitlement to approval and love from anyone whose happiness one has promoted. This idea of merit itself explains beneficent action, since the benefactor will assume the beneficiary will accept the benefactor's entitlement to esteem and other positive returns. Nor, Gay argues, does this ultimately self-interested motivation undermine the very idea of merit in such a case: what matters is the agent's non-ultimate end—viz., the happiness of the other. It may be that Gay is here offering mere psychology, and it certainly makes sense that a self-interested patient would wish to encourage further acts of beneficence towards her, regardless of their ultimate motivation. But as psychology, as Gay is aware (see below), it leaves unexplained what seems to be genuinely ultimate other-regarding motivation. (It may be thought that Gay is suggesting that the merit in question is genuinely normative. But it is hard to see how to make sense of such a notion without a conception of moral obligation which is itself independent of self-regarding practical necessity. My 'obligation' to esteem a benefactor, that is to say, is itself based on a recognition that by so favouring that benefactor I increase the chance of further benefits, either from that benefactor or others who see how I 'resent Favours or Injuries' (xxvii).)

---

[5] Cf. Hutcheson E 159.
[6] See Halévy 1928: 22. Carlyle (1901: 272) rightly notes that the view most similar to Gay's among his predecessors is that of Cumberland. But, as Albee (1897: 140) points out, there are no perfectionist elements in Gay's position.

Gay goes on to elucidate his claim about the source of our evaluative and conative states and attitudes in hedonic love and hate. Shame, for example, is the uneasiness felt at losing esteem. He then faces a 'grand Objection' (xxviii), returning to the issue of immediate moral approval and disapproval, unmediated by a concern for the agent's own happiness, even when the subject herself recognizes that what she is approving will decrease her own happiness. In effect, the objector is resurrecting Hutcheson's notion of the moral sense.

Gay accepts the phenomenon, but claims that it is the result of the agent's having already categorized the type of action in question as a means to her happiness and so to be pursued without any need for reference to that happiness in the particular case. In other words, as one might put it, the agent sees the keeping of a promise as 'to be done', rather than as 'to be done as a means to my happiness'. Gay compares the phenomenon to that of reliance on non-ultimate axioms when forming beliefs, describing such axioms, whether epistemic or practical, as 'RESTING PLACES' (xxx).

What about the cases in which the agent is quite aware of the detrimental effects some object of moral approval will have on their happiness? Gay's explanation of these and similar cases is that we tend to forget our ultimate end, and hence treat the practical 'resting places' as if they were themselves ultimate principles. Gay's position, then, is a version of what I earlier called split-level psychological egoism. He elucidates the mechanism involved using an analogy with money, which almost certainly inspired J.S. Mill to make the same move in his 'proof' of utilitarian to explain how virtue can become a 'part of happiness' (1998: 4.5–6; see Crisp 1996). Many begin by desiring money as a means to happiness. They take pleasure in money as a means, but gradually the association between money and happiness leads to money's becoming an end in itself.

Gay speaks of the 'fantastical pleasure of having' money, and it might seem that what he means is that these people desire money because they enjoy its possession. If that were so, Gay's suggestion that money itself is desired as an end would be misleading. Further, his analogy would be unhelpful in elucidating immediate approval and disapproval, which he has already said are quite independent of happiness. In other words we must take him seriously when he says: '[T]he Connection between Money and Happiness remains in the Mind; tho' it has long since ceased between the things themselves' (xxxi).

Gay ends by noting that the establishment of associations can arise through our learning from others, particularly those we admire, or whose esteem we would welcome. His conclusion makes clear that his main difference with Hutcheson does not concern the notion of the moral sense itself, so much as its origin: 'I deny that this Moral Sense, or these Public Affections are innate, or *implanted* in us: they are acquired either from our own *Observation* or the *Imitation* of others'. It has to be admitted that Gay provides little evidence for this crucial claim, and it is tempting to think that his associationist hypothesis is introduced primarily to sustain his egoistic psychological hedonist orthodoxy and to avoid any reference to 'occult qualities'.

2. Tucker: Regulus and Virtue Re-enlarged

Abraham Tucker (1705–74) was a comfortably off English gentleman, with a solid legal and classical education. After the death of his beloved wife, in 1754, Tucker spent much of the rest of his life on a vast, nine-volume work on ethics, metaphysics, and theology, *The Light of Nature Pursued*.[7] Tucker often cites Locke as an influence, and his position has much in common with that of Gay. Paley expresses a deep debt to him (1804: xxiv), and there is no doubt that, though his work is hardly read today, it was highly significant in the development of utilitarianism.

Tucker is a psychological egoist, a rational egoist, and an evaluative hedonist. Our motivations ultimately all arise from our own pleasure—or rather the representation of pleasure (1.105–6)—or pain, and that aggregate balance of pleasure or pain constitutes our happiness and our ultimate end (2.160, 186–7, 328). The only exception is weakness of will, when our representations of future good or evil lack their appropriate motivational force (1.109–10). Tucker understands pleasure broadly, using Locke's term 'satisfaction' to distance himself from any conception of pleasure in which it is opposed to 'business, duty, works of use and necessity' (1.98; also 2.11, 182), each of which can be enjoyed as effectively as bodily or sensual pleasure. And this is the only good: 'All that men esteem valuable or think it worth their while to pursue derives its value either directly from enjoyment or from something else first recommended thereby' (2.124; also 186–7). Satisfaction is the same in all cases: pleasures do not differ in kinds, *qua* pleasures, whether they arise from listening to music, tasting dainty food, performing virtuous actions, or contemplation (2.183).

Tucker's ideal agent will act for the glory of God, but even they must always do so in the firm belief that so acting is most beneficial for them (9.19). This is not to say that they, or anyone else, will at all times have that belief at the forefront of their minds, or as some kind of ultimate premise in any process of practical reasoning (2.195–7). Tucker follows Gay in his split-level psychological egoism. Like travellers, we should not constantly keep our eyes on our destination, but once we have set ourselves in the right direction we should concentrate on what is nearby. Indeed we very rarely aim directly at our own happiness.

Like Gay—and Cumberland, though to a lesser extent—Tucker's ethical position contains enough of the elements now typically attributed to utilitarianism for him to be characterized as an early proponent of the position. Tucker is a consequentialist, seeing no moral value or disvalue in actions independently of the pleasure or pain they produce (2.147). In language that resonates with the work of Hutcheson and Smith, Tucker suggests that we can often assess the value of our own actions best by imagining

---

[7] The first five volumes were published in 1768. The first two published volumes Tucker describes as a single volume in two parts, on 'Human Nature'. The final three he classifies as a second volume in three parts, on 'Theology'. The final four published volumes Tucker sees as parts of his third volume, on 'Lights of Nature and Gospel Blended'. I shall refer by number of published volume (1–9), and page number. All unattributed references are to this work.

the hedonic effects on us were we to be objects of the same actions performed by others:

[A]ctions have not an intrinsic turpitude necessarily touching the sense when contemplating them naked, but we must place them in other subjects where their tendency to bring trouble and inconvenience upon ourselves casts a turpitude upon them, having frequently seen them…we then practice the art of removing ourselves to a distance from ourselves, through which channel we derive that skill of discernment called the moral sense. (2.158)

It emerges also that Tucker's conception of impartiality is strong and impersonal. In one of his earlier volumes Tucker objects to 'violent attachments to particular persons' as morally equivalent to selfishness (2.334–5), later making it clear that any such attachment will count as 'violent' if it is not in line with the promotion of 'the general stock of happiness' (7.419). In scriptural language, we must see each of our fellow citizens in the universe as our neighbour, and—since each of us is a citizen—count their good equally with our own (benevolence) and our good equally with theirs (prudence) (7.419–20). As one might expect, Tucker is also committed to the maximization of overall happiness. The 'wiseman' will not ignore relative 'trifles', such as subscribing to a concert or making polite conversation, but his constant aim is 'the greater good' (2.323; also 6.251; 9.445), and that aim is prior to all others (2.342).

Tucker's utilitarianism is especially salient in his discussions of punishment: 'the use of punishment is not to repair the damage sustained, to which it will by no means contribute, but to mend the manners and direction the intention of mankind to the forbearance of injury' (2.128). Our principles of justice themselves are valuable only in so far as they promote happiness (2.157, 294), as is the case with all other common-sense moral principles (2.147; 5.43–4). Even fulfilling our duty to glorify God consists only in our promoting overall happiness, since that was God's own aim in creating us (6.18). Tucker is an act utilitarian—the rightness of an action consists in its promoting the good, impartially construed. And like most act utilitarians he recognizes the value of common-sense moral rules, but also allows that there can be times when 'a judicious discernment of the greater general good' (2.367) requires that they be broken. But it is important, when we believe that violating a rule will promote the overall good, to take into account the effect of breaking the rule on our own future actions or those of others (2.154), and also to bear in mind the difficulties in computing pleasures arising from our different tastes, the fact that we cannot directly compare past pleasures with future, and so on (2.113–16). In practice, promoting overall happiness is similar to guessing the number of sheep in a flock.

The dominance of the utilitarian principle over others also legitimizes appeal to it in cases of lower-level conflict between principles: 'I know of no other way to determine the matter than by a reference to use' (2.145). Lower-order rules should also be 'tested' occasionally in the light of the utilitarian principle, to ensure that they are still maximally effective in current circumstances.

The split-level nature of Tucker's egoism enables him to sidestep the objection that his virtuous agents can never be genuinely or disinterestedly virtuous, since they are always aiming directly at their own good. Because the virtuous person can on particular occasions be moved directly by concern for others, virtue is, Tucker suggests, like a flower which emerges untainted by the soil in which it grew (2.328-9; 7.351). But Tucker is quite clear that 'virtue' has no non-instrumental value (2.220-1). Actions are good only in so far as they lead to satisfaction; and virtue is good only in so far as it leads to actions, so that it is at 'two removes from the summum bonum'. It is there merely 'to rectify the disorders of our nature'. Nevertheless, virtuous action is generally attractive. There is a joy, or 'complacence', in acting rightly, and unpleasant shamefulness in acting wrongly (1.135), and each agent will be 'more or less happy' in proportion to his virtue (2.234-5). There are also less direct benefits (2.330-3). Benevolence will often be reciprocated; its aims will more often be achieved than those of malevolence; it provides opportunities for enjoyable activity, for enjoying others' happiness; it prevents others thinking badly of us, and by leading us to focus on the well-being of others it advances our understanding of the world and the role of fortune in it.

Do virtue and self-interest overlap for Tucker? Not entirely. Tucker allows that it might be the case that someone could love virtue so much that they were happy even when suffering great pain, but he thinks it likely to be highly unusual among 'the sons of Adam' (1.136-7). Virtue can only be, in most circumstances, the best bet from the self-interested point of view.

Consider again the story of Regulus, the Roman general who kept his promise to return to the Carthaginians and was tortured to death (see above pp. 126-7). In 'The Limitation of Virtue' (2.364-84), the final chapter of the first of his three 'volumes', Tucker faces the question whether Regulus sacrificed himself for virtue, and answers that he did. First, he admits that a person close to death may well find himself in a position where vice is profitable: why should someone with little time left, who loves their food, and takes little or no pleasure in temperance, not overindulge (2.367-73)? He then considers all that might be said in favour of the claim that Regulus's virtuous action promoted his happiness (2.376-9). We might assume that he was one of those who took such pleasure in virtue that he was overall happy even while being tortured. But it is implausible that this pleasure could be of greater value than the many future pleasures he gave up. Perhaps he knew that he would have been stricken by such terrible and enduring guilt had he broken his promise that enjoyments would have been out of the question. If so, that would have been the result of a virtuous disposition, and then we must ask what reason anyone would have to cultivate such a disposition in the first place. A rational agent should recognize that what is 'good and laudable at one time may become mischievous and blamable by a change of circumstances', and build moral flexibility into his character from the start. The wise man cultivates virtue because he believes it will make him happy, and he will not allow his commitment to virtue to defeat the very purpose for which he adopted it.

What about the afterlife? Tucker admits that he has found nothing in his research in his first volume, on human nature, which leads him to believe that there is such a thing (2.381). He then considers someone's objecting that his stating his views on virtue and self-interest is inconsistent with his own egoism: it is surely in his interest that others believe that virtue always coincides with self-interest, even if he himself does not? Here Tucker drops a strong hint that the rest of *The Light of Nature* is going to provide arguments for theism and the afterlife that will enable him to deny his earlier position.

In the thousands of pages that follow, Tucker is as faithful as Regulus in fulfilling his earlier promise. The main prop for his arguments for the existence of God is the notion of design, and he uses the analogy between God and a watchmaker, found in Cicero and used by many later writers, including Descartes, Newton, and Paley (6.216; also 5.95–7), who was perhaps influenced by Tucker. As we might expect, Tucker's God is—as far as we can discern—a utilitarian, and hence, for example, punishes only for reasons of deterrence (5.237–8, 380–2). The Christian doctrine of eternal punishment, for Tucker, 'has no foundation in human reason' (5.457). When considering present evils, we should take into account the pleasures to come. Doing some rough calculations comparing the numbers now living with those already in heaven, Tucker draws an analogy with a person who lives to the age of Methusalah and is perfectly happy except for one minute of pain every twenty-two years (8.148–9).

Tucker's position on morality and responsibility contains some tensions. On the one hand, we are told that God gives us free will, and so we are accountable for the choices we make (5.387–91). On the other, Tucker recognizes that, if God created everything, it is hard to see how anything is ultimately up to us, and he accepts a form of hard determinism, grounded in divine providence (6.186–7). Hard determinism causes few major problems for utilitarian ethics, according to which what ultimately matters is the actualization of the best possible world rather than the attribution of responsibility, blame, praise, punishment, or reward to individuals for what they have done in the past. But at this point Tucker's commitment to a utilitarian God fails. He cannot accept that God could allow inequalities between individuals which are not their own fault, and so insists that, in the end, the goods bestowed on any one of us, here and in the afterlife, will be equal. Tucker sees no 'hindrance that whatever measure of bounty is thought proper for the creatures may be diffused equally among them' (3.259; also 265; 5.305–6).

The upshot is that Regulus's sacrifice was only apparent, and virtue has been 're-enlarged'. Each of us will be compensated for any pain we suffer for the sake of others. Further, since Tucker avoids the perils of the mathematics of infinity, by undergoing such pain, we increase the total amount of good to be redistributed, and hence end up being *rewarded*, since by increasing the total we have increased our own share of that total (5.384–5, 489).[8] Tucker sees the universe as a business rather than a zero-sum game: 'The universe may be justly regarded as an innumerable host of partners, dealing together in the traffic of happiness' (5.356). Regulus, indeed, far from being imprudent, 'acted like a thrifty merchant' (5.504).

---

[8] Tucker is thus immune to the objection levelled at him by Stephen (1876: 120), who describes him as a 'solitary and half-trained thinker', that his view on divine equity makes all actions indifferent.

3. Paley: Rules for Happiness

William Paley (1743–1805) was a clergyman in the Church of England whose essays in Christian apologetics led to his being offered a stall in St Paul's cathedral and the rectory of Bishopwearmouth. He was educated at Cambridge, and went on to lecture there on moral philosophy. He is now best known for his use of the analogy between God and a watchmaker with which he begins his *Natural Theology*, a book which impressed Darwin. His *Principles of Moral and Political Philosophy* soon became hugely influential, and as late as 1933 was described by John Maynard Keynes as 'an immortal book' (1933: 108n1).[9] Paley was a close friend of John Law, the son of Edmund Law, in whose book John Gay's *Dissertation* had been published, and he played a significant role in the transmission and development of utilitarian theory from the late-eighteenth into the nineteenth centuries.

Paley again saw God's primary virtue as benevolence (1.74, 76), indeed infinite benevolence (N 319), and argued that the very presence of pleasure in the world is evidence of that benevolence, since God could have motivated his creatures solely by pain (N 299–300). 'It is a happy world after all', Paley claims, since there is a 'prepollency' of good over evil—pleasure over pain—in the human species (N 303). Serious evil is uncommon, which explains why it becomes a matter of note when it occurs. Paley uses here and elsewhere (e.g. 1.24) what is in effect an early version of the 'utilitarian calculus', influenced here by William Wollaston (1659–1724), according to whom happiness consists in an excess of pleasure over pain, such that, for example, 'nine degrees of pleasure, less by nine degrees of pain, are equal to nothing: but nine degrees of one, less by three degrees of the other, give six of the former' (1726: 36). On the value of pleasure, Paley, as elsewhere, appears to commit himself to positions that were later seen as opposed. On the one hand, pleasures differ only in 'continuance and intensity'; on the other, happiness consists not in the pleasures of sense, but in those of the social affections, the exercise of our faculties, and so on (1.26–46).

Paley is a psychological egoist, and defines virtue as '*the doing good to mankind, in obedience to the will of God, and for the sake of everlasting happiness*' (1.47; also 2.154). Other apparently different positions he sees as essentially equivalent: the notion of fitness in the claim that virtue consists in doing what is fit, for example, must be understood as fitness to promote happiness (1.62). He understands obligation in a Hobbesian sense: it is a '*violent motive resulting from the command of another*', that other here of course being God, and a motive can be violent only in so far as it affects our own wellbeing (1.64–5). Like Wollaston (1724: 128), Paley sees the promotion of general happiness

---

[9] References to *Natural Theology* will be to the online Oxford Classics edn., itself based on the first edn. of 1802, and prefaced by 'N'. Unattributed references without a prefix are to the 15th edn. of the *Principles*, published in 1804. For an excellent discussion of Paley within the theological voluntarist tradition, see Irwin 2008: ch. 64. For a very helpful account of theological utilitarianism, see Crimmins 1998, and the notes preceding each of the selections in Part One ('Religious Utilitarians') (in addition to Gay, Tucker, and Paley, Crimmins includes John Brown, Soame Jenyns, and Edmund Law).

as the ultimate end of society and its rules,[10] but unlike him (1724: 216–17) does not stop to calculate whether vice may be rational if there is no afterlife (unsurprisingly Wollaston thinks it would not be, because of the insipidness and ephemerality of vicious pleasures and their bad consequences in the form of regret). Paley is clear: our rewards in heaven will be proportionate to our earthly virtue (1.54–5).

'Whatever is expedient is right' (1.80), Paley claims, and the value of an action consists in its 'tendency' to promote overall happiness. He then recognizes that some apparently immoral actions—such as those of an assassin—may be for the best overall. Like almost every utilitarian, Paley refuses to allow utilitarianism entirely to usurp the morality of common sense. Virtue lies in the formation of habits, and in particular habits or dispositions to follow the rules of common-sense morality, such as those requiring veracity (1.50–3). This view provides Paley with a response not only to the 'assassin' argument, but to the objection that his psychological egoism is excessively egocentric. He is, that is to say, both a utilitarian and yet another proponent of split-level psychological egoism.

The response to the assassin argument leads Paley again to appear to straddle what later became a significant divide between act and rule versions of utilitarianism (see Sidgwick 1902: 238n1). We should consider not only the 'particular' consequences of an action, but also any 'general' consequences that may arise through its violating some useful general rule (1.82). Such rules may be beneficial through their preventing harmful actions, as well as their enabling agents to plan and co-ordinate their actions (1.85; 2.456–7).

The expedience of an action consists in all its consequences, and so any potential assassin must take into account the effect his action may have on others (1.89–90; 330). Paley then faces up to the obvious challenge: what about the case of an assassination that remains secret for all time (1.867–8)? His first response is that, if one accepts a secret violation of this rule, then one must accept a new rule—that secrecy can justify any action. But this will be true, of course, only if accepting that new rule itself promotes the overall good. He then notes that no actions will remain secret at the day of judgement. But this is by the by, since the deterrent effects on which he has based the prohibition of killing take place before the day of judgement. It is at this point that Paley's view might seem to be heading in the direction of rule utilitarianism, since he suggests that one can assess general consequences by asking what would be the consequences if the type of action in question were generally permitted (1.89). But in fact he is probably making the same point made no less confusingly by the act utilitarian J.S. Mill, which has also led Mill to be misinterpreted as a rule utilitarian (Mill 1961–91: 17.1881; see Crisp 1997: 117). Act utilitarians who advocate the

---

[10]   See also the claim by Joseph Priestley (1733–1804) that 'the good and happiness of the members, that is the majority of the members of any state, is the great standard by which every thing relating to state must finally be determined... all arguments in favour of any law being always drawn from a consideration of its tendency to promote the public good' (1771: 13). Again, this claim rests on a view of God as primarily benevolent (1771: 14). Like Paley, Priestley believed God has designed the world in such a way that objective sacrifice is impossible; see Matsumoto 2010.

following of rules can suggest that a good way to approach assessing the actual value of some rule is to ask what might be the consequences of such a rule's being generally ignored or followed. This is far from suggesting that an act's being right consists in its being in accordance with a rule which would be maximally valuable were it generally followed. That Paley is indeed an act utilitarian emerges in his admission at 1.93 that it is *rarely* advantageous to violate a moral rule, which implies of course that such violation is sometimes permitted or even required.

Paley's being an act utilitarian has as a consequence that his appeal to rules in an attempt to avoid the apparently counter-intuitive consequences of his view is a failure, a failure repeated many times by act utilitarians since his day. The objection to him is that, on his view, actions judged very wrong by the lights of common-sense morality are not only right, but required. Paley should admit that, though he would be well advised to question the reliability of common sense.

Paley explicitly states that our only moral duty is to promote happiness, that duty itself requiring us in almost every case to follow the non-fundamental rules of common-sense morality (2.2). The rules of property (1.119–24), promising (139–41), and veracity (1.207), for example, all have a utilitarian basis. The value of liberty and indeed politics as a whole lies ultimately solely in their advancing well-being (2.179; 381), and Christ himself judges virtues by their utility rather than by any standard of intrinsic rightness (1.303). But because his utilitarianism permits the use of the language of common-sense morality, Paley frequently exhibits another vice characteristic of the less careful act utilitarian: to fall into common-sense moral argument without explaining the act utilitarian case for the common-sense moral rules to which he appeals (see Irwin 2008: 844). Consider, for example, his discussions of irreverence to God (1.159), or rights of bequest (1.254). Act utilitarianism can be a highly radical doctrine, but complacency can result in its becoming just another prop for conservatism.[11]

God is always in the background of Paley's ethics, as also is the deep question, faced explicitly by Butler, but not by Paley himself, of whether benevolence is God's only virtue. Again we find different strands of thought in Paley. On the one hand, as we have seen, he frequently states that God's sole aim is to promote happiness, and that we should follow him in that. So, for example, punishment is for deterrence, and never for retribution (1.297; 2.295), since utility is the foundation of justice (2.459). On the other hand, Paley does not struggle with the issue of how posthumous punishment can serve as a deterrent. Rather he claims that 'the retribution of so much pain for so much guilt... [is] the dispensation we expect at the hand of God, and which we are accustomed to consider as the order of things that perfect justice dictates'. Once again, for dialectical reasons of his own, we see Paley sliding from a conception of a common-sense moral rule as instrumental to one that attributes to it an independent status. Bentham has a much clearer grasp on the radical implications of utilitarianism, and,

---

[11] There are, however, radical elements in Paley's thought as a whole: see Le Mahieu 2002: xii; cf. xviii–xix; xxiv–v.

like Hume, cannot fall back on posthumous reward and punishment to explain and justify virtue. But as we shall see his position also faces its own difficulties, both internal and external.

4. Bentham: Legislating for the Good

Jeremy Bentham (1748–1832), like Hume, attended university as a child, and, perhaps unsurprisingly, did not enjoy his three years at Oxford. He went on to train as a lawyer, but practised only for a short time before dedicating himself to a life of research, writing, and political and legal reform. Somewhat remarkably, the process of publishing his manuscripts is still incomplete, though the Bentham Project at University College London has made steady progress since 1968. So far thirty-four of an expected eighty volumes of the *Collected Works* have appeared, and the structure and detail of Bentham's ethical thought emerges in several of them.[12]

Bentham's (somewhat hesitant, as we shall see) commitment to psychological egoism and to psychological and evaluative hedonism are manifest in one of his most famous pronouncements—the opening of the *Introduction to the Principles*:

Nature has placed mankind under the governance of two sovereign masters, *pain* and *pleasure*. It is for them alone to point out what we ought to do, as well as to determine what we shall do. On the one hand the standard of right and wrong, on the other the chain of causes and effects, are fastened to their throne.[13]

And later he notes: 'A motive is substantially nothing more than pleasure or pain, operating in a certain manner' (I 10.9; see T 11, 61). Each person sees their own happiness as consisting in the greatest balance of pleasure over pain in their life as a whole (D 250; DAS 336), and virtue is, and is thought to be, no part of happiness (A 301); each person has that happiness as their only actual ultimate end. Several qualities of happiness are relevant to its measurement and valuation (I 4.4–8; T 66–7, 88–9). Only two of these— intensity and duration—are intrinsic properties of the pleasurable or painful experience itself, constituting its 'magnitude'. The others are extrinsic: its 'certainty' (in effect, probability) and 'propinquity' (distance in the future), and 'fecundity' and 'purity' (its productiveness of further pleasures or pains).[14] Further, pleasure and pain can be aggregated across persons, according to their 'extent'.

---

[12] For our purposes, the most important texts are the 1776 *Fragment on Government* (F), the *Introduction to the Principles of Morals and Legislation* (I) (mostly written in 1780, though not published with a later 'concluding note' until 1789), the *Table of the Springs of Human Action* (T) (written 1813–17), *Deontology* (D) (written 1814–31), *Dedacologia: Art and Science Division* (DAS) (written in 1815), 'Constitutional Code Rationale' (C) (written in 1822), and the *Article on Utilitarianism* (A) (written in 1829). All of these have been published in the *Collected Works*, T, DAS, and A alongside D in a single volume.

[13] I 1.1; see F 417–18. The passage is almost certainly influenced by Helvétius. As noted by several commentators, Bentham closes this opening section with: 'enough of metaphor and declamation: it is not by such means that moral science is to be improved'. But this comment on style does not imply any doubt on Bentham's part about the content of the claims themselves.

[14] On propinquity, see Gustafsson 2018: 90n6.

It is important to note that each person has their own happiness as their ultimate end in the sense that their own pleasure and ease from pain is the 'efficient' or 'exciting' cause of their actions (I 4na; see e.g. Kelly 1990: 23). Since human beings naturally sympathize with others, they can be moved immediately and without conscious reflection on their own good to pursue the happiness of others (T 36). But it is an implication of this position that, if it becomes clear to the agent that such pursuit will be costly to them, they will desist. It is an 'incontrovertible fact…that no man ever has done or ever can do any act which at the moment of action is not (in the largest sense…that can be given to the word "interest") in his own eyes at least, his interest to do' (D 175; see 192, 250). It is unsurprising, then, to find Bentham ruling out genuine subjective sacrifice by individuals for the sake of others: 'man cannot be made to sacrifice what he thinks happiness' (T 38; see Ayer 1959: 251).[15] There has never been a truly 'disinterested' action (T 12, 99–100), and 'in the general tenor of life the act of sacrifice is neither possible nor so much as desirable' (because, Bentham thinks, morality need not be seen as making painful demands on us) (D 121–3).

It might seem that Bentham is not entirely consistent on these matters. His suggestion (T 35, 50, 65; D 190; C 233; DAS 333–4) that self-regarding interests predominate over other-regarding in human motivation is consistent with psychological egoism, since, as we have seen, he allows for the self-interested advantages of sympathy (see D 194n4). But in his discussion of 'extra-regarding' virtue, he does appear to allow for the possibility of genuine subjective sacrifice:

[F]or the sake of producing a more extensive and thence upon the whole a greater mass of good receivable by another person or assemblage of persons, a man forbears possession of, or does what depends upon him for sacrificing, a lesser mass of good receivable by himself. (D 154)

Such sacrifice may include not only a person's sacrificing pleasure, but also accepting pain, for the sake of others. But it has its natural limits, and in explicating them Bentham puts forward a possible elucidation of what he may mean by 'sacrifice':

[B]eneficence which is accompanied with any degree of self-sacrifice is not exercised without being to a certain amount exercised at the expense of self-regarding prudence: although it may be no otherwise at the expense of self-regarding prudence than as the seed sown by the husbandman is sown at the expense of self-regarding prudence. (D 185)

This passage—though it would be clearer were 'may be' replaced by 'is'—may be read as suggesting that the 'sacrifice' in extra-regarding virtue is merely apparent. The agent believes that they will be rewarded through, say, reciprocity (see e.g. D 184–6, 278), so that the action in question is to their overall advantage. But in fact Bentham shortly afterwards appears to allow for genuine, if pointless, self-sacrifice, when 'neither the greater future happiness of the agent in question is considered as being promoted, nor

[15] Baumgardt (1952: 416) suggests that, according to Bentham, 'self-sacrifice implies a self-contradiction, the assumption of an interest to do something combined with the denial of any interest in the case in question'.

the happiness of others' (D 188). This is 'asceticism—the offspring of delusion'. And later he considers a case in which the agent's own interests are incompatible with those of others, and raises as a genuine question when the agent should give preference to the interests of others (D 214–15).

These unclarities arise out of the breadth of Bentham's ethical focus. His primary concern is to ensure that the 'sanctions' of morality are working as effectively as possible, and with that in mind he is especially interested in addressing legislators (see e.g. Mill 1961–91: 10.7; Dinwiddy 1982: 295–6; 1989: 29–31; Schofield 2009: 4).[16] And he can be understood as following Hume in adopting what Postema (1986: 385–9) calls 'strategic egoism' at the political level, assuming that each person should be taken to be a psychological egoist even if this is not universally the case.[17] The art of legislation seeks to explain how a community as a whole can most effectively promote the happiness of all through the shaping of motives by the law (I 1.7, 17.20), and is hence a central part of 'ethics at large' (I 17.2). There is then, as Bentham sees it, a moral justification for his decision to concentrate on jurisprudence.

At I 3.2–6, Bentham lists four sanctions: the *physical* (the immediate pleasure or pain following from any action); the *political* (the hedonic consequences attached to an action by law); the *moral* or *popular* (pleasures and pains resulting from the spontaneous, non-rule-governed responses of others in the agent's community); and the *religious* (consequences flowing from the action of a supernatural being, in this or some future life). Later in the *Introduction*, Bentham describes the moral sanction as involving a 'sense of honour' (I 6.16), and allows for a 'sympathetic sensibility' which leads to pleasure at the happiness and pain at the unhappiness of others (I 6.20; D 129). By the time of the *Table* and *Deontology*, he was prepared to add the sympathetic as a sanction independent of the other four (T 8; D 151–2n1, 176–7, 197). The task of the legislator is to ensure that, as far as possible, the optimific political sanctions (which of course operate via the physical (I 3.11; see 5.33)) are attached to actions falling within the scope of law, particularly through punishment (I 6.45; 17.20). The scope of the 'deontologist' is broader, covering what is to be done in general, and will include as far as possible encouraging good conduct through redirection of the moral sanction (T 71–2; see D 125).[18] This task for the deontologist is largely consistent with pointing out to each individual what is best for them, through 'hunting' for consequences and reporting one's findings (D 251). Each of us has a duty of *prudence* to promote our own happiness, and duties of *probity* and *beneficence* respectively to refrain from harming

---

[16] This point is not to be exaggerated. Bentham was interested in ethics for individuals, and also insisted on limits to the scope of legislation beyond which only moral norms were applicable (see e.g. Rosen 2003: 93). It is worth noting the potential tension between Bentham's advocacy of legislation and his view that individuals are the best judges of their own interests. As Schofield suggests (2009: 5), any such tension is at least partly alleviated through Bentham's later commitment to democracy.

[17] Consider D 132: 'To better his condition, to acquire for the future some means of enjoyment more than at present he is in possession of, is the aim of every man. Not perhaps in the character of a universal proposition, true; but for argument sake, let it be so.'

[18] On Bentham's 'practical philanthropism', see Sidgwick 1906: 243–4.

and to benefit others (elsewhere the two latter duties are reasonably enough described simply as those of beneficence (e.g. D 122, 180; cf. A 306)). Conflict between the interests of self and of others is decreased through sympathy, and the 'semi-social motives of love of amity and love of reputation' (I 17.6–7). 'According to utility, *proper* end: greatest happiness of greatest number. Actual end: each man's own' (T 37; see C 238).[19] The task for the legislator or moralist, then, is straightforward: 'Cause duty and interest to coincide' (T 50; see 67).

Bentham tells us that he was converted to utilitarianism by a pamphlet of Priestley's he read in Harper's Coffee-house in Oxford in 1768, in which 'the greatest happiness of the greatest number' was stated to be 'the only rational foundation, of all enactments in legislation and all rules and precepts destined for the direction of human conduct in private life'.[20] (Bentham later dropped the reference to 'the greatest number' as unnecessary and potentially confusing (A 309–10). What matters is the greatest happiness overall, not, for example, the greatest happiness of the majority.[21]) On the first page of the preface to F, he refers to the 'discovery' of this 'fundamental axiom' (F 393), later describing it as the principle which lies behind all others (e.g. the principle that promises should be kept), which provides the sole mode of assessment of legislation, and which 'furnishes us with that *reason*, which alone depends not upon any higher reason, but which is itself the sole and all-sufficient reason for every point of practice whatsoever' (F 446–8, 483). Utility, indeed, is the only ground of assessment for any 'act, habit, disposition, or propensity' (D 209; also I 1.1).

Given his attraction to psychological hedonism, it is not entirely surprising to find Bentham implying that only utility will be taken by anyone to justify any legal or other

[19] As Sidgwick notes (1906: 244; see Shaver 1999: 150–1), Bowring (Bentham 1843: 560) cites a document from 1827 in which Bentham says: 'Constantly *proper* end of action on the part of every individual at the moment of action, his real greatest happiness from that moment to the end of life' (my italics). But this should not be taken as a commitment to any kind of rational egoistic principle. The passage closes with 'See Deontology, private'; Bentham has in mind 'private ethics', which advises individuals on what will be best for them independently of the interests of others (I 17.12 suggests that one of the roles of private ethics is to censure pernicious acts, but this may be because Bentham wrote some parts of the chapter before fully realizing the potential for inconsistency between private ethics and legislation: see Dinwiddy 1982: 294–5). As Dinwiddy points out (1989: 31–2), by increasing the happiness of a single individual, the deontologist will increase aggregate happiness. What happens when the deontologist sees that what is most in the interests of the person they are advising will decrease the good overall? Nothing Bentham says commits him to the view that the deontologist will here depart from utilitarianism in deciding which advice to offer. Sidgwick also suggests that in his later life Bentham came to the view that there is never any conflict between the happiness of any agent and the general happiness. But his expressions of this view might be taken to be further examples of his practical philanthropism (see previous note), or at least optimistic generalizations.
[20] A 291–2; see 1843: 79. Bentham allowed that he may have read it in Beccaria (1843: 142).
[21] Bentham's statements are not always straightforward, and there are passages which allow for a satisficing rather than maximizing interpretation of his utilitarianism. Given the number of passages in which he clearly accepts a maximizing view, it is more charitable to charge him with looseness of expression than with inconsistency. An ingenious and yet more charitable view is presented by Gustafsson (2017), who argues that the correct understanding of Bentham's 'binary' view (in which each act is to be compared with its non-performance) allows one to interpret the passages apparently advocating satisficing as in fact committing Bentham to maximization.

institution (F 416). But he also recognizes the possibility of—as he sees it, entirely erro-neous—opposition to utilitarianism. As Bentham saw it, there are only two alterna-tives: asceticism, and the principle of sympathy and antipathy, or 'ipsedixitism' (I 2.1–18; A 304–5, 312–16). The ascetic principle is in direct opposition, advocating the pursuit of unhappiness; ipsedixitism is indirect and consists in the appeal to any other alleged reason or value. Bentham provides an error theory to explain non-utilitarian theories: their proponents are suffering from the 'prejudices of the religious class, or hurried away by the force of what is called sentiment or *feeling*' (F 417nz).[22] Not all ascetics are religious; some philosophers, while not going so far as to see positive value in pain, have nevertheless criticized certain pleasures (I 2.5–6). And it is important to note that the 'sympathy' and 'antipathy' Bentham has in mind in connection with the second class of principles is not with others, but with the principles in question. According to Bentham, those who advocate non-utilitarian principles for non-reli-gious reasons are claiming that their own approval or disapproval is itself a sufficient ground for their principles (I 2.11–12). Bentham is perhaps led to this view by his attraction to psychological hedonism. Since all human beings in fact see happiness hedonistically construed as the only valuable goal, they cannot sincerely advocate any-thing else—such as justice—as valuable. And since they must be aware that we know their true views, they must be understood as claiming that their own approval provides reasons (though presumably they cannot sincerely believe that those who act so as to meet their approval will, by so doing, promote some non-hedonic value). Further, given that pleasure itself is approved, and pain disapproved, it is not surprising that the implications of the principles of sympathy and antipathy overlap to a large extent with those of the principle of utility (I 2.15).

Since each of us finds pleasure attractive and pain unattractive, the onus of proof is on the ascetic to show that there are cases in which our usual evaluations are mistaken. As for ipsedixitism, 'no worse progenitor can by any the most ill humoured adversary be ascribed to it than the Genius of Nonsense'. Bentham is led to this view by his philosophy of language, in which no distinction is drawn between sense and reference: 'a proposition having for its subject a fictitious entity has neither truth nor meaning' (T 5; see 74–5; Ogden 1951). Consider, for example, an anti-utilitarian theory based on the attribution of basic rights. This theory is nonsense: 'What [is] a right? Answer: a right is not *a* any thing' (T 7). It is important to note that this does not mean we should avoid using terms such as 'right', or indeed 'obligation' (D 206–7). They can be useful, as for example in elucidating the sympathetic sanction (T 8), if they are rationally related to real entities, viz., pleasures and pains (T 98).

So Bentham's utilitarianism is best understood as a split-level version, in which con-stant application of the utility principle in every choice situation is not required

---

[22] For an interesting reconstruction of Bentham's argument according to which it rests on appeal to utility as the only ground for rational public discussion, see Harrison 1983: ch. 7. See also Shaver 2013: 299–302.

(I 4.6).[23] Just as laws are to be judged by the amount of happiness they produce through the acts they influence (F 418a1, 486), so the same is true of practical moral principles in general, such as the principle that promises be kept:

> But, after all, for what *reason* is it, that men *ought* to keep their promises? The moment any intelligible reason is given, it is this: that it is for the *advantage* of society they should keep them; and if they do not, that, as far as *punishment* will go, they should be *made* to keep them. It is for the advantage of the whole number that the promises of each individual should be kept: and, rather than they should not be kept, that such individuals as fail to keep them should be punished. (F 444; see I 11.2)

Nor does this throw the principle of utility into doubt, since the reasons for adopting the secondary principles are themselves grounded in utility (I 1.13; see T 37).

Bentham's position on human nature is that human beings are either entirely or largely motivated by their own interest, though they sometimes demonstrate an irrational bias towards the nearer future and possibly on occasion sacrifice their overall interests for other reasons, perhaps even the well-being of others. But at the normative level Bentham is a utilitarian, not a rational egoist: the end we *should* pursue is the greatest happiness overall, not our own greatest happiness. The task of the legislator, as we have seen, is to seek to align self-interested motives with utility-maximizing actions. Here an obvious and serious practical difficulty emerges. Bentham is fully aware of the danger of morally corrupt leadership:

> The predominance of self-regarding over social interest being not only undeniable but necessary, thence of the ruling few it cannot but be the constant object to sacrifice to their own interests that of the subject many.

> To this purpose it will be their constant aim to preserve and increase abuses by which this, their sinister interest, is promoted, [and] to prevent every improvement by which it may be thwarted—thence to give currency to whatsoever notions tend to reconcile men to this sacrifice, or to prevent their seeing it. (T 65; see C 230; Schofield 2009: 11–13)

In a 'civilized' society (T 73), the pleasures of the moral, religious, and sympathetic sanctions will be strong, and one might reasonably hope for rulers and legislators who will most enjoy trying to produce the greatest overall happiness. But even in such a society Bentham will have little to say to a less civilized powerful individual. That is not because he has nothing to say: he believes they should follow the greatest happiness principle. But Bentham is aware that their capacity for so doing so is limited by their own nature to the point that engaging with them on the issue will be pointless. As Schofield (2009: 93) and others have noted, Bentham began to see democratic reform

---

[23] Bentham sometimes writes as if he has failed to recognize the utilitarian case against applying the utility principle. E.g.: 'Of the greatest happiness principle, application cannot be made upon too large a scale: it cannot be carried on too far' (A 318). But in fact he is clearly aware of it: see e.g. T 37.

as an important part of the solution to the problem of sinister interests in Britain, along with the recognition of various 'political fallacies'.

The same clash of perspectives emerges at the level of individual decisions.[24] At least in most cases, agents will not align their actions with the principle of utility unless they believe it will be in their own interest to do so, and to that extent one 'ought' to maximize utility impartially only to the extent that doing so is consistent with one's own good (see e.g. Halévy 1928: 476–7; Ayer 1959: 254). The ancient philosophers faced a problem similar to Bentham's, wishing to justify potentially costly virtue to self-interested agents, and it is not uncommon to find a blurring of the distinction between what is morally good or virtuous and what is good for the agent (see e.g. Crisp 2003). The same is true in Bentham's work. Consider the following passage from the *Fragment*:

> Now then, with respect to actions in general, there is no property in them that is calculated so readily to engage, and so firmly to fix the attention of an observer, as the *tendency* they may have *to*, or *divergency* (if one may so say) *from*, that which may be styled the common *end* of all of them. The end I mean is *Happiness*: and this *tendency* in any act is what we style its *utility*: as this *divergency* is that to which we give the name of *mischievousness*. With respect then to such actions in particular as are among the objects of the Law, to point out to a man the *utility* of them or the mischievousness, is the only way to make him see *clearly* that property of them which every man is in search of; the only way, in short, to give him *satisfaction*. (F 415–16)

When he first mentions happiness in this passage, Bentham attaches a footnote referring to Aristotle's use of *eudaimonia*, and it is clear also from his reference to the 'property ... which every man is in search of' that he has the agent's own good in mind. But what justifies a law, or obedience to it, is not the agent's own happiness but the general happiness. Bentham could be charged with complacency (see e.g. Stephen 1900: 315). Consider for example his alternative title for *Deontology*:

> *Morality made easy:*
> *Shewing how*
> *Throughout the whole course of every person's life*
> *Duty coincides with interest rightly understood*
> *Felicity with Virtue*
> *Prudence extra-regarding as well as self-regarding with*
> *Effective benevolence.* (D 119)

But given Bentham's awareness of the duties on him as a moralist, and given his own obvious sympathetic tendencies, it is perhaps more charitable to think that he sought to play down the gap between self-interest and morality in order to encourage his readers, and that he was attracted to the view common in his day that there is a natural tendency for interests to converge over time (Gomberg 1986: 439).

---

[24] Bentham's 'pessimism' about human nature is counterbalanced by an optimistic view of morality's contribution to happiness. In general, his view is that the best chance for happiness lies in aligning oneself with the forces working for the general good (see Sprigge 1999: 303–4).

Bentham's problem is a practical one, arising from the demand by beneficence that individuals sacrifice their own well-being, and its resolution depends less on philosophy than on psychology, political science, and other empirically grounded disciplines. Any plausible moral theory will include a potentially demanding principle of impartial beneficence, and, given the current state of the world, that demandingness is clearly not only potential but actual. Human beings face many challenges, but the greatest and most urgent, as Bentham recognized, is how to deal with our extreme partiality to ourselves and those close to us.

5. Conclusion: The Shaping of Modern Moral Philosophy

Bentham's lack of clarity about psychological egoism and psychological hedonism is partly a result of his focus on legislation and the protreptic aims of his moral philosophy. But it is also the beginning of a sustained move away from psychological egoism, which despite the work of Cumberland, More, and the philosophers discussed in this book from Hutcheson to Price, retained at the close of our period much of the grip it had had on Hobbes at the beginning. Evaluative hedonism also remained dominant throughout, though again we find exceptions in Cumberland, Mandeville, and Reid. Another theme common to all these post-Hobbesian philosophers is their denial of rational egoism, and their acceptance of M-reasons (though the views of both Cumberland and Shaftesbury incorporate an egoistic veto). These reasons were standardly seen alongside S-reasons, and in that sense the dualism of practical reason can be seen emerging early, in More, though it is not made fully explicit until Hutcheson. Another highly significant pre-modern aspect of the period, alluded to in my title, is the belief in the afterlife of all these writers until Hume, which meant that any subjective or objective sacrifice could be only mundane, and therefore not truly a sacrifice of oneself at all. It was Hume who changed British moral philosophy, turning it towards the secular point of view that is now standard and regaining for philosophy a common-sense notion of sacrifice which the ancient and Christian traditions had made impossible.

The broadly Sidgwickian characterization of the central debate in normative ethics—as between rational egoism, deontology, consequentialism, and various forms of dualism—seems to me both exhaustive and accurate.[25] It should now be clear how Sidgwick's grasp of this structure emerged in part from his own insightful readings of the British moralists from Hobbes to Bentham. The debate has continued within this structure until the present day, though in Britain after Bentham it began to be ever more informed by positions developed on the European continent and later the United States. I hope that this book has shown how much the British moralists still have to contribute to it.

---

[25] In Crisp 2015b I show that virtue ethics is best understood not as an alternative to consequentialism and deontology but as a version of the latter.

Bibliography

Primary Texts

Bentham, J. 1843. *Memoirs (Part I) and Correspondence*, *Works* vol. 10, ed. J. Bowring. Edinburgh: William Tate.

Bentham, J. 1977 [1776]. *A Fragment on Government* [F] in his *A Comment on the Commentaries and a Fragment on Government*, ed. J. Burns and H.L.A. Hart. Oxford: Clarendon Press.

Bentham, J. 1983. *Deontology* [1834; D] *together with a Table of the Springs of Action* [1817; T] *and Article on Utilitarianism* [A], ed. A. Goldsworth. Oxford: Clarendon Press.

Bentham, J. 1989. 'Constitutional Code Rationale' [C], in his *First Principles Preparatory to Constitutional Code*, ed. P. Schofield. Oxford: Clarendon Press.

Bentham, J. 1996 [1789]. *An Introduction to the Principles of Morals and Legislation* [I], ed. J. Burns and H.L.A. Hart. Oxford: Clarendon Press.

Butler, J. 1900. *Works*, ed. J.H. Bernard. London: Macmillan.

Butler, J. 2006. *Works* [*Fifteen Sermons Preached at the Rolls Chapel* [S], 2nd edn., 1729; *The Analogy of Religion, Natural and Revealed, to the Constitution and Course of Nature* [A], 2nd edn., 1736, incl. 'A Dissertation on the Nature of Virtue' [D]], ed. D. White. Rochester: University of Rochester Press.

Butler, J. 2017. *Fifteen Sermons and Other Ethical Writings*, ed. D. McNaughton. Oxford and New York: Oxford University Press.

Clarke, S. 1721. *Three Practical Essays, on Baptism, Confirmation, and Repentance* [P], 4th edn. London: J. Knapton.

Clarke, S. 1728. *A Discourse concerning the Being and Attributes of God, the Obligations of Natural Religion, and the Truth and Certainty of the Christian Revelation* [D], 7th edn. London: J. and J. Knapton.

Cudworth, R. 1731. *A Treatise concerning Eternal and Immutable Morality*. London: J. and J. Knapton.

Cumberland, R. 2005 [1672, Latin], *A Treatise of the Laws of Nature*, trans. J. Maxwell [1727], ed. J. Parkin. Indianapolis: Liberty Fund.

Gay, J. 1731. *Preliminary Dissertation concerning the Fundamental Principle of Virtue or Morality*. In W. King, *An Essay on the Origin of Evil*, tr. E. Law, xi–xxxiii. Cambridge: Thurlbourn; London: R. Knaplock, J. and J. Knapton, and W. Innis.

Hobbes, T. 1840 [1668]. 'An Answer to Bishop Bramhall's Book, called *The Catching of the Leviathan*' [AB], in *English Works*, ed. W. Molesworth, vol. 4. London: Bohn, 279–384.

Hobbes, T. 1889 [1650]. *The Elements of Law*, ed. F. Tönnies. London: Simpkin, Marshall, and Co.

Hobbes, T. 1991. *Man and Citizen* (*De Homine* [DH] [1658, Latin] and *De Cive*), ed. B. Gert, tr. (DH) C. Wood, T. Scott-Craig, and B. Gert. Indianapolis: Hackett.

Hobbes, T. 1998. *On the Citizen* (*De Cive* [DC] [1642, Latin]), ed. and tr. R. Tuck and M. Silverthorne. Cambridge: Cambridge University Press.

Hobbes, T. 2012 [1651]. *Leviathan* [L]. Vol. 2, *The English and Latin Texts (i)*, ed. N. Malcolm. Oxford: Clarendon Press.

Hume, D. 1932. *Letters*, ed. J. Greig. Oxford: Clarendon Press.

Hume, D. 1975 [1748]. *An Enquiry concerning Human Understanding*, ed. L.A. Selby-Bigge, 3rd edn, rev. P.H. Nidditch. Oxford: Clarendon Press.

Hume, D. 1987 [1742/1752]. *Essays, Moral, Political, and Literary* [E], ed. E.F. Miller, rev. edn. Indianapolis: Liberty Fund.

Hume, D. 1998 [1751]. *An Enquiry concerning the Principles of Morals* [E], ed. T. Beauchamp. Oxford: Clarendon Press.

Hume, D. 2007 [1739–40]. *A Treatise of Human Nature* [T], ed. D.F. and M.F. Norton. 2 vols. Oxford: Clarendon Press.

Hutcheson, F. 1735. *Letters between the late Mr Gilbert Burnet and Mr Hutcheson, concerning the True Foundation of Virtue or Moral Goodness. Formerly Published in the London Journal* [L], with preface and postscript by Burnet. London: R. Wilkins.

Hutcheson, F. 1750. *Reflections upon Laughter and Remarks upon the Fable of the Bees* [R]. Glasgow: R. Urie.

Hutcheson, F. 1755. *A System of Moral Philosophy* [S], ed. F. Hutcheson. 2 vols. Glasgow: R. and A. Foulis.

Hutcheson, F. 1993. *Two Texts on Human Nature* [*Reflections on the Common Systems of Morality* [CS] [1724]; *Inaugural Lecture on the Social Nature of Man* [IL] [1730]], ed. T. Mautner. Cambridge: Cambridge University Press.

Hutcheson, F. 2002 [1725]. *An Essay on the Nature and Conduct of the Passions and Affections, with Illustrations on the Moral Sense* [E], ed. A. Garrett. Indianapolis: Liberty Fund.

Hutcheson, F. 2006 [1756/1749/1730, Latin]. *Logic, Metaphysics, and the Natural Sociability of Mankind* [LM], ed. J. Moore and M. Silverthorne, tr. M. Silverthorne. Indianapolis: Liberty Fund.

Hutcheson, F. 2007 [1745, Latin]. *Philosophiae Moralis Institutio Compendaria*, with *A Short Introduction to Moral Philosophy* [English tr., 1747] [SI], ed. L. Turco. Indianapolis: Liberty Fund.

Hutcheson, F. 2008 [1725]. *An Inquiry into the Original of Our Ideas of Beauty and Virtue* [I], rev. edn., ed. W. Leidhold. Indianapolis: Liberty Fund.

Locke, J. 1975 [1700, 4th edn]. *An Essay concerning Human Understanding*, ed. P. Nidditch. Oxford: Clarendon Press.

Locke, J. 1997. *Political Essays* [PE], ed. M. Goldie. Cambridge: Cambridge University Press.

Locke, J. 2000 [1695]. *The Reasonableness of Christianity*, ed. J. Higgins-Biddle. Oxford: Clarendon Press.

Mandeville, B. 1729. *Free Thoughts on Religion, the Church, and National Happiness* [F], 2nd edn. London: J. Brotherton.

Mandeville, B. 1732. *An Enquiry into the Origin of Honour, and the Usefulness of Christianity in War* [E]. London: J. Brotherton.

Mandeville, B. 1732. *A Letter to Dion, Occasion'd by his Book Call'd Alciphron, or The Minute Philosopher* [L]. London: J. Roberts.

Mandeville, B. 1924 [1732]. *The Fable of the Bees: or Private Vices, Publick Benefits*, ed. F. Kaye, 2 vols. Oxford: Clarendon Press.

Mandeville, B. 2006 [1724]. *A Modest Defence of Publick Stews, or, An Essay upon Whoring, as it is now practis'd in these kingdoms* [M], ed. I. Primer. New York: Palgrave Macmillan.

More, H. 1690 [1667, Latin]. *An Account of Virtue, or Dr Henry More's Abridgement of Morals*, tr. E. Southwell. London: B. Tooke.

Paley, W. 1804. *The Principles of Moral and Political Philosophy*, 15th edn. London: R. Faulder.

Paley, W. 2006 [1802]. *Natural Theology* [N], ed. M. Eddy and D. Knight. Oxford: Oxford University Press. Online edn.

Price, R. 1974 [1787, 3rd edn]. *A Review of the Principal Questions in Morals*, ed. D.D. Raphael. Oxford: Clarendon Press.

Reid, T. 2002 [1785]. *Essays on the Intellectual Powers of Man*, ed. K. Haakonssen and D.R. Brookes. Edinburgh: Edinburgh University Press; University Park, PA: Pennsylvania University Press.

Reid, T. 2007. *On Practical Ethics*, ed. K. Haakonssen. Edinburgh: Edinburgh University Press.

Reid, T. 2010 [1788]. *Essays on the Active Powers of Man*, ed. K. Haakonssen and J. Harris. Edinburgh: Edinburgh University Press.

Shaftesbury, 3rd Earl of. 1698. 'Preface' to B. Whichcote, *Select Sermons of Dr Whichcot* [P]. London: Awnsham and John Churchill, 1. [i–xviii].

Shaftesbury, 3rd Earl of. 1716. *Several Letters Written by a Noble Lord to a Young Man at the University* [NL]. London: J. Roberts.

Shaftesbury, 3rd Earl of. 1750. *Letters of the Earl of Shaftesbury, Author of the Characteristicks, Collected into One Volume* [L]. [London?].

Shaftesbury, 3rd Earl of. 1900. *The Life, Unpublished Letters, and Philosophical Regimen of Anthony, Earl of Shaftesbury* [R], ed. B. Rand. London: Swan Sonnenschein.

Shaftesbury, 3rd Earl of. 1914. *Second Characters or the Language of Forms*, ed. B. Rand. Cambridge: Cambridge University Press.

Shaftesbury, 3rd Earl of. 1999 [1711]. *Characteristics of Men, Manners, Opinions, Times*, ed. L. Klein. Cambridge: Cambridge University Press.

Shaftesbury, 3rd Earl of. 2011. *Standard Edition* II,6: *Askêmata*, ed. W. Benda, C. Jackson-Holzberg, P. Müller, and F. Uehlein. Stuttgart and Bad Cannstatt: frommann-holzboog.

Shaftesbury, 3rd Earl of. 2013 [1706]. *Pathologia*, ed. and trans. L. Jaffro, C. Maurer, and A. Petit, *History of European Ideas* 39: 221–40.

Smith, A. 1979 (1790; 1st edn. 1759). *The Theory of the Moral Sentiments*, ed. D.D. Raphael and A.L. Macfie. Oxford: Oxford University Press.

Tucker, A. 1768. *The Light of Nature Pursued*. 5 vols. London: T. Jones.

Tucker, A. 1777. *The Light of Nature Pursued*. 4 vols. London: W. Oliver.

Waterland, D. 1730. *The Nature, Obligation, and Efficacy, of the Christian Sacraments*. London: John Crownfield.

Secondary Texts

Aaron, R. 1955. *John Locke*, 2nd edn. Oxford: Clarendon Press.

Adams, R.M. 1976. 'Motive Utilitarianism', *Journal of Philosophy* 73: 467–81.

Adams, R.M. 1998. 'Self-love and the Vices of Self-preference', *Faith and Philosophy* 15: 500–13.

Ainslie, D. 2007. 'Character Traits and the Humean Approach to Ethics', in S. Tenenbaum (ed.), *Moral Psychology*. Amsterdam: Rodopi, 79–110.

Ainslie, D. and A. Butler (ed.) 2015. *Cambridge Companion to Hume's Treatise*. Cambridge: Cambridge University Press.

Akhtar, S. 2006. 'Restoring Bishop Butler's Conscience', *British Journal for the History of Philosophy* 14: 581–600.

Albee, E. 1896. 'The Relation of Shaftesbury and Hutcheson to Utilitarianism', *Philosophical Review* 5: 24–35.

Albee, E. 1897. 'Gay's Ethical System', *Philosophical Review* 6: 132–45.

Albee, E. 1902. *A History of English Utilitarianism*. London: Swan Sonnenschein.

Anscombe, G.E.M. 1997. 'Modern Moral Philosophy', repr. in R. Crisp and M. Slote (eds), *Virtue Ethics*. Oxford: Oxford University Press, 26–44.

Åqvist, L. 1960. *The Moral Philosophy of Richard Price*. Lund: CWK Gleerup.

Aristotle 1855. *The Ethics of Aristotle*, 4th edn., ed. A. Grant, 2 vols. London: Longmans, Green.

Aristotle 1894. *Ethica Nicomachea*, ed. I. Bywater. Oxford: Clarendon Press.

Aristotle 1959. *Rhetorica*, ed. W.D. Ross. Oxford: Clarendon Press.

Aristotle 1984. *Collected Works*, ed. J. Barnes. Princeton: Princeton University Press.

Arrington, R.L. 1998. *Western Ethics: An Historical Introduction*. Malden, MA: Blackwell.

Ashford, E. 2005. 'Utilitarianism with a Humean Face', *Hume Studies* 31: 63–92.

Ayer, A.J. 1959. 'The Principle of Utility', repr. in *Philosophical Essays*. London: Macmillan, 250–70.

Ayers, M. 1993. *Locke: Epistemology and Ontology*. London: Routledge.

Baier, A. 1991. *A Progress of Sentiments*. Cambridge, Mass.: Harvard University Press.

Baier, A. 2008. 'Enquiry concerning the Principles of Morals: Incalculably the Best?', in E. Radcliffe (ed.), *A Companion to Hume*. Malden, MA: Blackwell, 293–320.

Baier, A. 2009. 'Kinds of Virtue Theorist: A Response to Christine Swanton', in C. Pigden (ed.), *Hume on Motivation and Virtue*. Basingstoke: Palgrave Macmillan, 249–58.

Baier, A. 2013. 'Hume's Place in the History of Ethics', in R. Crisp (ed.), *Oxford Handbook of the History of Ethics*. Oxford: Oxford University Press, 399–420.

Baier, K. 1991. 'Egoism', in P. Singer (ed.), *A Companion to Ethics*. Oxford: Blackwell, 197–204.

Baillie, J. 2000. *Hume on Morality*. London: Routledge.

Barnes, W. 1942. 'Richard Price: A Neglected Eighteenth Century Moralist', *Philosophy* 17: 159–73.

Batson, C. 2011. *Altruism in Humans*, Oxford: Oxford University Press.

Baumgardt, D. 1952. *Bentham and the Ethics of Today*. Princeton: Princeton University Press.

Baumgold, D. 1988. *Hobbes's Political Theory*. Cambridge: Cambridge University Press.

Beauchamp, T. 1998. 'Editor's Introduction', in D. Hume, *An Enquiry Concerning the Principles of Morals*. Oxford: Oxford University Press, 7–53.

Beck, L.W. 1937. 'A Neglected Aspect of Butler's Ethics', *Sophia* 5: 11–15.

Beiser, F. 1996. *The Sovereignty of Reason: The Defense of Rationality in the Early English Enlightenment*. Princeton: Princeton University Press.

Beiser, F. 1998. 'Cambridge Platonism', in E. Craig (ed.), *Routledge Encyclopedia of Philosophy*. London: Routledge.

Beiser, F. 2005. *Schiller as Philosopher: A Re-examination*. Oxford: Clarendon Press.

Bishop, J. 1996. 'Moral Motivation and the Development of Francis Hutcheson's Philosophy', *Journal of the History of Ideas* 57: 277–95.

Blackstone, W.T. 1965. *Francis Hutcheson and Contemporary Ethical Theory*. Athens, Georgia: Georgia University Press.

Blair, H. 1755. Review of Hutcheson, *A System of Moral Philosophy*, *Edinburgh Review* 1: 9–23.

Boonin-Vail, D. 1994. *Thomas Hobbes and the Science of Moral Virtue*. Cambridge: Cambridge University Press.

Botwinick, A. 1977. 'A Case for Hume's Nonutilitarianism', *Journal of the History of Philosophy* 15: 423–35.

Bowle, J. 1951. *Hobbes and his Critics*. London: Jonathan Cape.

Bowlin, J. 2000. 'Sieges, Shipwrecks, and Sensible Knaves: Justice and Utility in Butler and Hume', *Journal of Religious Ethics* 28: 253–80.

Brandt, R.B. 1979. *A Theory of the Good and the Right*. Oxford: Clarendon Press.

Bredvold, L. 1952. 'The Invention of the Ethical Calculus', in R.F. Jones et al., *The Seventeenth Century: Studies in the History of Literature from Bacon to Pope*. Stanford: Stanford University Press, 165–80.

Brinton, A. 1991. '"Following Nature" in Butler's Sermons', *Philosophical Quarterly* 41: 325–32.

Broad, C.D. 1930. *Five Types of Ethical Theory*. London: Kegan Paul, Trench, Trübner, and Co.

Broad, C.D. 1950. 'Egoism as a Theory of Human Motives', *Hibbert Journal* 48: 105–14.

Broadie, A. 2006. 'Sympathy and the Impartial Spectator', in K. Haakonssen (ed.)., *Cambridge Companion to Adam Smith*. Cambridge: Cambridge University Press, 158–88.

Broadie, A. 2017. 'Scottish Philosophy in the 18th Century', in E. Zalta (ed.), *Stanford Encyclopedia of Philosophy* (winter 2017 edn.), https://plato.stanford.edu/archives/win2017/entries/scottish-18th/.

Brogan, A. 1959. 'John Locke and Utilitarianism', *Ethics* 69: 79–93.

Broiles, R.D. 1964. *The Moral Philosophy of David Hume*. The Hague: Martinus Nijhoff.

Brown, K. (ed.) 1965. *Hobbes Studies*. Oxford: Blackwell.

Brown, V. 1994. *Adam Smith's Discourse: Canonicity, Commerce and Conscience*. London and New York: Routledge.

Brownsey, P. 1995. 'Butler's Argument for the Natural Authority of Conscience', *British Journal for the History of Philosophy* 3: 57–87.

Burgess-Jackson, K. 2013. 'Taking Egoism Seriously', *Ethical Theory and Moral Practice* 16: 529–42.

Burnet, T. 1989. *Remarks on John Locke, with Locke's Replies*, ed. G. Watson. Doncaster: Brynmill Press.

Bykvist, K. 2010. *Utilitarianism: A Guide for the Perplexed*. London: Continuum.

Campbell, T. 1971. *Adam Smith's Science of Morals*. London: George Allen and Unwin.

Campbell, T. 1982. 'Francis Hutcheson: "Father" of the Scottish Enlightenment', in R. Campbell and A. Skinner (eds), *The Origins and Nature of the Scottish Enlightenment*. Edinburgh: John Donald, 167–85.

Capaldi, N. 1989. *Hume's Place in Moral Philosophy*. New York: Peter Lang.

Carey, D. 1997. 'Method, Moral Sense, and the Problem of Diversity: Francis Hutcheson and the Scottish Enlightenment', *British Journal for the History of Philosophy* 5: 275–96.

Carey, D. 2015. 'Francis Hutcheson's Philosophy and the Scottish Enlightenment: Reception, Reputation, and Legacy', in A. Garrett and J. Harris (eds), *Scottish Philosophy in the Eighteenth Century*, vol. 1: *Morals, Politics, Art, Religion*. Oxford: Oxford University Press, 36–76.

Carlsson, P.A. 1964. *Butler's Ethics*. The Hague: Mouton.

Carlyle, E.I. 1901. 'Gay, John (1699–1745)', in S. Lee (ed.), *Dictionary of National Biography*, Supplement, 2.272–3. London: Smith, Elder.

Carrasco, M. 2011. 'Hutcheson, Smith, and Utilitarianism', *Review of Metaphysics* 64: 515–63.

Carritt, E. 1935. *Morals and Politics*. Oxford: Clarendon Press.

Cassirer, E. 1970. *The Platonic Renaissance in England*, tr. J. Pettigrove. New York: Gordian Press.

Castiglione, D. 1986. 'Considering Things Minutely: Reflections on Mandeville and the Eighteenth-century Science of Man', *History of Political Thought* 7: 463–88.

Cicero, M.T. 1994. *De Officiis*, ed. M. Winterbottom. Oxford: Clarendon Press.

Cléro, J.-P. 2013. 'Hume et l'Utilité', *Revue Internationale de Philosophie* 263: 99–122.

Cockburn, C.T. 1702. *A Defence of the Essay of Human Understanding, written by Mr Lock. Wherein its Principles with Reference to Morality, Reveal'd Religion, and the Immortality of the Soul, are Consider'd and Justify'd: In Answer to Some Remarks on that Essay*. London: W. Turner, J. Nutt.

Cohon, R. 1997. 'The Common Point of View in Hume's Ethics', *Philosophy and Phenomenological Research* 57: 827–50.

Cohon, R. 2006. 'Hume's Artificial and Natural Virtues', in S. Traiger (ed.), *Blackwell Guide to Hume's Treatise*. Malden, MA: Blackwell, 256–75.

Cohon, R. 2008. *Hume's Morality: Feeling and Fabrication*. Oxford: Oxford University Press.

Cohon, R. 2018. 'Hume's Moral Philosophy', in E. Zalta (ed.), *Stanford Encyclopedia of Philosophy* (fall 2018 edn.), https://plato.stanford.edu/archives/fall2018/entries/hume-moral/.

Colman, J. 1972. 'Bernard Mandeville and the Reality of Virtue'. *Philosophy* 47: 125–39.

Colman, J. 1983. *John Locke's Moral Philosophy*. Edinburgh: Edinburgh University Press.

Cook, H. 1999. 'Bernard Mandeville and the Therapy of the 'Clever Politician'', *Journal of the History of Ideas* 60: 101–24.

Cook, H. 2002. 'Bernard Mandeville', in S. Nadler (ed.), *Companion to Early Modern Philosophy*, 469–82. Oxford: Blackwell.

Crimmins, J. 1990. *Secular Utilitarianism: Social Science and the Critique of Religion in the Thought of Jeremy Bentham*. Oxford: Clarendon Press.

Crimmins, J. 1998. 'Religious Advocates of the Utility Principle', introduction to J. Crimmins (ed.), *Utilitarians and Religion*. Bristol: Thoemmes Press, 3–25.

Crimmins, J. (ed.) 1998. *Utilitarians and Religion*. Bristol: Thoemmes Press.

Crimmins, J. 2014. 'Bentham and Utilitarianism in the Early Nineteenth Century', in B. Eggleston and D. Miller (eds), *Cambridge Companion to Utilitarianism*. Cambridge: Cambridge University Press, 38–60.

Crimmins, J. 2018. 'Jeremy Bentham', in E. Zalta (ed.), *Stanford Encyclopedia of Philosophy* (spring 2017 edn.), https://plato.stanford.edu/archives/sum2018/entries/bentham.

Crisp, R. 1994. 'Aristotle's Inclusivism', *Oxford Studies in Ancient Philosophy* 12: 111–36.

Crisp, R. 1996. 'Mill on Virtue as a Part of Happiness', *British Journal for the History of Philosophy* 4.2: 367–80.

Crisp, R. 1997. *Mill on Utilitarianism*. London: Routledge.

Crisp, R. 1999. 'Teachers in an Age of Transition: Peter Singer and J.S. Mill', in D. Jamieson (ed.), *Singer and his Critics*. Oxford: Blackwell, 85–102.

Crisp, R. 2003. 'Socrates and Aristotle on Happiness and Virtue', in R. Heinaman (ed.), *Plato and Aristotle's Ethics*. Aldershot: Ashgate, 55–78.

Crisp, R. 2006. *Reasons and the Good*. Oxford: Clarendon Press.

Crisp, R. 2014. 'Nobility in the *Nicomachean Ethics*', *Phronesis* 59: 231–45.

Crisp, R. 2015a. *The Cosmos of Duty: Henry Sidgwick's Methods of Ethics*. Oxford: Clarendon Press.

Crisp, R. 2015b. 'A Third Method of Ethics?', *Philosophy and Phenomenological Research* 90: 257–73.

Crisp, R. 2017. 'Moral Luck and Moral Equality of Opportunity', *Proceedings of the Aristotelian Society*, suppl. vol. 91: 1–20.

Cullity, G. and B. Gaut 1997. 'Introduction' to their (ed.) *Ethics and Practical Reason*. Oxford: Clarendon Press, 1–27.

Cuneo, T. 2004. 'Reid's Moral Philosophy', in T. Cuneo and R. van Woudenberg (eds), *Cambridge Companion to Thomas Reid*, 243–66. Cambridge: Cambridge University Press.

Cuneo, T. 2010. 'Duty, Goodness, and God in Thomas Reid's Moral Philosophy', in S. Roeser (ed.), *Reid on Ethics*, 238–57. Basingstoke: Palgrave Macmillan.

Cuneo, T. 2018. 'Reid's Ethics', in E. Zalta (ed.), *Stanford Encyclopedia of Philosophy* (summer 2018 edn.), https://plato.stanford.edu/archives/sum2018/entries/reid-ethics.

Curley, E. 1990. 'Reflections on Hobbes: Recent Work on his Moral and Political Philosophy', *Journal of Philosophical Research* 15: 169–226.

Darwall, S. 1992. 'Conscience as Self-authorizing in Butler's Ethics', in C. Cunliffe (ed.), *Joseph Butler's Moral and Religious Thought*. Oxford: Clarendon Press, 209–41.

Darwall, S. 1994. 'Hume and the Invention of Utilitarianism', in M.A. Stewart (ed.), *Hume and Hume's Connexions*, 58–82. Edinburgh: Edinburgh University Press.

Darwall, S. 1995. *The British Moralists and the Internal 'Ought'*. Cambridge: Cambridge University Press.

Darwall, S. 1997. 'Hume on Practical Reason', *Hume Studies* 23: 73–89.

Darwall, S. 1998. 'Price, Richard (1723-91)', in E. Craig (ed.), *Routledge Encyclopedia of Philosophy*. London: Routledge.

Darwall, S. 1999. 'Sympathetic Liberalism: Recent Work on Adam Smith', *Philosophy and Public Affairs* 28: 139–64.

Darwall, S. 2000. 'Normativity and Projection in Hobbes's *Leviathan*', *Philosophical Review* 109: 313–47.

Darwall, S. 2004. 'Equal Dignity in Adam Smith', *Adam Smith Review* 1: 129–34.

Darwall, S. 2006. *The Second-Person Standpoint: Morality, Respect, and Accountability*. Cambridge, Mass.: Harvard University Press.

Davis, W.C. 2006. *Thomas Reid's Ethics: Moral Epistemology on Legal Foundations*. London: Continuum.

Debes, R. 2012. 'Adam Smith on Dignity and Equality', *British Journal for the History of Philosophy* 20: 109–40.

Debes, R. 2016. 'Adam Smith and the Sympathetic Imagination', in R. Hanley (ed.), *Adam Smith: His Life, Thought, and Legacy*. Princeton and Oxford: Princeton University Press, 192–207.

Deigh, J. 1996. 'Reason and Ethics in Hobbes's *Leviathan*', *Journal of the History of Philosophy* 34: 33–60.

Deigh, J. 2003. 'Reply to Mark Murphy', *Journal of the History of Philosophy* 41: 97–109.

Den Uyl, D. 1998. 'Shaftesbury and the Modern Problem of Virtue', *Social Philosophy and Policy* 15: 275–316.

Den Uyl, D. 2001. 'Foreword' to 3rd Earl of Shaftesbury, *Characteristicks of Men, Manners, Opinions, Times*. Indianapolis: Liberty Fund, vii–xii.

De Stier, M. 1993. 'Individual Egoism as Motivation for Human Praxis'. *Hobbes Studies* 6: 43–57.

Dinwiddy, J. 1982. 'Bentham on Private Ethics and the Principle of Utility', *Revue Internationale de Philosophie* 36: 278–300.

Dinwiddy, J. 1989. *Bentham*. Oxford: Oxford University Press.

Dolson, G. 1897. 'The Ethical System of Henry More', *Philosophical Review* 6: 593–607.

Dorsey, D. 2010. 'Hutcheson's Deceptive Hedonism', *Journal of the History of Philosophy* 48: 445–67.

Dreier, J. 1993. 'Structure of Normative Theories', *The Monist* 76: 22–40.

Driver, J. 2004. 'Pleasure as the Standard of Virtue in Hume's Moral Philosophy', *Pacific Philosophical Quarterly* 85: 173–94.

Driver, J. 2014. 'The History of Utilitarianism, in E. Zalta (ed.), *Stanford Encyclopedia of Philosophy* (winter 2014 edn.), http://plato.stanford.edu/archives/win2014/entries/utilitarianism-history/.

Duncan, S. 2017. 'Hobbes, Thomas', in E. Zalta (ed.), *Stanford Encyclopedia of Philosophy* (summer 2017 edn.), https://plato.stanford.edu/archives/sum2017/entries/hobbes/.

Duncan-Jones, A. 1952. *Butler's Moral Philosophy*. Harmondsworth: Penguin.

Dunn, J. 1984. *Locke*. Oxford: Oxford University Press.

Dyck, A. and C. Padilla 2009. 'The Empathic Emotions and Self-love in Bishop Joseph Butler and the Neurosciences', *Journal of Religious Ethics* 37: 577–612.

Edwards, T. 1964. 'Mandeville's Moral Prose', *English Literary History* 31: 195–212.

Engelmann, S. 2001. 'Imagining Interest', *Utilitas* 13: 289–322.

Epictetus 2014. *Discourses, Fragments, Handbook*, trans. R. Hard. Oxford: Oxford University Press.

Estlund, D. 1990. 'Mutual Benevolence and the Theory of Happiness', *Journal of Philosophy* 87: 187–204.

Ewin, R. 1991. *Virtues and Rights: The Moral Philosophy of Thomas Hobbes*. Boulder: Westview.

Farrell, D. 1984. 'Reason and Right in Hobbes' *Leviathan*', *History of Philosophy Quarterly* 1: 297–314.

Farrell, D. 1985. 'Hobbes as Moralist'. *Philosophical Studies* 48: 257–83.

Ferguson, J.P. 1976. *An Eighteenth Century Heretic: Dr Samuel Clarke*. Kineton: Roundwood Press.

Findlay, J.N. 1961. *Values and Intentions*. London: George Allen and Unwin.

Flage, D. 2000. 'Locke on Natural Law', in G. Fuller, R. Stecker, and J. Wright (eds), *John Locke: An Essay concerning Human Understanding in Focus*. London: Routledge, 249–70.

Fleischacker, S. 1991. 'Philosophy in Moral Practice: Kant and Adam Smith', *Kant-Studien* 82: 249–69.

Fleischacker, S. 1999. *A Third Concept of Liberty*. Princeton: Princeton University Press.

Fleischacker, S. 2004. *On Adam Smith's Wealth of Nations: A Philosophical Companion*. Princeton: Princeton University Press.

Fleischacker, S. 2017. 'Adam Smith's Moral and Political Philosophy', in E. Zalta (ed.), *Stanford Encyclopedia of Philosophy* (spring 2017 edn.), https://plato.stanford.edu/archives/spr2017/entries/smith-moral-political/.

Fogelin, R. 1985. *Hume's Scepticism in the Treatise of Human Nature*. London: Routledge and Kegan Paul.

Foot, P. 1988. 'Utilitarianism and the Virtues', rev. and repr. in S. Scheffler (ed.), *Consequentialism and its Critics* (Oxford: Oxford University Press), 224–42.

Forman-Barzilai, F. 2010. *Adam Smith and the Circles of Sympathy: Cosmopolitanism and Moral Theory*. Cambridge: Cambridge University Press.

Forsyth, M. 1982. 'The Place of Richard Cumberland in the History of Natural Law Doctrine', *Journal of the History of Philosophy* 20: 23–42.

Fowler, T. 1882. *Shaftesbury and Hutcheson*. London: Sampson Low, Marston, Searle, and Rivington.

Frankena, W. 1955. 'Hutcheson's Moral Sense Theory', *Journal of the History of Ideas* 16: 356–75.

Frankena, W. 1973. *Ethics*, 2nd edn. Englewood Cliffs, NJ: Prentice-Hall.

Frankena, W. 1976. Review of Monro 1975. *Dialogue* 15: 321–7.

Frankena, W. 1983. 'Concepts of Rational Action in the History of Ethics', *Social Theory and Practice* 9: 165–97.

Frey, R. 1992. 'Butler on Self-love and Benevolence', in C. Cunliffe (ed.), *Joseph Butler's Moral and Religious Thought*. Oxford: Clarendon Press, 243–67.

Fricke, C. 2013. 'Adam Smith: The Sympathetic Process and the Origin and Function of Conscience', in C. Berry, M.P. Paganelli, and C. Smith (eds), *Oxford Handbook of Adam Smith*. Oxford: Oxford University Press, 177–200.

From, F. 1944. 'Mandeville's Paradox', *Theoria* 10: 197–215.

Fuss, P. 1964. 'Conscience', *Ethics* 74: 111–20.

Fuss, P. 1968. 'Sense and Reason in Butler's Ethics', *Dialogue* 7: 180–93.

Gallie, R.D. 1998. *Thomas Reid: Ethics, Aesthetics and the Anatomy of the Self*. Dordrecht: Kluwer.

Garnett, J. 1992. 'Bishop Butler and the *Zeitgeist*: Butler and the Development of Christian Moral Philosophy in Victorian Britain', in C. Cunliffe (ed.), *Joseph Butler's Moral and Religious Thought*. Oxford: Clarendon Press, 63–96.

Garrett, A. 2007. 'Francis Hutcheson and the Origin of Animal Rights', *Journal of the History of Philosophy* 45: 243–65.

Garrett, A. 2012. 'Reasoning about Morals from Butler to Hume', in R. Savage (ed.), *Philosophy and Religion in Enlightenment Britain: New Case Studies*. Oxford: Oxford University Press, 169–86.

Garrett, A. 2013a. 'Seventeenth Century Moral Philosophy: Self-help, Self-knowledge, and the Devil's Mountain', in R. Crisp (ed.), *Oxford Handbook of the History of Ethics*. Oxford: Oxford University Press, 229–79.

Garrett, A. 2013b. 'Clarke, Samuel', in H. LaFollette (ed.), *International Encyclopedia of Ethics*. Chichester: Wiley-Blackwell.

Garrett, A. 2018. 'Joseph Butler's Moral Philosophy', in E. Zalta (ed.), *Stanford Encyclopedia of Philosophy* (spring 2018 edn.), https://plato.stanford.edu/archives/spr2018/entries/butler-moral.

Garrett, A. 2020. '*Pulchrum non honestum*: Mandeville and Modern Moral Philosophy', in *The View From the Devil's Mountain: The Making of Modern Moral Philosophy*. Oxford: Oxford University Press.

Garrett, D. 2015. *Hume*. New York: Routledge.

Gauthier, D. 1969. *The Logic of Leviathan*. Oxford: Clarendon Press.

Gauthier, D. 1977a. 'Why Ought One Obey God?', *Canadian Journal of Philosophy* 7: 425–46.

Gauthier, D. 1977b. 'The Social Contract as Ideology', *Philosophy and Public Affairs* 6: 130–64.

Gauthier, D. 1979. 'Thomas Hobbes: Moral Theorist', *Journal of Philosophy* 76: 547–59.

Gauthier, D. 1986. *Morals by Agreement*. Oxford: Clarendon Press.

Gauthier, D. 1987. 'Taming Leviathan', *Philosophy and Public Affairs* 16: 280–98.

Gauthier, D. 1990. *Moral Dealing: Contract, Ethics, and Reason*. Ithaca: Cornell University Press.

Gauthier, D. 1992. 'Artificial Virtues and the Sensible Knave', *Hume Studies* 18: 401–27.

Gert, B. 1965. 'Hobbes, Mechanism, and Egoism', *Philosophical Quarterly* 15: 341–9.

Gert, B. 1967. 'Hobbes and Psychological Egoism', *Journal of the History of Ideas* 28: 503–20.

Gert, B. 1988. 'The Law of Nature and the Moral Law', *Hobbes Studies* 1: 26–44.

Gert, B. 1991. 'Introduction' to Hobbes 1991, 3–32.

Gert, B. 1996. 'Hobbes's Psychology', in T. Sorell (ed.), *Cambridge Companion to Hobbes*, 157–74.

Gert, B. 2001. 'Hobbes on Reason'. *Pacific Philosophical Quarterly* 82: 243–57.

Gert, B. 2010. *Hobbes*. Cambridge: Polity.

Gert, B. 2015. 'Hobbes, Thomas', in R. Audi (ed.), *Cambridge Dictionary of Philosophy*, 3rd. edn. Cambridge: Cambridge University Press.

Gill, M. 2006. *The British Moralists on Human Nature and the Birth of Secular Ethics*. Cambridge: Cambridge University Press.

Gill, M. 2014a. *Humean Moral Pluralism*. Oxford: Oxford University Press.

Gill, M. 2014b. 'Moral Pluralism in Smith and his Contemporaries', *Revue Internationale de Philosophie* 269: 275–306.

Gill, M. 2018. 'Lord Shaftesbury [Anthony Ashley Cooper, 3rd Earl of Shaftesbury]', in E. Zalta (ed.), *Stanford Encyclopedia of Philosophy* (spring 2018 edn.), https://plato.stanford.edu/archives/spr2018/entries/shaftesbury/.

Glassen, P. 1957. 'A Fallacy in Aristotle's Argument about the Good', *Philosophical Quarterly* 7: 319–22.

Glossop, R.J. 1967. 'The Nature of Hume's Ethics', *Philosophy and Phenomenological Research* 27: 527–36.

Goldie, M. 1991. 'The Reception of Hobbes', in J. Burns and M. Goldie (ed.), *Cambridge History of Political Thought* 1450–1700. Cambridge: Cambridge University Press, 589–615.

Goldsmith, M. 1966. *Hobbes's Science of Politics*. New York: Columbia University Press.

Goldsmith, M. 1985. *Private Vices, Public Benefits: Bernard Mandeville's Social and Political Thought*. Cambridge: Cambridge University Press.

Goldsmith, M. 1988. 'Regulating Anew the Moral and Political Sentiments of Mankind: Bernard Mandeville and the Scottish Enlightenment', *Journal of the History of Ideas* 49: 587–606.

Goldsmith, M. 1998. 'Mandeville, Bernard (1670–1733)', in E. Craig (ed.), *Routledge Encyclopedia of Philosophy*.

Goldworth, A. 1969. 'The Meaning of Bentham's Greatest Happiness Principle', *Journal of the History of Philosophy* 7: 315–21.

Goldworth, A. 1987. 'The Sympathetic Sanction and Sinister Interest in Bentham's Utilitarianism', *History of Philosophy Quarterly* 4: 67–78.

Gomberg, P. 1986. 'Self and Others in Bentham and Sidgwick', *History of Philosophy Quarterly* 3: 437–48.

Gordon, R. 1995. 'Sympathy, Simulation, and the Impartial Spectator', *Ethics* 105: 727–42.

Graham, G. 2016. 'Adam Smith and Religion', in R. Hanley (ed.), *Adam Smith: His Life, Thought, and Legacy*. Princeton and Oxford: Princeton University Press, 305–20.

Grave, S. 1952. 'The Foundation of Butler's Ethics', *Australasian Journal of Philosophy* 30: 73–89.

Grean, S. 1964. 'Self-interest and Public Interest in Shaftesbury's Philosophy', *Journal of the History of Philosophy* 2: 37–45.

Grean, S. 1967. *Shaftesbury's Philosophy of Religion and Ethics: A Study in Enthusiasm*. Athens, Ohio: Ohio University Press.

Green, T.H. 1885. *Works*, vol. 1, 5th imp., ed. R. Nettleship. London: Longmans, Green.

Green, T.H. and T.H. Grose, 1889. 'History of the Editions', in D. Hume, *Essays, Moral, Political, and Literary*, ed. Green and Grose, vol. 1, new edn. London: Longmans, Green, 15–84.

Griffin, J. 1986. *Well-Being: Its Meaning, Measurement and Moral Importance*. Oxford: Clarendon Press.

Griffin, J. 1996. *Value Judgement*. Oxford: Clarendon Press.

Griswold, C. 1999. *Adam Smith and the Virtues of Enlightenment*. Cambridge: Cambridge University Press.

Griswold, C. 2010. 'Smith and Rousseau in Dialogue: Sympathy, *Pitié*, Spectatorship and Narrative', in V. Brown and S. Fleischacker (eds), *Essays on the Philosophy of Adam Smith*. Abingdon: Routledge, 59–84.

Gustafsson, J. 2018. 'Bentham's Binary Form of Maximizing Utilitarianism', *British Journal of the History of Philosophy* 26: 87–109.

Guyer, P. 2004. 'The Origins of Modern Aesthetics: 1711–1735', in P. Kivy (ed.), *Blackwell Guide to Aesthetics*. Oxford: Blackwell, 15–44.

Haakonssen, K. 1981. *The Science of a Legislator: The Natural Jurisprudence of David Hume and Adam Smith*. Cambridge: Cambridge University Press.

Haakonssen, K. 1988. 'Moral Philosophy and Natural Law: From the Cambridge Platonists to the Scottish Enlightenment', *Political Science* 40: 97–110.

Haakonssen, K. 1996. *Natural Law and Moral Philosophy: From Grotius to the Scottish Enlightenment*. Cambridge: Cambridge University Press.

Haakonssen, K. 2000. 'The Character and Obligation of Natural Law according to Richard Cumberland', in M. Stewart (ed.), *English Philosophy in the Age of Locke*. Oxford: Clarendon Press, 29–47.

Halévy, E. 1928. *The Growth of Philosophic Radicalism*, tr. M. Morris. New York: Macmillan.

Hampton, J. 1986. *Hobbes and the Social Contract Tradition*. Cambridge: Cambridge University Press.

Hanley, R. 2009. *Adam Smith and the Character of Virtue*. Cambridge: Cambridge University Press.

Hanley, R. 2013. 'Adam Smith and Virtue', in C. Berry, M.P. Paganelli, and C. Smith (eds), *Oxford Handbook of Adam Smith*. Oxford: Oxford University Press, 219–40.

Hardin, R. 2007. *David Hume: Moral and Political Theorist*. Princeton: Princeton University Press.

Hare, R.M. 1981. *Moral Thinking: Its Methods, Levels, and Point*. Oxford: Clarendon Press.

Harman, G. 1986. 'Moral Agent and Impartial Spectator', Lindley Lecture. Lawrence: University of Kansas.

Harris, J. 2008. 'Religion in Hutcheson's Moral Philosophy', *Journal of the History of Philosophy* 46: 205–22.

Harrison, J. 1976. *Hume's Moral Epistemology*. Oxford: Clarendon Press.

Harrison, J. 1981. *Hume's Theory of Justice*. Oxford: Clarendon Press.

Harrison, R. 1983. *Bentham*. London: Routledge.

Harrison, R. 2003. *Hobbes, Locke, and Confusion's Masterpiece*. Cambridge: Cambridge University Press.

Hart, H.L.A. 1962. 'Lecture on a Master Mind: Bentham', *Proceedings of the British Academy* 48: 297–320.

Hart, H.L.A. 1982. *Essays on Bentham*. Oxford: Clarendon Press.

Hart, H.L.A. 1996. 'Bentham's Principle of Utility and Theory of Penal Law', in Bentham 1996, lxxix–cxii.

Harth, P. 1969. 'The Satiric Purpose of the Fable of the Bees', *Eighteenth-Century Studies* 2: 321–40.

Hayek, F. 1966. 'Dr Bernard Mandeville'. *Proceedings of the British Academy* 52: 125–41.

Heath, E. 1988. 'Mandeville's Bewitching Engine of Praise', *History of Philosophy Quarterly* 15: 205–26.

Heath, E. 1999. 'Critical Study: J. Martin Stafford's *Private Vices, Public Benefits?*', *Hume Studies*: 225–40.

Heath, E. 2013. 'Adam Smith and Self-interest', in C. Berry, M.P. Paganelli, and C. Smith (eds), *Oxford Handbook of Adam Smith*. Oxford: Oxford University Press, 241–66.

Hebblethwaite, B. 1992. 'Butler on Conscience and Virtue', in C. Cunliffe (ed.), *Joseph Butler's Moral and Religious Thought*. Oxford: Clarendon Press, 197–207.

Henry, J. 2016. 'Henry More', in E. Zalta (ed.) *Stanford Encyclopedia of Philosophy* (winter 2016 edn.), https://plato.stanford.edu/archives/win2016/entries/henry-more/.

Henson, R. 1988. 'Butler on Selfishness and Self-Love', *Philosophy and Phenomenological Research* 49: 31–57.

Herbert, G. 1989. *Thomas Hobbes: The Unity of Scientific and Moral Wisdom*. Vancouver: University of British Columbia Press.

Herzog, L. 2016. 'Adam Smith and Modern Ethics', in R. Hanley (ed.), *Adam Smith: His Life, Thought, and Legacy*. Princeton and Oxford: Princeton University Press, 340–53.

Hills, A. 2015. 'The Intellectuals and the Virtues', *Ethics* 126: 7–36.

Hittinger, J. 1990. 'Why Locke Rejected an Ethics of Virtue and Turned to an Ethics of Utility', *Proceedings of the American Association of Catholic Philosophers* 64: 267–76.

Hoekstra, K. 1997. 'Hobbes and the Foole', *Political Theory* 25: 620–54.

Hoekstra, K. 2003. 'Hobbes on Law, Nature, and Reason', *Journal of the History of Philosophy* 41: 111–20.

Hood, F. 1964. *The Divine Politics of Thomas Hobbes*. Oxford: Clarendon Press.

Hooker, B . 2000. *Ideal Code, Real World*. Oxford: Clarendon Press.

Hope, V. 1989. *Virtue by Consensus: The Moral Philosophy of Hutcheson, Hume, and Adam Smith*. Oxford: Clarendon Press.

Horne, T. 1978. *The Social and Political Thought of Bernard Mandeville: Virtue and Commerce in Early Eighteenth-Century England*. London: Macmillan.

Hruschka, J. 1991. 'The Greatest Happiness Principle and Other Early German Anticipations of Utilitarian Theory', *Utilitas* 3: 165–77.

Hubin, D. 1980. 'Prudential Reasons', *Canadian Journal of Philosophy* 10: 63–81.

Hudson, W.D. 1970. *Reason and Right: A Critical Examination of Richard Price's Moral Philosophy.*

Hume, L.J. 1978. 'Revisionism in Bentham Studies', *Bentham Newsletter* 1: 3–20.

Hundert, E. 1994. *The Enlightenment's Fable: Bernard Mandeville and the Discovery of Society.* Cambridge: Cambridge University Press.

Hurka, T. 2013. 'Aristotle on Virtue: Wrong, Wrong, and Wrong', in J. Peters (ed.), *Aristotelian Ethics in Contemporary Perspective.* New York: Routledge, 9–26.

Hutton, S. 1998. 'Ralph Cudworth (1617–88), in E. Craig (ed.), *Routledge Encyclopedia of Philosophy.* London: Routledge.

Hutton, S. 2013. 'The Cambridge Platonists', in E. Zalta (ed.), *Stanford Encyclopedia of Philosophy* (winter 2013 edn.), http://plato.stanford.edu/archives/win2013/entries/cambridge-platonists/.

Hutton, S. 2015. *British Philosophy in the Seventeenth Century.* Oxford: Oxford University Press.

Immerwahr, J. 1989. 'Hume's Essays on Happiness', *Hume Studies* 15: 307–24.

Irwin, T. 2003. 'Stoic Naturalism in Butler', in J. Miller and B. Inwood (eds), *Hellenistic and Early Modern Philosophy.* Cambridge: Cambridge University Press, 274–300.

Irwin, T. 2008. *The Development of Ethics*, vol. 2, *From Suarez to Rousseau.* Oxford: Clarendon Press.

Jack, M. 1975. 'Religion and Ethics in Mandeville', in Primer (ed.), 34–42.

Jack, M. 1976. 'Progress and Corruption in the Eighteenth Century Mandeville's "Private Vices, Public Benefits"', *Journal of the History of Ideas* 37: 369–76.

Jackson, R. 1943. 'Bishop Butler's Refutation of Psychological Hedonism', *Philosophy* 18: 114–39.

James, E. 1975. 'Faith, Sincerity and Morality: Mandeville and Bayle', in Primer (ed.), 43–65.

James, E. 1981. 'Butler, Fanaticism and Conscience', *Philosophy* 56: 517–32.

James, W. 1979. 'The Moral Philosopher and the Moral Life', in *The Will to Believe and Other Essays in Popular Philosophy, Collected Works*, vol. 6, ed. F. Burkhardt, F. Bowers, and Ignas K. Skrupskelis. Cambridge, Mass.: Harvard University Press, 141–62.

Jensen, H. 1971. *Motivation and the Moral Sense in Francis Hutcheson's Ethical Theory.* The Hague: Martinus Nijhoff.

Johnston, D. 1986. *The Rhetoric of Leviathan.* Princeton: Princeton University Press.

Jolley, N. 1999. *Locke: His Philosophical Thought.* Oxford: Oxford University Press.

Kail, P.J.E. 2001. 'Hutcheson's Moral Sense: Skepticism, Realism, and Secondary Qualities', *History of Philosophy Quarterly* 18: 57–77.

Kant, I. 2002. *Groundwork for the Metaphysics of Morals*, ed. T. Hill and A. Zweig, trans. A. Zweig. Oxford: Oxford University Press.

Karlsson, M.K. 2006. 'Reason, Passion, and the Influencing Motives of the Will', in S. Traiger (ed.), *Blackwell Guide to Hume's Treatise.* Malden, MA: Blackwell, 235–55.

Kavka, G. 1983. 'Right Reason and Natural Law in Hobbes's Ethics', *Monist* 66: 120–33.

Kavka, G. 1986. *Hobbesian Moral and Political Theory.* Princeton: Princeton University Press.

Kelly, P. 1990. *Utilitarianism and Distributive Justice: Jeremy Bentham and the Civil Law.* Oxford: Clarendon Press.

Kelly, D. 2013. 'Adam Smith and the Limits of Sympathy', in C. Berry, M.P. Paganelli, and C. Smith (eds), *Oxford Handbook of Adam Smith.* Oxford: Oxford University Press, 201–18.

Kemp, J. 1982. 'Hobbes on Pity and Charity', in J. van der Bend (ed.), *Thomas Hobbes: His View of Man*. Amsterdam: Rodopi, 57–62.

Kemp Smith, N. 1941. *The Philosophy of David Hume*. London: Macmillan.

Kerkof, B. 1995. 'A Fatal Attraction? Adam Smith's *Theory of Moral Sentiments* and Mandeville's *Fable*', *History of Political Thought* 16: 219–33.

Keynes, J.M. 1933. *Essays in Biography*. London: Macmillan.

King, P., Lord 1830. *The Life of John Locke*. London: Colburn and Bentley.

Kirk, L. 1987. *Richard Cumberland and Natural Law: Secularisation of Thought in Seventeenth-Century England*. Cambridge: James Clarke.

Kivy, P. 2003. *The Seventh Sense: Francis Hutcheson and Eighteenth Century British Aesthetics*. Oxford: Clarendon Press.

Kleer, R. 1995. 'Final Causes in Adam Smith's *Theory of Moral Sentiments*', *Journal of the History of Philosophy* 33: 275–300.

Kleinig, J. 1969. 'Butler in a Cool Hour', *Journal of the History of Philosophy* 7: 399–411.

Korsgaard, C. 1997. 'The Normativity of Instrumental Reason', in G. Cullity and B. Gaut (eds.), *Ethics and Practical Reason*. Oxford: Clarendon Press, 215–54.

Kraus, P. 1984. 'Locke's Negative Hedonism', *Locke Newsletter* 15: 43–63.

Kupperman, J. 1985. 'Francis Hutcheson: Morality and Nature', *Journal of Value Inquiry* 2: 195–202.

Kydd, R. 1946. *Reason and Conduct in Hume's Treatise*. London: Oxford University Press.

Kyle, W. 1929. 'British Ethical Theories: The Place and Importance of Bishop Butler', *Australasian Journal of Psychology and Philosophy* 7: 252–62.

Laird, J. 1932. *Hume's Philosophy of Human Nature*. London: Methuen.

Lamprecht, S. 1918. *The Moral and Political Philosophy of John Locke*. New York: Columbia University Press.

Lamprecht, S. 1926. 'The Fable of the Bees', *Journal of Philosophy* 23: 561–79.

Lear, G.R. 2006. 'Aristotle on Moral Virtue and the Fine', in R. Kraut (ed.), *Blackwell Guide to Aristotle's Nicomachean Ethics*. Oxford: Blackwell, 116–36.

LeBuffe, M. 2003. 'Hobbes on the Origin of Obligation', *British Journal for the History of Philosophy* 11: 15–39.

Lecaldano, E. 2008. 'Hume's Theory of Justice, or Artificial Virtue', in E. Radcliffe (ed.), *A Companion to Hume*. Malden, MA, 257–72.

Lefevre, A. 1899. 'The Significance of Butler's View of Human Nature', *Philosophical Review* 8: 128–45.

Lefevre, A. 1900a. 'Self-love and Benevolence in Butler's Ethical System', *Philosophical Review* 9: 167–87.

Lefevre, A. 1900b. 'Conscience and Obligation in Butler's Ethical System', *Philosophical Review* 9: 395–410.

Leites, E. 1975. 'A Problem in Butler's Ethics', *Southwestern Journal of Philosophy* 6: 43–57.

Le Mahieu, D.L. 2002. 'Foreword' to W. Paley, *Principles of Moral and Political Philosophy*. Indianapolis: Liberty Fund, xi–xxvii.

Lent, A. 2009. 'What's in it for Me? Butler's Complaint against Collins', *British Journal for the History of Philosophy* 17: 333–49.

Le Rossignol, J. 1892. *The Ethical Philosophy of Samuel Clarke*. Leipzig: G. Kreysing.

Levy, S. 1999. 'Thomas Reid's Defense of Conscience', *History of Philosophy Quarterly* 16: 413–35.

Lewis, C. and C. Short 1879. *A Latin Dictionary*. Oxford: Clarendon Press.

Lloyd, S. 1992. *Ideals as Interests in Hobbes's* Leviathan. Cambridge: Cambridge University Press.

Lloyd, S. 2009. *Morality in the Philosophy of Thomas Hobbes*. Cambridge: Cambridge University Press.

Lloyd, S. and S. Sreedhar 2018. 'Hobbes, Thomas: Moral and Political Philosophy', in E. Zalta (ed.), *Stanford Encyclopedia of Philosophy* (summer 2018 edn.), https://plato.stanford.edu/archives/sum2018/entries/hobbes-moral.

LoLordo, A. 2012. *Locke's Moral Man*. Oxford: Oxford University Press.

Long, A.A. 2003. 'Stoicism in the Philosophical Tradition: Spinoza, Lipsius, Butler', in J. Miller and B. Inwood (eds), *Hellenistic and Early Modern Philosophy*. Cambridge: Cambridge University Press, 7–29.

Long, D. 1990. ' "Utility" and the "Utility Principle": Hume, Smith, Bentham', *Utilitas* 2: 12–39.

Louden, R. 1995. 'Butler's Divine Utilitarianism', *Philosophy and Phenomenological Research* 12: 265–80.

Lyons, D. 1991. *In the Interest of the Governed: A Study in Bentham's Philosophy of Utility and Law*, rev. edn. Oxford: Clarendon Press.

Mabbott, J.D. 1973. *John Locke*. London: Macmillan.

MacIntyre, A.C. 1959. 'Hume on Is and Ought', *Philosophical Review* 68: 451–68.

Mack, M. 1962. *Jeremy Bentham: An Odyssey of Ideas* 1748–92. London: Heinemann.

Mackie, J.L. 1980. *Hume's Moral Theory*. London: Routledge and Kegan Paul.

Mackie, J.L. 1982. *The Miracle of Theism*. Oxford: Oxford University Press.

Mackinnon, D.M. 1957. *A Study in Ethical Theory*. London: A. and C. Black.

MacLachlan, A. 2010. 'Resentment and Moral Judgement in Smith and Butler', *Adam Smith Review* 5: 161–77.

MacNabb, D.G. 1951. *David Hume: His Theory of Knowledge and Morality*. London: Collins.

Malcolm, N. 2002. *Aspects of Hobbes*. Oxford: Clarendon Press.

Marcus Aurelius 2013. *Meditations, Books* 1–6, tr. C. Gill. Oxford: Oxford University Press.

Marshall, J. 1994. *John Locke: Resistance, Religion and Responsibility*. Cambridge: Cambridge University Press.

Martineau, J. 1885. *Types of Ethical Theory*. Oxford: Clarendon Press.

Martinich, A. 1992. *The Two Gods of* Leviathan. Cambridge: Cambridge University Press.

Martinich, A. 1997. *Hobbes*. Basingstoke: Macmillan.

Masham, D. 1705. *Occasional Thoughts in reference to a Vertuous or Christian Life*. London: A. and J. Churchil.

Matsumoto, A. 2010. 'Happiness and Religion: Joseph Priestley's "Theological Utilitarianism"', *Kyoto Economic Review* 79: 55–66.

Maurer, C. 2006. 'Two Approaches to Self-love: Hutcheson and Butler', *European Journal of Analytic Philosophy* 2: 81–96.

Maurer, C. 2009. *Self-Love in Early 18th-Century British Moral Philosophy: Shaftesbury, Mandeville, Hutcheson, Butler and Campbell*. PhD. dissertation, University of Neuchâtel.

Maurer, C. 2010. 'Hutcheson's Relation to Stoicism in the Light of his Moral Psychology', *Journal of Scottish Philosophy* 8: 33–49.

Maurer, C. 2013. 'Self-interest and Sociability', in J. Harris (ed.), *Oxford Handbook of British Philosophy in the Eighteenth Century*. Oxford: Oxford University Press.

Maurer, C. 2014. 'What Can an Egoist Say Against an Egoist? On Archibald Campbell's Criticisms of Bernard Mandeville', *Journal of Scottish Philosophy* 12: 1–18.

Maurer, C. and L. Jaffro 2013. 'Reading Shaftesbury's *Pathologia*: An Illustration and Defence of the Stoic Account of the Emotions', *History of European Ideas* 39: 207–20.

Mautner, T. 2002. 'Introduction' to Hutcheson 2002, 1–87.

Maxwell, J. 1951. 'Ethics and Politics in Mandeville', *Philosophy* 26: 242–52.

McAteer, J. n.d. 'The Third Earl of Shaftesbury (1671–1713)', in J. Feiser and B. Dowden (eds), *Internet Encyclopedia of Philosophy*, http://www.iep.utm.edu/shaftes/.

McClintock, T. 1994. 'The Meaning of Hobbes's Egoistic Moral Philosophy', *Philosophia* 23: 247–63.

McCosh, J. 1875. *The Scottish Philosophy: Biographical, Expository, Critical from Hutcheson to Hamilton*. London: Macmillan.

McNaughton, D. 1992. 'Butler on Benevolence', in C. Cunliffe (ed.), *Joseph Butler's Moral and Religious Thought*. Oxford: Clarendon Press, 269–91.

McNaughton, D. 1996. 'British Moralists of the Eighteenth Century: Shaftesbury, Butler and Price', in S. Brown (ed.), *Routledge History of Philosophy, vol. 5: British Philosophy and the Age of Enlightenment*, 203–27.

McNaughton, D. 1998. 'Shaftesbury, Third Earl of (Anthony Ashley Cooper) (1671–1713)', in E. Craig (ed.), *Routledge Encyclopedia of Philosophy*. London: Routledge.

McNaughton, D. 2013. 'Butler's Ethics', in R. Crisp (ed.), *Oxford Handbook of the History of Ethics*. Oxford: Oxford University Press, 377–98.

McNeilly, F. 1966. 'Egoism in Hobbes', *Philosophical Quarterly* 16: 193–206.

McNeilly, F. 1968. *The Anatomy of Leviathan*. London: Macmillan.

McPherson, T. 1948. 'The Development of Bishop Butler's Ethics', *Philosophy* 23: 317–31.

McPherson, T. 1949. 'The Development of Bishop Butler's Ethics. Part 2', *Philosophy* 24: 3–22.

Mehta, P. 2006. 'Self-interest and Other Interests', in K. Haakonssen (ed.), *Cambridge Companion to Adam Smith*. Cambridge: Cambridge University Press, 246–69.

Mijuskovic, B. 1971. 'Hume and Shaftesbury on the Self', *Philosophical Quarterly* 21: 324–36.

Mill, J.S. 1961–91. *Collected Works*, ed. J. Robson. Toronto: University of Toronto Press.

Mill, J.S. 1998. *Utilitarianism*, ed. R. Crisp. Oxford: Oxford University Press.

Millar, A. 1988. 'Following Nature', *Philosophical Quarterly* 38: 165–85.

Millar, A. 1992. 'Butler on God and Human Nature', in C. Cunliffe (ed.), *Joseph Butler's Moral and Religious Thought*. Oxford: Clarendon Press, 293–315.

Mintz, S. 1962. *The Hunting of Leviathan*. Cambridge: Cambridge University Press.

Monck, W. 1878. 'Butler's Ethical System', *Mind* 3: 358–69.

Monro, H. 1975. *The Ambivalence of Bernard Mandeville*. Oxford: Clarendon Press.

Montes, L. 2004. *Adam Smith in Context: A Critical Reassessment of Some Central Components of his Thought*. Houndmills and New York: Palgrave.

Montes, L. 2016. 'Adam Smith: Self-interest and the Virtues', in R. Hanley (ed.), *Adam Smith: His Life, Thought, and Legacy*. Princeton and Oxford: Princeton University Press, 138–56.

Moore, J. 1990. 'The Two Systems of Francis Hutcheson: On the Origins of the Scottish Enlightenment', in M.A. Stewart (ed.), *Studies in the Philosophy of the Scottish Enlightenment*. Oxford: Clarendon Press, 37–59.

Moore, J. 2002. 'Utility and Humanity: The Quest for the *Honestum* in Cicero, Hutcheson, and Hume', *Utilitas* 14: 365–86.

Moore, S. 1971. 'Hobbes on Obligation, Moral and Political: Part One: Moral Obligation', *Journal of the History of Philosophy* 9: 43–62.

Moore, S. 1972. 'Hobbes on Obligation, Moral and Political: Part Two: Political Obligation', *Journal of the History of Philosophy* 10: 29–42.

Moses, S. 2009. ' "Keeping the Heart": Natural Affection in Joseph Butler's Approach to Virtue', *Journal of Religious Ethics* 37: 613–29.

Murphy, M. 1994. 'Deviant Uses of "Obligation" in Hobbes' *Leviathan*', *Journal of the History of Philosophy* 11: 281–94.

Murphy, M. 2000a. 'Desire and Ethics in Hobbes's *Leviathan*: A Response to Professor Deigh', *Journal of the History of Philosophy* 38: 259–68.

Murphy, M. 2000b. 'Hobbes on the Evil of Death'. *Archiv für Geschichte der Philosophie* 82: 36–61.

Nagai, Y. 1982. 'Jeremy Bentham on Richard Price', *Enlightenment and Dissent* 1: 83–7.

Nagel, T. 1959. 'Hobbes's Concept of Obligation', *Philosophical Review* 68: 68–83.

Nagel, T. 1979. 'Moral Luck', repr. in *Mortal Questions*. Cambridge: Cambridge University Press, 24–38.

Nanay, B. . 2010. 'Adam Smith's Concept of Sympathy and its Contemporary Interpretations', in V. Brown and S. Fleischacker (eds), *Essays on the Philosophy of Adam Smith*. Abingdon: Routledge, 85–105.

Nelson, W. 1994. 'Mutual Benevolence and Happiness', *Journal of Philosophy* 91: 50–1.

Newey, G. 2008. *GuideBook to Hobbes and* Leviathan. Abingdon: Routledge.

Nichols, R. and G. Yaffe 2016. 'Thomas Reid', in E. Zalta (ed.) *Stanford Encyclopedia of Philosophy* (winter 2016 edn.), http://plato.stanford.edu/archives/win2016/entries/reid/.

Nilsson, P. 2013. 'Butler's Stone and Ultimate Psychological Hedonism', *Philosophia* 41: 545–53.

Norton, D.F. 1977. 'Hutcheson on Perception and Moral Perception', *Archiv für Geschichte der Philosophie* 59: 181–97.

Norton, D.F. 1982. *David Hume: Common-Sense Moralist, Sceptical Metaphysician*. Princeton: Princeton University Press.

Norton, D.F. 1985. 'Hutcheson's Moral Realism', *Journal of the History of Philosophy* 23: 397–418.

Norton, D.F. 1998. 'Hutcheson, Francis (1694–1746)', in E. Craig (ed.), *Routledge Encyclopedia of Philosophy*. London: Routledge.

Norton, D.F. and M.F. Norton 2007. 'Historical Account of *A Treatise of Human Nature* from its Beginnings to the Time of Hume's Death', in Hume 2007, 2.433–588.

Norton, D.F. and J.C. Stewart-Robertson 1980. 'Thomas Reid on Adam Smith's Theory of Morals', *Journal of the History of Ideas* 41: 381–98.

Nozick, R. 1974. *Anarchy, State, and Utopia*. New York: Basic Books.

Nunan, R. 1989. 'Hobbes on Morality, Rationality, and Foolishness', *Hobbes Studies* 2: 40–64.

Nussbaum, M. 1990. *Love's Knowledge: Essays on Philosophy and Literature*. Oxford: Oxford University Press.

Nussbaum, M. 2019. ' "Mutilated and Deformed": Adam Smith on the Material Basis of Human Dignity', in *The Cosmopolitan Tradition: A Noble but Flawed Ideal*. Cambridge, Mass.: Harvard University Press.

Oakeshott, M. 1975. 'Introduction to *Leviathan*', repr. in *Hobbes on Civil Association*. Indianapolis: Liberty Fund, 1–79.

Oakley, F. 1999. 'Locke, Natural Law and God – Again', repr. in J. Milton (ed.), *Locke's Moral, Political, and Legal Philosophy*. Dartmouth: Ashgate, 213–40.

O'Brien, D. 2012. 'Hume and the Virtues', in A. Bailey and D. O'Brien (eds), *Continuum Companion to Hume*. London: Continuum, 288–302.

O'Brien, W. 1991. 'Butler and the Authority of Conscience', *History of Philosophy Quarterly* 8: 43–57.

Ogden, C.K. 1951. *Bentham's Theory of Fictions*, 2nd edn. London: Routledge and Kegan Paul.

Olsthoorn, J. 2014. 'Worse than Death: The Non-preservationist Foundations of Hobbes's Political Philosophy', *Hobbes Studies* 27: 148–70.

Oslthoorn, J. 2015. 'Why Justice and Injustice have No Place Outside the Hobbesian State', *European Journal of Political Theory* 14: 19–36.

Otteson, J. 2013. 'Adam Smith', in R. Crisp (ed.), *Oxford Handbook of the History of Ethics*. Oxford: Oxford University Press, 421–42.

Owen, G.E.L. 1971–2. 'Aristotelian Pleasures', *Proceedings of the Aristotelian Society* 72: 135–52.

Paletta, D. 2011. 'Francis Hutcheson: Why be Moral?', *Journal of Scottish Philosophy* 9: 149–59.

Parfit, D. 1984. *Reasons and Persons*. Oxford: Clarendon Press.

Parkin, J. 1999. *Science, Religion and Politics in Restoration England: Richard Cumberland's De Legibus Naturae*. Woodbridge: Boydell Press.

Parkin, J. 2002. 'Probability, Punishments and Property: Richard Cumberland's Sceptical Science of Sovereignty', in I. Hunter and D. Saunders (ed.), *Natural Law and Civil Sovereignty: Moral Right and State Authority in Early Modern Political Thought*. Basingstoke: Palgrave Macmillan, 76–90.

Parkin, J. 2005. 'Foreword', in R. Cumberland, *A Treatise of the Laws of Nature*, ed. J. Parkin (Indianapolis: Liberty Fund), ix–xix.

Parkin, J. 2007. *Taming the Leviathan*. Cambridge: Cambridge University Press.

Peacock, M. 2010. 'Obligation and Advantage in Hobbes' *Leviathan*', *Canadian Journal of Philosophy* 40: 433–58.

Penelhum, T. 1985. *Butler*. London: Routledge and Kegan Paul.

Persson, I. and J. Savulescu 2012. *Unfit for the Future*. Oxford: Oxford University Press.

Peters, R. 1956. *Hobbes*. Harmondsworth: Penguin.

Pigden, C. 2012. 'A "Sensible Knave"? Hume, Jane Austen and Mr Elliott', *Intellectual History Review* 22: 465–80.

Plamenatz, J. 1965. 'Mr Warrender's Hobbes', repr. in K. Brown (ed.) 1965, 73–87.

Plamenatz, J. 1966. *The English Utilitarians*, 2nd rev.edn. Oxford: Blackwell.

Plato 2003. *Respublica*, ed. S. Slings. Oxford: Clarendon Press.

Postema, G.J. 1986. *Bentham and the Common Law Tradition*. Oxford: Clarendon Press.

Postema, G.J. 2006. 'Interests, Universal and Particular: Bentham's Utilitarian Theory of Value', *Utilitas* 18: 109–33.

Priestley, J. 1771. *An Essay on the First Principles of Government, and on the Nature of Political, Civil, and Religious Liberty*. London: J. Johnson.

Primer, I. (ed.) 1975. *Mandeville Studies: New Explorations in the Art and Thought of Dr. Bernard Mandeville (1670–1733)*. Hague: Martinus Nijhoff.

Primer, I. 1975. 'Mandeville and Shaftesbury: Some Problems', in Primer (ed.) 1975, 126–41.

Prince, M. 1996. *Philosophical Dialogue in the British Enlightenment*. Cambridge: Cambridge University Press.

Prior, A.N. 1949. *Logic and the Basis of Ethics*. Oxford: Clarendon Press.

Pritchard, M. 1978. 'Conscience and Reason in Butler's Ethics', *Southwestern Journal of Philosophy* 9: 39–49.

Purviance, S. 2004. 'Shaftesbury on Self as a Practice', *Journal of Scottish Philosophy* 2: 155–63.

Quinn, M. 2012. 'Which Comes First, Bentham's Chicken of Utility or his Egg of Truth?', *Journal of Bentham Studies* 14: 1–46.

Quinton, A. 1973. *Utilitarian Ethics*. London: Macmillan.

Radcliffe, E. 1986. 'Hutcheson's Perceptual and Moral Subjectivism', *History of Philosophy Quarterly* 3: 407–21.

Radcliffe, E. 2013. 'Moral Sentimentalism and the Reasonableness of Being Good', *Revue Internationale de Philosophie* 263: 9–27.

Raphael, D.D. 1949. 'Bishop Butler's View of Conscience', *Philosophy* 24: 219–38.

Raphael, D.D. 1969. *British Moralists 1650–1800*. 2 vols. Oxford: Clarendon Press.

Raphael, D.D. 1972–3. 'Hume and Adam Smith on Justice and Utility', *Proceedings of the Aristotelian Society* 73: 87–103.

Raphael, D.D. 1977. *Hobbes: Morals and Politics*. London: Allen and Unwin.

Raphael, D.D. 2007. *The Impartial Spectator: Adam Smith's Moral Philosophy*. Oxford: Clarendon Press.

Rashdall, H. 1907. *The Theory of Good and Evil*. Oxford: Clarendon Press.

Rogers, G.A.J. and A. Ryan (eds) 1988. *Perspectives on Thomas Hobbes*. Oxford: Clarendon Press.

Rauscher, F. 2003. 'Moral Realism and the Divine Essence in Hutcheson', *History of Philosophy Quarterly* 20: 165–81.

Rawls, J. 1999. *A Theory of Justice*, rev. edn. Oxford: Oxford University Press.

Reichlin, M. 2016. 'Hume and Utilitarianism: Another Look at an Age-old Question', *Journal of Scottish Philosophy* 14: 1–20.

Rendall, J. 1978. *The Origins of the Scottish Enlightenment*. London: Macmillan.

Rick, J. 2007. 'Hume and Smith's Partial Sympathies and Impartial Stances', *Journal of Scottish Philosophy* 5: 135–58.

Riddle, G. 1959. 'The Place of Benevolence in Butler's Ethics', *Philosophical Quarterly* 9: 356–62.

Rivers, I. 1991. *Reason, Grace, and Sentiment: A Study of the Language of Religion and Ethics in England, 1660–1780*, vol. 1: *Whichcote to Wesley*. Cambridge: Cambridge University Press.

Rivers, I. 2000. *Reason, Grace, and Sentiment: A Study of the Language of Religion and Ethics in England, 1660–1780*, vol. 2: *Shaftesbury to Hume*. Cambridge: Cambridge University Press.

Roberts, T.A. 1973. *The Concept of Benevolence: Aspects of Eighteenth-Century Moral Philosophy*. London: Macmillan.

Roberts, T.A. 1992. 'Butler and Immortality', in C. Cunliffe (ed.), *Joseph Butler's Moral and Religious Thought*. Oxford: Clarendon Press, 169–87.

Rogers, A. 1925. 'The Ethics of Mandeville', *International Journal of Ethics* 36: 1–17.

Rogers, G.A.J. 1981. 'Locke, Law, and the Laws of Nature', in R. Brandt (ed.), *John Locke: Symposium Wolfenbüttel, 1979*. Berlin: De Gruyter, 146–62.

Rogers, G.A.J. (ed.) 1995. Leviathan: *Contemporary Responses to the Political Theory of Thomas Hobbes*. Bristol: Thoemmes.

Rorty, A. 1978. 'Butler on Benevolence and Conscience', *Philosophy* 53: 171–84.

Rosen, F. 1996. 'Introduction' to Bentham 1996, xxxi–lxxviii.

Rosen, F. 2003. *Classical Utilitarianism from Hume to Mill*. London: Routledge.

Ross, W.D. 1930. *The Right and the Good*. Oxford: Clarendon Press.

Russell, B. 1970. 'The Elements of Ethics', repr. in W. Sellars and J. Hospers (eds), *Readings in Ethical Theory*, 2nd edn. New York: Appleton-Century-Crofts, 3–28.

Russell, P. 2008. *The Riddle of Hume's Treatise: Skepticism, Naturalism, and Irreligion*. Oxford: Oxford University Press.

Ryan, A. 1974. *J.S. Mill*. London: Routledge and Kegan Paul.

Ryan, A. 1996. 'Hobbes's Political Philosophy', in T. Sorell (ed.), *Cambridge Companion to Hobbes*, 208–45.

Sayre-McCord, G. 1994. 'On Why Hume's "General Point of View" isn't Ideal – and Shouldn't Be', *Social Philosophy and Policy* 11: 202–28.

Sayre-McCord, G. 1996. 'Hume and the Bauhaus Theory of Ethics', in P.A. French, T.E. Uehling (Jr.), and H.K. Wettstein (eds.), *Midwest Studies in Philosophy 20: Moral Concepts*. Notre Dame: University of Notre Dame Press, 280–98.

Sayre-McCord, G. 2010. 'Sentiments and Spectators: Adam Smith's Theory of Moral Judgment', in V. Brown and S. Fleischacker (eds), *Essays on the Philosophy of Adam Smith*. Abingdon: Routledge, 124–44.

Sayre-McCord, G. 2015. 'Hume and Smith on Sympathy, Approbation, and Moral Judgment', in E. Schliesser (ed.), *Sympathy: A History*. New York: Oxford University Press, 208–46.

Scanlon, T.M. 1998. *What We Owe to Each Other*. Harvard: Belknap Press.

Scheffler, S. 1982. *The Rejection of Consequentialism*. Cambridge: Cambridge University Press.

Schliesser, E. (ed.) 2015. *Sympathy: A History*. New York: Oxford University Press.

Schliesser, E. 2016. 'The Theory of Moral Sentiments', in R. Hanley (ed.), *Adam Smith: His Life, Thought, and Legacy*. Princeton and Oxford: Princeton University Press, 33–47.

Schmitter, A. 2016. 'Hobbes on the Emotions', suppl. to '17th and 18th Century Theories of Emotions', in E. Zalta (ed.) *Stanford Encyclopedia of Philosophy* (winter 2016 edn.), https://plato.stanford.edu/archives/win2016/entries/emotions-17th18th/LD3Hobbes.html.

Schneewind, J.B. 1977. *Sidgwick's Ethics and Victorian Moral Philosophy*. Oxford: Clarendon Press.

Schneewind, J.B. 1990 (ed.). *Moral Philosophy from Montaigne to Kant: An Anthology*. 2 vols. Cambridge: Cambridge University Press.

Schneewind, J.B. 1994. 'Locke's Moral Philosophy', in V. Chappell (ed.), *Cambridge Companion to Locke*. Cambridge: Cambridge University Press, 199–225.

Schneewind, J.B. 1995. 'Voluntarism and the Origins of Utilitarianism', *Utilitas* 7: 87–96.

Schneewind, J.B. 1998. *The Invention of Autonomy: A History of Modern Moral Philosophy*. Cambridge: Cambridge University Press.

Schneider, L. 1987. *Paradox and Society: The Work of Bernard Mandeville*. New Brunswick and Oxford: Transaction.

Schofield, P. 2006. *Utility and Democracy: The Political Thought of Jeremy Bentham*. Oxford: Oxford University Press.

Schofield, P. 2009. *Bentham: A Guide for the Perplexed*. London: Continuum.

Schultz, B. 2017. *The Happiness Philosophers*. Princeton: Princeton University Press.

Scott, W.R. 1900. *Francis Hutcheson: His Life, Teaching and Position in the History of Philosophy*. Cambridge: Cambridge University Press.

Scott-Taggart, M. 1966. 'Mandeville: Cynic or Fool?', *Philosophical Quarterly* 16: 221–32.

Scott-Taggart, M. 1968. 'Butler on Disinterested Actions', *Philosophical Quarterly* 18: 16–28.

Selby-Bigge, L.A. (ed.) 1897. *British Moralists, being Selections from Writers Principally of the Eighteenth Century*. 2 vols. Oxford: Clarendon Press.

Sellars, J. 2016. 'Shaftesbury, Stoicism, and Philosophy as a Way of Life', *Sophia* 55: 395–408.

Sen, A. and B. Williams 1982. 'Introduction: Utilitarianism and Beyond', in their (ed) *Utilitarianism and Beyond*. Cambridge: Cambridge University Press, 1–21.

Sharp, F. 1912. 'The Ethical System of Richard Cumberland and its Place in the History of British Ethics', *Mind* 21: 371–98.

Shaver, R. 1992. 'Hume's Moral Theory?', *History of Philosophy Quarterly* 12: 317–31.

Shaver, R. 1999. *Rational Egoism*. Cambridge: Cambridge University Press.

Shaver, R. 2006. 'Virtues, Utility, and Rules', in K. Haakonssen (ed.). *Cambridge Companion to Adam Smith*. Cambridge: Cambridge University Press, 189–213.

Shaver, R. 2013. 'Utilitarianism: Bentham and Rashdall', in R. Crisp (ed.), *Oxford Handbook of the History of Ethics*. Oxford: Oxford University Press, 292–311.

Shaver, R. 2017. 'Egoism', in E. Zalta (ed.), *Stanford Encyclopedia of Philosophy* (winter 2017 edn.), https://plato.stanford.edu/archives/win2017/entries/egoism/.

Shelton, G. 1992. *Morality and Sovereignty in the Philosophy of Hobbes*. Basingstoke: Macmillan.

Sheridan, P. 2007. 'Pirates, Kings and Reasons to Act: Moral Motivation and the Role of Sanctions in Locke's Moral Philosophy', *Canadian Journal of Philosophy* 37: 35–48.

Sheridan, P. 2016. 'Locke's Moral Philosophy', in E. Zalta (ed.), *Stanford Encyclopedia of Philosophy* (summer 2016 edn.), https://plato.stanford.edu/archives/sum2016/entries/locke-moral/.

Shiner, R. 1979. 'Butler's Theory of Moral Judgement', in S. Brown (ed.), *Royal Institute of Philosophy Lectures* 12 (1978): Philosophers of the Enlightenment. Brighton: Harvester, 199–25.

Sidgwick, H. 1902. *Outlines of the History of Ethics*, 5th edn. London: Macmillan.

Sidgwick, H. 1907. *The Methods of Ethics*, 7th edn. London: Macmillan.

Skinner, Q. 1966. 'The Ideological Context of Hobbes's Political Thought', *Historical Journal* 9: 286–317.

Smart, J. 1956. 'Extreme and Restricted Utilitarianism', *Philosophical Quarterly* 6: 344–54.

Smith, J. 1950. 'The British Moralists and the Fallacy of Psychologism', *Journal of the History of Ideas* 11: 159–78.

Smyth, D. (ed.) 1992: *Francis Hutcheson*, suppl. to *Fortnight* 308.

Sobel, J.H. 1997. 'Hume's Utilitarian Theory of Right Action', *Philosophical Quarterly* 47: 55–72.

Sobel, J.H. 2009. *Walls and Vaults: A Natural Science of Morals (Virtue Ethics according to David Hume)*. Hoboken: John Wiley.

Sober, E. 1992. 'Hedonism and Butler's Stone', *Ethics* 103: 97–103.

Sober, E., and D. S. Wilson 1998. *Unto Others*. Cambridge, Mass.: Harvard University Press.

Sorell, T. 1986. *Hobbes*. London: Routledge and Kegan Paul.

Sorell, T. 1998. 'Hobbes, Thomas', in E. Craig (ed.), *Routledge Encyclopedia of Philosophy*. London: Routledge.

Sprague, E. 1954. 'Francis Hutcheson and the Moral Sense', *Journal of Philosophy* 51: 794–800.

Sprigge, T.L.S. 1999. 'The Relation between Jeremy Bentham's Psychological, and his Ethical, Hedonism', *Utilitas* 11: 296–319.

Stearns, J.B. 1974. 'Bentham on Public and Private Ethics', *Canadian Journal of Philosophy* 5: 583–94.

Stephen, L. 1876. *History of English Thought in the Eighteenth Century*. 2 vols. London: Smith, Elder.

Stephen, L. 1900. *The English Utilitarians*, vol. 1. London: Duckworth.

Stephen, L. 1904. *Hobbes*. London: Macmillan.

Stephens, J. 2000. 'Conscience and the Epistemology of Morals: Richard Price's Debt to Joseph Butler'. *Enlightenment and Dissent* 19: 133–46.

Stewart, J.B. 1963. *The Moral and Political Thought of David Hume*. New York: Columbia University Press.

Stewart, R. 1982. 'John Clarke and Francis Hutcheson on Self-love and Moral Motivation', *Journal of the History of Philosophy* 20: 261–77.

Stewart, R. 1992. 'Butler's Argument against Psychological Hedonism', *Canadian Journal of Philosophy* 22: 211–21.

Strasser, M. 1987. 'Hutcheson on the Higher and Lower Pleasures', *Journal of the History of Philosophy* 25: 517–31.

Strasser, M. 1990. *Francis Hutcheson's Moral Theory: Its Form and Utility*. Wakefield, NH: Longwood Academic.

Strauss, L. 1936. *The Political Philosophy of Hobbes*, tr. E. Sinclair. Oxford: Clarendon Press.

Street, S. 2006. 'A Darwinian Dilemma for Realist Theories of Value'. *Philosophical Studies* 127: 109–66.

Stroud, B. 1977. *Hume*. London: Routledge and Kegan Paul.

Sturgeon, N. 1976. 'Nature and Conscience in Butler's Ethics', *Philosophical Review* 85: 316–56.

Superson, A. 2009. *The Moral Skeptic*. New York: Oxford University Press.

Swanton, C. 2015. *The Virtue Ethics of Hume and Nietzsche*. Chichester: Wiley Blackwell.

Szabados, B. 1976. 'Butler on Corrupt Conscience', *Journal of the History of Philosophy* 14: 462–9.

Taylor, A.E. 1926. 'Some Features of Butler's Ethics', *Mind* 35: 273–300.

Taylor, A.E. 1938. 'The Ethical Doctrine of Hobbes', *Philosophy* 13: 406–24.

Taylor, C. 1989. *Sources of the Self: The Making of the Modern Identity*. Cambridge: Cambridge University Press.

Taylor, J. 1998. 'Justice and the Foundations of Social Morality in Hume's *Treatise*', *Hume Studies* 24: 5–30.

Taylor, J. 2002. 'Hume on the Standard of Virtue', *Journal of Ethics* 6: 43–62.

Taylor, J. 2016. 'Adam Smith and Feminist Ethics: Sympathy, Resentment, and Solidarity', in R. Hanley (ed.), *Adam Smith: His Life, Thought, and Legacy*. Princeton and Oxford: Princeton University Press, 354–70.

Tennant, B. 2011. *Conscience, Consciousness and Ethics in Joseph Butler's Philosophy and Ministry*. Woodbridge: Boydell Press.

Thomas, D.O. 1977. *The Honest Mind: The Thought and Work of Richard Price*. Oxford: Clarendon Press.

Tiberius, V. 2015. *Moral Psychology: A Contemporary Introduction*. New York: Routledge.

Tilley, J. 2016. 'Hutcheson's Theological Objection to Egoism', *Journal of Scottish Philosophy* 14: 101–23.

Tolonen, M. 2013. *Mandeville and Hobbes: Anatomists of Civil Society*. Oxford: Voltaire Foundation.

Townsend, H. 1926. 'The Synthetic Principle in Butler's Ethics', *International Journal of Ethics* 37: 81–7.

Tranöy, K. 1959. 'Hume on Morals, Animals and Men', *Journal of Philosophy* 56: 94–103.

Trianosky, G. 1978. 'On the Obligation to be Virtuous: Shaftesbury and the Question, Why be Moral?', *Journal of the History of Philosophy* 16: 289–300.

Tuck, R. 1989. *Hobbes: A Very Short Introduction*. Oxford: Oxford University Press.

Tuck, R. 1996. 'Hobbes's Moral Philosophy', in T. Sorell (ed.), *Cambridge Companion to Hobbes*, 175–207.

Tuveson, E. 1948. 'The Origins of the "Moral Sense"', *Huntington Library Quarterly* 11: 241–59.

Vandenberg, P. and A. DeHart n.d. 'Francis Hutcheson (1694–1745)', in J. Feiser and B. Dowden (eds), *Internet Encyclopedia of Philosophy*, http://www.iep.utm.edu/hutcheso/.

Vandenberg, P. and A. DeHart n.d. 'Bernard Mandeville (1670–1733)', in J. Feiser and B. Dowden (eds), *Internet Encyclopedia of Philosophy*, http://www.iep.utm.edu/mandevil/

Van Mill, D. 2001. *Liberty, Rationality, and Agency in Hobbes's Leviathan*, Albany: State University of New York Press.

Vienne, J.-M. 1995. 'La Morale au Risque de l'Interpretation: L'*Enchiridion Ethicum* d'Henry More', *Archives de Philosophie* 58: 385–403.

Vitz, R. 2002. 'Hume and the Limits of Benevolence', *Hume Studies* 28: 271–95.

Voitle, R. 1955. 'Shaftesbury's Moral Sense', *Studies in Philology* 52: 17–38.

Voitle, R. 1984. *The Third Earl of Shaftesbury, 1671–1713*. Baton Rouge: Louisiana State University Press.

Von Leyden, W. 1954. 'Introduction' to J. Locke, *Essays on the Law of Nature*, ed. W. Von Leyden. Oxford: Clarendon Press.

Voorhoeve, A. 2002. 'Bernard Mandeville'. *Philosophers' Magazine* 20: 53.

Walsh, J. n.d. 'Locke: Ethics', in J. Feiser and B. Dowden (eds), *Internet Encyclopedia of Philosophy*, http://www.iep.utm.edu/locke-et/.

Wand, B. 1962. 'Hume's Non-utilitarianism', *Ethics* 72: 193–6.

Warrender, J. H. 1957. *The Political Philosophy of Hobbes*. Oxford: Clarendon Press.

Watkins, J. 1973. *Hobbes's System of Ideas*, 2nd edn. London: Hutchinson.

Wedgwood, R. 2008. 'Butler on Virtue, Self-interest, and Human Nature', in P. Bloomfield (ed.), *Morality and Self-interest*. Oxford: Oxford University Press, 177–204.

Welchman, J. 2007. 'Who Rebutted Bernard Mandeville?', *History of Philosophy Quarterly* 24: 57–74.

White, A. 1952. 'Conscience and Self-love in Butler's Sermons', *Philosophy* 27: 329–44.

Wilde, N. 1898. 'Mandeville's Place in English Thought'. *Mind* 7: 219–32.

Williams, B. 1972. *Morality*. Cambridge: Cambridge University Press.

Williams, B. 1981a. 'Internal and External Reasons', repr. in *Moral Luck*. Cambridge: Cambridge University Press, 101–13.

Williams, B. 1981b. 'Persons, Character, and Morality', repr. in *Moral Luck*. Cambridge: Cambridge University Press, 1–19.

Williams, B. 1981c. 'Moral Luck', repr. in *Moral Luck*. Cambridge: Cambridge University Press, 20–39.

Williams, B. 1985. *Ethics and the Limits of Philosophy*. London: Fontana.

Williams, B. 2014. *Review of Iris Murdoch, The Fire and the Sun*, repr. in *Essays and Reviews 1959-2002*, 142–5.

Williams, G. n.d. 'Thomas Hobbes: Moral and Political Philosophy', in J. Feiser and B. Dowden (eds), *Internet Encyclopedia of Philosophy*, http://www.iep.utm.edu/hobmoral/.

Wilson, C. 2007. 'The Moral Epistemology of Locke's *Essay*', in L. Newman (ed.), *Cambridge Companion to Locke's* Essay concerning Human Understanding. Cambridge: Cambridge University Press, 381–405.

Winkler, K. 1985. 'Hutcheson's Alleged Realism', *Journal of the History of Philosophy* 23: 179–94.

Wollaston, W. 1724. *The Religion of Nature Delineated*, repr. London: S. Palmer.

Wolterstorff, N. 2010. 'Reid on Justice', in S. Roeser (ed.), *Reid on Ethics*. Basingstoke: Palgrave Macmillan, 187–203.

Worsnip, A. 2015. 'Hobbes and Normative Egoism', *Archiv für Geschichte der Philosophie* 97: 481–512.

Worthen, J. 1995. 'Joseph Butler's Case for Virtue: Conscience as a Power of Sight in a Darkened World', *Journal of Religious Ethics* 23: 239–61.

Worthen, J. 1999. 'Joseph Butler on the Enemies of Virtue', *Studies in Christian Ethics* 12: 48–56.

Yenter, T. and E. Vailati 2018, 'Samuel Clarke', in E. Zalta (ed.), *Stanford Encyclopedia of Philosophy* (fall 2018 edn.), https://plato.stanford.edu/archives/fall2018/entries/clarke/.

Yolton, J. 1985. *Locke: An Introduction*. Oxford: Blackwell.

Zellner, H. 1999. 'Passing Butler's Stone', *History of Philosophy Quarterly* 16: 193–202.

Index

aesthetics, ethics and 83–4
Aristotle 1
  on contemplation 29–30
  and doctrine of the mean 28, 45, 76n.8,
    160n.8, 161
  on happiness 28–9, 183–4
  on justice 51–2
  on pleasure 28–9, 31–2
  and practical wisdom 164
  psychological egoism of 14, 79
  on sacrifice 14
  on virtuous person 31–2

Bacon, Francis 38n.11
Bentham, Jeremy
  on alternatives to utilitarianism 201–2
  on leadership 203–4
  on sanctions 200–1
Bramhall, Bishop 14n.12
Burnet, Thomas 52n.4
Butler, Joseph 1, 11–12
  on abstract and naturalist methods 93
  on Hobbes on compassion and
    benevolence 99
  on 'ought implies can' 102
  on piety 105
  on psychological hedonism 98
  on Shaftesbury on scepticism 107–8
  on virtue and nature 93–7
  welfarism of 103–5

Cambridge Platonists 27, 33
Campbell, Archibald 2n.4
Clarke, Samuel
  on fittingness 128
  hedonism of 130
  welfarism of 129–30
Cockburn, Catharine Trotter 52n.4
cosmological argument 37–8
Cudworth, Ralph 27
Cumberland, Richard
  conservatism of 45
  non-hedonism of 2–3, 39–40
  on non-human animals 43
  on non-moral good 43–4
  on probability 44
  on rights 45
  on sacrifice 35–6
  value-based account of action 33–4

dualism of practical reason 1, 47–8
  Smith compared with Sidgwick 167
  dual source view 154–5

egoism
  moralistic 4
  predominant 14
  psychological 1–4
  rational 1, 6–9
  rule 20n.31
  split-level 6–8, 13–14, 20–2, 80–1, 121,
    190–191, 196
  strategic 200
  veto 6, 107
evil, as privation of good 40
experience machine 32

Foot, Philippa
  on beneficence 103, 171–2

Gauthier, D. 23n.37
Gay, John
  and Hutcheson 188, 190
  influence of 187–8, 190
Grotius, Hugo 36
Gyges, ring of 3–4

hedonism
  evaluative 2–3
  psychological 5–6
Hobbes, Thomas 1
  on authority of God 25–6
  influence of 2
  on natural law 15–18, 22–3
  on natural rights 17–21
  sacrifice in 2
  self-interest in 11–12, 13n.9,
    14–15
  on the sovereign 25
Hume, David
  on character 145–6
  on justice 142–4
  on Mandeville 69n.21
  on politicians and virtue 67
  on practical reason 141–2
  sacrifice in 2–3
  and Smith 151n.38
  on sympathy 143
  on utility 147–8

Hutcheson, Francis
  on deathbed beneficence 120–1
  against deontology 119
  on good and evil 111–12
  on Hume 139n.7
  internalism about reasons of 120n.16
  on moral sense 112–13, 115, 121–2
  motivational utilitarianism of 112–13
  on piety 116–17
  on rights 117–19

Kames, Lord 180
Kant, Immanuel
  on duty 182

Leibniz, Gottfried 113n.5
Locke, John
  and Aristotle 51–2
  Calvinism of 53
  hedonic turn in 49
  and utilitarianism 56–7, 154n.42

Mandeville, Bernard 2
  Jansenism of 60, 62–3, 72–3
  non-hedonism of 2–3, 69–71
  on self-love and self-liking 60n.3,
    66–7
  on Stoicism 69–70
  and utilitarianism 71
Masham, Damaris Cudworth 57n.13
Mill, J.S. 1, 31–2
  as act utilitarian 196–7
  on dignity 32, 127
  on happiness 123
  on maximization 149–50
  on pleasure 123–4, 126
Moore, G.E.
  on Mill 124n.21
moralists, British 1–2
  hedonism of 2–3
morality question, the 3–4
More, Henry
  Aristotelianism of 28
  on glory 32
  on qualities of pleasure 31–2

Paley, William
  on benevolence of God 195
  psychological egoism of 195–6
  and rule utilitarianism 196–7
paradox of self-denial 68, 70–1
Plato 1, 139n.4
  on pleasures 31–2, 89, 125, 141n.9
  on reason and desire 15n.18, 76, 163
  sacrifice in 4n.6, 139n.4
  on vice 87

pluralism, ego-restricted and
    non-ego-restricted 6
Price, Richard
  on atheism 176–7
  and 'consequentializing' 171–2
  on future generations 171
  on 'heads' of virtue 170–1, 177–8
  on impiety 176–7
  and moral luck 174–6
  on repentance 179
  on unity of virtue 177–9
Priestley, Joseph
  influence on Bentham of 201
  and utilitarianism 196n.10
Pufendorf, Samuel von 36
punishment, divine 2, 31–2, 39, 43, 75
  in Butler 104–5, 108–9
  in Clarke 130–1
  and deterrence 46
  in Hutcheson 111–12
  in Price 184–6
  in Smith 166
Pythagoreans, the 27

reasons
  M- and S- 3–4, 7
Reid, Thomas
  Butler's influence on 132
  dualism of practical reason of 134–5
  non-hedonism of 2–3
  objections to egoism of 133–5
  on pleasures of virtue 134
  on principles of action 133
  on virtue and self-interest 135–6
Ross, W.D. 170–2

sacrifice
  subjective and objective 2
Schiller, Friedrich 80n.15
self-interest 1
  modern conceptions of 2–3
  virtue and 2, 27
Shaftesbury, 3rd Earl of
  and alienation 80
  Aristotelianism of 78–91
  and Hutcheson 81n.17
  influences on 79n.13
  and Locke 74–5
  psychological egoism of 78, 81
  on Stoicism 75–8
  teleology of 77
  and utilitarianism 85–6
Sidgwick, Henry 1–2
  on Bentham 201n.19
  on Cumberland 39n.14
  on distinction between oneself and others 47

on 'profoundest problem of ethics' 3–4
on rational egoism 122
on supererogation 181
Smith, Adam
 and Berkeley 162–3
 and Butler 158, 164
 contrasted with Aristotle 168–9
 on Mandeville 72
 on moral luck 163–4
 on propriety 161–2
Stephen, Leslie
 on Tucker 194n.8
Stoicism
 in Butler 93n.5
 and compassion 125
 on greatest happiness 113n.5
 in Mandeville 70–3
 and Shaftesbury 74–91
 on virtue 44, 127

Tucker, Abraham
 influences on and influence of 191
 on punishment 192

utilitarianism
 act and rule 196–7
 motive 146, 150
 split-level 44–5, 104, 144, 192, 202–3

virtues, amiable and awful 164–5

watchmaker, divine 194–5
Waterland, Daniel 187n.3
well-being see self-interest
Whichcote, Benjamin 74–5
Williams, Bernard
 internalism of 55n.11, 157n.45
Wollaston, William
 and utilitarian calculus 195–6